WORKS ISSUED BY
THE HAKLUYT SOCIETY

Series Editors
W. F. Ryan
Gloria Clifton
Joyce Lorimer

THE ARCTIC WHALING JOURNALS
OF WILLIAM SCORESBY THE YOUNGER

VOLUME II
THE VOYAGES OF 1814, 1815 AND 1816

THIRD SERIES
NO. 20
(Issued for 2007)

Donations

The Hakluyt Society gratefully acknowledges donors in 2007–2008. The Society thinks it appropriate that the generosity of donors should be recorded not only in its Annual Report, but also in the book which these donations have helped to make possible. Donations and legacies, and, for British members, Gift Aid, are a valuable supplement to the Society's subscription income which rarely matches the steadily increasing cost of producing our books to the high standard we seek to maintain. The officers of the Society, and the editors and series editors, receive no remuneration and are proud to continue the endeavour which Richard Hakluyt himself inspired, and which we have maintained for 162 years – the endeavour to record, to understand and to interpret the means by which, for better or worse, the different regions and different peoples of the world have become connected with one another.

Mr Edward Alsip
Mr Robert C. Baron
Ms Astrid Anderson Bear
Mr Sanford Bederman
Mr Theodore Benttinen
Mr Matthew Blum
Dr John Bockstoce
Mr Bruce Bogert
Mr James Breckenridge
Mr Chuck Elk
Mr Neil E. Fahy
Dr Norman Fiering
Mr Paul Garber
Dr Martin Greene
Mr Manuel Guerra
Mr Thomas Haas
Mr Gary Haines
Mr Todd Hansen
Professor William Harris
Mr Richard Hawkis
Mr Warren Heckrotte
Mr Paul Herrup
Dr Stephen Kanter
Dr John Libcke

Ms Dee Longenbaugh
Dr Ross MacPhee
Mr William McKinstry
Mr Glen McLaughlin
Mr Robert M. Norris
Mr Thomas Peckham
Mr William Reese
Mr Rudy L. Ruggles, Jr
Professor David Harris Sacks
Mr Robert Sandstrom
Dr Jeffrey Schauer
Mr Werner Schuele
Mr Harold Schwab
Professor Paul Seaver
Mr Kenneth Siple
Mr David Stam
Mr Robert B. Stephenson
Mr Stuart Thro
Mr Edgar Weber
Mr James West
Dr Thomas White
Mr Ted Widmer
Mr Thomas Winter

The Hakluyt Society is deeply grateful to the Gladys Krieble Delmas Foundation of New York which made a substantial grant to the American Friends of the Hakluyt Society as a contribution to the cost of publishing this volume. Dr David Stam's advice over the preparation of the application is much appreciated. The President and Council would wish also to acknowledge the co-operation of the American Friends organization and especially the help of Dr Ross MacPhee in connection with this donation and other financial aid for the Society.

Flensing a whale

William Marshall Craig's 'Greenland Whale Fishery' was probably created in the artist's London studio, which may account for the peculiar representation of the polar bear in the foreground. However, the engraving clearly shows the flensing process, as a large piece or 'slip' of blubber, weighing half a ton or more, is hoisted by speck-tackle from the whale carcass on to the ship. It was published in October 1805, shortly before William Scoresby's father's invention, the crow's-nest, was introduced and widely adopted by whalers. (National Maritime Museum PAH 3384)

THE
ARCTIC WHALING JOURNALS
OF
WILLIAM SCORESBY THE YOUNGER

VOLUME II
THE VOYAGES OF 1814, 1815 AND 1816

Edited by
C. IAN JACKSON

With an Appendix by
GEORGE HUXTABLE

Published by
Ashgate
for
THE HAKLUYT SOCIETY
LONDON
2008

Published for The Hakluyt Society by

Ashgate Publishing Limited
Wey Court East
Union Road
Farnham
Surrey GU9 7PT
England

Ashgate Publishing Company
Suite 420
101 Cherry Street
Burlington
VT 05401-4405
USA

Ashgate website: http://www.ashgate.com

British Library Cataloguing in Publication Data
Scoresby, William, 1789–1857
The Arctic whaling journals of William Scoresby the younger
(1789–1857)
Vol. 2: The voyages of 1814, 1815 and 1816 – (Hakluyt Society
third series)
1. Scoresby, William, 1789–1857 – Diaries 2. Whaling –
Arctic regions 3. Arctic regions – Description and travel
I. Title II. Jackson, C. Ian III. Hakluyt Society
919.8'04

Library of Congress Cataloging in Publication Data
PCN 2004445100

ISBN 978–0–904180–92–3

Typeset by Waveney Typesetters, Wymondham, Norfolk
Printed and bound in Great Britain by
the University Press, Cambridge

Contents

Illustrations and Maps

Illustrations

Maps

Preface and Acknowledgements

This volume of Scoresby's journals, like its predecessor, is based on the manuscript transcripts of the original journals that form part of the Scoresby Papers in the Whitby Museum of the Whitby Literary and Philosophical Society. The 1814 journal forms part of WHITM:SCO1253; those for 1815 and 1816 form part of WHITM:SCO1254. I remain very grateful to the officers and staff of the Society and Museum for the invaluable help and advice they have provided and the continuing interest that they have shown in this project.

In addition to Scoresby's own journals, this volume includes the journal of the 1814 voyage that was maintained by a young supernumerary, Charles Steward, shortly before he joined the shipping service of the East India Company. That manuscript is in the library of the New Bedford Whaling Museum in Massachusetts. The Hakluyt Society and I are grateful to the Museum and to Michael Dyer and Laura Pereira for permission to publish Steward's account. It was a personal pleasure for me to work in that library, beneath the Museum's portrait of William Scoresby, Senior.

A small query raised by George Huxtable about a footnote in volume I rapidly led to an invitation from me that he should prepare an appendix on Scoresby's navigation. Despite a weekend of patient explanation at Mystic Seaport in Connecticut, I know that I could never be trusted to determine my longitude by lunar distances, even on dry land, but I am sure that others besides myself will appreciate Scoresby's navigational skills all the more as a result of George's contribution.

My relocation from Long Island Sound to the banks of the St Lawrence River has not lessened my gratitude to Yale University for its continuation of my honorary appointment as an Associate Fellow of Timothy Dwight College. One measure of this will be found in the online sources listed in the 'Works Cited' in this volume, because access to many of them depended on the link through Yale's library.

George Huxtable and I acknowledge the care that Professor Joyce Lorimer and Professor Will Ryan have given to the final editing of our texts. Finally, I should like to express my personal gratitude to the Gladys Krieble Delmas Foundation of New York for its substantial grant to the Hakluyt Society specifically for the publication of this volume. The third and final volume of Scoresby's journals, covering the voyages of 1817, 1818 and 1820, will be published in due course.

Montreal, Quebec   IAN JACKSON
May 2008

Table of Quantities and Conversions
(approximations in most cases)

Length
1 inch = 2.5 cm   1 foot = 30 cm   1 yard (3 feet) = 91 cm
1 fathom (6 feet) = 1.8 m   1 mile = 1.6 km

Weight
1 pound (lb) = 0.45 kg   1 quarter (28 lb) = 12.7 kg
1 hundredweight (cwt, 112 lb) = 50.8 kg   1 ton (20 cwt, 2240 lb) = 1016 kg
1 chaldron (Whitby measure) = 4927 lb or 2235 kg

Temperature
A difference of 10°C is equivalent to a difference of 18°F and the Celsius and Fahrenheit scales converge at −40°, so:

0°F = −18°C   10°F = −12°C   20°F = −7°C   32°F = 0°C
40°F = 4°C   50°F = 10°C   60°F = 16°C

Atmospheric pressure
One inch of mercury is equivalent to 33.864 millibars or hectopascals. Therefore:

Inches of mercury	Millibars	Inches of mercury	Millibars
28	948	29.5	999
28.5	965	30.0	1016
29	982	30.5	1033

Cask capacities
In Scoresby's day, volumes and other dimensions were generally imprecise. The cask capacities listed below are therefore very approximate, and it is the hierarchy of cask sizes (e.g. as listed in the 'Manifest' at the end of the 1811 voyage) that is more important than the measure of capacity, especially because the casks contained blubber and not liquids.

Leaguer	=	159 imperial gallons	Butt	=	126 gallons, wine-measure
Puncheon	=	72 gallons	Barrel	=	31½ gallons

Miscellaneous
1. According to Scoresby (see note to journal entry for 26 May 1813),'Four tons of blubber by measure, generally afford three tons of oil.' and 'The ton or tun of oil is 252 gallons wine measure.' A butt cask could hold half the latter amount of oil.
2. Value of the pound sterling. The source (Twigger) used in volume 1 was later revised and updated to 2002 (see 'Works Cited' s.v. Allen). This revision may slightly alter the comparison with 1998 shown in volume 1. The equivalent purchasing power in 2002 of £1 in each of the years in volumes 1 and 2 was: 1811: £49.65; 1812: £43.72; 1813: £42.64; 1814: £48.95; 1815: £54.73; 1816: £59.92.

Glossary

These entries supplement those in the glossary in volume I of these *Journals*. As there, many of the definitions are taken from Smyth's *Sailor's Word Book*, with others derived from Scoresby's *An Account of the Arctic Regions* and other sources.

A lee. 'A-LEE. The contrary of *a-weather*: the position of the helm when its tiller is borne over to the lee-side of a ship, in order to go about or put her head to windward.' (Smyth)

Bolt-rope. 'A rope sewed all round the edge of the sail, to prevent the canvas from tearing.' (Smyth)

Cable. 'A thick, strong rope or chain which serves to keep a ship at anchor; the rope is cable-laid, 10 inches in circumference and upwards.' (Smyth)

Calf. '[I]n the Arctic regions, a mass of floe ice breaking from under a floe, which when disengaged rises with violence to the surface of the water; it differs from a tongue, which is the same body fixed beneath the main floe.' (Smyth)

Cant fall. 'SPIKE TACKLE AND CANT-FALLS. The ropes and blocks used in whalers to sling their prey to the side of the ship.' (Smyth)

Canvas. 'A cloth made of hemp, and used for the sails of ships. It is ... numbered from 1 to 8, rarely to 9 and 10. Number 1 being the coarsest and strongest, is used for the lower sails, as fore-sail and main-sail in large ships.' (Smyth). However, Layton's *Dictionary* states that canvas is 'Graded in numbers from 0 to 7, 0 being the heaviest.'

Ceiling. According to Smyth, synonymous with FOOT-WALING: 'The inside planking or lining of a ship over the floor-timbers; it is intended to prevent any part of her ballast or cargo from falling between her floor-timbers.'

Cloth. 'CLOTHS. In a sail, are the breadths of canvas in its whole width.' (Smyth)

Crang/krang. In most dictionaries, the whale carcass after removal of the blubber, but used by Scoresby in a narrower sense, and as a verb as well as a noun. See footnote to journal entry for 12 May 1814.

Cross jack yard. 'CROSSJACK-YARD (pronounced *crojeck-yard*). The lower yard on the mizen-mast, to the arms of which the clues of the mizen top-sail are extended.' (Smyth)

Downs. '[T]he anchorage or sea-space between the eastern coast of Kent and the Goodwin Sands, the well-known roadstead for ships, stretching from the South to the North Foreland, where both outward and homeward-bound ships frequently make some stay, and squadrons of men-of-war rendezvous in time of war.' (Smyth)

Fish. 'FISH, OR FISH-PIECE. A long piece of hard wood, convex on one side and concave on the other; two are bound opposite to each other to strengthen the lower masts or the yards when they are sprung, to effect which they are well secured by bolts and hoops, or stout rope called woolding.' (Smyth)

Fothering. '[A] peculiar method of endeavouring to stop a leak in the bottom of a ship while she is afloat. It is performed by drawing a sail, by means of ropes at the four corners, beneath the damaged or leaky part, then thrusting into it a quantity of chopped rope-yarns, oakum, wool, cotton, &c.; or by thrumbing the sail, that is, sewing long bunches of rope-yarn all over it, before it is placed beneath the ship. These materials being sucked into the leaky part, the flow of the water into the ship is interrupted, or at least diminished.' (*Account of the Arctic Regions*, II, p. 448.) See also Smyth.

Fox. '[A] fastening formed by twisting several rope-yarns together by hand and rubbing it with hard tarred canvas'. (Smyth)

Foy-boat. Layton (*Dictionary*): 'Used in Tyne and other N.E. coast ports. About 15 ft. long, 4 ft. 6 in. beam. Pulls two oars and has a lugsail. Attended mooring of ships.'

Gote. Robinson (*Glossary*): 'a narrow opening or slip from a street to the shore.'

Hake's teeth. 'A phrase applied to some part of the deep soundings in the British Channel; but it is a distinct shell-fish, being the *Dentalium*, the presence of which is a valuable guide to the Channel pilot in foggy weather.' (Smyth)

Head cloth. 'A canvas screen for the head of a ship.' (*OED*)

Heaving down. 'The bringing one of a ship's sides down into the water, by means of purchases on the masts, in order to repair any injury which is below her water-line on the other.' (Smyth). See also *Account of the Arctic Regions*, II, p. 450.

Leewardly. 'Said of a ship which presents so little resistance to the water, when on a wind, as to bag away to leeward.' (Smyth)

Meck/mik. 'MECK. A notched staff in a whale-boat on which the harpoon rests.' (Smyth)

Oakam/oakum. Layton (*Dictionary*): 'Rope that has been unlaid and the yarns teased out. Used for caulking seams, filling fenders, and other purposes.'

Points/reef-points. 'Small flat pieces of plaited cordage or soft rope, tapering from the middle towards each end, whose length is nearly double the circumferences of the yard, and used for the purpose of tying up the sail in the act of reefing.' (Smyth)

Pump spear. 'The rod of iron to which the upper box is attached – and to the upper end of which the brake is pinned – whereby the pump is set in motion.' (Smyth)

Roomstead. '[T]he space between any two ribs or frames of timber in a ship.' (*Account of the Arctic Regions*, II, p. 461.)

Rough-Tree. An unfinished mast or spar, to be used in case of need, and meanwhile carried horizontally at the side of the ship's deck. See Smyth, *s.vv.* ROUGH-TREE and ROUGH-TREE TIMBER.

Russia mat. '*Russia-matting*: matting manufactured in Russia from the inner bark of the linden.' (*OED*)

Ruttling. Robinson (*Glossary*) defines 'ruttle' as 'to gurgle like water pressing through a pipe'.

Sandstrake. '*Garboard-strake* or *sand-strake*, is the first range of strakes or planks laid upon a ship's bottom, next the keel, into which it is *rabitted* below, and into the stem and stern-post at the ends.' (*Account of the Arctic Regions*, II, p. 448.) See also Smyth, s.v. GARBOARD-STRAKE, OR SAND-STRAKE.

Sinus. 'A bay, gulf, or arm of the sea.' (*OED*)

Sky-larking. Falconer (*Dictionary*): 'a term used by seamen, to denote wanton play about the rigging, and tops, or in any part of the ship, particularly by the youngsters.'

Slip. See *Speck/slip*.

Snatch block. 'A single iron-bound block, with an opening in one side above the sheave, in which the bight of a rope may be laid, instead of reeving the end through.' (Smyth)

Speck/slip. 'The fat or blubber of a whale.' (*OED*). Hence 'specksioneer'. In *Account of the Arctic Regions*, Scoresby preferred the term 'slip'.

Stomach piece. 'APRON, OR STOMACH-PIECE. A strengthening compass timber fayed abaft the lower part of the stem, and above the foremost end of the keel; that is, from the head down to the fore dead-wood knee, to which it is scarfed. It is sided to receive the fastenings of the fore-hoods or planking of the bow.' (Smyth)

Sway. 'To hoist simultaneously; particularly applied to the lower yards and topmasts, and topgallant-masts and yards.' (Smyth)

Swim. 'To cause to float; to buoy up.' (*OED*)

Editorial Note

The transcription of the manuscript text follows the original with the following exceptions:

1. Occasionally missing punctuation or letters are supplied in square brackets for greater clarity.
2. The layout of the original text in columns has been simplified for economy and ease of reading. Variations in layout are indicated in editorial notes in square brackets in the text. Marginal headings giving dates, coordinates, wind direction etc. have been placed at the head of the entry to which they refer. Dates in headings have been emboldened for ease of location, and the form of coordinates in headings has been standardized.
3. Asterisks in square brackets indicate unreadable words.
4. Words in square brackets with a question mark indicate an uncertain but probable reading.
5. Where Scoresby himself uses brackets this is normally indicated in a footnote as ('Brackets in transcript').

Introduction

[I]n all instances of reaching high Northern latitudes, for which the authority of the ship's journal may be required, it is almost impossible to procure this sort of evidence, except the voyages have been recent; … I find that, if the ship's journal is not wanted by the owners in a year or two (which seldom happens) it is afterwards considered as waste paper.

Daines Barrington, *The Probability of Reaching the North Pole Discussed*, 1775.

After a whaling ship returned to port, the journal was immediately important, as evidence that the voyage qualified for the 'bounty' or subsidy paid to the owners of whaling vessels by the British government.[1] The journal was presumably also important to the owners in deciding whether to retain a master's services for the next voyage, especially if the vessel had brought back fewer whales than the owners had anticipated. However, when such immediate concerns had been dealt with, the journals became, for most owners and masters except the Scoresbys, 'waste paper'. What Barrington lamented in 1775 was reiterated by Ross two centuries later: whalers made more than 29,000 voyages to the Spitsbergen, Davis Strait and Hudson Bay fisheries, but few journals survived, and, even at the time, little of the knowledge they contained circulated beyond the whaling community.[2]

The three voyages described in the journals in this volume each have a particular interest. In 1814, when the *Esk* returned with the blubber from as many as twenty-three whales, we have the unique advantage of a second journal, kept by a young and educated supernumerary, Charles Steward. His account stands comparison, though it does not rival, the journal kept by William Scoresby himself, and is particularly valuable because it mentions a few topics that Scoresby omitted, probably deliberately. The following year, when the relative absence of whales from the Greenland Sea frustrated Scoresby and the other captains (8 June 1815: 'The ships scour about the country in the utmost disorder – the oldest commanders are at their wits' end'), Scoresby's narrative skill is at its best in the straightforward but sympathetic account of the destruction by fire of the Hull whaler *Clapham* (15 May 1815 'Thus by an act of presumptive carelessness was destroyed the finest ship that ever engaged in the whale fishing trade').

However, it will be the 1816 voyage to which most readers will turn most eagerly. The dramatic events that began on 29 June, when part of the *Esk*'s keel was torn off by ice in latitude 78°N, and that ended with her safe return to Whitby almost a month later, were described in considerable detail in the final chapter of the second

---

[1] See vol. I of these *Journals*, p. xxii.
[2] Ross, 'Commercial Whaling in the North Atlantic Sector', p. 553.

volume of *An Account of the Arctic Regions*, based on the journal. There is nevertheless an inevitable level of detachment in that chapter, describing events several years earlier.[1] It is also easy to assume that elements of that chapter reflect that detachment, when in fact we find in the journal that they were part of that narrative. The most outstanding example is the pages (pp. 479–81 in the *Account*) devoted to calculating how much water entered the *Esk* between 29 June and 7 July. Scoresby stated (p. 479) that 'I now made some experiments to ascertain the quantity of water discharged by the pumps' but it still seems incredible to discover in the journal that the complex calculations based on these experiments were made on 13 July, when the *Esk* was still north of 70°N and the attempts at fothering had failed,[2] so that the ship was afloat only by 'swimming its ceiling'[3] and 'The leak continues moderate, it does not much exceed 10 tons p hour'!

Beyond the immediate interest of the voyages themselves, these journals also document the gradual emergence of both Scoresby the scientist and Scoresby the future minister of religion. His scientific investigations in this period are considered below, but there is clearly a growth in confidence in observation and experiment, as compared to the earlier voyages, and a willingness to develop explanatory hypotheses based on what he observed. As a member of Edinburgh's Wernerian Natural History Society, he had earlier been gratified that the Society published his arctic meteorological data. Now, during the winter of 1814–15, he completed his first major scientific paper for the Society, more than seventy printed pages 'On the Greenland or Polar Ice' (see below, p. xxxi) and announced at the end of the paper his intention to write what would later become the *Account of the Arctic Regions*. His journals show evidence of the reading needed for that book, including Hudson's first voyage in 1607, presumably from Samuel Purchas's *Purchas his Pilgrimes* of 1625, and Phipps's Royal Navy explorations in 1773 in the *Racehorse* and *Carcass*.[4]

The Voyages

1814. This voyage began with a near-catastrophe when, approaching the Shetlands, the *Esk* was caught in the tidal race known as the Sumburgh Röst on 26 March. It is remarkable that the existence of this race was unknown to Scoresby, and presumably also to his father, because its dangers had been known for centuries and both of them must have crossed the race many times on previous voyages.

---

[1] In his manuscript autobiography (WHITM:SCO843.7) Scoresby made the rather surprising comment that the 1816 voyage 'proved the most adventurous expedition (*my voyage to Copenhagen perhaps excepted*) that I had ever encountered' [*emphasis added*]. Chapter 3 of Scoresby-Jackson's *Life* is devoted to Scoresby's description of the 1807 voyage to bring Danish naval vessels from Copenhagen to Britain.

[2] For a description of this process see p. xxiii below.

[3] I.e. with nothing but the floorboards of the hull keeping out the water where the outer hull had been lost.

[4] There are no recorded editions of Purchas after the seventeenth century until the 1905 MacLehose reprint of the 1625 edition, also issued as Hakluyt Society extra series vols 14–33. Asher, who edited the Hakluyt Society's 1860 volume *Henry Hudson the Navigator*, used the 1625 edition. Edinburgh University Library has the four volumes of 1625, and this may be where Scoresby read Hudson's journal.

The *Esk* left Lerwick on 4 April, the same date as in 1813, and again encountered an 'open season' so that the ship was in the whaling area west of Spitsbergen three weeks later.[1] By 9 May three whales had been captured, all 'size' (i.e maximum length of whalebone 6 feet or greater), but Scoresby was complaining that with so many whales in sight, 'favoured by a smiling Providence we should have expected a Dozen at least'. Another three were caught in the following week, a much more successful start to the season that in the three preceding years.

By 10 May, however, the *Esk* and other ships were trapped in the ice, and by the 17th Scoresby was contemplating the possibility that they would remain so throughout the season, 'augmented by the probability of being exposed to continual danger of being crushed by the Ice'. With the aid of teams from the other ships, the *Esk* achieved a partial escape on 24 May, but the others ships were not so fortunate, and Scoresby went 'personally to thank each Captain for his timely aid to us' before moving on to seek open water, which was not achieved until 28 May.

Early June was a period of very successful whaling, with eight captured in four days, 2–5 June. The journal from 15 to 22 June provides graphic reminders of the dangers and difficulties encountered even in a successful season. On 15 and 16 June, a harpooned whale was pursued for nearly sixteen hours, and avoided its pursuers even when dragging several whaleboats and whale lines that, even when dry, weighed over half a ton. Scoresby was forced to abandon the chase because the boat crews were exhausted, 'many of them being sparingly wrapped in clothes drenched in Oil' from making off immediately before the chase, all this taking place during periods of thick fog and a heavy swell. The whale was never caught, but by a combination of forethought, careful navigation and good luck, two days later (17 June) the *Esk* found the boat and whale lines that it had been forced to abandon. The dangers continued: on 22 June another large whale destroyed a whale boat and damaged another.

The *Esk* caught her twenty-third and last whale of the season on 1 July. Scoresby gave up the hunt on 17 July, and arrived back off Whitby on 9 August, though it was not until 14 August that there was sufficient water depth for the *Esk* to enter harbour.

1815. This was yet another 'open' year. The *Esk* left Whitby on 24 March, and Lerwick a week later. By 12 April the ship was north of 76°N before seeing any ice. The season began well, with three large whales taken by 21 April. The main event of the month was however the severe storm of 27–28 April when 'Our situation was now highly alarming – a dreadful storm blowing from the west, a lee pack of ice only a few miles distant, and a rocky lee shore not more than 5 or 6 leagues off; the sails reduced to three close reefed top sails, fore, foretop and main stay sails, each of which seemed ready to blow away'.

The *Esk* survived the storm, but only two whales were taken throughout the month of May. The bad luck continued: only three whales were taken in June and these were the last to be captured by the *Esk*, though a dead whale was encountered on 4 July which provided some blubber 'though all the back part was eaten of sharks'. John

---

[1] See journal entry for 25 April 1814, and the Introduction to the 1811–13 voyages, pp. liv–lv.

Hebden, the Cook's mate, was struck by an unknown disease, and died on 13 July. By the 19th, Scoresby concluded that 'the fishery for the present season did apparently close with the month of June, and ... the prospect here is as hopeless as may be imagined'.

Scoresby's account of the return journey is interesting mainly because of the entry for 29 July, in which he contrasted the lack of information on navigation charts for the Shetlands, as compared to those of the English Channel. 'The charts extant are replete with errors and omissions.' To a modern reader, the contrast between the Shetlands and the English Channel at that date might not appear surprising, but it is easy to forget the importance of the 'Greenland & Archangel trades' in the early nineteenth century. Scoresby returned to this theme in *An Account of the Arctic Regions*, extending it to the need for lighthouses 'on two or three of the most dangerous and prominent parts of the coast' (II, p. 373). Because of his experience in the Sumburgh Röst in 1814, he was glad to learn that such lighthouse building was about to begin at Sumburgh Head. It would, however, require several more decades before the Muckle Flugga lighthouse was constructed on the extreme northern tip of Shetland in the 1850s, and that was initiated as a response to the needs of the Crimean War, not maritime commerce.

The *Esk* was back in Whitby on 4 August, and Scoresby cannot have been happy to find that the *Aimwell* (11 whales, 140 tons of oil), *Henrietta* (24 whales, 140 tons) and *Valiant* (14 whales, 190 tons) had all had more successful voyages.

1816. In much of the Northern Hemisphere, this was 'the year without a summer'.[1] For Scoresby, long accustomed to spending summerless months in the Arctic, the main climatic event was the severe gale that he encountered at about 77°N at the end of April. In calmer conditions, he would presumably have encountered an ice barrier at this latitude, defining 1816 as a 'close' season, but the strength of the gale on 30 April and 1 and 2 May broke up the barrier into 'a vast number of large masses, in violent agitation'. The combination of gale force winds, heavy swell, moving masses of ice and poor visibility kept Scoresby in the crow's-nest for seven or eight consecutive hours, and he was later to write in *An Account of the Arctic Regions* that 'In the course of fourteen voyages ... I passed through many dangers ... but the present case ... far surpassed in awfulness, as well as actual hazard, any thing that I had before witnessed.'

Even after the gale subsided, ice remained a problem during May, with a frequent danger of besetment. Nevertheless, by 24 May the *Esk* had captured seven whales, one of them in a joint operation with the crew of the *Mars*, captained by William Scoresby, Senior. This attempt at cooperation seems mainly to have emphasized the competitive nature of whaling, at least as seen by the ordinary seamen, whereas the impression given by Scoresby's earlier journals is that the masters were generally well aware of the need for mutual assistance and information sharing, because of the dangers inherent in arctic whaling.

[1] Harington, *The Year without a Summer? World Climate in 1816*. The phenomenon is usually attributed to atmospheric ash from a succession of major volcanic eruptions in the preceding years.

For almost three weeks up to 12 June, the *Esk* was beset, but the rest of the month was productive, so that another six whales were caught, even though Scoresby complained on 24 June that three large whales had 'been lost in 8 days by the unskill-fulness of the harpooners'. A few days later, such concerns were forgotten, after Scoresby discovered on 29 June that part of the hull below the water line had been torn off by ice 'unseen and consequently unfeared' but also unnoticed until the ship 'was directly observed to sink in the water above a foot'.

The image of the disaster that has come down to us during the last two centuries is the 'Representation of the Ship Esk of Whitby, Damaged by Ice and Almost Full of Water' that forms the frontispiece of volume I of the *Account* and appears as Figure 7 of the present volume. Although it is no doubt an accurate representation of what was happening at about 3 p.m. on the afternoon of 1 July,[1] it tends to give a false impression of what Scoresby was trying to achieve at that point. One imagines that the men from the *Esk* and the *John* were attempting to tilt the *Esk* so as to expose and then repair the damage on the port quarter. That approach – to '*heave the ship down*' had been the plan 'particularly recommended to me by all the masters who visited me, and by most of the carpenters'.[2]

Scoresby, however, had concluded the previous day that this solution was 'utterly impossible without the help of some ships to take the Esk alongside & heave her stern upwards'[3] and there were no ships willing to accept the risk of besetment that was involved. The alternative was normally to *fother*, i.e. to plug the leak from the outside by a piece of sail held in place by ropes and containing oakum, rope-yarns and other materials. This also proved to be impractical, because the torn portion of the hull projected outwards and prevented an effective seal, and even after this wood was removed, subsequent fothering attempts failed because the iron bolts remained projecting outwards. A third approach, to *well the ship*, i.e. to create a watertight bulkhead separating the after part of the ship from the rest of the hold, was rejected as impractical because such a bulkhead could only be constructed and installed if the entire hold could be pumped dry.

What is portrayed in the frontispiece therefore is Scoresby's attempt at a fourth solution, that even he described as a 'desperate experiment', to '*turn the ship keel upward*', i.e. 'to discharge the cargo, and to unrig the ship, then letting her fill with water, after securing the cabin windows and hatches, to turn her keel up'.[4]

What prevented this 'desperate experiment' from being implemented was the discovery that the ship could not be turned sufficiently because of its buoyancy and stability. 'This remarkable stability encouraged us to persevere and attempt to take the ship home at all events, for it appeared she would neither sink nor upset.'[5]

---

[1] Scoresby, *Account of the Arctic Regions*, II, p. 457.

[2] Ibid., p. 450.

[3] Journal entry 30 June 1816.

[4] Scoresby, *Account of the Arctic Regions*, II, p. 451. All these options, together with the successful one of 'caulking the ceiling' are described on pp. 449–51.

[5] Journal entry 1 July 1816.

Scoresby appears to have been using the 'royal we' in that entry, as it is clear that his enthusiasm was not shared by his crew, at least initially. Scoresby may have been prepared to attempt the return voyage, relying on fothering and on caulking the ceiling, or floor of the hold, so that it became the barrier to the sea instead of the missing part of the keel, but his crew were unwilling to see the *John*, by 3 July the only ship remaining to assist, sail away to continue whaling.

At this point it seems necessary to question Scoresby's judgement, exhausted as he was.[1] On 3 July he wrote in his journal that 'I had for some time back discovered that one half of my crew were most despicable, spiritless, and altogether weak characters; their want of perseverance & their cowardice were alike evident and disgraceful'. Even in *An Account of the Arctic Regions*, several years later, he modified this only to 'many of my crew ... proved themselves to be in general a spiritless set of men' (II, p. 464). If, however, the crew 'being quite overcome with fatigue, dispirited, and even yet hopeless of being able to keep the ship at sea, were determined to leave the ship if the John sailed away',[2] then it seems reasonable to conclude that the crew were entirely justified, and that Scoresby should have been more willing to recognize this than he was.[3] Thereafter, however, his account reverts to its normal objectivity and generosity of spirit.

Charles Steward

Much of what is known at present about Charles Steward is contained in Scoresby's brief journal entry for 2 March 1814:

> Son of Timothy Steward Esqr of Yarmouth, a young Gentleman of promising talents, 16 years of age, educating for the East India Sea Service, and who by prior agreement purposes to take a trip in the Esk to Greenland by the way of obtaining nautical information & spending the interval of time until the sailing of the autumn East India fleet; in a new ship of which he is to embark in the capacity of Sixth Mate [4]

---

[1] 'During 120 hours I have only rested about 12' (4 July 1816, repeated in almost identical form in *Account of the Arctic Regions*, II, p. 472).

[2] Journal entry 3 July.

[3] He did admit in his journal (3 July) that 'The men had indeed cause for apprehension' and in *Account of the Arctic Regions* (II, p. 464) he also admitted that 'these importunities I constantly resisted, until, finding the necessity of the case, I at length, at the unanimous request of my whole crew, made the proposal to Captain Jackson' that the *John* should escort the *Esk* as far as Shetland under terms set out in the written agreement of 3 July. By the time he came to write about the events in his autobiography, criticism of the crew had disappeared almost entirely: 'If the John left us ... which was now also designed, we had little or indeed no hope by ourselves of accomplishing all the labour that lay before us, the ship at that time being a mere wreck – and, indeed, the stay of the men by the ship, could not be secured if we were likely to be totally deserted.'

[4] Perhaps surprisingly, Scoresby made no mention of Steward when writing about the 1814 voyage in his manuscript autobiography. As noted below (p. 4, note 4) at least four large ships (1,200 tons or more) made their first voyages for the East India Company in 1814. Tracing Steward's family in Yarmouth is difficult, because there were a large number of mariners in that town with the name of Timothy Steward. Most, from their burials at St. Nicholas Church, appear to have been Anglicans, but Charles was probably the son of Timothy Steward and Mary Fowler, who were married at the Yarmouth Old Meeting Unitarian Chapel on 16 March 1794, where Charles was christened on 16 March 1798. Another son, Thomas, had been christened there in

His father, Timothy Steward, appears to have been involved in commercial shipping in Yarmouth, including the Archangel trade.[1] In his own journal, Steward noted on 30 March 1814 that 'I have seen the poor houses in Russia – but I really hardly think them inferior to the Shetland ones' suggesting that he may have travelled to Archangel himself before 1814.

It may appear strange that Charles Steward would choose (or at least happily agree) to spend part of what nowadays might be termed a 'gap year' in a whaling journey to an area that was characterized by sea and weather conditions totally unlike those he was likely to encounter in his career with the East India Company Shipping Service. One response, of course, is that this is precisely what such gap years are for: the opportunity for new experiences that are unlikely to be offered in the future. It seems reasonable to anticipate that a whaling summer at 80°N might command a certain respect among Steward's future colleagues in the Service. There were also more direct benefits. Experience in handling a sextant (18 and 24 April) was valuable in any ocean, and high latitudes were a good place to learn that magnetic compass readings should be read with caution. Although most of the ships in which he would serve would probably be much larger than the *Esk*, Steward must have learned much that would be useful about the handling of sails and other features of navigation in the confined waters of an ice-strewn sea.

Last, but by no means least, Steward must have learned much that would be valuable in the future by sailing with Scoresby as captain. Less than ten years separated them in age, but the younger man must surely have been impressed by Scoresby's abilities as a navigator and master of a crew, as well as by his scientific knowledge and interests. As the *Esk* sailed along the Northumberland coast on 8 August, Steward could justifiably conclude 'I have been most thoroughly pleased with my voyage; although it may be in many people's eyes one that would not have been undertaken by a person who expects to immediately set out for the East Indies.'

Like Scoresby's own journal, Steward's account is full and wide-ranging; that may have been something else he learned from Scoresby. Understandably, much of what it contains is merely another view of the same situation; what is of greater interest is where the accounts diverge, and in particular what Steward includes that Scoresby omits. Probably the most significant omission by Scoresby is any mention of the 'bloody conflict' between the specksioneers of the *Esk* and the *Fountain* on the streets of Lerwick that Steward described in his entry for 1 April 1814. It is inconceivable that Scoresby was unaware of this, especially as it needed 'some Highland soldiers being

---

1796, and another brother to Charles was born in 1801. The India Office Library records in the British Library list a 'Captain Charles Steward' in command of the East India Company's vessel *Lord Lowther* on two voyages in 1826–7 and 1828–9, a few years before the Company's Shipping Service ended in 1833. An 1839 directory (Pigot) of Yarmouth lists Arthur and Charles as shipowners and there are two listings for 'Thomas Fowler Steward' as banker and attorney. I am grateful to Edwin King for his assistance, but both he and I regard these identifications as tentative.

[1] The Emmanuel Henry Brandt collection in the Archives of the University of Illinois at Urbana-Champaign contains (Packet 86, Bundle 86–1) several letters between Brandt and a Timothy Steward of Yarmouth that, though very brief, specifically mention Archangel.

called out' to quell what had become 'a general confusion in the town', but Scoresby's entry for that day mentions nothing but weather and the prospects for sailing. It is also noticeable that Scoresby never mentioned, in any of the journals from 1811 to 1816, the rats and mice that Steward memorably recorded on 15 July 1814: 'The whole ship was swarmed with these troublesome vermin ... . Indeed I could not sleep at night, without having these creatures running all over me. My face and everywhere else.'

It would of course have been unusual if the *Esk* had been relatively free of rats and mice, but the contrast between Steward's graphic description and Scoresby's complete silence on the subject is striking. Two possible reasons for Scoresby's omissions suggest themselves, though this is only speculation. As a good manager of the men under his command, Scoresby seems deliberately to have avoided any criticism of his crew in his journals that could lead to an individual being identified later by the owners or others. Discipline had to be maintained, and punishments presumably ordered and carried out, but there is no mention of them in the journals. In 1814 (23 March) and again in 1815 (24 March) he noted that all of the crew were sober; this implies that some of them may have been inebriated at the outset of other voyages, but he never said so in his journals. On occasion he mentioned that an officer of the watch did not carry out his orders, either through neglect or misunderstanding (e.g. 28 May 1814 and 30 May 1815) but the officer was never named. The nearest to named criticism that can be found is on 4 April 1814, when the cooper had to be retrieved from a cock fight so that the *Esk* could sail from Lerwick.[1]

A second possible reason for some of Scoresby's omissions may be that he did not want the owners and others to second guess his decisions and actions, long after the events. That this was always liable to happen seems to be shown in the entry for 12 June 1816, when the *Esk* escaped from ice that had beset the ship for several days. Scoresby recognized that the failure to escape the previous day 'might construe a great deficiency of judgement and experience' but argued that the difference between success and failure was a matter of very slight changes in wind direction. This sounds more like an explanation for others than the personal soliloquies that are more usual in his journals.

Returning to Steward's journal, it seems significant that on 9 May he quoted Marten's description of the moon at midnight in 1671, and on 1, 6 and 8 July Phipps's account of his voyage in 1773. It is possible, but surely very improbable, that Steward either carried editions or transcripts of these voyages with him on the *Esk*, or that he could recall so accurately what he had read in anticipation of the voyage. It seems much more likely that he was shown these items, in print or transcript, by Scoresby during the voyage, and we are left wondering about the size and content of the latter's personal library on board. Again, however, there is little or nothing on the subject in Scoresby's journal, apart from the mention of collections of sermons to be used in Sunday services, the occasional newspaper and Scoresby's own mention of the Greenland Sea voyages of Phipps and Hudson (e.g. 7 July 1814 and 16 May 1815).

---

[1] Scoresby's tolerance, like that of other good managers, did not extend to those in a similar position of responsibility. See the outrage expressed at the master of the *Valiant* (and Scoresby's former first mate) in the journal entry for 17 June 1815.

In summary, there is little or nothing in Steward's account of the 1814 voyage that conflicts with Scoresby's journal. That is to be expected. In a few places, Steward included or expanded on items that Scoresby omitted or mentioned very briefly. Overall, however, Steward's account, written by someone who was educated, articulate, and youthfully eager to record a once-in-a-lifetime experience, serves mainly to enhance still further one's respect for Scoresby's literary skill, intellectual curiosity, management ability, and personal integrity.

Scoresby's Personal and Religious Development

As in the earlier journals, it is clear that Scoresby believed in an omnipotent and all-knowing but benevolent God. This is demonstrated very clearly in his entry for 6 July 1816, as the *Esk* was preparing to attempt the dangerous voyage back to Whitby:

> I know that in fothering the Almighty could easily direct my hand in the application of a bundle of oakum so as to produce an extraordinary effect, as well as the same merciful being could influence our carpenters to exert their energies with their best will & with the best effect …

That is entirely in character and, given the severity of the situation, one might perhaps have expected more religious expression in the entries for July and August than is there. What is more surprising is the lengthy prayer that forms part of the journal entry for 10 April 1814. One can easily imagine Scoresby using such a prayer during his regular Sunday services at sea, but its inclusion in the journal is difficult to explain. One can only speculate that, because 10 April was a Sunday, it was a prayer that he had in fact used earlier that day, and wished to preserve, or perhaps that it was inserted in lieu of holding a service on that date.[1]

Despite that prayer, Scoresby later claimed that, at the beginning of the 1814 voyage, not merely was he already looking forward to a life beyond whaling, but also

> there was a sensible diminution in my desire after the favour of God, and in consequence a great falling off of even my former attention, to religious ordinances. Worldly things had obtained a great hold of my attention. My prosperity so far had excited the hope of a speedy independence [*sic*], and encouraged me to think that with a due regard to the improvement of my little property, I might in a few years be able to relinquish an occupation so full of dangers and privations, and to which I had

[1] It should be noted, however, that the accomplished preacher and lecturer of later years was probably far from evident at this time. The Scoresby Papers in Whitby include an undated fragmentary note (WHITM:SCO872.2), apparently one of several in which he listed topics to be included in his autobiography. The writing in pencil is small and difficult to read: 'My extraordinary diffidence in public speaking – the way it was overcome. In speaking to the sailors it required an amazing effort to use a sentence of my own & for years I never could [venture?] upon. I used to blush & was overwhelmed with feeling. An [indelicacy?] almost suspended my breathing! First efforts at public speaking – Studied speeches – short – difficult to remember – always carried the writing. First instance of liberty at Liverpool.' As his journals record (e.g. 9 April 1815), he used printed sermons when conducting Sunday services at sea.

no very decided preference or regard. Hence my chief aim was that of the major part of the world – to get wealth.[1]

After the relatively unsuccessful voyage of 1815, Scoresby noted in his autobiography that

God in his great mercy, was now beginning to call upon me by the voice of his providence, which at length was so determinate and so irresistable, that his gracious designs, in my behalf, were at length accomplished.

This did not, however, prevent Scoresby and his wife from spending more than two months in London, staying with relatives, a period that he described in his autobiography as 'thrown away in vanities and idleness', during which he 'spent a considerable sum of money in pleasures and trifles'. Not all the time was misspent; he

visited Sir Joseph Banks, indeed, several times at his conversaziones, where I of course met with men of science & received some attention from Dr. Thompson, [now?] Professor of Chemistry of the Glasgow University, Sir Everard Home, and some other men of science. But my chief and most obliging friend was the liberal President of the Royal Society.[2]

The visit to London ended when 'I received my father's command to proceed directly to Greenock'.[3] If the term 'command' seems unexpected in regard to a son

---

[1] Quoted in Scoresby-Jackson's *Life* (pp. 90–91) from the manuscript autobiography (WHITM:SCO 843.6). In the autobiography, written with the benefit of hindsight probably in the early 1820s, Scoresby explained that, during the winter of 1813–14 he had 'entered … on the hazardous adventure of underwriting, leaving with a friend, letters of attorney, to write in my name on all proper risks that should be insured at Whitby'. Early in 1814 he had also 'proposed to the owners of the ship to be permitted to purchase a one-third share of her. To this I obtained a reluctant consent. But when the conditions of the purchase were made known to me I found the terms proposed so high (the ship being valued at 14,000£) that I was obliged to remonstrate with the proprietors on the subject; but could not obtain a reduction in the valuation, nor any better terms as to the mode of payment. As our conferences on the subject became at length rather unpleasant on both sides – the question was unexpectedly set at rest by an offer of an increase of wages of extraordinary liberality, provided I would relinquish my now acknowledged claim for a share of the Concern. This offer was no less than a premium of five per cent upon the quantity or value of oil obtained in the fishery, in addition to my former wages. I, therefore, immediately agreed to the new terms and every thing was soon amicably adjusted to my perfect satisfaction.'

[2] The Scoresby Papers in Whitby Museum include a copy of a letter of introduction (WHITM: SCO5762) from Banks to John Pond, the Astronomer Royal, describing Scoresby as 'the best informed person who uses the seas of Spitzbergen – he is always attentive to science & will I am sure if you will point out any thing for the "advancement" of science that can be done in the high latitudes undertake it with cheerfulness & execute it with zeal'. The letter is dated 11 December 1815, and it is not clear whether Scoresby, who left London in the middle of the month, actually met Pond at that time. 'Dr Thompson' was presumably Thomas Thomson MD, FRS (1773–1852), appointed Regius Professor of Chemistry at Glasgow University in 1818, but in 1815 the editor in London of the *Annals of Philosophy*. Sir Everard Home FRS (1756–1832) was sergeant-surgeon to King George III and a prolific writer on medical subjects.

[3] Autobiography, quoted in Scoresby-Jackson's *Life*, p. 95.

aged twenty-six, Scoresby's description of his return from Greenock is still more enlightening. Having left his wife with friends at Newcastle during the journey north, he returned to her via Edinburgh. In the stage coach from Edinburgh to Newcastle the lady seated next to him fell asleep on his shoulder. From subsequent conversation he learned that she was, at the age of twenty, the widow of an officer killed in the Peninsular War. What is surprising is the effect the incident had on Scoresby. The account in his autobiography extends to ten pages, far longer than the amount usually allocated to other topics, and ends as follows:

> It was perhaps well for me, & for my wife too, that I was so soon parted from this enchanting female. Though my wife was beloved with sincere affection, I yet found the external attraction of Mrs. Hansard so preeminent as to throw every other lady that I had ever known into the shade. And although, I had hitherto since my marriage, maintained a general correctness & propriety of conduct, this rectitude was not to be relied upon, where the heart was insensible to the pure and internal obligations of religion; for though my outward actions might be correct in the main, I now am conscious of an impurity of heart which could only require temptation & opportunities for its complete triumph over a mere external deportment of piety.[1]

Scoresby's increasing prosperity was next demonstrated in a change of address:

> The beginning of the year 1816 was occupied in removing from a house I had rented in Church Street, a low part of the town & not very genteel, to the New Buildings, an elevated situation & fashionable neighbourhood. I here took a lease of a house, at treble my former rent – which, however, was still low compared to other towns being only 34, a year for a handsome house (with 11 rooms) in the best situation in the town, having in front a very pretty flower garden, facing the south, & separating the house from the high road, – with a very commodious well [stocked?] kitchen garden behind & extending backwards 30 or 40 yards.[2]

In the 1816 voyage journal, Scoresby recorded in some detail the subsidized sale of bibles to the crew of the *Esk* (7 & 14 April). This was the work of the Whitby Marine Bible Association, one of several outgrowths of the Whitby Auxiliary Bible Society, established in 1812. Although Scoresby was one of the secretaries, the Marine Society seems to have been at least as much an initiative of William Scoresby Senior, who gave the substantial sum of fifty guineas to its support, as of his son.[3]

---

[1] Whether the lady was aware of the impression she made on Scoresby is not known, but during a change of horses after daybreak, on a clear but cold morning, she chose to spend the rest of the journey to Newcastle on top of the coach!

[2] Autobiography (WHITM:SCO843.7). What were then the New Buildings is now St Hilda's Terrace, adjacent to Whitby Museum. As described by George Young in 1817, 'The street ... is the finest in Whitby: it forms but one row of houses; but all of them are beautiful, and some magnificent. They front the south, on which side they have small gardens, or ornamental grass-plots, which, owing to the curvature of the street, are of various lengths ... Behind the back street, except at the lower part, are extensive gardens, generally belonging to the houses before them. The front street has a fine walk at the side, paved with flags' (*History of Whitby*, II, p. 510).

[3] Young, *History of Whitby*, II, pp. 631–2.

From Scoresby's autobiography, it appears that he was going through a religious experience that, then as now, was termed being 'born again'.[1] With, perhaps, too much benefit of hindsight, he related his progress in this direction to events during and after the 1816 voyage. During the violent storm at the beginning of May, he wrote that

> my mind was not a little harassed with various emotions resulting from apprehension of the loss of the ship, or failure in the fishery, or permanent detention. These feelings were the means of making me more strict in my religious duties & more earnest in my devotions. Sometimes I experienced something like a Spirit of Prayer; but still my heart was unsubdued & my will too stubborn to be perfectly obedient to Christ.

As noted already, the journal of the 1816 voyage acknowledged the hand of God in saving the *Esk* and bringing her safely to port after she was severely damaged at the end of June. However Scoresby's autobiography (WHITM:SCO 843.8) suggested that his achievement in returning the vessel to Whitby had a negative effect on his spiritual development.

> The dealings of Providence with me on this voyage were most remarkable. It was a series of difficulties and dangers, and abounded with striking displays of a Divine interposition for our eventual preservation. These various trying circumstances called forth an earnestness and occasionally an energy in my private Devotions, which, however, coldly performed were seldom omitted, such as I cannot but think were in some measure accepted; yet I am conscious that generally my secret reserve of Sin was not overcome, nor the total subjugation of my own will to that of God accomplished. I began to perceive through these trials the design of Providence: it appeared to me that the object was to turn me from vanity & the unsubdued love of Sin to the love of God. But on my arrival at home the adulation of friends and the universal applause that my successful exertions for saving my ship, under such circumstances that in the opinion of the most experienced Captains [around?] she must inevitably be lost, frustrated, as it were, the grace of God, by giving me satisfaction and honour, in place of humility, gratitude, and submission to the Divine will.

It was at this period that Scoresby came under the influence of the minister of the Anglican chapel in Baxtergate, Whitby, one James Thomas Holloway. Scoresby, who before this 'had seldom heard in the church anything but dry morality, and that delivered with total want of feeling in sermons of ten or fifteen minutes'[2] went to hear him 'with prejudice ... but was deeply impressed under his sermon'. Holloway 'soon became an intimate and beloved friend'.[3]

Although it is evident from both the autobiography and these journals that religion was becoming increasingly important in Scoresby's life, it should also be noted

---

[1] '... the means of effecting that renovation and surrender of heart which I was sensible must be yet wanting before I could be said to be "born again".' (Quoted in Scoresby-Jackson's *Life* (p. 108) from a passage in Scoresby's autobiography about his situation after returning from the 1816 voyage.)

[2] This is presumably a scarcely veiled criticism of Thomas Eglin, minister of Whitby parish church since 1773.

[3] Holloway's influence was described in more detail in Scoresby-Jackson's *Life of William Scoresby*, pp. 107–9 and 151.

that this did not make him less tolerant of the imperfections of others. In writing about the Marine Bible Society in the entry for 7 April he commented that 'This desire in seamen for possessing copies of the scriptures it were too sanguine to attribute entirely to the principle of religious feelings' but it was gratifying that so many were willing to purchase bibles. Though he always saw the annual Mayday celebrations as a 'routine of the ridiculous' (4 May 1816), he evidently understood the crew's need for such distraction from the hard life of whaling. He had a similar tolerance for the rough and dangerous 'skylarking' of his crew (25 May), a tolerance that was in marked contrast to the two hundred lashes round the fleet ordered by a Royal Navy court martial a few years earlier 'as an admonition against "skylarking"'.[1]

Scoresby the Scientist

Scoresby's lengthy paper for the Wernerian Natural History Society, 'On the Greenland or Polar Ice', was read on his behalf at four meetings of the Society in Edinburgh: on 17 December 1814, 21 January and 11 and 25 March 1815. It does not appear that Scoresby himself attended any of these meetings, and it is clear from the 1815 journal that he was in Whitby on 11 March and at sea two weeks later.[2] At the end of the printed version of the paper (pp. 335–8) Scoresby announced 'In a work which I am now preparing for the press, the preceding paper, amplified and illustrated, is intended to be introduced.' He then indicated the main headings of what would later become *An Account of the Arctic Regions*.[3]

Salinity. That Scoresby was becoming increasingly concerned with all aspects of arctic science is evident from the 1814 journal. Before the *Esk* sailed from Whitby, he had acquired two glass hydrometers with which to measure the salinity of sea water. The

---

[1] *Naval Chronicle*, 1808–9, p. 84. Smyth, *Sailor's Word Book*, defined 'round the fleet' as 'A diabolical punishment, by which a man, lashed to a frame on a long-boat, was towed alongside of every ship in a fleet, to receive a certain number of lashes by sentence of court martial'.

[2] The dates of the meetings, and the officers responsible for the readings, are recorded on pp. 654–5 of the second volume of the Society's *Memoirs*. Scoresby-Jackson, in his *Life of Scoresby* (p. 92), stated that the paper was 'read by Mr. Scoresby on two occasions before the Wernerian Society' but he does not seem to have had access to the *Memoirs*. In his autobiography, Scoresby noted that he renewed the preparation of this paper after returning from the 1814 voyage, but did not complete the task until early in 1815.

[3] Because this statement appeared at the very end of the paper, which was not published until 1818, it might appear that the statement was a later insertion. However, in his autobiography, when describing the paper's preparation in 1814–15, Scoresby clearly stated that 'At the close of the paper I announced my intention of preparing for publication a history of Greenland & of the Whale fishery, and gave the outline of my then projected plan.' Elsewhere in the autobiography, he noted that 'My leisure, during the year now brought to a conclusion [1815], was generally occupied in drawing up a History of the Northern Whale-fishery, as part of my projected work. I made some little progress in the collection of materials & even in the writing of the chronological part – but owing to the time spent in London, what I accomplished was very little. The only thing done in London to the furtherance of this object, was the procuring of a translation of part of a Description of the Whale-fishing in Dutch – a language for which I had neither taste nor patience to master, that I might translate for myself.'

subject had interested him for several years, and he had begun measuring salinities in
1810. At page 182 in *An Account of the Arctic Regions*, I, there is a table of sixty-two
such measurements between 1810 and 1817. The vast majority of these were taken at
latitudes of 70°N or higher; the measurement on 25 March 1814 at 57°22′ is the
most southerly of the series.

As described in the journal entry for the latter date, Scoresby's hydrometers were
calibrated by himself on an arbitrary scale from zero to a saturated solution at 100.
By experiments adding known amounts of marine salt to rainwater, he was then able
to approximate this arbitrary scale to relative density (then termed specific gravity).
In view of the results he obtained, however, it seems that he was working in imperial
measure rather than the wine measure stated in the journal entry. He was aware that
specific gravity varied with the water temperature (because water expands in volume
and therefore becomes less dense as its temperature increases.) He included a table of
corrections for temperature, derived again from experiment, in *An Account of the
Arctic Regions*, I, p. 183, and the specific gravity that he listed for each of his voyage
measurements was corrected to 60°F (15.6°C).

Scoresby was also aware that specific gravity could provide only a close approximation to salinity, because the density of the water was also influenced by the minute
solids it contained. In the table of sixty-two measurements in *An Account of the
Arctic Regions*, the lowest specific gravity was 1.0231 (salinity 31‰) on 14 March
1810 when the *Resolution* was near the head of the Moray Firth, where salinities
lower than in the open sea were to be expected. The highest value (1.0280, 37.5‰)
was measured two days earlier at the same latitude but in the open North Sea. North
of 70°N, the specific gravities he measured varied only between 1.0259 (35‰) and
1.0272 (36.5‰). Although the individual measurements he made between 1810 and
1817 were of questionable accuracy by modern standards, he was able to arrive at
the valid conclusion that 'The sea in the Arctic regions is of somewhat less specific
gravity, than it is in temperate or torrid regions; and consequently less salt' (*An
Account of the Arctic Regions*, I, p. 181).

Depth and temperature soundings. On 18 April 1815, in latitude 77°37′, Scoresby
noted that the sea water temperature at a depth of two or three feet was 38°F, or nearly
10°F above the freezing point of sea water at normal salinity. From this he concluded
that 'an undercurrent sets along the W. coast of Spitzbergen to the N^d whilst an upper
current conveys the ice in a southwestern direction from the high Polar regions'.

He was wrong: the pattern of inflow and outflow in the Greenland Sea is separated
horizontally, not vertically[1] and the fact that the temperature a few feet below the
surface was warmer than at the surface was simply the result of surface cooling. In *An
Account of the Arctic Regions*, he came closer to the truth, recognizing that

> In some situations near Spitzbergen, the warm water not only occupies the lower and
> mid regions of the sea, but also appears at the surface. … [E]ven among ice, the tem-
> perature of the sea at the surface, has been as high as 36° or 38°, when that of the air has

[1] Gyory et al., 'The Spitsbergen Current'.

been several degrees below freezing. This circumstance, however, has chiefly occurred near the meridians of 6° to 12° east ... (I, pp. 210–11)

A year later, encouraged by his father, Scoresby used his 'marine diver' to take temperature soundings at great depths at about 79°N on 20 and 21 May 1816. The main purpose was to measure the effect of deep immersion on different wood samples, but it was the depth of the sounding that is perhaps of greater scientific interest. Using all the lead lines available on the *Esk* and the *Mars*, 'The marine diver with the pieces of wood attached was sent down the whole length of our lines or 730 fathoms'. He estimated that, allowing for drift, the actual depth attained was 'probably about 660–670 fathoms or 4000 feet'.[1] This is consistent with present knowledge. The bathymetry of the Greenland Sea west of Spitsbergen is extremely variable; along the relatively short length of the 79th parallel between 3°E and the Spitsbergen coast at 11°E, the depth rises from over 3000m in the west to the shoreline. At 79°N 6°E, where Scoresby's soundings were made in May 1816, the sea bottom is close to 2000 m (6500 ft) below the surface.[2]

Ice crystals, hoar frost and rime. Scoresby's powers of observation and deduction are well shown in the comments on ice formation that form the bulk of the journal entry for 11 May 1814. This entry provided much of the material for his discussion of 'frost-rime' and 'hoar-frost' in *An Account of the Arctic Regions*, I, pp. 434–40, where he mentioned specifically the weather and ice conditions of that day.[3] In the *Account* (pp. 437–8), Scoresby's description of what he observed on 11 May is more detailed, and perhaps better structured, than in the journal, and is therefore worth quoting for comparison.

> At midnight the temperature fell to 10°[F], and the frozen vapour made its appearance. It soon increased to the density of frost-rime, and was carried by the wind in clouds or showers. In the course of the night, the rigging of the ship was most splendidly decorated with a fringe of delicate crystals. The general form of these, was that of a feather having half of the vane removed …. Many of these crystals, possessing a perfect arrangement of the different parts corresponding with the shaft, vane, and rachis of a feather, were upwards of an inch in length, and three-fourths of an inch in breadth. Some consisted of a single flake or feather; but many of them gave rise to other feathers … There seemed to be no limit to the magnitude of these feathers, so long as the producing cause continued to operate, until their weight became so great, or the action of the wind so forcible, that they were broken off, and fell in flakes to the deck of the ship.

In the *Account,* Scoresby drew a clear distinction between the formation of this hoar frost and the frost-rime that he had described earlier (pp. 434–5).

---

[1] This allowance was not made in the table on p. 187 of *Account of the Arctic Regions*, I, where the depth in feet of the sounding is given as 4,380 feet, i.e. the 730-fathom length of the sounding lines.

[2] Leier, *World Atlas of the Oceans*, p. 212.

[3] The actual date is not mentioned in the *Account* and the longitude is given as 'about 2°E' whereas it was stated as 4°10′ E in the journal; however the latitude is identical and the descriptions in the journal and the *Account* use the same words and phrases in many places.

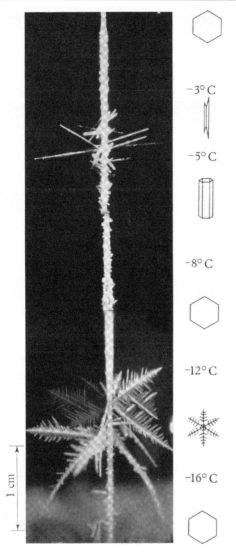

Figure 1. Diffusion chamber
Ice crystals of differing shapes growing on a filament suspended in a diffusion chamber with controlled temperature gradient. The crystals take characteristic forms at different temperatures as indicated along the right edge of the photograph. Reading from the top, the symbols represent: thin hexagonal plates, needles, hollow prismatic columns, hexagonal plates, branched fern-like crystals (or dendrites), and hexagonal plates. At temperatures below −25°C, prisms appear again. This photograph and description appeared as Plate XIII in B. J. Mason's *Clouds, Rain and Rainmaking* (Cambridge, 1962).

It [frost-rime] consists of a dense frozen vapour, apparently rising out of the sea or any large sheet of water, and ascending, in high winds and turbulent seas, to the height of 80 or 100 feet; but in light breezes and smooth water, creeping along the surface. The particles of which it consists are as small as dust, and cleave to the rigging of ships, or almost any substance against which they are driven by the wind, and afford a coating of an inch or upwards in depth. These particles adhere to one another, until the windward surface of the ropes is covered; and form long fibres, somewhat of a prismatical or pyramidal shape, having their points directed towards the wind …

Frost-rime sometimes appears at a temperature of 20° or 22°; but generally; it is not observed until the cold is reduced to 14°. It is most abundant in the lowest temperatures, with a high sea and strong winds; but diminishes as the swell and wind subside, or whenever the sea begins to freeze.

Scoresby could have been forgiven if he had considered these two forms of ice formation as essentially a single phenomenon, but with a different appearance depending on whether the sea surface was frozen or open water. The *Oxford English Dictionary*, for example, originally defined 'rime' as 'hoar-frost; frozen mist'; only in its *Supplement* did it add the comment 'In scientific use now distinguished from hoar-frost'.

Although Scoresby perceived that the two forms arose from different atmospheric causes, he was unable to explain these, nor could any other scientist of the period. The notion of polarity and the analogy with a magnet that he suggested in both the journal and the *Account* for the formation of hoar frost followed the physical thinking of his time. Compare his journal entry of 1814, for example, with the following quotation from Neill Arnott's *Elements of Physics, or Natural Philosophy* (1827), cited in *OED*, s.v. 'polarity':

> When atoms are allowed to cohere according to their natural tendencies, they always assume a certain regular arrangement and form, which we call crystalline. Because in this circumstance they seem to resemble magnets, which attract each other only by their poles; the fact has been called the polarity of atoms.

What Scoresby was observing was the growth of ice crystals from supercooled water droplets, at temperatures between 0°C and −40°C. Because of a shortage in the atmosphere of nuclei on which ice formation is efficient, the water droplets that form on the abundant condensation nuclei as cloud or fog continue to exist below 0°C in a supercooled state, but are readily converted to ice when they come into contact with an ice crystal. In effect a small number of ice crystals grow at the expense of a multitude of supercooled water droplets.

Scoresby's observation on 11 May 1814 is particularly significant because of the ambient air temperature that he noted: falling below 10°F (−12°C) A century and a half later, laboratory experiments showed that the form adopted by a growing ice crystal is closely related to the air temperature and the degree of supersaturation that this represents. Fig. 1 shows that crystals growing at different temperatures on a fibre in a diffusion chamber take different forms at different temperatures, and only at temperatures between −12°C and −16°C do the ice crystals take the dendritic form so carefully observed and described by Scoresby.[1]

Magnetism and the navigational compass. Scoresby's well-established interest in terrestrial magnetism, and the variation of the compass when moved to different places on the ship, continued during these voyages, but only the observations made on 30 June 1815 would be included in the paper that he presented to the Royal Society in 1819. In a very useful review of the state of knowledge at this time, Yost[2] noted that, by the second decade of the nineteenth century,

> interest in terrestrial magnetism specifically focused on Captains Flinders' discovery of local attraction. During his surveying voyages, Flinders had recognized that increased amounts of iron in and on ships were causing navigational errors. Before, these errors had been blamed on imperfect compasses, unnoticed ocean currents, or simply bad seamanship. … Local attraction and terrestrial magnetism would require more systematic, accurate observations before they would be truly understood.

Scoresby's observations, made with increasing care in latitudes where the horizontal component of the magnetic field was very weak, were therefore of general importance.

Marine biology and sea colour. In his journal entry for 4 July 1814, Scoresby noted that the colour of the sea in the whaling area was apt to change between blue and green 'the blue is a sort of indigo colour, the other a kind of bottle Green'. The change in colour

---

[1] Mason, *Clouds, Rain and Rainmaking*, where Fig. 1 appears as Plate XIII.
[2] Yost, *Observations, Instruments and Theories.*

could not be linked to 'the State of the Atmosphere with regard to clouds or the influence of the Sun's unclouded rays', nor was it due to the 'nature of the bottom', because 'a deeply immersed tongue of ice' appeared very different in the two situations. Scoresby went on to comment:

> I have often noticed some particles of a yellow substance floating in the Green water which probably occasions its peculiar colour & turpidity [sic] & which sometimes is observed to tinge the edges of the Ice with a deep yellow hue.

In 1815 he returned to the topic in lengthy journal entries on 16 and 17 May, and expanded the 'yellow substance' comment of the year before into a microscopic study and description of the zooplankton that caused it:

> it is very evident that these substances give the peculiarity of colour to the sea in these parts, and from their appearance & great profusion are evidently sufficient to occasion the great diminution of transparency which always accompanies the colour. (16 May)

It is somewhat surprising that Scoresby's comments on these localized concentrations of zooplankton have not been given much notice in modern studies of bowhead feeding habits, even though much of what he recorded in 1815 provided the basis for pages 175–81 of volume I of *An Account of the Arctic Regions*.[1] Würsig and Clark ('Behavior', p. 171) noted that

> Bowhead whales take advantage of prey concentrations that occur sporadically in time and place. Although zooplankton patchiness has been studied in the Beaufort Sea, it is not possible to predict reliably where and when any of the feeding types will occur.

It seems that either the concentrations Scoresby described are less common in the Beaufort Sea, where most of the modern research reported in *The Bowhead Whale*[2] has been carried out, than west of Spitsbergen, or that such concentrations do not occur nowadays, because of the change in trophic relationships consequent on the decline in whale numbers, or other factors.

Although it is not explicit in the journals, Scoresby recognized the existence of a food chain in the arctic seas, and, indeed, it seems probable that in 1820 he was the first to use the term 'chain' in this context. The relevant paragraph in *An Account of the Arctic Regions* is as follows (I, p. 546):

> The economy of these little creatures, as constituting the foundation of the subsistence of the largest animals in the creation, has already been noticed.[3] The common whale feeds on medusæ, cancri, actiniæ, sepiæ, &c. and these feed probably on the minor medusæ,

---

[1] There is a citation to Scoresby in Lowry, 'Foods and Feeding Ecology', p. 202, but the citation appears to be inaccurate. It mentions earlier work that had used 'figures in Scoresby (1823) that "depicted organisms often encountered in the surroundings of the [bowhead]"' but there are no such illustrations in the 1823 text, *Journal of a Voyage to the Northern Whale-Fishery*. The citation should presumably be to Plate XVI, 'Medusæ &c', in vol. II of *Account of the Arctic Regions*.

[2] Burns et al., *The Bowhead Whale* (1993).

[3] Scoresby was probably referring to his discussion of the food of the bowhead whale, *Account of the Arctic Regions*, I, p. 469.

and animalcules. The fin-whales and dolphins feed principally on herrings and other small fishes, these subsist on the smaller cancri, medusæ, and animalcules. The bear's most general food is probably the seal; the seal subsists on the cancri, and small fishes; and these on lesser animals of the tribe, or on the minor medusæ and animalcules. Thus the whole of the larger animals depend on these minute beings, which, until the year 1816,[1] when I first entered on the examination of the sea-water were not, I believe, known to exist in the polar seas. And thus we find a dependent chain of existence, one of the smaller links of which being destroyed, the whole must necessarily perish.

The term 'food-chain' was not included in the *Oxford English Dictionary* until the second *Supplement*, where the earliest citation is 1927.

Conclusion
Throughout the journals in this volume, there is clear evidence that William Scoresby had become a true scientist. His descriptions are as clear and detailed as they were in the earlier voyages, but by 1814, and certainly by 1815, he was no longer content with description. He was equipping himself with the available tools, such as a microscope, to investigate phenomena, and he was prepared to suggest explanations for what he observed. His hypotheses were sometimes inaccurate or incomplete, but that is to be expected. What is undeniable is that the author of *An Account of the Arctic Regions* is clearly evident in the journals of 1814 to 1816.

---

[1] In fact 1815, in his journal entry for 17 May of that year.

Journal for 1814

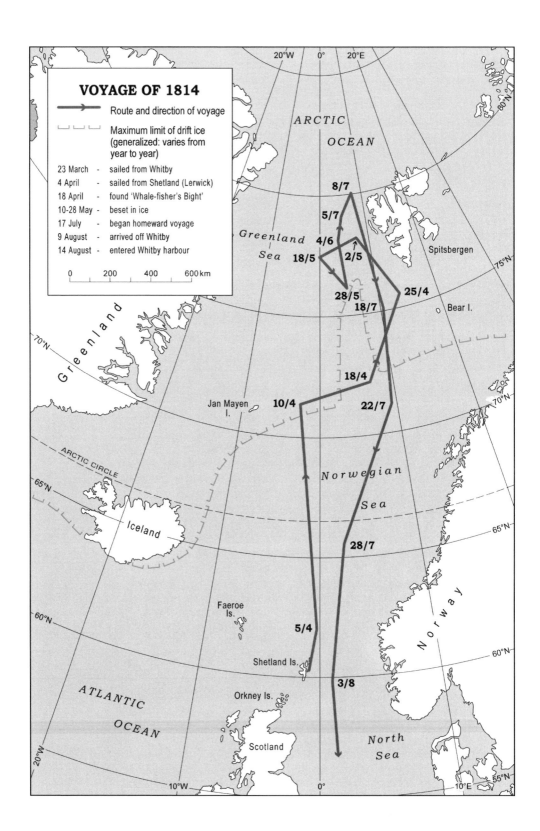

VOYAGE OF 1814

→ Route and direction of voyage

⌐ ⌐ ⌐ Maximum limit of drift ice
(generalized: varies from
year to year)

23 March - sailed from Whitby
4 April - sailed from Shetland (Lerwick)
18 April - found 'Whale-fisher's Bight'
10-28 May - beset in ice
17 July - began homeward voyage
9 August - arrived off Whitby
14 August - entered Whitby harbour

0   200   400   600 km

20°W   0°   20°E

ARCTIC

OCEAN

80°N

8/7

5/7

4/6

Greenland   18/5   2/5   Spitsbergen

Sea

25/4   75°N

28/5   Bear I.

18/7

70°N

18/4

Jan Mayen   10/4   22/7   70°N

I.

ARCTIC CIRCLE   Norwegian

65°N   Sea   65°N

Iceland

28/7

Faeroe

Is.   60°N

5/4

Shetland Is.

3/8   60°N

ATLANTIC   Orkney Is.

OCEAN

Scotland   North   Norway

Sea

20°W   10°W   0°   10°E   55°N

Greenland

Journal of the Second Greenland Voyage Under Divine Providence of the Ship Esk of & from Whitby by William Scoresby Junr. Commander. 1814

Introduction

Monday the 21st of February. Attended tide in the Afternoon with 6 Men & 2 Boys and removed the Ship with some difficulty from her winter birth in the <u>Bell Gote</u>[1] to the middle of the channel nearly opposite to Brown's Quay but too late in the tide to haul alongside. Moored; & left the Ship at 7 Pm. The exertion of this day so aggravated an illness which for some time had oppressed me, that my disorder was very much increased on the following day.

Tuesday the 22^d. The disease preying on me with increasing force, prevented me attending the removal of the Ship this day which was in consequence left to the Pilot.[2] A corn vessel kept the Esk from the Quay.

23^d. The Mate arrived in the Flora Brig, bringing in her 12 Tons <u>pig iron</u>, well <u>squared</u> Ballast, purchased in London for £5..10/- p Ton. The Ship hauled alongside the Quay & was moored.

24. The Boatswain with a few hands prepared for masting & rigging, by conveying some of the necessary stores to the Ship.

25. The process of rigging forwarded.

26. Rigging &c. continued.

27. Sunday. ☽ (Moon.).[3]

28th. Monday. The Iron Ballast was placed in the angles between the ceiling[4] on the floor timbers & the Kelson, and the stowing of the Casks in the Hold commenced by the Mate, 2^d mate, Specksioneer, &c. The process of rigging continued.

---

[1] A 'gote' was defined in Robinson's 1855 *Glossary* as 'a narrow opening or slip from a street to the shore'. This definition is cited in *OED*. The Bell was the large sandbank, exposed at low tide, in the middle of the inner harbour. As in the similar mention in the journal for 11 February 1815, this spelling appears to have been erroneously 'corrected' to 'gate' by a later hand.

[2] Actually 'pivlot' in the transcript, with 'v' crossed through.

[3] The moon was at First Quarter on this date. In general, on the coasts of Britain, neap tides are encountered around first and third quarters; spring tides coincide with new and full moons. See the journal entries for 6 and 21 March.

[4] 'The lining or planks on the inside of a ship's frame: these are placed on the flat of the floor, and carried up to the hold-beams' (Smyth, *Sailor's Wordbook*). Terms such as 'kelson' that were included in the Glossary of vol. 1 are not normally redefined here.

Hitherto the disorder wasting my flesh & enfeebling my frame continued its ravages without interruption: fever & inflammation prevented any appetite for food, whilst my strength was continually diminished by the effects of relaxing medicines,[1] & violent perspiration, it was not until Tuesday the 1st of March, that any abatement of the morbid symptoms was observable, when an <u>All</u> Gracious Providence [blessed?] the means made use of, removed the severity of the disorder and exhibited marks of amendment.

The process of stowing the Hold & rigging continued.

Wednesday 2d of March. Further signs of amendment; food taken with some degree of relish, pleasing prospects of convalescence.

Arrived at our house as temporary inmate Mr Charles Steward, Son of Timothy Steward Esqr of Yarmouth,[2] a young Gentleman of promising talents, 16 years of age, educating for the East India Sea Service, and who by prior agreement purposes to take a trip in the Esk to Greenland[3] by the way of obtaining nautical information & spending the interval of time until the sailing of the autumn East India fleet; in a new ship of which he is to embark in the capacity of Sixth Mate with Captain [*blank space*].[4]

March 3d, 4th & 5th The rigging in a great measure completed. The stowing of the Hold & filling of water as ballast prosecuted with vigour & despatch. The <u>ground tier & wingers</u> completed & filled to an extent as usual but the second tier allowed to remain empty except beneath the space allotted for the stowing of the fresh water.

Sunday March 6th ◯ (Full Moon.)

Monday the 7th Five tons of Beer in 10 Casks & 4 Casks of Ale containing about 160 Galls were received on board from [Comn?] Clark's; likewise Seven Chaldrons of coals, whereof One Chaldron is meant the use of the Armourer.

Tuesday the 8th Five tons of Beer & 4 Casks of ale were received from Mr. Geo. Stonehouse.[5] The Stowing of the hold & filling of water for Ballast, continued by the mate

[1] From the context, probably a 'laxative', but *OED* does not include a definition of 'relaxing' in this sense.

[2] See Introduction, p. xxiv.

[3] 'The name *Greenland*, is here to be taken in its common and most general acceptation, which is meant to signify, not only Greenland properly so called, but more especially the land of Spitzbergen and adjacent islands, together with the seas intermediate between these two coasts, extending from the farthest navigable point north, to the southern margin of all ice; or by act of Parliament, to 59°30'N. latitude. – 26th Geo. III. c.41. §16.'(Scoresby, 'On the Greenland or Polar Ice', p. 261, footnote.) Scoresby quoted the relevant legislation in *Account of the Arctic Regions*, II, p. 504, but cited the paragraph as 18, not 16.

[4] As many as four large ships (1200–1300 tons) made their first voyages for the East India Company Shipping Service in 1814: *General Kyd*, *Herefordshire*, *Vansittart*, and *Warren Hastings*. The on-line documentation of the Service (www.eicships.info) has not yet reached the stage of listing the officers on these voyages.

[5] In Young's *History of Whitby* (1817) he noted (II, p. 577) that there were twelve brewers in the town, although he hastened to add in a footnote that 'There are only 4 breweries'.

with 6 or 8 officers & men & 6 small Boys. In the Evening the empty fresh water casks were conveyed up the river & after the tide had fallen away they were filled with the water flowing down the channel of the <u>Esk</u> which is always found to be perfectly good.

Wednesday March 9th 14 Casks of 300 Galls capacity each were taken on board filled with fresh water & stowed in the 3^d tier immediately before the Main-Mast – 41 cwt. of Ship bread was received from Hamilton's & emptied into lockers adapted for the purpose.

Thursday 10th Rec^d on board 50 cwt. of Ship Bread from Nettleship, great part of which was obliged, from the want of room, to be put into casks whereof [*blank space*] of [*blank space*] Gall^s contained the remnant. 8 Sacks or One Ton of Flour was likewise received from Mr. Wm Elgie of Ruswarp.[1] The Guns also were taken on board this day – The winds during the whole of this week have prevailed from the NE. or E.ward accompanied by daily falls of snow, whereby the roads in many places are rendered impassible, a circumstance very uncommon at so late a period of the Spring.[2]

The bad weather prevented me taking exercise in the open air & thereby considerably retards the recovery of my wonted strength. I made but one essay out of doors since Tuesday the 22^d of February.

The Courier of March the 7th gives the following.

"<u>Covent Garden Market</u>. The extreme severity of the weather has rendered all the fruits and & vegetables of the Season scarce, & consequently dear beyond all precedent. The following is a State of the prices on Saturday. Asparagus 24/- p hundred; Cucumber 21/- a brace; best pines 52/- each: grapes 63/- p lb, endive 8/- a Dozen; best brocoli 16/- p bundle [***]; french beans 8/- a hundred; mushrooms 5/6 p pottle,[3] best Kale 12/- a basket; nonpariel [*sic*] apples 8/- p Dozen; Colmar pears 30/- p Dozⁿ; Coss lettuce 4/- p Dozⁿ; Mint 1/6 a Bunch, greens 16/- p Dozⁿ bunches, Spanish Onions 12/- per Dozen["]! !![4]

Friday March 11th Wind still from the East. The Snow yet remains on the neighbouring grounds. Thermometer during the day for this past week has been from 33° to 40°.

During the cold of February we had several times a temperature of as low as 18° at 9 or 10 Pm. Once indeed 17 or 16° & ½ a mile from the Town on a little elevation 14

[1] Elgie was a subscriber to Young's *History*, as were several Nettleships, including Thomas Nettleship who supplied bread for Scoresby's 1812 voyage (see journal entry for 28 February 1812).

[2] Not so: see the journal entries for 14–26 March 1812, especially 23 and 26 March.

[3] 'A measure of capacity for liquids (also for corn and other dry goods, rarely for butter), equal to two quarts or half a gallon, now abolished.' *OED*.

[4] In most cases, the superscripts 's' and 'd' (i.e. shillings and pence) were inserted above these prices. Scoresby's exclamation marks seem justified: because £1 in 1814 had approximately the purchasing power of £48.95 in 2002, the price of grapes in 1814 was equivalent to £154.19 per pound in 2002 (Allen, Table 1).

or 15° was the Tem*peratur*e. The frost continued with <u>all</u> winds, Easterly as well as westerly though not quite so severe. The great mortality which has of late prevailed throughout Great Britain proves that a severe winter is a most unhealthy Season especially to aged and weak persons.

Took on board four five oared whale-boats & stowed them in the twin-decks.

The Steward having arrived the preceding Evening, commenced his occupations of arranging the stores, cleaning & airing the Cabin, &c. &c.

Saturday March 12th Wind continues at East, weather the same: Sundry stores taken on board, various operations performed, Cabin washed, Coppers cleaned, hold nearly completed, &c. &c.

Sunday 13th Morning Cloudy, weather more mild & Evening Calm[.] Wind inclined from the SW^d. Enjoyed the air half an hour on the Staith-Side.

Monday 14th Charming fine day, wind SW. Received 80 Bushels of Potatoes on board & sundry other stores. Entered into [fray?][1] by preparing provisions for the Crew – about 35 partook. Enjoyed the air on board the Ship.

Tuesday 15th **March.** Weather cloudy, wind Southwesterly & Cold. Bent Sails, and brought on board 59 Whale-lines, lacking one of the N^o required by act of Parliament.[2] Seamen & officers Signed articles of agreement to the amount of thirty seven.

Wednesday 16th **March.** Weather Cloudy: wind S.erly, Air Cold. Took on board our three remaining Whale-Boats & my own Barge. Painted the Gun-carriages green, the colour of the inside of the Bulwark. Received from Gile & Brown stock of spirits for Harbour & Sea use, also 10 Doz^n Bottles of Porter: & from [Pierson?] & Frankland 5 Doz^n Port; 1½ Doz^n Sherry & 1 Doz^n of Vidonia Wine.[3] Completing my Sea & Harbour Stock of Wines, Spirits & Porter.

---

[1] Possibly 'pay'.

[2] In *Account of the Arctic Regions*, II, pp. 493–4, Scoresby quoted the relevant requirements from the Act of 42d Geo. III. c. 41. §2, and in a footnote summarized the requirements in the following table:

Tonnage of Ships	Harpooners	Boat-Steerers	Linemen	Seamen	Greenmen	Apprentices	Total, including Master & Surgeon	No. of Boats	Fishing lines	Harpoons
150 and under 200	3	3	3	7	3	3	24	3	30	30
200 _____ 250	4	4	4	8	4	4	30	4	40	40
250 _____ 300	5	5	5	9	5	5	36	5	50	50
300 and upwards	6	6	6	10	6	6	42	6	60	60

[3] 'A dry white wine made in the Canary Islands.' *OED*.

Agreeable to an engagement accompanied by M^rs S & Mr Steward I took a ride to Mr Mead's residence in a Chaise for the benefit of my health. We were there regaled by a substantial & agreeable dinner, & had the pleasure of spending the afternoon with M^r & Mrs Langbourne in addition to Mr Mead's family.[1]

Thursday 17th March. The Crew was mustered by the Surveyor of the Customs agreeable to the usual forms, consisting of Master, Surgeon, 6 Harponeers, 6 Boatsteerers, 6 Linemanagers, 16 Seamen, 7 extras, & 7 Boys, in all 50 <u>hands</u>.[2] After which advanced each man one month's pay, paid hand-money to Harponeers, & all arrears of wages, agreeable to table in last years journal under date 12th of March. Finished by 1 Pm and dined 18 persons in the Cabin.

18th Sundry stores received on board, consisting of Gun-Powder, &c. &c. In the Morning Cleared ship at the Custom house.

Saturday 19th Took on board fresh stocks consisting of the Beef of one & a half oxen, the legs were retained uncut & the finer parts in large pieces for the purpose of preserving fresh, which can be effected for several months by slightly covering them with salt, or immersing them a few times in Sea water & then suspending them in the air. The coarser pieces we cut up for the Seamens present use.

Sunday 20th A moderate breeze of wind at SW with fine weather. The Henrietta lying in the Bridge way floated & went to Sea, the tide was not sufficiently high for the other Ships, & the Esk did not float by 6 or 8 Inches.

Monday 21st of March. (New Moon.)[3] Nearly calm all day; light airs occasionally from the South^d or Eastw^d[.] Much rain in the Afternoon and Evening; a SW.erly Breeze in the Night. – Attended morning tide but the Ship did not float. In the afternoon all the remaining Ships intended for the Greenland Whale-fishery, viz. the W^m & Ann, Aimwell, Resolution, Volunteer, & Lively were towed or hauled out of the Harbour & got to Sea. The Esk by means of strong mechanical powers was dragged from her dock and hauled down the Harbour, about half the distance between her former birth & the Bridge, where upon a gravel bed she grounded, & moved no farther during the continuance of the tide of flood & was left nearly dry on the ebb.

Tuesday 22^d Frequent thick fog during the day – In the morning attended tide & moved the ship about 50 yards over a part of the highest ground in the whole navigation & was again stopped by the efflux ['egress' *inserted above previous word*] of the

---

[1] The names of Peirson [*sic*], Frankland, Mead and Langborne [*sic*] are among the list of subscribers to Young's *History of Whitby*.

[2] The process of mustering, and the qualifications of the different categories of the crew, are summarized in *Account of the Arctic Regions*, II, pp. 513–14.

[3] In addition to this parenthetical statement, the transcript also included a non-standard symbol for the new moon.

tide. The wind at this time blew lightly from the N^d or NE^d. In the afternoon the ship floated & was hauled down to the Bridge, but on account of a Strong breeze at NW & the prevalence of an uncommonly thick fog, we did not think it prudent to attempt to get to Sea. The Rain which fell the preceeding [*sic*] day, increased by the melting of the Snow in the Country occasioned by this day's fog & mild atmosphere, has caused a very strong efflux of fresh water from the River into the Sea. This is supposed to be the first general thaw in this County[1] of three months past! – Secured the Ship by strong moorings against the powerful action of the rapid <u>fresh</u>.

Wednesday 23^d In the morning Calm or light airs of wind from the Eastward prevailed; this with the force of the effluxion of fresh water deterred us from attempting to sail. The fresh had just attained its maximum velocity by the co-operating influence of the ebbing tide, when a fine Breeze of wind sprung up from the SW^d – We were now anxious to quit the harbour, which from its shallow water and ebbing dry prevents large ships from sailing by the lack of sufficient depth of water; except during a few days on the action of the Spring tides; unfavourable winds occurring at this period must altogether prevent ships of considerable draught from proceeding until another springs – This uncertainty made the owners grow uneasy & anxious to get the Ship to Sea, & all concerned hailed the favourable appearances of this day as promising a fulfillment of their wishes.

The favourable breeze continuing & the Ship floating at 3 Pm. was soon hauled through the Bridge; I then parted with my Dear Mrs S. & our Beloved Boy & in a few minutes the ship was under sail, with the assistance of a foy[2] Boat & lines to the pier we proceeded to Sea.

[*At this point the normal three-column format ('Dates', 'Winds', 'Occurrences, Remarks, &c. 1814') is adopted, and the first page of this format has the following heading:*]

The Journal

Wednesday 23^d of March
SW, W, & SW
At 4 Pm we passed the limits of the Harbour & cheered the crowd of spectators on the West Pier with the usual Huzzas, which were duly & cordially returned with every ['sign' *deleted*] indications of good wishes for the prosperity of the voyage. The Crew were ['Whitby Abbey in Lat 54°.28½ Lon. 0°.31½ W.' *in margin*] immediately mustered, all hands were found on board and every man sober! – Reached a little to the Northw^d & at 4¼ Pm the Pilots left us; tacked soon afterwards & stood close to the pier end, where we again tacked, parted with the only remaining shore Boat and

---

[1] *Sic*. Both 'Country' earlier and 'County' here are clearly written in the transcript.

[2] Layton, *Dictionary*: 'Foy Boat. Used in Tyne and other N.E. coast ports. About 15 ft. long, 4 ft. 6 in. beam. Pulls two oars and has a lugsail. Attended mooring of ships.' See also *OED*, s.v. 'foy'.

made sail on a NNE course – At 6 Pm Whitby Abbey bore SbW One Mile distant – In the Evening we had a brisk breeze from the NW^d propelling the ship with a velocity of 6 knots per hour. At Mig-N^t [*sic*] fine weather & clear – Several coasters seen.

Thursday 24th March Lat. 55°36′ Lon. 44′W.
NW^d – SW^d[,] Calm[,] SE to E.
Fine cloudy Morning with a fresh breeze of wind until 4 am. from 8 to 12 Calm, afterwards a fine breeze of wind from the SE^d[.] In the afternoon the clouds assumed a universal dense appearance with faint softened streaks of black in various places like as if faintly darked with a pencil of indian Ink, having something the appearance of the grain of old polished Oak: they were of the description ['described' *deleted*] mentioned by Luke Howard Esqr and by him called Cirro-Stratus: he notes two kinds,[1] these were of the dark grained sort; the position was nearly horizontal of most of the darkes: this modification of the clouds always predicts rain & that speedily: this form was assumed at 2 Pm. at 5 Rain commenced which increased to a strong continuous fall at 7 Pm.[2] – Course p Compass NNE. 4 Sail of vessels seen during the day. The Esk under all sails.

Friday 25th March Lat. 57°29′ Long. 1.17′W.
East
A moderate breeze of wind all day, attended with occasional Showers of Rain – Reaching close hauled by the wind to the NNE with a velocity of 3 to 5½ miles p hour. The Crew employed in sundry useful & needful work. Carpenters, & Cooper preparing the fishing apparatus. Temperature of the air during the day 39° to 42°. Of the water at the surface 41° at 10 am, Hydrometer 14.1 at Temp. 60° from whence the quantity of Salt in a wine gallon of this Sea water appears to be 5 ounces 10 drams.[3] Lat. 57°22′ Lon.1°.16W. – To ascertain the specific gravity of Sea water and its relative saltness*[4] therefrom, I procured from a Glass Blower two Glass Hydrometers: one of which had a small bulb & thick stem as N°. 1. of the following figures & the other a large bulb & very small stem. The former immersed in Rain water at temp.

---

[1] In his description 'Of the Cirro-stratus' (*Philosophical Magazine*, 1803, pp. 103–4) Howard did not recognize two forms of this cloud type. Scoresby seems to have been referring to the two illustrations of the type in Plate VI (*Philosophical Magazine*, 1804), but the difference in these illustrations appears to be caused by the way light falls on the cloud. See also Hamblyn, *Invention of Clouds*, ch. 10.

[2] Cirriform clouds, including but not limited to cirrostratus, are normally the first visible signs of an advancing depression, as they appear to have been on this occasion.

[3] Ocean salinities, measured in parts per thousand, generally range between 33‰ and 38‰, with 35‰ as the normal (i.e. 3.5% by weight). Scoresby's wine gallon is equivalent to the modern US gallon (231 cubic inches), so that his readings would indicate a salinity of about 40‰. However, if the quantity of water was the larger imperial gallon, the salinity would be 35‰. In *Account of the Arctic Regions*, I, the table at p. 183 gives a specific gravity of 1.0269 at 60°F for this measurement, equivalent to a salinity of 36‰. See also Introduction, p. xxxi.

[4] Footnote in MS: '*This is going on the supposition that the Salt of the Sea is in all places of the same description as to its property of raising the specific gravity by solution, in the same exact ratio.'

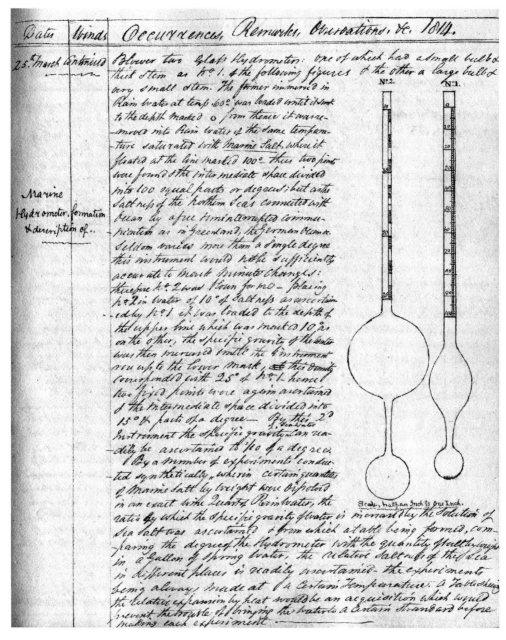

Figure 2. Scoresby's sketch of his 'hydrometers'
The modern term for similar instruments that measure atmospheric humidity is 'hygrometers' (Transcripts SCO1253, 25 March 1814). Photograph courtesy of the Whitby Museum.

60° was loaded until it sank to the depth marked o from thence it was removed into Rain water of the same temperature saturated with <u>Marine Salt</u>, where it floated at the line marked 100° – thus two points were found & the intermediate space ['Marine Hydrometer, formation & description of.' *in margin*] divided into 100 equal parts or degrees; but as the Saltness of the Northern Seas connected with Ocean by a free & uninterrupted communication as in Greenland, the German Ocean &c. seldom varies more than a single degree this instrument would not be sufficiently accurate to mark minute changes: therefore N°. 2 was blown for me – placing N° 2 in water of 10° of saltness as ascertained by N°. 1 it was loaded to the depth of the upper line which was marked as 10° as on the other, the specific gravity of the water was then increased until the instrument rose up to the lower mark, ['at' *deleted*] this density corresponded with 25° of N°. 1 – hence two fixed points were again ascertained & the intermediate space divided into 15° & parts of a degree – By this 2^d Instrument the specific gravity of sea water can readily be ascertained to $\frac{1}{10}$ of a degree.

By a number of experiments conducted synthetically, wherin certain quantities of marine salt by weight were dissolved in an exact wine Quart of Rain water, the ratio by which the specific gravity of water is increased by the solution of sea salt was ascertained & from which a table being formed, comparing the degree of the Hydrometer with the quantity of salt by weight in a gallon of spring water, the relative saltness of the Sea in different places is readily ascertained, the experiments being always made at a certain Temperature. A Table showing the relative expansion by heat would be an acquisition which would prevent the trouble of bringing the water to a certain standard before making each experiment.

Saturday 26 March Lat. 58°58′ Lon. 1°30′W.
Eerly[,] Calm[,] SSW. South, SSW[,] S.West, WSW
Calm in the Morning fine cloudy W^r[.] At 3 am. a breeze of wind sprang up from the S^d which by noon had increased to a fresh gale – Continued upon a NNE Course with Stearing [*sic*] Sails & all other canvass which could be of service spread to the wind. Saw two sail of Ships to the Westward of us – At noon steered North by the way of making Fair Island & at ½ Pm saw Land, Fair Isle at NNE p Compass distant about 20 miles – Dark cloudy weather. Several Gulls seen. A Starling pitched upon the Ship. At 5 Pm. Fair Island bore WNW p Compass distant 3 or 4 miles, the wind then blowing a ['fresh' *deleted*] strong Gale so powerful indeed that by continuing under all sails the Ship would have run the distance of Lerwick by 11 Pm. this however not being, scarcely indeed practicable owing to the haze which prevailed, further observing the darkness of the Sky, so as the [*sic*] render every object invisible at more than a miles distance: the great number of Ships likewise, which are generally at this Season collected together for the purpose of procuring men, renders taking the harbour in the night attended with great risque of receiving or ['giving' *deleted*] doing damage: by the way therefore of keeping astern reduced the sail, to three close reefed Top Sails under which we scudded NE. easterly 14 miles p Log & then hauled our wind to the ESE, Sumbrough head p account bearing NEbN 10 miles off. The weather was now stormy & hazy with Rain in Showers – We proceeded thus for two ['& ½' *deleted*]

hours (to 10 ['½' *deleted*] Pm.) when to our astonishment Land was descried under our lee at a very short ['Rapid tides & singular dangerous effects' *in margin*] distance: supposing it to be Sumborough head from the faint view the thickness & darkness of the night allowed us to take of it, we immediately set the Foresail, Mainsail, Mizen, Jib & Mizen Stay sail & reached rapidly to the Eastward – At 10½ Pm. Land was descried, on the lee bow, ahead, & to windward no part of which could be two miles distant, so that we were completely embayed; all hands sprang upon deck in a moment, the Ship was wore & all sail made on the contrary tack, by which we soon cleared the danger which threatened us & which might have been of the most serious consequences had we kept a bad look out, or the weather been thick foggy.[1] I perceived we had reached into Quedall Bay lying 3 or 4 miles to the NW^d of Sumbro' Head and hitherto we must have been driven by the tide in a direction p Compass N¼E or 11 miles in distance from the [place?] of the Ship as ascertained by the nicest calculation. From our wearing place in <u>Quedall Bay</u>, where Fitfil Head bore North, we steered by the wind, ['**Sunday 27 March** SW' *in margin*] WNW 6' & NW½ N, 5 miles & wore again at 1¼ am then proceeded SEbS 1¼ miles, SSE 6 miles & SE, 3 miles – thus at 5 am. from these courses & distances our Latitude should have been 59°.49′N & Lon. 1°.29W. instead of which from the bearing of Fair Isle, West p Compass, & Sumbro' Head NNE 12 miles off our true Lat. proved to be 59°.38 & Long. 1°.20′W from which it appears that the flood tide had set us in the contrary direction to the former ebb, whereby we were carried in a S¼W course p compass a distance of 12 miles by the action of the tide.*[2] Fair Isle & Sumbro Head made their appearance at 5 am in the above directions; we immediately bore up NEbN & set all sails, the wind being more moderate & sky clear. The sun rose from behind a low heavy cloud at 5^h 43′ am. the sky was serene & clear & bedecked with light fleeces of the \ & ⌒ description of cloud*[3] which shortly changed into the _of both the light and dark description, foreboding rain. At 7½ am. passed Sumbro Head at WNW – 5 Sail of ships then seen, two steering to the W^d & the rest apparently for Lerwick. Reduced our sails on approaching the Harbour & at 11½ am. anchored in Brassey

[1] See Appendix, p. 300.

[2] There is an addition to the text in the margin (not at the foot of the page): '*The tides about Fair Isle are said to set with a velocity of 7`miles p hour on Spring & 3`p hour on neap tides, & in different directions according to the situation.' It is somewhat surprising that Scoresby was not already aware of the tidal race known as Sumburgh Röst, as its existence and dangers had been known for centuries:

'Sumburgh Röst, a race of great violence, forms S of Sumburgh Head and Horse Island (1¼ miles W) during both the SE-going and NW-going tidal streams. At springs the race can be fully 3 miles wide if the wind, or the residual swell after a gale, is against the tidal stream. Within the race tidal streams set broadly E and W ...

Although it has not been definitely established, there appears to be no period of no race between the end of the W-going and commencement of the E-going race. Locally the W-going race is said to prevail for about 9 hours and the E-going for about 3 hours which is then followed by The Still of about 30 minutes duration.

In rough weather Sumburgh Röst is said to be dangerous at all times for vessels up to the size of small coasters.' (United Kingdom, Hydrographic Office. *North Coast of Scotland Pilot*, p. 192.)

[3] Footnote in transcript: '*Modifications of the clouds – \ signifies cirrus, ⌒ cumulus, _ stratus, \⌒ cirrocumulus, _ cirro-stratus, ⌒_cumulo stratus, & \⌒_ nimbus or cirro-cumulo-stratus.'

Sound with the ['Castle' *deleted*] Fort Charlotte at W. amidst a fleet of Fishing Ships amounting to 27 Sail, most ['anchored in Lerwick Harbour or Brassa Sound – Lat. 60°09′ Lon. 1°W.' *in margin*] of which want from 10 to 20 men each & expect to make up their deficiency at this place. Men are in great demand, consequently the wages high, beyond any former precedent – £3 or Guineas p month & 15/- p Size fish are given to the Shetland fishermen whilst from the port of Hull,*[1] prime Seamen are hired for [*blank space*] /- p mo. & 10/6 p fish ['generally far' *inserted above the line*] <u>infinitely</u> superior to most of <u>the best men, the produce of these Islands</u>.

We found all the Whitby fleet safe at anchor: they <u>all</u> arrived but yesterday. – We had fresh gales of wind the following part of the day with a constant cloudy rain threatening sky; some small showers fell. Having brought with me the Courier of the 21st Inst. containing the dispatches from Lord Wellington relative to the defeat of Soult by the armies under his command, and his subsequent entrance into Bordeaux in consequence thereof,[2] I was pressed on all hands on my landing for a sight of the news, mine being the only paper later than the 19th yet brought here: hence my Courier was esteemed as a valuable gift by the gentry here who seize with avidity any late news from the metropolis especially when of such masculine importance. I speedily put the paper into such a channel of circulation, that seemed best calculated to satisfy the interested & curious, the patriotic & the politician. Came in 4 Hull or Aberdeen Ships.

Monday 28th March
SW.erly

Fresh or Strong Gales of wind, squally with cloudy weather. Came in three Sail of Fishing ships & 5 Sailed for Greenland. All hands busily employed filling water in the after hold for Ballast to accomplish which all the Beer was taken upon ['Crew employed filling water for Ballast' *in margin*] deck & after the 2d tier of Casks were filled it was returned upon the top. Sent down the Gallant Yards. Made a trial of my Gig under Sail, she answered delightfully, & navigated the Sound with astonishing velocity & with great stability. This was the first trial with any suitable wind; she rigged with two <u>Settee</u> sails[3] together containing 50 yards of Canvass. At the time she was working up the sound two or three Ships drove with their anchors from the power of the wind. In the afternoon I went on shore after amusing myself for a while by Sailing across the Sound. – My friends here as usual I found kind & attentive: a few of the inhabitants I esteem but in general even those who are considered respectable are mercenary, fastidious, cringing, artful, characters: persons who do nothing without a motive of interestedness, or show ['Character, manners, dispositions, habits, &c, &c,&c. of the Zetlanders.' *in margin*] respect & attention but in the perspective ['prospect' *inserted above line*] of future benefit. The lower class of

---

[1] Footnote in transcript: '*The Seamen in Hull were particularly scarce this spring which causes the great demand here.'

[2] Bordeaux fell to Wellington's army on 12 March.

[3] The term 'settee' normally referred to a Mediterranean vessel with lateen sails (see Smyth, *Sailor's Word Book*, s.v. SETTEE) but *OED* cites a 1794 definition of a settee sail: 'This sail is quadrilateral. The head is bent to a lateen-yard.' See also Layton, *Dictionary*, s.v. 'Settee Rig'.

people are in their manners mean & wretched – wretched in their living, dirty beyond what can be found in Britain in the worst of circumstances, an outward shew of civility, respect, great consideration & servile humility: they are poor & <u>starve</u> through existance without complaint; their food is indulged but sparingly & of the ['most' *deleted*] worst kind. Potatoes, oatmeal & fish, form the extent of their bill of fare & frequently the latter is a desideratum which they cannot obtain. – They supply the Ships with Eggs, poultry, & milk, but on such terms as charity alone can warrant the accepting (or dire necessity) – They will not part with any article for money but always require a barter; – I never in my experience could bargain or truck with them under at least a double value of any article which they preferred, but more frequently 3 or 4 times the worth of their articles would scarcely content them. I once tried the experiment, how far self interest would induce a ['poor' *deleted*] servile wretch to outstop the value of the articles he had offer in return. He was a man in <u>moderate</u> cicumstances, by no means in necessity ['indigence' *inserted above line*] I ordered the Steward to give him of every article he should require at least the intrinsic worth of what he brought – He was presented with Beef & looked very gloomy, though fully the worth of his Eggs, & fowl, supposing he would get nothing more, in fact he would not have taken it on those terms: bread was then given him, & oatmeal & Barley: he then required spirits, & afterwards <u>drugs</u>: the Steward's patience was exhausted & he sent him off with about a Guinea's value of food for 1ˢ/6ᵈ of Shetland produce. – This over-reaching character, this bartering for high advantage prevails amongst I should suppose at least 9/10 of the population, it seems connected with their very nature, for many, nay most of the inhabitants ['Manners & disposition of Zetlanders Continued' *in margin*] of genteelest appearance discover the same trait if opportunity serve. There are exceptions, in Lerwick I have met with some families whom I value & respect, but thinly are they sown! – This disposition of the poor starving wretches who form the principal part of the population may be excused from the consideration of their wants, but in the opulent it is disgusting & hateful. – The lower rank, in costume seem to resemble the Icelanders: seal skin, or rather sheep skin [dresses?] are much worn by them. Instead of shoes sandals of the same material are worn laced across the foot & ancle, but many spare the use of either, by using that skin which a vital principal supplies on being removed or worn, by another of stronger texture, which is likewise as surely & duly removed. Their houses or huts are miserable hovels: the places of window & chimney are supplied by holes in the roof,whilst the same dwelling affords shelter for the family, the Cattle, the pigs & the fowls & occasionally without any separation but that of <u>respect</u>, the lower animals being removed farther from the fire! They all enter at the same door & differ but little in their manner of living. Their ideas are contracted, their wants few, they are supplied at the most moderate cost, whilst content & if possible happiness abides with them so long as food sufficient for the preservation of life can be procured.

Tuesday 29ᵗʰ March
SW, S.erly.
Very strong Gales the whole day attended with dark cloudy weather & some little rain. – Arrived two ships – Several made Signals for sailing but none departed,

owing the strength of the wind. Extraordinary wages yet continue to be paid for Shetland Seamen: £3 or Guineas p[1] ['Extraordinary wages obtained by the Shetlanders.' *in margin*] Month, with One Guinea p size fish, or 1/6 p Ton on Oil has been given by several ships. – This enormous rate of wages arises from the great number of men required by the fleet at present here, for completing their crews – Of 36 or 38 Ships, which we have seen here since our arrival I do not hear of one, except ourselves, ['but' *deleted*] that was obliged to be indebted to this port for the completion of their crew.[2] A great many require from 10 to 15 hands, a considerable number 20 & some few several more! No doubt the best of the men will be procured at these high wages, yet it is highly probable that towards the close of the engagements very good hands may be procured for one half of the present remuneratives – Besides it often happens that some of those youths who are too modest to presume on such high rewards for their services, & who will come forward towards the close, may be equal in abilities & practical capacity with those whose confidence induces them to consider themselves as first rate Seamen.

Completed the Ballast watering having filled about 80 tons of Casks with Sea water & brought the Ship down to a draught of 12^{ft} 6^{in} – forward & 13^{ft} 2^{in} abaft.[3] Replaced the pump which had been removed for the purpose filling these Casks. Ther*mometer* 44°, 45 & 40°. –

Wednesday 30th March Bar*ometer* 29.89 Ther*mometer* 40°–42°
SSW
Strong Gales all the day with dark cloudy weather – Came in the Harmony: Several Ships made Signals for Sailing but none departed. The People employed in procuring a supply of sand, in defending the rigging by mats, overhauling & repairing sundry stores, &c &c –

Thursday 31st March
S.erly SSE. or SE
Strong Gales all the day, in the Evening very hard gales accompanied with rain – arrived a vessel from Berwick brings no news. Sailed the Henrietta of Whitby although the weather was very tempestuous, sea high, & wind very oblique to the course insomuch that [it?] is expected she would not weather the Skerries but must go within the Islands & even then must experience great difficulty in clearing the northern extremity of the Island.[4]

---

[1] Possibly '12' from the handwriting, but unlikely from the context.

[2] There seems to be a transcription error in this sentence. As written, it implies that the *Esk* was the only vessel requiring additional crew members, but the sense of the journal entry is precisely the opposite; the *Esk* appeared to Scoresby to be the only ship that arrived in Lerwick fully manned.

[3] See p. 93, note 1.

[4] Scoresby seems to be saying that the *Henrietta* was unlikely to be able to pass to the east of the Out Skerries (60°25′N 48′W) and might subsequently have difficulty in passing the north tip of Unst.

The wind at Sea seems to be about SE or ESE whilst in the Harbour it blows from the SSE. At 6 Pm. gave the ship a long Service of Cable[1] on the small Bower after dropping the sheet anchor.

[*At this point, the bottom of a left-hand page, the journal format is temporarily abandoned. The facing page is devoted to a description, and large diagram, drawn to scale, of a floating anchor (Fig. 3). The following left-hand page is blank; then follow three tables regarding personnel, each occupying one page.*]

Afloating [*sic*] Anchor

Length of each Bar 16 feet; Breadth 2½ Inches & ⅜ to ⅝ in thickness: The Bars turn upon an Eyebolt center [*sic*] at <u>A</u>[2] passing through the [under?] one with square shoulder & turning on the upper one by a round shoulder & screwed fast by a nut. It is covered with Nº 1[3] Canvass upon a 2½ Inch Bolt rope,[4] having diagonal bands or linings for protection from chafes by the Iron – There are 4 eyebolt upon each bar besides the Center one which is common to both, the [*sic*] have all square shoulders & are screwed on by nuts.

In the Centre of the Canvass is a large eye ['bolt' *deleted*] let hole through which passes the center eye-bolt before it is screwed fast. The rest of the eyebolts are withdrawn & when the Canvass is stretched to the 4 extremities of the bars, the eyebolts are passed thro' eyelet holes into their places and screwed at the back.

Scale half an Inch to a Foot.

1814. Copy of the Articles of agreement between the Master & Crew of the Esk

Nº	Men's Names	Quality & Stations	Sea Pay p Month	Striking Money	Fish Money	Oil Money p Ton	Hand Money
			£ s d	£ s d	£ s d	£ s d	£ s d
1	Christ.ʳ Crawford	Surgeon	4 0 0	—	1 1 0	—	—
2	George Sinclair[5]	Mate & Harponeer	2 2 0	0 10 6	1 1 0	0 6 0	7 7 0
3	John Trueman	Specksioneer & Harponeer	—	0 10 6	0 10 6	0 6 4	8 8 0
4	Robert Dowell	Second Mate & Harponeer	1 1 0	0 10 6	—	0 6 0	7 7 0
5	John Dunbar	Boatswain, [Gun.ʳ?] & H.	1 6 0	0 10 6	—	0 6 0	7 7 0

[1] Smyth, *Sailor's Word Book*: 'A thick, strong rope or chain which serves to keep a ship at anchor; the rope is cable-laid, 10 inches in circumference and upwards ...'.

[2] The 'A' is not marked on the sketch in the transcript, though the location of the bolt is obvious.

[3] Smyth, *Sailor's Word Book*, s.v. 'CANVAS': 'It is ... numbered from 1 to 8, rarely to 9 and 10. Number 1 being the coarsest and strongest, is used for the lower sails, as fore-sail and main-sail in large ships.' However, Layton's *Dictionary* states that canvas is 'Graded in numbers from 0 to 7, 0 being the heaviest.'

[4] Smyth, *Sailor's Word Book*: 'A rope sewed all round the edge of the sail, to prevent the canvas from tearing.'

[5] See the criticism of Sinclair in Scoresby's journal entry for 17 June 1815, after Sinclair had become master of the *Valiant*.

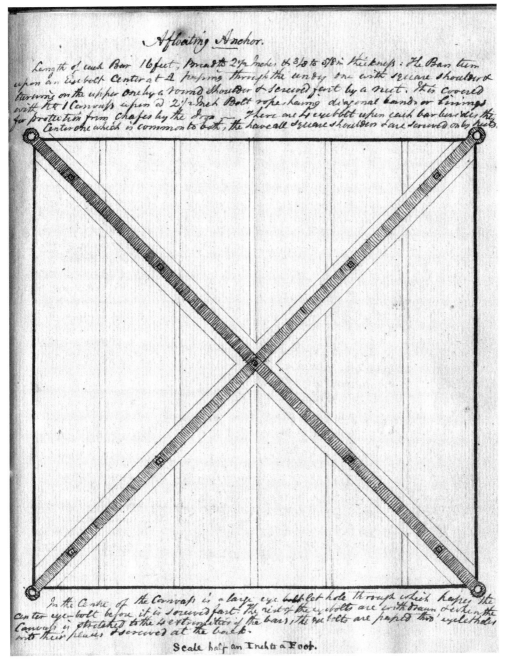

Figure 3. Scoresby's sketch of his floating anchor

The scale indicated is inaccurate as reproduced here. Photograph courtesy of the Whitby Museum. See also the journal entry and illustration for 19 April 1813, where Scoresby described it as a 'tracking machine, or floating anchor'.

Nº.	Men's Names	Quality & Stations	Sea Pay p Month	Striking Money	Fish Money	Oil Money p Ton	Hand Money
			£ s d	£ s d	£ s d	£ s d	£ s d
6	Thomas Welborn	Harponeer	—	0 10 6	—	0 6 0	7 7 0
7	George Bulman	Skeeman & Loose Harponeer	4 1 0	1 1 0	—	0 1 6	—
8	William Watson	Boatsteerer	3 0 0	1 1 0	—	0 1 6	—
9	Thomas Hewson	do	3 0 0	—	—	0 1 6	—
10	James Storm	do	3 0 0	—	—	0 1 6	—
11	Thomas Parsey¹	do	3 0 0	—	—	0 1 6	—
12	John Nicholson	do	3 0 0	—	—	0 1 6	—
13	John Webster	Boatsteerer & Cooper	4 9 0	—	—	0 1 6	—
14	Samuel Gaskoyne	Linemanager	2 17 6	—	—	0 1 6	—
15	Thomas Anderson	do	2 17 6	—	—	0 1 6	—
16	Thomas Schorfield	do	2 17 6	—	—	0 1 6	—
17	James Carthew	do	2 17 6	—	—	0 1 6	—
18	John Hutcheson	do	2 17 6	—	—	0 1 6	—
19	Richard Anderson	do	2 17 6	—	—	0 1 6	—
20	Richard Slytom	Carpenter	4 15 0	—	1 1 0	—	—
21	John Stamp	do mate	3 5 0	—	—	0 1 6	—
22	John Hebdon	Cook's mate	2 17 6	—	—	0 1 6	—
23	Anderson Graham	Cook & Seaman	3 0 0	—	—	0 1 6	—
24	Richard Simpkin	Steward & do	3 0 0	—	—	0 1 6	—
25	Richard Simpkin Junior	Seaman	2 15 0	—	—	0 1 6	—
26	John Harrison	do	2 15 0	—	—	0 1 6	—
27	Edwin Messenger	do	2 15 0	—	—	0 1 6	—
28	William Standen	do	2 15 0	—	—	0 1 6	—
29	Francis Brown	do	2 15 0	—	—	0 1 6	—
30	George Mackenzie	do	2 15 0	—	—	0 1 6	—
31	Thomas Piercy	Seaman & Armourer	3 15 0	—	1 1 0	—	—
32	Robert Potts	do	2 15 0	—	—	0 1 6	—
33	Martin Hall	do	2 15 0	—	—	0 1 6	—
34	Thomas Innis	do	2 15 0	—	—	0 1 6	—
35	George Maclane	do	2 15 0	—	—	0 1 6	—
36	William Dawson	do	2 15 0	—	—	0 1 6	—
37	Joseph Pierson	do	2 15 0	—	—	0 1 6	—
38	Thomas Shippy	do	2 15 0	—	—	0 1 6	—
39	Jonathan Wright	½ Seaman	2 10 0	—	—	0 1 0	—
40	John Jones	Seaman (Italian)	2 10 0	—	—	0 1 6	—
41	William Shepherd	½ Seaman	2 15 0	—	—	0 1 0	—
42	Thomas Smith	½ do	2 15 0	—	—	0 1 0	—
43	John Mowatt	Shetland Boy	1 10 0	—	0 5 0²	—	—
44	Charles Steward	Supernumary & 7 Boys apprentices with the Master makes 52 in Nº.					

[*The following note was included in the table, running from bottom to top at the side of the final column:* 'NB. All the persons in this List, excepting Nᵒˢ 2, 3, 4, 5, 6, & 43 have 5ˢ/- p month more wages if the Ship procures a Cargo 100 Tons of Oil.']

¹ Or 'Passey'; it is also doubtful in the following table of watches and boat's crews.
² There is also a dash, like those above, beneath this entry, but the amount seems clearly aligned with Mowatt's name.

Distribution of the Crew of the Esk into Watches, Boat's Crews, &c. 1814

Mate's Watch		Specksioneer's Watch		Captain's Watch	
Boat N⁰ 2		Boat N⁰ 4		Boat N⁰ 6	
George Sinclair (Mate)	H	John Trueman (Speck)	H	Robert Dowell (2[d] Mate)	H
Thomas Hewson	B	Thomas[1] Parsey	B	William Watson	B
Richard Anderson	Li	James Carthew	Li	Samuel Gascoyne	Li
Geo. McKenzie	S	Richard Simpkin	S	Edwin Messenger	S
Robert Potts	S	Joseph Pierson	S	Thomas Innis	S
William Shepherd	½S	John Jones	½S	Thomas Smith	½S
David Robinson	Ap	Geo. McLane	S	John Mowatt	Boy
Boat N⁰ 1		Boat N⁰ 3		Boat N⁰ 5	
John Dunbar	H	Thomas Welburn	H	George Bulman	H
John Nicholson	B	James Storm	B	John Webster	B
John Hutcheson	Li	Thomas Schofield	Li	Thomas Anderson	Li
John Harrison	S	William Standen	S	Francis Brown	S
John Stamp	La[2]	Martin Hall	S	William Dawson	S
Thomas Shippy	S	Richard Slytom (Carp.)	S	Jonathan Wright	½S
James Wells	Ap	John Hebdon	La	George Sair	Ap
Extras.		Extras.		Extras.	
Nelson Corner	Ap	Thomas Wilson	Ap	Robert Dowell	Ap
Ralph Elden	Ap	Thomas Piercy	Armourer	Anderson Graham	Cook
Christopher Crawford	Surg[n]	Richard Simpkin	Steward	Mr Charles Steward	Supernumary

[1] 'James' deleted.

[2] *Sic.* John Stamp is shown in the crew list as carpenter's mate; John Hebdon, in the next column, was the cook's mate.

Comparative Table of Wages paid to different Classes of Men & Officers in the Whale fishery trade from various ports of Great Britain

Stations	Whitby. Sea pay p month	Striking money	Fish money	Oil money p Ton	Hand money	London. Sea pay p month	Striking money	Fish money	Oil money off 1/25	Hand money	Hull. Sea pay p month	Striking money	Fish money p Ton	Oil money	Hand money
Harponeer	–	0.10.6	–	6/-	7 7 0	–	0.10.6	–	6/-	7 7 0	–	10/6	–	6/-	7 7 0
Boatsteerer	3 0 0	1 1 0	–	1/6	–	2 10 0	–	0 5 0	1/0	–	2 10 0	–	10/6	–	–
Linemanager	2 17 6	–	–	1/6	–	2 10 0	–	0 5 0	1/0	–	2 10 0	–	10/6	–	–
Seaman	2 15 0	–	–	1/6	–						2 10 0	–	10/6	–	–
Landmen	2 0 0 / 2 10 0	–	–	1/- / 1/6	–										
Mate (Single[l])	3 0 0	1 1 0	1 1 0	1/6 / 3/-	–										
Mate & H. (Extra)	2 2 0	0 –	1 1 0	–	–	2 10 0	–	1 1 0	–	–	2 0 0	–	21/-	–	–
2d Mate "	1 1 0	–	–	–	–						1 1 0	–	10/6	–	–
Boatswain "	1 1 0	–	–	–	–										
Specksioneer "	–	–	0 10 6	0/4	1 1 0	–	–	0 10 6	0/8	1 1 0	–	–	10/6	–	1 1 0
Surgeon	4 0 0 / 5 5 0	–	1 1 0	–	–	5 0 0	–	1 1 0	–	–	3 13 6	–	21/-	–	–
Carpenter	4 15 0	–	1 1 0	–	–						7 0 0	–	21/-	–	–
Cooper	4 4 0	–	–	1/6	–						4 4 0	–	31/6	–	–
Carp. mate	3 5 0	–	–	1/6	–						3 0 0	–	10/6	–	–
Cook	3 0 0	–	–	1/6	–										
Carpenter & H						3 0 0	10/6	1 1 0	6/0	7 7 0					
Skeeman & H. (Extra)	1 1 0	–	–	–	–						0 15 0	–	10/6	–	–
Loose H & Boatswain	3 0 0	1 1 0	–	1/6	–						3 10 0	1 1 0	21/-	–	–

[The normal three column format of the Journal now resumes, after a blank left-hand page.]

Friday 1ˢᵗ April
SE to SSW to SbE

Very strong Gales in the night accompanied with Rain: moderate weather in the morning, in the night thick fog. The opportunity seeming favourable a great part of the Ships in the Sound weighed & proceeded to Sea: I was dubious on account of the high Sea without & the apparent unsettled state of the weather, at length determined to stay. No arrivals this day – Bar*ometer* 29.52 Therm*ometer* 42° to 46°.

Saturday 2ᵈ of April
SSE, SE, E. SSE var.

Light or fresh Gales in the morning with Rain or thick fog. Variable weather & winds. Prepared for sailing but relinquished the thought on account of the wind blowing much more Easterly at Sea, so much indeed as to render the certainty of clearing the land very critical.

Distributed our Crew consisting of 51[1] hands (one additional Boy having been engaged here for 30/- p month & 5/- p size fish) & Mʳ Steward a supernumary into Boats' Crews of Seven Men each, & also into three divisions for three watches – Likewise lotted for their respective Boats, for the purpose of getting them properly fitted.

In the Evening much Rain. <u>No arrivals although</u> all the London Ships are expected to be on their passage.

Sunday 3ᵈ of April
SE. SSE.variable S.

Fresh or moderate Gales all this day with showers of Rain & constant dark heavy weather. No arrivals: no ships sailed.

Monday 4ᵗʰ of April Lat. 60°14′ Long. 50′W.
S.erly. var. SW. W or WNW

Light airs with fine weather in the Morning – at 6 am. prepared for sailing & at 8 weighed anchor: we had not proceeded far before we found the Cooper was not on board: lay too in the Sandy Bay to the northward of the Town & sent a Boat on shore for him. They returned in about an hour, having discovered the absentee very busily engaged in assisting at the ceremonies of a <u>Cock fight</u>![2] Immediately made sail & at 10½ am. having reached the Ocean discharged the Pilot & proceeded upon an East or EbS cruise to clear the <u>Soulden Rock</u>[3] from whence an EbN course likewise cleared the Skerries at 3½ Pm. All the Fishing Ships in the Harbour (19 Sail) except two

---

[1] Could also be read as '57' but the crew list earlier, including Charles Steward and the seven apprentices, is clearly 51, plus Scoresby.

[2] This was legal at the time, and may have remained so in Scotland until 1895, although it had been banned in England by the middle of the century.

[3] This name did not appear on the Hydrographic Office's chart of the Orkney and Shetland Islands that was published in 1807.

accompanied us to Sea. Squally in the Evening with Rain. At 8 Pm. the north end of Shetland lying in Lat. 60°53' & Long. 0°38'W bore due West 3 Lea*gue*s off.

['I cannot' *deleted*] Before entering another day I may mention a remarkable house I saw near Lerwick, situated in the angle of two rocks ['Remarkable house near Lerwick' *in margin*] on the west edge of the Garrison – it increased on the outside 6 feet in breadth 6 feet from the ground to the summit of the roof & about 8 feet in length: it is built of rough stones without lime or clay & forms an habitation for a wretched woman of the name of ['Inge'(?) *inserted above line*] Phillips, a poor crea-ture of shallow mind & the most miserable means of life. Her house is said to have been formed by her own hands.

Tuesday 5th April Lat. 62°14' Long. 0°18'W
West WNW variable

Fresh or moderate breezes of wind, rainy in the Night, but charming fine weather during the day – All hands employed making matts for the rigging & spanning Harpoons: viz, the operation of affixing 4 to 4½ or 5 fathoms of untarred rope of 2½ Inches circumference called a Foreganger to each Harpoon as a precursor to the less suple [*sic*] Whale line, & securing a Stock or handle to the Harpoon thereby – at the same time, wrapped the cutting part of the previously cleansed Harpoon in Oiled paper to prevent its rusting. Beneath the Service of rope yarns on the Socket of the Harpoon is placed ['Spanned Harpoons' *in margin*] a leathern [mark?], bearing the Characters **Esk Scoresby 1814**, written with Ink in which has been dissolved a portion of lunar Caustic[1] or Blue vitriol[2] to prevent its washing out. A similar mark is likewise placed within the strands of each foreganger: a usual precaution to prevent mistakes with regard to the priority of claim to any whale struck between two vessels.

Unbent the Cables & hauled the wetted parts upon the deck to dry.

All the fleet which sailed with us are yet in sight, all excepting three are astern. At noon, after steering all night & the morning upon a NNE course, we found ourselves in Latitude 62°14'N.

Light winds in the Evening & variable; & cloudy sky.

Wednesday 6th of April Lat. 63°44' Lon. 0°39'W.
Werly SW, SSW South SSW

At 2 am. the wind veered to the S[d] set steering sails. During the day we had moderate to fresh Gales, delightful fine weather in the morning, cloudy at noon. Several of the fleet in sight chiefly astern. Two sail far ahead. Aroused all hands at 8 am; cleared the cable stage of ropes, & 5 provision casks, & in the afternoon placed the cables theron.

In the Cable Tier coyled all the Ice ropes, in such a way as to leave every one at liberty & clear of each other.

This being the anniversary of M[rs] Scoresby's Birth['day' *deleted*] as likewise of my mother's served out to the Crew an additional allowance of ['the' *deleted*] spirits,

---

[1] Silver nitrate ($AgNO_3$). See *OED*, s.v. 'lunar'.
[2] Copper (II) sulphate pentahydrate ($CuSO_4.5H_2O$).

wherewith they failed not to improve its enlivening influence by every species of jollity which they could command – music, singing, & dancing closed the harmonious hours of the Evening.

In the cabin likewise we were not backward in celebrating the occasion.

In the Evening we had dark hazy weather with a Strong Gale of wind – Parted C^o with all the fleet, some steering more Easterly, some more westerly but the chief part were left astern. Shortened sail.

Thursday 7th April Lat. 66°52' Lon. 0°36'W
SSW, West. to NW
In the morning dark rainy weather: Sea very high from the SW^d the Ship ['roll' *deleted*] laboured considerably. The wind blowing strong, veered more westerly during the rain. At noon we found ourselves in Latitude 66°52'N, having run a distance of 188 miles During the preceding 24 hours or nautical day. At 2 Pm. the ship went with a velocity of 10 Knots p hour. At 7 the wind increasing & the atmosphere stormy [we?] reduced our Canvass to 2 treble reefed Topsails & [F.T.?] Staysail[.] very hard Gales the rest of the night.

Friday 8th April Lat 68°35' Long. 0°38'E
NNW, NW Var SSW
Towards morning the wind moderated somewhat, but the Sea was still very heavy. At 6 am. set the Main & Foresails reefed, and at 10 am made more sail. Two sail in sight ahead.

At 6 Pm. sent up Top Gall*ant* Yard & made sail NNE before the wind. Dark weather with snow or sleet.

Saturday 9th April Lat. 70°17'+ Lon. 0°24'W
WNW EbN
Steering NNE: at 5 am. the wind suddenly veered from WNW to EbN[;] at 8 strong Gales with squally weather, towards noon more moderate. Constant snow – Ship close hauled by the wind on the starboard tack. In the Afternoon the Therm*omete*r fell from 32 to 25° – Snow finely crystallized. The lengthening day now proclaims our rapid approach towards the pole. In this Latitude we have scarcely 4 hours night, though the twilight commences before 8 in the Evening. At 7 pm. temp*erature* of the Sea at surface 37½° saltness Hydrom*ete*r ≃ 14.3 at Temp. 60°.[1] The night was fine.

Sunday 10th April Lat. 71°14+ Lon. 2°35'W[2]
ESE
Fresh Gales with squally blasts prevailed during this day. The intensity of the frost advanced ['increased' *above line*] with our approach towards Ice. At 6 am. whilst steering under a brisk sail to the North, close hauled; observed appearance of young

---

[1] See Introduction, p. xxxii.
[2] This position is preceded in the margin by 'at noon', presumably to distinguish it from the other coordinates in the margin that indicate the location where the *Esk* reached the ice.

Ice on the surface of the Sea & shortly afterwards entered an extensive sheet of Bay Ice, wherin by the motion ['Make the Ice but not the main body in Lat. 71°8′N Lon. 2°40′W' *in margin*] or undulation of the swell this prevented from freezing into a continuous sheet but became divided, the separate pieces being [urged?] against each other assume a roundish form whilst ['crushed?' *deleted*] their edges are thickened by the incorporation of the crushed fragments: this description ['Pancake Ice' *in margin*] of young Ice is by the sailors called <u>pancakes</u> or <u>pancake</u> Ice. These masses are at first very small but as they gain thickness they are enlarged by acquisition, many being cemented by the [frost?] into one mass, until at length they are sufficient to bear the weight of a man, at the same time, they have great power in allaying the force of the Sea. The thinnest film of Ice on the water, smoothens the surface however agitated: similar to the remarkable effect produced by Oil.[1]

At 8 am. saw two ships ahead of us – At 9¼ am. having come amongst Ice of several days formation, the ship made small progress; tacked least the wind should abate & the frost arrest us in our course. At ['Temp. air 5°!' *in margin*] 6 am. the Temp*erature* of the air was 14 at 10 am 5°! Frost rime makes its appearance on every portion of vacant surface of the Sea this [*sic*] [exposed?], or uncovered by Ice. At Noon were in Lat. 71°14′ – 2 strange sail to lee-ward – Within 24 hours the Temp*erature* of the Air has been reduced more than 20°: this great variation of necessity has a wonderful effect on the human frame: it calls into use, wigs, mitts, Peajackets, Comforters, & every other invention for retaining and accumulating heat in the system.

It is in the use of these resources that we are enabled to support with any degree of comfort cold so intense. At 8 Pm. Temp*erature* 4°.

About 8 Pm. a fiery meteor was observed consisting of a <u>Bluish</u> ['Fiery Meteor' *in margin*] <u>Ignited</u> Ball followed by a Red luminous tail. It took a direction descending from EbN to WbS & disappeared behind a dark horizonal [*sic*] cloud.[2]

[*The following paragraph extends the full width of the page, across the margins headed 'Dates' and 'Winds.'*] O thou inexhaustible Source of Life & Light, the protector of the faithful, the God of Salvation – Behold now in tender compassion thy humble dependants. In the hope of thy care and guidance we have ventured forth on the bosom of the mighty deep, where occasionally we behold thy wonders on the stormy Ocean. Nevertheless that we are unholy, unworthy & undeserving of any of thy mercies; yet, in consideration of the meritorious sacrifice of the Blessed ['precious' *above line*] Jesus, we hope for thy blessing on this our adventurous voyage. Be thou O God our guide, our strong-hold, our defence; the Rock of our Salvation & the director of our lives – Blessed by thee, nothing can fail us, no human malice can harm us, no danger overcome us, no fear appal us. We trust in humble confidence, O thou God of omnipotence, that as thou hast heretofore graciously manifested thy self as our preserver from ['amidst' *above line*] the most alarming dangers, that as thou hast done these mighty things for us whereof we are glad, we diffidently hope thou wilt

---

[1] *Brewer's Dictionary*, s.v. 'oil', notes that this effect was mentioned as far back as Bede's *Ecclesiastical History* of 731.

[2] This would nowadays be termed a 'fireball'. The colours described by Scoresby are explained in the website of the American Meteor Society: www.amsmeteors.org/fireball/faqf.htm.

not on this occasion desert us. Prosper us O Lord in all our justifiable undertakings; be thou our support in all dangers and difficulties, & if we are spared to return crowned with Success enable us to devote to thy cause & glory, liberally of those benefits with which thou so bountifully crownest our exertions. May we perform every act & work with humble dependence on thee, & may every dispensation of thy providence, whether for good or apparent ill, be sanctified unto us, be submissively and patiently received impressed with the confidence that thou dost all things well. Into thy Fatherly Care O Lord we would commend those of our kindred, our nearest & dearest [ties?]: Be thou their support their defence, afford them comfort under every privation, & preserve them in health for our future comfort & happiness. If we are mutually spared for the realizing of this, the purest Blessing of Sense; May Thou the Great First Cause receive due thanks & praise for thy wonderful works to us the Children of Men. Lord if thy providence ordains that we should not meet again on Earth; O grant that we may rest submissive to thy Holy Will in a well grounded confidence of a joyous communion in the realm of Glory, with them, with thee the Glorious three in One for the sake of the Great High Priest Jesus Christ Amen.[1]

During the night we continued plying to windward with a fresh Gale of wind from the ENE amongst young Ice, ['for Shelter' *deleted*] which afforded shelter from the chief part of the Sea. The Augusta & William of London occasionally near us. Frost rime all the night.

Monday 11th April Lat 71°17′+ Lon. 2°5 W
ENE NE.
At 4 am. the Thermometer stood at 4° at 11 am 6° & another coated with Ice & exposed to the wind sank to +4½°. At noon the Temperature of the Cabin 4½ feet from the front of a brisk fire was 25°! In the steerage & store-room almost every liquid freezes – water freezes within 2 feet of the Stove. At 4 pm. the mean of two Thermometers was 3°. The air at this time seemed absolutely humid as, on one thermometer being coated with Ice it showed ['indicated' *above line*] the same temperature as the dry one in a simultaneous Experiment.[2]

Blowing a Gale of wind all day attended with intense frost & thick frost rime. Stood in amongst the Bay Ice until it became strong & almost impervious, then tacked (at 11 am) & reached to the Eastward all the ['night ***' *deleted*] afternoon & night amidst streams of Bay ['**Tuesday 12 April** Lat. 71°20 Lon. 2°E[.] NE, NNE, var. East. very variable' *in margin*] Ice with here and there a piece of older formation. At day light the Weather was fine but still intensely cold: the Thermometer stood at the Zero & even at mid-day only indicated a temperature of +1½°! Frost rime very thick. The wind being more moderate, made sail & reached about 20 miles amongst Bay intermixed with a few pieces of heavy Ice, aggregated into Streams: these streams

---

[1] This unusual supplication contrasts with what Scoresby later wrote in his autobiography about his feelings at the outset of the 1814 voyage. See Introduction, p. xxvii.
[2] The difference in temperature shown by 'dry bulb' and 'wet bulb' thermometers (the latter either covered by a moist wick or the bulb coated with ice) is the standard method of measuring atmospheric relative humidity. As Scoresby stated, no difference in temperature indicates a saturated atmosphere (100% relative humidity).

lay widely scattered with unfrozen space between & apparently highly favourable for sealing, however we saw but one the whole day. In the Evening the wind Eastering & seeming inclined from the Southward, we hastened towards the verge of the Ice under a brisk sail – Saw two ships – at 8 Pm. obtained the Sea edge, reduced sails & stood off until 2 am. ['**Wednesday 13**th **April**[,] Lat. 70°00′ Lon. 2°20′E[,] ESE (5′/ Calm?).[1] West. or WSW.' *in margin*] when we tacked & again made the Ice at 7 am, in large washed pieces; tacked off – The wind now increasing to a very hard Gale accompanied by snow, close reefed the Top Sails & in the afternoon furled all sails but the reefed Fore Sail & Close reefed Main Top Sail. I dont recollect ever observing in this country or indeed elsewhere such remarkable changes in the state of the Atmosphere both with regard to pressure & temperature, within the space of 24 hours as occurred ['remarkable changes in the Atmosphere' *in margin*] at this time. Yesterday at 4 Pm the Thermometer indicated a temperature of 1½° or 2° to day at 4 Pm it stood at 34° & at 6 at 36°, a variation of 32° in 24 hours & 34° in about 26 hours! the Barometer at the same time was far from a state of quescience [*sic*] having fallen from 30.10 to 29.10 Inches from 6 Pm of the preceeding to 6 Pm of the present day, a variation of One Inch in 24 hours! At this time (6 Pm.) the wind from blowing furiously hard suddenly abated, the sky cleared in the SW quarter & ['Sudden change of wind' *in margin*] became beautifully bedecked with clouds of the Cirro-Cumulus & the bold Cirri extending across the Heavens in a NW and SE direction. The sky clearing in any other quarter than the windward is generally a token ['Correct indications of Atmospheric appearances' *in margin*] of a speedy change of wind from that ['dir' *deleted*] point. So it proved in this instance for after a few minutes Calm, western coursing waves were observed to project their sprays into the air which were immediately arrested by a western Breeze & deflected backward from their source. Speedily the wind ['(WSW)' *above line*] was felt in the sails it rapidly increased insomuch that at 10 Pm. a very hard Gale resulted attended with rain, agreeable to the indications of _[2] clouds & the low state of the Barometer. Steering ENE under two close reefed T. Sails & foresail. Sea excessively turbulent.

Thursday 14th **April** Lat. 71°49′+ Lon. 3°10′E
WSW to NNW variable EbS, E
At 2 am. made a progress of 7 knotts p hour against a strong <u>head Sea</u> on an ENE course & soon afterwards the wind veered to the NWd & abated. The Morning was fine & clear. Employed all hands, in repairing the Chafes of the late Gales, in stowing 4 of the Guns below, suspending a Boat by the Quarter Davits, Airing Sails, &c, &c. At 11 am a strong Easterly swell prevailed, the sky became dark in the East, & very shortly afterwards a strong Gale attended with thick snow commenced momentarily from that ['same' *deleted*] quarter augmented by tremendous squalls. Having advanced a short distance amongst some scattered pieces of Ice we ['at noon Barometer 29.34 Thermometer 32' *in margin*] tacked the ship, & although every exertion

---

[1] From what is narrated in the journal, Scoresby probably intended this to mean a calm lasting five minutes.
[2] Cirrostratus.

was used it was with the greatest difficulty that we [saved?] the smaller ['lighter' *above line*] sails. Had I paid the wonted respect to my Barometer we should have been prepared for the event, but really the clear <u>syren</u>[1] morning induced me to spread all sails to the refreshing influence of a warm Sun. Treble reefed the Top sails & proceeded on a SSE or S. course by the wind under as much sail as we could prudently carry.

In the Evening we had heavy squalls, thick Snow & high Sea.

Friday 15ᵗʰ April Lat. 71°4′+ Lon. 3°20′E
ESE
In the morning the Gale became less violent, tacked at 8 am, & made sail towards the Ice: ['with' *deleted*] fine cloudy weather & <u>Temperate</u>. At 8 Pm. saw two ships standing off the Ice; at 10 we tacked. Sun set at 8ʰ 0′ Pm.

Saturday 16ᵗʰ April Lat. 71°46′+ Lon 4°E[2]
ENE or East
Brisk Gales all the day & fine cloudy weather – at 8 Am. tacked near some streams of Ice, returned at 11 am & at 3 Pm. we reached in amongst scattered Ice which led us to the edge of a ragged <u>Pack</u>, somewhat slack on the border but apparently solid within; seeing no Seals we again tacked off. A strange sail to windward.

Sunday 17ᵗʰ April Lat. 71°43′+ Lon. 4°[***]E
E, NE, NNE
Most delightful weather, wind moderate, sea smooth. This day passed over without the Sun being obscured for a moment & scarcely ['uncommon fine weather' *in margin*] a cloud could be discerned at any time, except some very few faint toutches near the Southern Horizon – I don't recollect ever seeing so clear a day throughout in the Greenland Seas. At 4 am. tacked in & at 4 Pm approaching the verge of the Ice tacked off: three sail of Ships in sight; names not known. Nevethess [*sic*] the Sun shone unclouded throughout the day the Temp*erature* of the air constantly decreased – at 8 am. the Therm*ometer* was at 27°, at Noon 25° & at 4 Pm. 20°. At 6 pm saw seven ships.

[1] Presumably a variant spelling of 'serene', but not shown as such in the *OED* entry for 'serene' as an adjective.
[2] The value of this longitude, and those for several successive days (16–21 April and 23 April, are in pencil, apparently as later additions to the ink transcript, which was left blank in all cases. The value for 22 April is complete in ink, and that for 24 April has no longitude value in ink or pencil. Steward's journal does include the following coordinates in the margin: 15 April 71°04N [3?]°0E; 16 April 71°46′N 3°28′E; 17 April 71°45′N 3°34′E; 18 April 72°15′N 7°0′E; 19 April 72°51N 8°22′E; 20 April 72°46′N 8°30′E; 21 April 72°46′N 11°21′E; 22 April 73°29′N 12°30′E; 23 April 73°55′N 10°24′E; 24 April 74°00′N 14°26′ [*indicated, as explained in Steward's journal for this date, as obtained by observation, with a longitude of 13°0′ by account (i.e. dead reckoning) also noted in the margin*]; 25 April 76°10′N 13°[5?]′N; 26 April 76°54′N 13°0′E. Note that Steward's and Scoresby's values frequently differ by small amounts, here and elsewhere in the two journals. See also Appendix, p. 297.

Monday 18ᵗʰ April Lat. 72°15′+ Lon. [7 E?]
N, NNE, N to NW

We had light winds most of this day, towards Evening a moderate Breeze. This day like the last, past over without a cloud in the Atmosphere, except towards Sun set when a few bold Cirri or faint _ made their appearance in the north. The Sun set at 8ʰ 32′[.] The Sun shone with uncommon splendour; such two successive days as the past never witnessed in these Regions.

In the Morning steering NE by the wind, passed several loose pieces of Ice and desultory streams. Towards noon the main Ice made its appearance, exhibiting a heavy pack of varied Ice, which trended ['Thermom*eter* 8 am. 20° noon 25°, 8 Pm 15° Bar. 29.90′ *in margin*] more Easterly afterwards so that we steered about an ENE course from Noon to 8 Pm & from thence to 3 am. SE along the edge of the Ice. At ['**Tuesday 19ᵗʰ April** Lat 72°50′ Lon. 11°E[.] NWbN. [North?]. Calm. N.' *in margin*] this time passed what appeared to be a long peninsula & hauled up by the wind & whilst steering NEbN soon lost sight of the Ice. At 6 am. the wind veered to [north?] & obliged us to furl the small sails & reef top sail: Snow showers then prevailing. At 10 am. the Snow abated & the usual hard north wind [sky?] of Greenland presented itself. It consists of horizontal <u>bales</u> ['packs' *above line*] of clouds, purple or Black on the lower edge & yellow above: they have the appearance of an enlarged _ but should ['(do?)' *above line*] I think predict dry weather instead of foul. A bright Ice blink shows itself to the NW where for 3 or 4° of altitude not a cloud its [*sic*] to be seen whilst the rest of the firmament is darkened by their abundance.

Made several Experiments on the reduction of the freezing point of Sea water by concentration in the process of freezing; from which the freezing point of water of specific Gravity equal to that of water ['Experiments on the freezing of salt water' *in margin*] containing in solution 5ᵒᶻ 12ᵈʳ of Marine Salt in every wine gallon, (which is about the common saltness of the Northern Ocean)[1] the Temp*erature* was 28½° when equal to 12ᵒᶻ 10ᵈʳ of salt in the gallon the freezing point was 23½ ° & with 18ᵒᶻ 11ᵈʳ in the gallon the freezing point was reduced to 18½°.

Early in the afternoon the sky cleared, the wind abated & a delightful Evening was the result. Having tacked at 11 am, we reached the edge of an open pack ['of Ice' *deleted*] by 5 Pm where we saw some thousands of Seals basking on the Ice – A considerable Easterly swell prevailing lay the ship a mile from the Pack & sent three Boats in pursuit of Seals ['Killed 29 Seals' *in margin*] They returned at 8 to 11 pm. bringing with them 29 Seals whereof 3 were very small, were brought on board alive & irritated our feelings by their cries which very much resembled those of a child. The other 26 were all old animals but not fat.

We should have got many more but the agitation caused in the Ice by the swell prevented the boats from penetrating into the Ice & the men from travelling across its

---

[1] Here again, as in the measurement taken in the North Sea on 25 March, the quantity of salt suggests an imperial gallon rather than a wine gallon; if the imperial gallon is correct, the salinity would be 35.9‰. The freezing point of sea ice at 35‰ is about 28.6°F. The salinity of sea-ice is initially about 4–5‰, but tends to decrease over time as the ice is raised above the surface, is diluted by snow, and as the salts drain downwards. (King, p. 112.)

surface by means of its laborious motion. Seals are killed by means of a Club (vide plate ...)¹ wherewith they are struck a blow between the eyes, a little above the nose, which ['method of killing Seals' *in margin*] seldom fails to bring them down in a moment. The Hooded Seal having this tender part defended by its natural appendage of a Hood, requires piercing with the sharp point of the Club before he can be overcome – the Capture of these large [***] of Seals is frequently attended with danger from their fierceness, great strength, activity, Hooded defence & large Dentes Canines.²

Wednesday 20ᵗʰ April Lat. 72°44′ Lon. 9°40′E
North NNE.
Fine weather most part of this day with fresh Breezes of wind: towards night fresh Gales with prodigious squalls accompanied with Showers of fine crystallized lamellar Snow.

We reached off & on by the edge of the Ice until 4 Pm when being amongst large streams of Young Ice, which extended in a single sheet as far as could be seen to the [Wᵈ?], prevented thereby from approaching the ['Thermo*meter* all day about 16° *in margin*] Sealing Ice, we stood off under a brisk sail – 5 Sail of ships were in sight in the morning, but parted Co*mpany* by continuing their reach to the Eastward. In the night we met a heavy Easterly swell; about midnight the wind fell to a calm & suddenly a Strong Gale arose at East ['**Thursday 21ˢᵗ April** Lat. 72°16′ Lon. 10°[50′?][.] East, ENE, NE. *in margin*] & blew tremendously in a moment. A cross Sea prevailed at the same time with thick snow. Put the Ship under a snug sail & continued our reach larboard tacked. At 10 am. the wind abated: made sail. At 11 tacked, had very squally weather, & at 6 pm. again tacked & reached to the NEbE the rest of the day.

Friday 22ᵈ April Lat 73°29′ Lon 11½°E
NbW ENE, Calm NEbE
Singular weather; intermittent Gales, heavy squalls, snow showers & high sea. The wind blew so strong in the squalls that we were reduced to treble reef'd ['Courses &'[?] *deleted*] Topsails & courses, whilst in the intervals we could have carried Royals. At 3 Pm. we had a sudden calm in a Shower of [Snow?] which continued about an hour & the Gale recommenced with greater severity in an instant. It continued until 9 Pm. when the wind flew round from NNW to ENE in an instant at

---

¹ Although this parenthesis appears in the transcript, there is no accompanying illustration. However, the club is illustrated as Plate XIX, fig. 6 in *Account of the Arctic Regions*, II (see also vol. I, p. 512). This may possibly indicate that the transcript was prepared after the publication of the *Account* in 1820.

² In *Account of the Arctic Regions*, I, pp.508–11, Scoresby recognized that there were several species of seal in the Greenland Sea. 'The Phoca Vitulina is more abundant in the Greenland Sea, than any other species, especially near Jan Mayen. The Hooded Seal is common near Spitzbergen.' The Hooded Seal is *Cystophora cristata*; *Phoca vitulina* is the Harbour Seal. However, the vast majority of seals near Jan Meyen at present are Harp Seals (*P. groenlandica*) and it is probably this species that Scoresby identified as *P. vitulina*.

the same time falling to near Calm. From 9 to 12 pm. the Snow fell 6 Inches thick upon the deck. The ship sailed on each tack according as the wind suited for getting to the N^d.[1]

Saturday 23^d April Lat. 73°55+ Lon 11°[20′?]E
NEbE
Fresh Gales to moderate breezes during this day with snow in the Morning & Evening, having very squally [*weather*?] reached to the N^d under a moderate sail. No Ships or Ice to be seen.

Sunday 24th April Lat 74°40′+ Lon. [*blank space*]E
E.rly S.rly very var Calm. ESE
Delightful fine weather, calm most of the day, in the Evening a brisk breeze of wind sprang up from the E^d commencing with a very thick shower of snow. At [*blank space*] am. Longitude by the mean of 7 sets of observations = [*blank space*] East Lat [*blank space*] Pm. Long. by the mean of 5 sets of observations on the Sun & moon was ° ′ ″E.[2] Latitude of the ship at Noon. 74°40′N.

A heavy cloud in horizontal stratum lay all day to the Eastward of us & appeared precipitating its moisture for many hours: it was the description \\\frown_ or nimbus accurately defined: I imagine it lay over Cherry Island however that land could not be seen.[3] Saw 2 or 3 small Icebergs to the [***] & the main body of Ice not far distant lying in a direction about NNE & SSW.

Monday 25th April Lat. 76°0′54″+ Lon. 13°5′45″+E[4]
E.rly. SE. Var. N.erly. NW.erly Variable
The forepart of this day we had charming fine, mild, clear Weather. In the Morning saw the Land of Spitzbergen, which we took for the high mountains of the North of Bell Sound, at *[5] 9 am: it bore NE¼N p Compass, but from an ∠ taken between this Land & the Sun & compared with the ⊙'s azimuth as found by estimation its bearing appeared to be (according to the ['Situation of Point

---

[1] Using some of the same words and phrases, Scoresby used this day as an example of '*intermitting gales*' in *Account of the Arctic Regions*, I, pp. 402–3. See also the journal entry for 18 April 1815.

[2] The degree, minute and second signs are in the transcript, but no values. See Appendix, p. 298 and p. 27, note 2.

[3] Bear Island (Bjørnøya) is at 19° E; if Scoresby's longitude was 13°E, the island would have been more than 170 km from the *Esk*.

[4] Beneath this inked value of the longitude, there are two pencilled rows, '1.46' and beneath the latter, '14.51'. Note that the indicated noon longitude is identical to the earlier value calculated by lunar distance. Huxtable suggests that Scoresby later added an estimated 1°46′ to his longitude determination that morning to arrive at a revised noon longitude of 14°51′E. However, as well as the measured longitude being absurdly precise (see Appendix, p. 297), Huxtable also suggests that the difference of 1°46′ in 2 hours 36 minutes is doubtful, because at that latitude it represents a distance travelled eastward of 25.6 nautical miles, or a vessel speed (possibly combined with current) of almost 10 knots.

[5] Note in margin: '*ship's Latitude 9 am. = 75°54′N.*'

Look Out ascertained.' *in margin*] true North) N [*blank space*]°E whilst that of point Look Out which now appeared in sight was N [*blank space*]°E or ENE¼N by the Compass. At 9^h 23' 23" Am. the Longitude of the Ship as deduced from three sets of Observation on the Sun & Moon[1] appeared to be 13°5'45"E from which the Longitude of Point Look Out seems to be [*blank space*]E and that of the high cape lying on the North of ['Bell' *deleted*] sound in Lat. 77°20' ['76°49'' *above line*] = 14°51'E,[2] being by calculation [*blank space*] distant & Point Look Out [*blank space*] Miles. 4 ships in sight.

It now appears, from the deficit of Ice in this Latitude, that what is termed an open season, again occurs, as last year. Most commonly the shores of Spitzbergen cannot be approached so near at this Season as our present situation, whilst a firm barrier of Ice obstructs the navigation towards the regions where whales seek shelter in the greatest abundance. In an open season the Wern shores of Spitzbergen are exposed to waves of the North Sea, & the adjacent Seas are generally openly navigable to the extent of the 80th degree of Lat, ['Such' *deleted*] whilst the main body of Ice extends in a N & South or NE & SW direction a distance of 30 or 40 Leagues from the Land. Such Seasons, as was the last, often afford but a partial fishery, the greatest part of the adventures failing in their object & thence producing a serious loss to the Owners of their Ships. It to [*sic*] be hoped the present year may be more generally successful.[3]

Our advance to the N-ward since the preceeding day at Noon by account[4] falls more than 20 miles short of the observations; hence a northerly current or tide must have facilitated our progress.

Having now advanced to a Latitude frequently the resort of Whales, we ['Coyled Whale lines & fitted Boats for the Fishery' *in margin*] took advantage of the fine morning to fit the Boats for the fishery; which is effected by supplying each with six whales lines of 120 fathoms amounting to 1440 yards in length, which is neatly & singly coyled in battened partitions [*sic*] adapted for the purpose[5] – Each Boat is likewise ['supplied wit' *deleted*] furnished with 6 or 8 lances, a suitable number of oars, a Flag, spare tholls, grommets & Harpoon: Mallets, Piggings, an axe, a fid, a <u>meck</u>, <u>aftertow</u> & <u>fin tow</u>,[6] grapnel, a ball of fox as a

---

[1] See Appendix, p. 297.

[2] These values (but not the degree and minute superscripts and the 'E') are also in pencil, suggesting that they were inserted into blank spaces left by the transcriber of the journal.

[3] Scoresby summarized the open seasons of 1813 and 1814 in *Account of the Arctic Regions*, I, p. 281. See also his journal entry for 17 April 1813.

[4] I.e., from dead reckoning.

[5] In *Account of the Arctic Regions*, II, p.232, Scoresby made it clear that these lines 'are spliced to each other' and that a 'stray-line' is left uncovered 'for the facility of connecting the lines of one boat with those of another.'

[6] Smyth, *Sailor's Word Book*: 'MECK: A notched staff in a whale-boat on which the harpoon rests.' In *Account of the Arctic Regions*, II, p. 233, Scoresby termed it a 'mik'; it is illustrated in Plate XX, fig. 7 of that volume. Neither 'after-tow' nor 'fin-tow' is mentioned in the *Account*, Smyth, or *OED*; they may be devices that assist in securing a dead whale as it is towed back to the ship for flensing.

snatch block,[1] &c. &c Finished at 4 Pm & suspended one boat ['at' *deleted*] on the Starboard Main Chains Davits.

Having steered on a NbE course, whilst the wind would permit, our difference of Longitude at Noon from yesterday's Evening lunar observation was 1°10′W.

At 9 ['Pm' *deleted*] P.m. we were close by the edge of the E.ern pack, consisting of heavy Ice but not very close. The Land about 20′ off. Variable light winds detained us some hours.

Tuesday 26th April Lat. 76°49′+ Lon. 12°16′E.
WbS Variable
Light breezes in the morning, in the afternoon & night strong Gales with Snow Showers, Steering all day to the NW^d by the wind at the rate of 4½ to 8½ knotts p hour under a press of sail. At noon the high cape before mentioned bore E/S (due course) distant 41 miles or 2°35′ of difference of Longitude. Saw no Ice from leaving that adjoining the land at 2 am. until 8 Pm. when we fell in with several detatched streams & patches & many scattered loose pieces of Ice. Continued our course amongst them to the [N^d?] where we soon lost the tempestuous Sea which prevailed on the outside & had comfortable sailing. This night for the first time the Sun never withrew[2] his enlivening ['At Mid-Night. Lat. 77°52″ Long. 7°33′E. *in margin*] rays but continued to cheer the gloom of a Northern Latitude by his oblique presence ['beams' *above line*] at the midnight hour. Several Ships in sight.

Wednesday 27th April Lat. 78°29′ Lon 6°10′E
West, to NW & N. Variable. NNE.
Fresh ['Gales' *deleted*] variable Gales during this day more moderate breezes in the night, snow Showers prevailed in the former part & frost rime in the latter[.] Having met with a barrier of Ice within which seemed ample room we reached to W^d and then worked up under a brisk sail directly to windward (NW^d or N^d) amongst streams & patches of Ice with some large Floes & some bay Ice – at 10 am. saw a whale, the first this season & afterwards two or three more, had three Boats in pursuit which returned after 3 hours chasing without success. At noon we entered a wide channel between two compact patches of Ice & 7 Pm. reached the extremity of navigable water in this situation – Several Ships which preceeded us will probably reach a field lying 15 or 20 miles to the N^d as indicated by the blink,[3] having a free

---

[1] Smyth, *Sailor's Word Book*: 'FOX: … a fastening formed by twisting several rope-yarns together by hand and rubbing it with hard tarred canvas'; 'SNATCH-BLOCK: a single iron-bound block, with an opening in one side above the sheave, in which the bight of a rope may be laid, instead of reeving the end through'. The snatch-block illustrated in *Account of the Arctic Regions*, II, Plate XX, fig. 17, appears to be made of wood. It seems probable that there is a transcription error: 'as' was written instead of 'and'.

[2] *Sic*. Presumably 'withdrew' intended. The marginal note suggests that Scoresby determined his latitude by the altitude of the midnight sun (see Appendix, p. 293, and the journal entry for 3 May 1814).

[3] See Ice Blink in Glossary, vol. 1: an intense whiteness visible close to the horizon, closed by reflection of light by the ice-covered sea beneath.

navigation thither, which has been interrupted by the joining of two large patches of Ice. 22 Ships were in sight. The Leviathan of Shields in working to windward in the morning ran against a piece of Ice which has stove her very severely, breaking 14 timbers & leaving an indented wound 14 feet long & three deep. At night the channel up which we came, closing, we steered before the wind until we got into a more commodious situation then lay too.

Thursday 28ᵗʰ April Lat. 78°12'. Lon. 6°58'E
NNE Calm SW.erly.
We had ['little' *deleted*][1] wind or calms the fore part of the day, brisk Gales in the afternoon & Evening with fine cloudy Weather. Reached to the Eastward into very open Ice, saw 3 or 4 fish but could not come near them. In the Evening returned a few miles to the Westward & then worked up to the SW amongst streams of Ice ['&' *deleted*] patches & small floes in a roomy situation. The Aurora, William & Ann, British Queen, & Leviathan of Shields in Cᵒ.

Friday 29ᵗʰ April Lat. 77°40' Lon. 6°0'E
SW, SSW, South
Towards Morning we had Strong Gales of wind with Snow Showers. Proceeded in a ['W' *deleted*] SW direction for several miles, when observing large openings of water to the west advanced thither to a distance of 6 or 8 Leagues leaving the Ships above named to the Eastward. About 2 Pm. we had reached the extremity a firm [*sic*] barrier of Floes, cemented together by Bay Ice. A large narrow opening appeared to the SWᵈ & a large floe to the Sᵈ of us[.] Toward, the Floe made all speed, having the appearance of a likely place for whales & ere we reached it with the ship sent two Boats off to the edge of it. We lay too under its lee at 5 Pm. saw ['but' *deleted*] only 2 or 3 Fish at the Ice, but several to leeward. Owing however to the <u>wind lipper</u> or Sea urged by a strong Gale of wind the Boats could not ply to any advantage except near the Ice & under its shelter. During the day we had many near chances of striking Fish, one of the Harpoons actually wounded a stout whale, but the Harpoon did not hold. About 10 Pm. blowing hail with thick Snow moored to the Floe & furled the Sails. At Mid Night the Aurora & Leviathan came up to us the latter made fast near us, they had patched up the wound received the 27ᵗʰ Instant but it was still leaking we furnished them with some nails for covering it with sheathing. was much distressed to learn that one of the Leviathan's boats with a crew of 6 or 7 men which was alongside of the Esk on the Evening of Wednesday & which departed for the British Queen for the purpose of procuring planks & spike nails had never been heard of since leaving the British Queen to return to her Ship. The distance was only about 2 miles the weather though frost rimy & Showery was nevertheless tollerably clear at intervals. As there were no ships within several miles it is much to be feared that they have perished.

---

[1] Possibly not a deletion, but instead a careless extension of the crossings of the 't's.

Saturday 30th April
Lat. 77°45′ 5°40′E
WSW to NW & N. Calm. NErly
Strong Gales in the morning with snow showers – Frost rime at 8am. At & on account of the wind shifting & some loose Ice approaching our moorings we cast the ship off & lay too – afterwards worked up a narrow opening between two floes & found much water in a w.erly direction, where we also saw some whales. In the Evening falling Calm we were obliged to [tow?] out with 3 Boats in the same ['direction' *deleted*] place that we entered at: the Ice closed rapidly as we proceeded so that we with difficulty made our escape. 5 ships in sight.

In the evening was suspended a ribband clad garland, according to the usual custom,[1] on the main T.G. Stay attended with the usual forms of blacked faces ridiculous costumes; antique dances & strange fetes, accompanied by an excess of hilarity, excited by the music of a Fiddle, Drum, trambourine [*sic*], frying pans, tin kettles, &c. &c. The Garland is ['always' *deleted*] usually suspended immediately on the entrance of May day Morn, but in the present case interfering with the Sabbath, operations & ceremonies commenced at 8 or 9 Pm.

Sunday 1st May Lat.77°52′+ Lon. 6°40′E.
NNE, North. NNW. NE.erly
We had fresh Gales most of the day, with an increase towards night. At 6 am. the Foot rope of the Jib broke & the sail split from bottom to the head – Bent a fore T. M. stay sail in its place having no spare jib.

Plying to windward in the Morning amongst streams & patches of heavy Ice, lay too during the hour of ['Prayer' *deleted*] public worship, & the Evening stretched out to Sea on a NE course – at 10 pm. the Middle Hook of the Foreland at East distant 10 or 12 Leagues. The wind veering to the NE tacked at 8 Pm & afterwards worked to windward, saw several large Whales. At midnight one Ship in sight.

Monday 2d of May Lat. 78°20′ Lon. 7°50′E
NNE
Blowing exceptionally hard all day with frequent thick Snow Showers & keen frost. We were plying to windward the forepart of the day under [Fore?] close reef'd Top Sail with Fore & F.T. stay sails sheltered by streams of heavy Ice, but occasionally exposed to a heavy sea. Besides the Stream that afforded shelter, throughout the intermediate spaces was disseminated many detached pieces of Ice, incommoding our course & endangering our navigation. In the afternoon & Evening found shelter under a heavy Stream of Ice & which, though but 150 to 200 yards across, completely resisted the force of a furious Sea for several hours. The James of Liverpool near us.

---

[1] In the margin at this point are some comments in pencil, which do not appear to be similar in age to the transcript.

Tuesday 3ᵈ of May Lat. 77°48′ Lon8[½?]′¹
NNE
Still blowing furiously but with an abatement of the Snow. At 1 am the swell had overcome the cohesion of our sheltering stream, & the large flat pieces were urged to leeward with a most laborious motion & considerable velocity rendering sailing amongst them tedious & highly dangerous – a little westward we were for a while sheltered but at length found it prudent to steer to the Eastward with the expectation of soon obtaining an open ocean. In our progress we passed many immense pieces of Ice prodigiously agitated by the force of a most turbulent Sea. Such pieces as would in the hardest Gale with smooth Sea scarce have sensible drift even ['when' *deleted*] with a Ship ['was' *deleted*] moored thereunto, now are seen [***] before the foaming swell with a rate of 2 or 3 Knotts p hour. We found great difficulty in clearing some of the pieces & were frequently obliged to lay too for an hour together before we could get safely past them. We lashed the quarter Boats up to the Davits & took the waist boats upon deck on account of the tempestuous sea & furious Gale. Continued our reach to the Eastward during the whole day under Two close reefed Topsails: Shipped a good deal of water. At mid-night wore. Latitude by the Sun's altitude below the pole 77°30′N.

Wednesday 4ᵗʰ May at. 77°17+ Lon. 7°54′E
NNE
Continued our reach to the Westward occasionally passing pieces of Ice: the wind decreased to-wards noon, at the same time that we fell in with much scattered Ice. The Old Manchester of Hull was observed assiduously to keep company with us during the past Gale, she now displayed an ancient at her fore top masthead, as a signal to speak us. We lay too & on her coming up we were informed that that [*sic*] Captain was exceedingly ill. A Boat came on board for our surgeon & although the sea was very heavy I accompanied him. The Captain was indeed ill, we gave him different medicines which were judged serviceable for his complaint, (a kind of <u>stranguary</u>)² & left him [***] [shortly?] with great hopes of a speedy recovery. The Crew informed us of a great many Ships which had captured several fish each, chiefly those vessels that parted from us the 27ᵗʰ ult. & attained the edge of a Field as suspected.

In the Evening we fell in with streams of Ice & at 10 Pm. were at the edge of a Pack. Being now fine moderate weather made all sail to windward. Several Sail in sight. Cut the torn canvass out of the <u>split</u> Jib, & set the sail maker to repair it, by reducing it in removing one cloth³ of canvass. One whale seen.

---

¹ This is clearly in the form of a fraction; it is the denominator that is uncertain.
² *OED* s.v. 'strangury': 'A disease of the urinary organs characterized by slow and painful emission of urine.'
³ Smyth, *Sailor's Word Book*, s.v. 'CLOTHS: In a sail, are the breadths of canvas in its whole width.'

Thursday 5ᵗʰ of May Lat. 77°51′+ Lon. 6°50′E
W.erly, SW, SSW, SW West to N
A Westerly breeze prevailed early in the morning which veering to Sᵈ also increased to
a Strong Gale. We coasted the Ice along in a NNE direction, found it to consist of an
open pack – passed many ships & saw several fish. In the Afternoon we had Snow
Showers & began to experience a troublesome Sea, on the weather clearing however
about 3 PM. an opening was observed in the Ice to the North of us, we entered it &
proceeded under a smart sail a distance of about 20 miles in a NW direction amongst
much Ice & some floes. In the Evening (8 pm.) we came to the lee of impervious Ice at
the same time saw a great many whales, sent 5 Boats of [*sic*] which pursued the chase
for 4 hours without any success:– the wind had decreased it now again increased,
made sail to the NWᵈ towards the blink of a Field (to appearance) – Saw Fish
constantly but could not come at any. 5 ships in sight: Two made successful fishing
near us. We laboured unblessed & of course laboured in vain.

Friday 6ᵗʰ of May Lat 78°5+ Lon. 5°10′E
N or NNE
Fresh Gales of wind with some Snow during this day: worked to windward under a
brisk sail, soon made the edge of a Field along which in a NNE course we proceeded
with occasional stoppages for Whales, until noon – Two openings now presented
themselves the one to the NW to [*sic*] other to the NEᵈ we chose the latter &
presently after some difficult sailing gained a roomy situation & saw many whales.
Some ships also appeared Fishing, spoke the Sisters of Hull with 9! During the rest of
the day we were in constant pursuit of fish with 2, 3, or 4 Boats; we saw an
extraordinary number & although most of the ships around us were successful we
could not make a single Capture. A considerable field lies within sight to the NE &
much water to the [SWᵈ?] of us. At Mid-Night made sail to the NWᵈ[.] 10 or 12 Sail
in sight.

Saturday 7ᵗʰ May Lat 78°10′ Lon. 4°50′E
NNE. Variable
All this day fresh Gales of wind with snow showers the fore & [*sic*] part & constant
hard frost: thermometer from 16° to 10°. Early in the morning we came to the margin
of a Field of Young Ice; taking a more westerly situation than any accompanying ship
we had the opportunity of pursuing the chase of numerous whales for several hours
without interruption & although a great number were scared by our Boats, it was not
until

['Thos Welburn F.   No.1 + 9ᶠᵗ2‴ *in margin*]

2 Pm. that we were successful in entangling a Whale. She ran out a length of 3200
yards of line weighing 16¼ Cwt. After about an hour & half a second Harpoon was
struck, & the Capture completed in an hour more. One of the Boats was sunk, upset
indeed whilst lancing but the Crew providentially escaped uninjured. Moored to the
Ice & began to flinch.

Assailed by a considerable sea, generated in an extensive opening of the Ice close to the west of the Field where the fish was struck, it was with ['considerable' *deleted*] great care & difficulty that we succeeded in preserving the upset Boat. Her lines were part turned out, about half remained undisturbed notwithstanding that she was twice bottom up before we could get the tackles hookcd. Three active men then leaped into her speedily

['George Bulman.   Harpoon drew.' *in margin*][1]

bailed out all the water. She was hoisted up, the lines hauled & cleared. At 9½ Pm. whilst some of [the?] men were employed Flinching, some heaving in whale lines, the lone[2] Harponeer struck a Second fish – only two other Boats were fitted which proceeded to assist. Six lines were run out except a few yards before the first Boat arrived at the <u>Fast Boat</u>. The Fish soon made her appearance in the open water, but before a Boat could get near she disappeared. [He pursued?][3] to windward along the edge of the Ice & sometimes saw her <u>Blast</u> but never came near her. The Harpoon was supposed then to draw – a Ship ['to' *deleted*] about half a mile of we expected,[4] re-entangled the same fish as we observed his ['**Sunday** 8th **of May**[,] Lat. 78°3′ Lon. 4°50′E, NNE' *in margin*] Boat fast, & in a few minutes the fish was dead. The situation also was exactly that towards which she was last seen to proceed. Upwards of 20 Sail in sight. Owing to the severity of the weather, & our late inexperience in the arts of flinching &c, it was 2 or 3 am. before the Blubber was stripped from the whale & several hours more before all the lines were got in & coyled in their respective Boats.

The wind continuing from the NNE & blowing a fresh Gale, at Noon we cast the Ship off & made sail to windward on the west side of the Field supposing the Fish to have withdrawn thither of which we saw an amazing number & chiefly of large size during the precceeding [*sic*] day; not infrequently 4 or 5 were seen together. In the Evening as we plyed along the W. side of the Field fell in with a great number of Whales but were unsuccessful in the pursuit though of 5 ships around us, some got 2 others 3!

Monday 9th of May Lat 78°5′+ Long. 4°0′E
NNE
At Mid Night made sail to the NWd until we came to a western field about 15 miles from the Eastern one, both of which are connected together by an immense field lying to the North in an E&W direction. The frost being intense the water began to freeze in the NW angle of the fields[.] in this Bay Ice we found Whales sporting by hundreds, 15 or 20 might be counted within the space of two miles at the same moment. A small one

'Geo. Sinclair **M.**   No. 2 . 6ft4½ in' *in margin*]

[1] Note that Bulman's tail is outline only, as whale was not captured.
[2] Possibly 'loose'.
[3] Possibly 'The pursued', suggesting a transcription error for 'The boats pursued'.
[4] *Sic*. '… of where we expected' presumably intended.

we were favoured to entangle which died under water & was drawn up at 12½ hours of the day after being struck 4½ hours. Three ships near us all of which have fished successfully. Within this 4 days though we have taken two fish we have been peculiarly unfortunate, under similar

'Robert Dowell **M.**   No. 3. 6′3ⁱⁿ' *in margin*]

circumstances & favoured by a smiling Providence we should have expected a Dozen at the least. We continued to pursue fish during the rest of the day but without success until 10 Pm. when one made its appearance along side of the ship & lay until a Harponeer descended into a Boat that happened to be down & struck it. It descended 1440 yds perpendicularly downwards & returned to the surface after 40 minutes and in 5 minutes more was killed. As we flinched the water froze around us ['**Tuesday** 10th **of May** Lat. 78°5 Lon. 4°10′E[.] W.erly, Variable' *in margin*] so that the ship lay motionless in a few hours. We had light winds the rest of the day; the Ship remained fixed amongst the Bay Ice: the Ice amidst which we proceeded hither has so much approximated that no opening remains for us to escape by if even we could pass through the young Ice.[1] The northern field has for many hours been observed to move Eastward, the S.ern Ice has also set up so that the dimensions between the firm Ice where we lay is about 4 miles N & S & 15 or 20 East & West whereas 24 hours ago it was 6 times the dimensions – The vacancy (if so it may be called) still seems to contract by the overlapping of the Bay Ice which is many thickness all around us. The Augusta, Gilder, & another Ship near us: the Sisters, Duncomb, Perseverance & 4 others at a distance enclosed as well as ourselves.

At Mid Night for this & several days past we have had thick hoar frost, very much resembling frost rime & appearing to rise out of the Ice: it evidently has its origin from the warmth of the Sun's rays during the day & the great increase of cold towards night whereby the excess of moisture risen under the influences of a Meridian Sun is deposited on the Surface of the Ice & assumes the form of frost rime, [cleaving?] to the rigging & ship & forming a [***] of light fibrous <u>Snow</u> upon every rope.

Wednesday 11th **of May** Lat. 78°9′+ Long. 4°10′E.
Incl. to calm E.rly
Calms or light airs of wind from the Eastward with bright clear weather during the whole day. The situation of the Ice much the same as on the preceding day, but the Bay Ice much stronger being capable of carrying a man in almost every part. Finding ourselves [freezing?] into the centre of a large Bay floe & supposing the chance of catching a whale more probable were we near the Field we began at Noon to cut the Bay Ice by means of a Boat, a sufficient breadth for the Ship whereby she was drawn

---

[1] Scoresby used the events of 9 to 26 May in his paper to the Wernerian Society 'On the Greenland or Polar Ice' at pages 312–17. 'I have been thus minute in the relation of the progress of our extrication from an alarming, though not very uncommon, state of *besetment*, both for the purpose of giving a faint idea of the difficulties and dangers which those engaged in the whale-fishery have occasionally to encounter, and also more particularly to shew, the extraordinary manner in which ships are imperceptibly immured amidst the ice, by the regularity of its drift to the south-westward.'

forward by lines fastened with suitable anchors to the Ice: the distance was about a mile & ¼, at mid night we had approached within about 300 yards. Saw several Whales spouting or Blowing in different parts of the Ice but none very near the Ship. At noon a thermo*mete*r exposed to the rays of the Sun indicated a temp*erature* of 54° whilst the air in the shade was about 18°! & at mid night as low as 10°. An abundant hoar frost was observed ['remarks on crystallization – and curious fact' *in margin*] during the night.[1] Whatever may be the predisposing cause of crystallization, it is certain that regular crystals may be formed not merely by a simultaneous act but by a progressive formation. In the freezing of water, & the crystallizing of many salts, angular mass is ['embodied' *deleted*] consolidated by a single effect or sudden impulse: but in the deposition of a quantity of congealed vapour on the rigging of a Ship, the process must be gradual yet it occasionally produces the most regular forms & of the most beautiful texture. I never witnessed this circumstance in so distinct a conformation as ['during' *deleted*] on this Evening: when the Sun began to decline and its rays struggling through the density of an oblique atmosphere, their calorific effect is but very trifling, whilst his body can be viewed with impunity by the naked eye. At such time the humid atmosphere begins to deposit its excess of moisture, first making their appearance on the frigid surface of the Ice as if arising therefrom & when the precipitation becomes more abundant ['on crystallization & the formation of Snowy Crystals' *in margin*] the effect of a thick fog is produced. Such of the particles as are borne by the breeze into contact with the Ship's rigging, affix themselves thereunto & envelope its <u>weatheren</u> [*sic*] surface in a thick but light coat of this Snowy vapour. But it does not adhere in an indifferent manner like the falling of Snow, but every additional particle arranges itself in its proper situation for preserving & perfecting the form of the crystal. Thus the ropes are coated with large flakes of Ice exhibiting the harmonious texture of the most perfect feather. A small direct line of white particles form the stem or shaft whilst others of a finer description branch out collaterally in close & parallel order at angles of 60° with the ['original' *deleted*] [Stem?] form the <u>Vane</u> whilst this affords a <u>rachis</u>[2] or source of other finer fibers or rays which ['with' *deleted*] forming similar angles with <u>their</u> parent fill up every interstice. I saw many of these feather like crystals of the most complete formation, an inch in length & about ¼ in breath [*sic*] measured across the stem. This is a beautiful & evident instance of a crystal being formed by the gradual deposition of ['probably' *deleted*] <u>single particles</u> of congealed vapour each of which being [***] [***] exerts its polarity & [***] its self by its proper side & its proper place. This fact likewise proves the existence of an attraction between the particles of a crystal for were there no attraction the ropes would have been uniformly coated with these particles & could not have arranged themselves in so perfect order. It likewise shows that such a crystal might have increased to an indefinite size & their increase was observed until their gravity became too great for their slender connection whereby the [*sic*] were

[1] See Introduction, p. xxxiii.

[2] *OED*: 'The stem or shaft of a feather, especially the part bearing the vexillum, as distinguished from the quill.' The earliest citation of the term in an ornithological context in *OED* is not until 1874, but Scoresby used the term in 1820 in *Account of the Arctic Regions*, I, p. 438: 'corresponding with the shaft, vane, and rachis of a feather'. The vexillum is the vane or web of a feather.

constantly dropped about the deck in very large flakes or aggregations of flakes. [To?] many of the flakes were joined others by the planes of the former. This peculiar increase of crystals throws considerable light upon the formation of those beautiful particles ['spiculae' *above line*] of snow which so abound in the atmosphere in intense frosts. It would seem that they are formed from a nucleus & that the beauty of the whole consists in & is produced by the ballooning of their reciporacal [*sic*] attractions or polarities & that in whatever form the first few particles shall adventitiously assume, others which afterwards adhere can unite in no other than correspondent positions until the crystal is perfected by the ballancing of their [united?] polarities. and as the connecting the two poles of a magnet by a piece of iron suppresses the power of that magnet, so it seems the perfecting of a crystal suspends the attractive power of its particles for extraneous atoms but so long as one single atom is wanting the annexed surfaces exist[1] their attraction until some particle comes within its power. Thus then the particles of congealed water, or rather vapour must reciparily [*sic*] have the same form, probably the same size & have an attraction for each other & for every aggregation of particles wherein the polarities are not neutralized.

Thursday 12th of May Lat. 78°8′ Lon. 4°10′E
E.rly N.rly
Light winds, fine clear weather with keen frost: Numerous beautiful Snowy Crystals constantly seen floating ['constantly' *deleted*] in the air on this, ['Icy crystals in air' *in margin*] as well as ['the' *deleted*] several of the preceding days. Having approached within a convenient distance of the Field moored the ship thereunto & at 10 am. (after having without much success awaited for Whales in different watery holes around us) made preparations for making off, the operation of Skinning, cranging,[2]

---

[1] *Sic*. Presumably a transcription error for 'exert'.

[2] This use of 'crang' as a verb appears to be unique to Scoresby in printed form, though it may have been common spoken usage among the whaling fleet. Crang is defined in *OED*, Smyth, and Layton (where the spelling is 'krang') as the carcass of a whale after the blubber has been removed. Scoresby's spelling is 'crang' in the journals, but 'kreng' in *Account of the Arctic Regions*. More important, however, he normally used the term in a much narrower sense than the dictionary definitions (but see the journal entry for 16 May 1814), as what appears to be the *hypodermis* described and illustrated by Haldiman & Tarpley ('Anatomy and Physiology', p. 79 and Fig. 4.4). In Scoresby's words, 'Between the adipose and muscular substances surrounding the body of the whale, is interposed a kind of loose spongy fat, or in some places fat intermixed with muscular flesh. This substance, before alluded to under the name of *kreng*, affords so little oil in the usual way, that it is frequently thrown overboard' (*Account of the Arctic Regions*, II, p. 412). He then went on to mention his father's attempt to produce oil from it at sea in 1818, 'attended with such trouble and inconvenience, that he never afterwards repeated the operation'. In his description of the making-off process (*Account*, II, p. 308) he again left the impression that the substance was useless and indeed a hazard. The first stage of making off was for the blubber to be 'received upon deck by the "krengers", whose office is to remove all the muscular parts, together with such spongy fat, as is known to produce very little oil. When these substances, which go under the general denomination of Kreng, are included among the blubber in the casks, they undergo a kind of fermentation, and generate such a quantity of gas, as sometimes to burst the containing vessels, and occasion the loss of their contents.' It is therefore somewhat surprising to find that in most years, Scoresby returned to Whitby with a few barrels of 'crang', as well as many more containing blubber.

chopping the Blubber & ['Begin to make off' *in margin*] introducing it through the Bung holes of the Casks being so called. Cleared therefore all the Blubber out of the Main hold, & [unstowed?] the Second tier of Casks in the Hatch way & pumped the water out of <u>three longers</u> of the ground tier & 2 Casks more. Several small opening [*sic*] appeared in the Ice around us in which many whales were occasionally seen, one sported & amused us by leaping repeatedly out of ['The capture of a Whale facilitated by means of Ice Shoes' *in margin*] the water setting the Sea all in a foam.[1] Placed two Boats in elligable situations & at 8 Pm. one of the Boatsteerers struck a small Whale. The capture was difficult, the wounded fish appeared in different parts of the Bay Ice which was so thick that the Boats were removed very tardily yet, in places so weak that a man could not travel over it, as several of the Crew in attempting it slipt

['*Willia*m Watson. **M.**   No. 4 = 4 feet' *in margin*]

through repeatedly, they all escaped without any injury. A few days ago I caused the Carpenter to make me a defence for the feet whereby to travel across thin Ice, consisting of two pieces of deal 6 feet long & 6 Inches broad each – The shape of the Shoe is hollowed out in the middle & a leathern strap confines the it [*sic*] to the foot. By means of these <u>Ice Shoes</u> I travelled across every part indiscriminately carrying a Harpoon & dragging the line after me.[2] I twice got near the fish but owing to the tightness of the line I could not get fast. Having however coyled some spare rope on the Ice when she next appeared happening to be near I struck a Second Harpoon – A Boat now came to my assistance & in 15' the Whale was dispatched. Drew her to the Ship by means of the 2ᵈ <u>fast line</u>: Suspended the operation of Making off for that of flinching, which when completed resumed the former. 13 ships in sight Beset!

Friday 13ᵗʰ May Lat. 78°6' Lon. 4°10'E
SE.erly S.erly
Light winds with Snow Showers in the Evening. The heavy Ice approximating, caused a concentration of the Bay Ice enclosed within its boundaries whereby it is overlapped many thickness near the Ship & other obstructions. Completed the operation of making off having filled 37 Casks containing 74 Butts of Blubber & one Cask with One Butts [*sic*] of Crang.

At 6 pm. I observed an astonishing refraction of the atmosphere. A dense appearance was seen to arise to the Southward of us & to advance with the wind to the NWᵈ when it ['had' *deleted*] bore SW[.] I first noticed that the horizon

---

[1]This is now termed 'breaching'; see Würsig and Clark, 'Behavior', pp. 171–2.

[2] In his autobiography, Scoresby elaborated at length on these shoes, and the possible 'application of my ice-shoes to the saving of persons from drowning who break through ice in exercise of skating. I was not aware of any means that have hitherto been adopted that is [*sic*] capable of affording so immediate a relief to the persons in danger, or at so small an expence … . This plan I afterward suggested to the Humane Society of London; but never received any reply to my communication on the subject, nor any acknowledgment.'

['between' *deleted*] under this apparent density was higher by 7 minutes of altitude than the true horizon & formed therewith a break or division exactly similar in appearance to the horizon viewed through the Horizon Glass of a quadrant[1] ['when' *deleted*] having an index error of 7'. Viewed from the Mast Head the refracted Horizon was seen about 20° further westward than when viewed from the deck. Two ships beset about 14 miles distant the Hull of which could not be wholly seen before the approach of this density was afterwards distinctly visible & the horizon some miles beyond them! These ['Singular refraction of the Atmosphere.' *in margin*] ships appeared as having large long Hulls & exceedingly Short Masts – They seemed as if <u>careening</u> or with great <u>heel</u> to one side. I never but once before observed so singular & appearance. It was on the ....[2] when the excess of refraction was still greater. Snow showers followed in the Evening. Having three Boats on watch for <u>fish</u> which occasionally made their appearance in small openings of the Ice around us, at 10 Pm. one was entangled. I ordered a regular tight strain to be held on the line with a view of drowning the fish if it ['**Saturday 14**th **of May** Lat. 70°9' Lon. 3°2'E[.] ESE, SE, Variable' *in margin*] could be accomplished. We ran three Boats into eligible situations amongst the Bay Ice to await the Whales ascent & whilst [fratching?][3] the Mate struck another fish. I again proved the utility of my Ice shoes by travelling across Ice indiscriminately in the direction the lines, trended, I thereby after some time discovered the mate's fast fish & made a signal for a Harpoon but before any Boat or Harpoon could be brought the fish disappeared, after breaking through different places in the Bay Ice & tinging it with Blood at every stoppage. I afterwards procured a Harpoon, coyled a quantity of spare line on a firm part of the Ice & when the fish next appeared (which was not until near an hour) I struck the Harpoon through the Bay Ice & with the assistance of the second mate, after about 20 minutes, [succeeded?] in killing it. During the lancing the fish twice broke through the Ice under my feet obliging

['Tho*m*as Welburn **M.**　　　　　　No. 5 = 8ft4''' *in margin*]

me to skip off in a hurry. I then returned to the Ship, ordered an empty Boat to be launched to the fish (which was 1200 or 1400 yards from the ship) & found the Specksioneer with several men employed heaving the first struck fish up by the Capstern. It had died beneath the surface, by remaining immersed until suffocated. The Ice had pressed so much of late & still continued to squeeze up alongside the ship that we had great difficulty in getting the fish secured in a flinching posture. Contrary

---

　[1] According to Huxtable (personal communication) the term 'quadrant' was at this period also loosely applied to the sextant.

　[2] The ellipsis points imply that a date was to be inserted later. That date was probably 28 April 1811 and that phenomenon was described in Scoresby's journal for the following day, and again in *Account of the Arctic Regions*, I, pp. 389–90. This observation of 13 May 1814, and that of 16 May, were similarly related again in the *Account*, I, pp. 387–9.

　[3] Probably a transcription error.

to the Common practice[1] we were obliged to take the tail <u>Aft</u> when by applying the <u>Cant</u>, a <u>towline</u> & the specktacles, assisted by sawing the obstructing Ice we succeeded in getting it alongside. When flinching we discovered it was much eaten of Sharks: three were seen yet feeding on its body & were all caught & cut to pieces. These sharks are so tenacious of life & apparently insensible of wounds that unless the body be divided they will scarcely leave their prey.

Some men ['that' *deleted*] who were sent to bring the <u>mate's</u> fish to the Ship now returned having fastened a Whale line to the Boat, the other end to the Ship & the fish to the Boat. We attempted to assist them by heaving on the line but the Ice over-lapped the line & squeezed about the fish that after being dragged a short way, the progress was completely stopped & the assisting whale lines ['a good' *deleted*] considerably injured. At 2 Pm. I proceeded to the spot myself & ordered all hands to follow. I found the fish closely pressed by Ice of about 8 Inches thick, which by vari-ous folds was increased to 5 or 6 feet! Thinner Ice was on the right – we immediately sawed the hard Ice in small pieces & forced them into a small opening adjoining & upon or under the neighbouring Ice &

['Geo. Sinclair F.   No. 6 = 6 .. 2' *in margin*]

assisted by a <u>purchase</u> on the Boat we dragged it and the fish forth – By fixing a grapnel in the Ice before us & attatching to it a line reeved through a Block [lashed?] the Boat we doubled our power & thereby made good progress; choosing the thinnest Ice that presented itself. We were likely to be stopped by the Ice at one time by its overlapping near us with a velocity of near two knotts p hour. We however succeeded in avoiding the parts in motion until come within 250 or 300 yards of the Ship when we met with a ['thick' *deleted*] part 100 yards across a foot or 16 Inches in thickness & ['was' *deleted*] increased by different additions to its under surface. Through this we likewise advanced though with immense labour. by sawing two cuts 6 feet asunder & sinking the intermediate Ice beneath the sides or dragging it on the top. In this we could not have proceeded but for a line from the ship hove on our purchase with the capstern as much as the line would bear. In four hours the fish was at Ship from the commencement above half of the time we were stopped by the latter thick Ice which retarded us further by closing as we advanced & obliging us to cut through [a mass?] of 7 or 8 feet thick & dispose of all the pieces. During the day scarcely a man in the Ship except myself escaped a wetting – some sliped [*sic*] through the Ice different times but none sustained any injury, but became so accustomed to [break?] in that they cared very little for it, & what they did care for the inconvenience was amply compensated in some with an additional <u>dram</u>. After the fish was flinched sent all hands to bed, except a Boat's Crew ['which' *deleted*] who had been previously prepared to watch by 2 or 3 hours rest; 30 hours successive exertion produced an effect highly somniferous & entirely superceeded all necessity of opiates for the most <u>wakeful</u>.[2]

[1] 'Towards the stern of the ship the head of the fish is directed' (*Account of the Arctic Regions*, II, p. 296).

[2] In the form of laudanum, opium was frequently and legally used in the 19th century.

Sunday 15th of May Lat. 78°2 Lon. 2°0′E.
ESE to ENE
Fresh breezes of wind all day, clear frosty weather: thermometer from 23° to 11. Some small openings of water at a distance from us. The Ice having accumulated to an amazing thickness around us, whilst it was thin 100 yards off[,] together with the nauseous effluvia of the Carcase of the last whale which from being suspended so long after the extinction of Life, is swelled by air generated from putrescence & thereby refuses to sink – These circumstances induced us to attempt to remove the Ship by availing ['Saw several Whales & 2 or 3 Bears' *in margin*] ourselves of the wind, ropes & a Boat to break the Ice but without success. Dined of a leg of fresh mutton which was excellent. Finished our Yeasted bread!

Monday 16th of May Lat. 77°1 56′+ Lon. 1°10′E
ENE to NE, NNE, North
Charming clear weather with moderate winds. Barometer 30.50! The Bay Ice having divided considerably to leeward of us & separated from the field at a short distance to the NNW from us induced us again to attempt a removal. We laboured about 8 hours breaking thin Ice with a Boat into triangular patches & pushing them off into the Water. That Ice within 50 yards of the ship we were obliged to saw, to break & separate with handspikes. Saw several Sharks feeding on the Crang, at the time we succeeded in removing the Ship into the opening [in?] water: made sail & plyed to the N^d 3 or 4 miles close by the field edge which lay on the East side of us – not Seeing ['not' *deleted*] a single whale & the Bay Ice returning towards the field we drifted nearly into our former situation & made fast to the Bay Ice about 300 yards from the field edge. Saw some Bears.

Again observed a refraction similar to what occurred on the 13th instant,[2] the division of the Icy horizon ['occurred' *deleted*] <u>appeared</u> in the SE quarter forming a very small angle with the common horizon at an elevation of about ['Singular refraction again Observed' *in margin*] 6 minutes above it. It first appeared in a straight line, but afterwards toward the extremity was divided into several distinct unconnected portions inclined toward the refracted horizon. The thermometer at this time was at 12° to 10° the wind brisk at north & as a certain haziness appeared to the East & North of the division of refractions, I suspected it was caused by the formation of hoar frost over the chilly surface of the Ice, ['which being' *deleted*] in the North which by its greater Cold, than the Ice in the neighbourhood of the Sea, augmented by the North wind arising in Regions nearer the Pole, condenses the vapour absorbed by the warmer atmosphere of the day & as the Cold gradually ['Attempt to account for it.' *in margin*] advances towards the ['warm' *deleted*] South the hoar frost is gradually evolved whilst the air being drier from which the dew is precipitated becomes more dense & consequently causes a higher refraction of the rays of light & the appearance of a divided horizon between the humid & dry atmospheres. This seems the

---

[1] '77' written over '78'.
[2] This event was described again in *Account of the Arctic Regions*, I, pp.388–9. See p. 42, note 2.

probable cause, yet may not be correct, it is merely a conjecture. To account for similar appearances with a South wind could not perhaps be compatible with the theory. 13 Ships in sight all Beset.

Tuesday 17th of May Lat. 77°46′+ Lon. 0°30′E
North. to NW
The Ice continuing close with a north wind is a circumstance causing considerable alarm – it is to be feared we have drifted vastly to the westward & thereby become involved amidst the firm Ice at an increasing distance from the Sea to the Eastward – a North or NW wind was confidently hoped would afford our release & yet a brisk N. wind produces no advantageous effect. The idea of being beset during the remaining part of the fishing Season which is not improbible [*sic*] is replete with distress, augmented by the probability of being exposed to continual danger of being crushed by the Ice. God grant in his mercy that our fears may not be realized. When we first entered this place we had an open space of near 100 square miles & now were all the Bay Ice dissolved it would not amount to 20, perhaps not more than 10. Our present situation is on the SW side of an immense field, large floes are connected with its E.ern extremity and the North West the firm fields & floes, to the South likewise large floes 10 or 15 miles across. Our only comfort is the presence of several ships situated similarly. 3 lay a Mile of [*sic*]¹ to the W^d 2 more 2 miles of [*sic*] & 2 more about 5 miles distant all the W^d or SW^d[.] 4 lay about 3 miles to the SE & 2 more about 12 or 14 miles to the S^d. These 13 ships are all that can be seen. Since yesterday noon it appears by observation that we have set 10 miles to the South & probably considerable to the Westward as the variation of the compass is found increased to 2½ or near 3 points west! and from the change of time.
    The watch employed gumming whale-bone. No Whales.

Wednesday 18th May Lat. 77°36′ Long. 0.
NbW to E.rly
Light winds all this day: in the morning a considerable break was observed in the Bay Ice extending 2 or 3 miles to the Eastward & separated therefrom by a very narrow neck of Bay Ice was a second opening of still greater magnitude extending along the edge of the Field in an ESE direction apparently [bounded?] by the Eastern Floes but amidst which it seemed to penetrate, Though this was far from being the way we entered with regard to the Ice yet it appeared the most elligable [*sic*] road of escape & the only probable direction for a speedy release. It was therefore an object of importance to obtain it. Accordingly we soon reached the first sailable Space and proceeded to its extremity & made an attempt to pass the neck of division by making two cuts above a Ship's breadth asunder & breaking the intermediate Ice with a Boat: but though the distance was only 300 to 350 yards, yet after penetrating about ⅓ we were obliged to relinquish the design from the closing & overlapping of the Ice wherever we made an incision. This Ice which is scarcely more than a week's formation is so strong that in most places it will carry a Boat with its lines & Crew & where strengthened by different

---

¹ Both here and later in the sentence 'off' presumably intended.

strata it is in particular spots several feet in thickness! We retreated the [*sic*] a place where the Ice seemed at rest & moored with a small space of water on our stern. The Duncombe, Sisters, & Perseverance near us with 6 fish 35 Tons, 12 fish 80 Tons & 1 fish success the ['Saw a Seahorse bleeding on the Field' *in margin*] latter near us. The Harmony penetrated the Bay Ice & gained the opening at which we aimed & proceeded to the E^d to its extremity. Her success 2 fish.

Thursday 19th of May Lat. 77°34′ Long. 0′[*sic*]
Calm, NW. W. WSW
Calm in the beginning of the day with thick <u>dew frost</u>. About noon we proceeded to cut through the Bay Ice with an intention of gaining the edge of the field aided by a Brisk Gale of wind which now sprang up and increased towards night. At first we made slow progress being obliged to cut our way with a Boat, but gaining the track of the Perseverance we followed it 200 or 300 yards with very little trouble but the Ice then setting together we found it more advantageous to prepare a new track for ourselves. With the increase of the wind we made better progress & at length with the assistance of a Boat suspended beneath the Jib boom we proceeded briskly hauling up in thin Ice on a SE or E Course avoiding the thickest patches & even the field edge as the Ice seemed to close upon it, we continued our proceedings until supposing ourselves 3 or 4 miles from the place where we started & near the [point?] of the Field which however we could not determine on account of a thick heavy fog, we then hauled to the NE^d until we approached new formed Ice separating us from the ['**Friday 20th of May** Lat. 77°35′ Lon. 0°5′E[.] SW, SSW to SWbW' *in margin*] field & then rested at 1¼ am. The fog continued throughout the night & morning so thick that we could never see a distance of half a mile. Towards noon we observed the field edge to which we seemed rapidly approaching, the Ice at the same time pressing hard upon the Ship, overlapping with great velocity & considerably endangering the Rudder as well as agitating the Ship in a very disagreeable manner induced us to attempt to change our situation. To effect this we made two cuts forming an angle at the ship's Bow diverging to the edge of the thin Ice not above 30 yards distance & then by a powerful strain hove with an hawser & the thin Ice [outside?] being crushed with a Boat, the piece was forced out & the ship partly at liberty. Observing the field edge to recede as we advanced Eastward we sailed about half a mile when both the South & North Ice were seen, we then hauled up & moored to the South Ice sheltered from immediate danger by the prominence of a point of Ice at a little distance to the East of us. The Duncombe & Perseverance followed us & took a situation farther to the Eastward near where the Sisters lay. The fog cleared away in the Evening & we saw the Harmony 3 or 4 miles of [*sic*] to the SE^d where the Ice was smaller & apparently less heavy. Several inaccessible opening appeared in that direction some of which were free of Bay Ice. Fresh Gales of wind in the night, furled the sails. Saw a Bear.

Saturday 21st of May Lat. 77°34′ Lon. 15′E
WSW to NW. & to NE
In the morning we observed an opening on the SE side of the floe against which we lay, separated from us by Bay Ice of different ages. Cast off at 9 am. warped to windward into

a convenient situation & made sail passed the young Ice with little difficulty & the older Ice yielded to a fresh gale of wind & a Boat ahead of the ship. In 2 or 3 hours we were in the opening attended by the Sisters, ['Harmon' *deleted*] Duncombe & Perseverance, the Harmony likewise joined in the Evening. Mr Steward & myself took coffee with Mr R. Marshall[1] on board the Sisters & after we returned to the Esk at 8 Pm. we moored to a Floe & furled all sails having a Strong Gale of wind. Considerable water joins us to the SWd but not a fish to be seen. To the Ed likewise is a very large opening of the Ice, at present not accessible to us. 3 Strange Sail far to the SEd altogether 16 Sail in Sight.

Sunday 22d of May Lat. 77°23′ Lon. 0°15′E
NNE NE.
An opening of the Ice appeared to the Eastward & progressively extended towards us, whilst a fresh Gale of wind prevailing, at the same time contracts the vacancy to the lee of the floe at which we lay. We cast off at 9 am & worked up a very narrow lane of water on the East side of the floe but having gained the extremity found no navigable space leading to the other Eastern opening: Continued dodging until Evening when the Ice still closing around us & a possibility appeared of extricating ourselves we worked up to ['the' *deleted*] a weather corner & put the Ship between two small floes whereby the power of a strong towline aided by the vacillatory motion of Sallying we passed two points in about 1¼ hours then, working in a free place 400 yards to the North we came round the point of another patch of congealed ['Ice' *deleted*] drift Ice & soon made way through a quantity of Brash Ice which now alone obstructed us. Having gained a navigable spot we proceeded to the SE or SSE accordingly as the edge of a large floe lying on the NE directed us. At this time & indeed soon after ['**Monday 23d of May** Lat. 77°18′+ Lon. 0°40′E[.] N.erly Variable Incl. Calm' *in margin*] we began the attempt to pass between the floes a thick fog prevailed & the wind abated. The water presently had its surface covered with Bay Ice so that by 7 am. the Ship would scarcely work amongst it. This opening lead us about 8 miles to the SEbS from yesterdays situation, at the farthest extremity of which we stopped; no possibility of proceeding farther offering we remained at rest during a fine mild day – occasionally fog showers but in the afternoon charming clear weather. The before named 4 ships all near us. One of the three ships seen yesterday to the SEd & which this morning appeared about 8 miles to the ENE of us, parted with his fellow [*sic*] & seemed to escape from amongst the Ice: the two remaining are close beset. Lost sight of all the Ships left to the westward of us. The two sail noted lying 12 or 14 miles to the Sd of us on the 17th instant are now to the NW of us about 4 miles off. The one is the Aurora of London; the other supposed to be the Ellen of Orkney. Thus in all 8 sail are yet in sight.

Tuesday 24th of May Lat. 77°14 Lon. 0°40′E
Calm NE.erly
Thick weather in the night & morning, at 11 am being clearer I observed a considerable break of the Ice to the SEd & which there seemed a possibility of reaching could

---

[1] Richard Marshall was master of the Hull whaler *Sisters* in 1813 and 1814 (Credland, *Hull Whaling Trade*, p. 138).

we pass between the points of two Bay floes against which we lay. We sawed an angle from the N.ern floe to clear the Sisters & having dragged the piece out we hauled on her Bow: as the two Ships on their commencing operations rather interfered with each other & we being somewhat ahead they surrendered their labours & sent most of their Crew to our assistance meaning to follow & as breaking a passage was expected to produce a general good each of the other ships supplied about 20 men, ['each' *deleted*] increasing our Complement to about 150 men, by means of this force we employed three Boats breaking the Bay Ice which by the closing of the Floes had overlapped to an incredible thickness, about 20 men were stationed to the Capstern on a 7 inch towline, a gang likewise at the windlass & a considerable remnant for constantly sallying the Ship without which no progress could be made. With such means we succeeded in passing the Strait in about 6 hours. We were however highly grieved to find that the friendly assistance of our neighbours profitted them nothing, for the ['assist' *deleted*][1] Sisters unfortunately keeping a little too far astern[2] when we passed the most difficult part the Ice suddenly closed up our tract & completely barred the progress of all our friends. Having stopped the Ship when we reached a navigable part, I proceeded across the Ice to see if our assistance could avail any thing & at the same time personally to thank each Captain for his timely aid to us. Our help could be of no avail, after therefore visiting each Ship we made sail – at first we proceeded thro' Bay Ice of recent formation about 2 miles SW had then to make a circuit round a patch of heavy Ice to the west & had considerable difficulty of passing some Bay Ice lying in the way in the act of <u>closing</u>. By our usual resources we succeeded, then passed along an opening scarcely more than the breath [*sic*] of the ship at the edge of a heavy floe above a mile to the SE & SSW. We then reached a large triangular break, formed by three floes with straight sides. Steered to the SE[d] not expecting to pass the points between which there appeared to be no opening: on coming near however a partial vacancy was observed & though the enterprise was highly dangerous I determined to use every precaution & attempt the passage. All hands were called up, all sail set & we passed the danger in less than half an hour. The breadth was scarcely 15 yards, the Ice on each side tremendously heavy & so compact as to form actual fields, no crack or rent being observable from the mast head either to the NNE or SSW. Providence blessed our endeavours & we safely over-came the danger & surmounted every difficulty.

Wednesday 25th of May Lat. 77°6 Long. 1°0′E
NEerly Nerly
We now flattered ourselves we were at liberty to range at large, but alas we were disappointed. We proceeded ESE along the edge of a floe in an extensive opening, after about 8 miles sailing we reached the extremity to the E[d] though to the SSW[d] no end could be observed. Here we discovered what ['is doubtless' *deleted*] appeared to be an opening into the Sea: no Ice being therin seen & by the <u>blink</u> no obstruction whatever

---

[1] This deletion, followed immediately by 'Sisters', may indicate that the transcriber was hearing the original by dictation, rather than copying by eye.

[2] But note that Steward's account says that the *Sisters* 'followed up close in our rear'.

in a certain direction. It was however separated from us by the junction of a floe scarcely a mile in breadth, & open wide enough for the Ship half the distance. We hoisted our Ancient a predetermined Signal to acquaint the Ships we left of a favourable prospect, to induce them to strain every nerve to accomplish their expectation. Blowing fresh with Snow Showers in the Morning we made fast to the windward floes near the junction where we sanguinely hoped for a release. As the floes seemed cemented together by the frost we made an attempt to disunite them by forcing wedges into a small fissure near the point of union. Our labour was without effect as almost immediately a strong pressure ensued whereby Ice two feet in thickness or upwards was elevated into hummocks of 8 or 10 feet high containing immense masses of Ice. I went to point of collision to witness the effect of such tremendous powers where I found the floes overlapping each other with majestic pace, producing a noise like that of complicated machinery or distant thunder. In one place hummocks were seen which measured upwards of 20 feet from the surface of the Ice & might be supposed 25 or 30 feet above the water. The immense masses thrown up were several 100 tons in weight. Near this place I observed Snow on the level Ice 3½ feet deep, a Boat hook introduced into a perpendicular fissure proved the continuance of a firm solid & single sheet of Ice upwards of 12 feet from the surface. The immense pressure occasioned fissures in a hundred places, [repeated?] the Ice sent under my feet, the singular noise, majestic movement of such tremendous bodies had a most sublime & terrific effect.[1]

['NNE' in margin] Such was the minuteness of the Iceblink that it formed a distinct & beautiful map of the varied Ice & spaces of water for at least 10 leagues around us.[2] From which I observed that could we pass this narrow neck of Ice, we must steer SSE to pass a point of Ice extending from the firm body in the North when we might [***] round it to the ENE without any apparent obstruction unless a few separate pieces of Ice or Bay Ice, or in short a free navigation apparently into the Sea. The blink likewise shewed a lane of water extending completely out into the Same navigable space to lee-ward of the floe lying to the SEᵈ of us. We attempted to proceed that way but having to pass some thick Bay Ice the Ship stuck fast though steering before a very fresh Gale of wind; a Boat could not break it. We therefore proceeded to warp back again but owing to the coarcting[3] of the Ice on each side we endured a

[1] Scoresby appears to have described this event, as an example of 'the tremendous Concussions of Fields', in his paper 'On the Greenland or Polar Ice'. His description is, however, there introduced with the words 'In the month of May of the present year, (1813), I witnessed a more tremendous scene' (p. 280). The year was evidently *not* 1813, and this error therefore suggests an earlier date for the preparation of the paper than was in fact the case.

[2] '[W]hen the ice-blink occurs under the most favourable circumstances, it affords to the eye a beautiful and perfect map of the ice, twenty or thirty miles beyond the limit of direct vision, but less distant in proportion as the atmosphere is more dense and obscure. The ice-blink not only shows the figure of the ice, but enables the experienced observer to judge whether the ice thus pictured be field or packed ice: if the latter, whether it be compact or open, bay or heavy ice. Field-ice affords the most lucid blink, accompanied with a tinge of yellow; that of packs is more purely white; and of bay-ice, greyish. The land, on account of its snowy covering, likewise occasions a blink, which is more yellow than that produced by the ice of fields' (*Account of the Arctic Regions*, I, p. 300).

[3] *OED*: 'to press or draw together; to compress, constrict, contract, tighten.' *OED* regards the verb as obsolete, and has no citation for this definition later than 1604.

considerable Squeeze amongst the Bay Ice, & were employed 8 hours with 25 hands in warping to a situation ['**Thursday 26**th **of May** Lat. 76°50 Lon. 1°40°E[.] NE.erly Variable' *in margin*] from whence we could take sail, owing to the narrowing Ice, patches drifting foul of us & the strength of the wind. Plyed back to our former situation & laid in the watch for the opening of the Points of the Floes. The four ships we left on Tuesday seem to have been assiduously using every exertion to effect their release but without success as they retain their former position forming a line close at each other's stern.

Still Blowing fresh with fine weather[.] Occasional snow showers with a cold of 20° at 10 am. the agreeable prospect, the eye gladdening view of the division of the points of Ice was evident, in less than half they were at 50 to 100 yards distance; we tacked made all sail & steered finely & safely through close hauled by the wind & in a few minutes found ourselves in fine free navigation. Thanks be to God for all his mercies especially for his distinguishing deliverance in the present instance where of 16 sail we were the most western except three & consequently the furthest ['off' *deleted*] immersed amongst Ice yet in such wise have be been favoured that we have been enabled to escape the first, whilst the besetting of some it may be feared will not ['be libera' *deleted*] allow their liberation for many days, unless a peculiar effect ['change' *above line*] is produced on the Ice.

Immediately on our release steered SSE as directed by the blink & found the point of Ice situated precisely as expected at 16 miles distant which we passed at noon & then hauled by the wind under a press of sail. Having advanced 10 or 12 miles we met with much packed Ice, probably what we yesterday observed by the blink lying to the N^d of the sinuosity leading out to sea & which by the force of the wind has been Drifted until it has formed a junction with the lee-ward floes. Notwithstanding we now had a strong Gale of wind & frequent snow showers we entered the pack in a slackish part leading towards a small opening to the ENE, we gained the opening after some difficult serpentine sailing & half an hour's hard boring in which the Ship could not be preserved from receiving two or three hard blows from the Ice.

From hence we perceived another opening in the same direction, leading to a third of great magnitude. We had critical & occasionally dangerous sailing in passing from one opening to another where the pieces of Ice though very small compared with what we latterly navigated amidst, yet would in general be of many 1000 tons weight. A [cloth?] was sent across in the Jib & at the same time the Sheet broke & probably saved the sail as the wind was so powerful that we could scarcely carry double reefed Topsails. In the Evening we reached the third opening & found its western boundary formed of ['No ships in sight' *in margin*] fields & floes, other floes making their appearance to the SE^d of us, indicating that we had made a course too far Northerly. We however plyed to windward ['**Friday 27**th **of May** Lat. 77°0′ Lon. 4°16′[.] NNE, NE Variable' *in margin*] until our progress was barred by a Floe lying across from the Eastern to the W^n bounds of our navigation. We lay too, after attempting to make the Ship fast to the Floe which by the clumsiness of some of the Men, though she came within 3 or 4 yards of the Ice, they did not get the rope <u>landed</u> until she had drifted 60 fathom off & in bringing her up the anchor broke the hole out & the Ship narrowly escaped drifting against a heavy piece of the Ice astern that had an immense <u>calf</u> [passing?] from beneath it.[1] In two hours the floe parted, we worked out to windw*ard* & were presently in an immense piece of water extending further than could be seen in an ENE direction. We found it limited on the East by a narrow stream of Ice, apparently a Sea Stream, which from the size of the pieces, the Gale of wind, & the swell observed without we could not prudently attempt to pass. Lay too. Blowing hard with thick snow showers. For 18 days past the Barometer has stood above 30 Inches the whole time averaging indeed 30....[2] at one time as high as 30.51. This great pressure of the atmosphere is probably peculiar to situations far immersed among the Ice. A comparison with my Father's Meteorological Register may throw some light on the subject.

In the Evening the wind increased & blew a hard Gale accompanied with much Snow. The Beating of the Sea against the Sea Stream with a westerly impulse urged it rapidly in that direction thereby adding to its breath [*sic*] every piece of Ice, stream, or floe that lay within some miles of it. Hence we were obliged repeatedly to shift our situation, constantly keeping near the Stream when circumstances would admit. In the night our sails were reduced to treble reefed Top sails ['**Saturday 28**[th] **of May** Lat. 76°46′+ Long 4°6′E[.] NE.erly NNE, E.rly, ENE' *in margin*] Storm Jib, &c. By an error of judgement in the officer having the watch the ship struck a piece of Ice in the Sea Stream in stays, with great force, by which she was driven astern with great violence & struck a second piece on the starboard quarter which in all probability saved the Rudder.

In the morning 8 O'clock the weather cleared & the wind abated – Saw two Ships in the E[d] under all sails. Reached to the Stream & found it augmented to a mile in Breadth in every place except in a lee-wardly situation. The wind Eastering & the Ice closing fast upon a heavy floe to the Westward with a heavy stormy like atmosphere induced me to attempt to push to Sea. All hands being on deck we proceeded to narrowest point, where by the most judicious management of the Sails, aided occasionally by a line to the lee-Ice we succeeded to admiration.[3] We did not strike but one piece with any degree of force & this was towards the edge where the impulse of the Ship's way was augmented by a strong head swell. We made good a course nearly wind abeam & weathered a pack lying to lee-ward scarcely 100 yards. Having reached the Sea we made all sail to the SE[d] by the wind. In a short time it veered to the SE[d], tacked at 3Pm & steered to the ENE[d] delighted ['SE[d], S[d] SSW' *in margin*] once again to find ourselves in the open Ocean at liberty to proceed as we pleased, after 18 days <u>besetment</u> during which we drifted with the Ice 60 or 70 miles to the South & probably 40 or 50 to the Westward. For the last ten days we have not seen a Whale! In the Evening seeing no Ice, & the weather being fine with moderate wind bore away to the North or NNW until we fell in with much ['8Pm. Therm*ometer* 29° *in margin*] brash Ice scattered about & some streams, then steered to the N. NNE, NE or ENE

---

[1] Smyth, *Sailor's Word Book*, s.v. 'CALF': 'in the Arctic regions, a mass of floe ice breaking from under a floe, which when disengaged rises with violence to the surface of the water; it differs from a tongue, which is the same body fixed beneath the main floe.'

[2] Space, indicated by ellipsis points, apparently left to insert the calculated value.

[3] *OED* regards the phrase 'to admiration' as 'slightly archaic'.

accordingly as the Ice trended. Lat. by Obs*ervatio*n of the Sun's Mer. Alt. at Mid N^t 77°9′.

Sunday 29th of May Lat. 77°40′ Lon. 4°20′E.
SW.erly. W.erly – Variable
Light variable winds all the day. At noon we supposed ourselves in Latitude 77°40′ & Long. 4°20′E continued our course to the NNE^d along the edge of the Ice consisting of a close Sea Stream & brash Ice without it. About 6 Pm. Saw a fish: near about the same time two Foreign ships that had accompanied us in this day's run & appeared as just entering the Country, struck each of them a fish. A number of ships seen within the Ice in the Evening to the amount of between 30 and 40. [Ran?] a few miles farther to the North & then hauled out to the Sea ward. The Sea here is of a deep opaque green colour & consequently highly favourable for fishing.

Monday 30th of May Lat 78°0 Lon. 4°0′E
S.erly, SW.erly. Var. SE.erly East
The Weather Continuing fine & seeing no fish without hauled to the W^d observing a deep sinuosity to the NW^w we proceeded down it & sheltered ourselves behind

['Robert Dowell **M.** No. 7. = 8^ft 7^in' *in margin*]

a small patch of Ice. Saw 3 or 4 fish one of which we struck in 34 minutes it re-appeared on the surface, in 40 minutes a 2^d Harpoon was struck & in 15′ more the Capture was complete. Moored to a large piece of Ice & presently stripped the poor whale of its [fat?] leaving the Carcase a feast for the Birds, Sharks, & Bears. Near 30 ships in sight, several fishing.

As soon as the decks were washed we cast off from the Ice meaning to reach NW^d in search of Whales, but the weather changing & becoming thick the wind blowing strong with every appearance of an inchoative Storm caused me to alter my design & proceed to Sea ward. Several ships were observed plying out of the Ice [under?] a heavy press of sail. Towards Mid-Night a heavy S.erly swell – The ship sailing by the wind to the SSE^d. Thick Snow.

Tuesday 31st of May Lat. 77 50 Lon. 4°20E
E to NE
Fresh or strong Gales with constant thick Snow & heavy S.erly swell. Stood in to the [N?]^d for 6 hours in the morning when supposing ourselves near the Ice we tacked off under easy sail & commenced making off.

Wednesday 1st of June Lat. 77°45′ Lon. 4°0′E
NE.erly very Var.
The weather began to amend early this day, the Snow cleared away & the wind & Sea were reduced. Tacked soon after mid-night[.] at 10 am. were near the Ice tacked off. Completed ['Finished' *above line*] the making off having with the former making off completed 5 longers of two tiers of Casks extending from the Pump-well forward.

Consisting in all of 15 Casks of 300 Galls & upwards, 41 Tons, & 10 of 200 gall. capacity, 66 Casks containing 134 Butts of Blubber or about 50 Tons of oil.

In the Evening plying to windward off the edge of the Ice without seeing a single fish. Several ships observed within the Ice enclosed by a firm Sea Stream, 2 attempted to bore out, one succeeded. 30 sail in sight, except 3 or 4 all to leeward.

Thursday 2ᵈ of June Lat 78°Lon. 4°39′E
Nerly very var.
Very variable light winds all this day with occasional slight fog showers. Plying to windward under every sail at a distance from the Ice. Saw fish constantly had Boats always in pursuit but without success. 8 or 10 ships to windward apparently fishing, as many to leeward plying to the Nᵈ.

Friday 3ᵈ of June Lat. 78°5 Long. 4°10′E
N.erly very var. Calm W.erly
Light winds exceedingly variable or Calms. Made little progress to windward reached within sight of the Ice & met many whales. The Ice seems packed 3 ships beset near us – it extends to the N & Eastward of us forming a deep sinuosity in a NNW direction apparently favourable for whales. The water is of a deep Green Colour, very thick with <u>shrimps</u> seen floating therin. Spoke the Henrietta of Whitby with 13 fish near 140 Tons of Oil! gives account of the Resolution of Peterhead 240 Tons, Resolution Whitby 115 or 120, William & Ann 140 & many others well fished the chief part of which have been captured within the past fortnight, or during the time wherin we lay beset & never enjoyed the sight of a fish! We enquired concerning the John

['Geo. Bulman **F.**   No.8 = 9.4' *in margin*]

but she had not been seen of some weeks. These news exhibiting our backwardness in the fishery excited great anxiety, proving at the same time an urgent stimulus towards calling forth our utmost exertions. We were somewhat relieved at 8 am. by the gladdening sound of "<u>a fall, a fall</u>." The fish was struck at a distance proved very active, <u>thrashing</u> in a furious manner, but was overcome in 1¼ hours. The fore-ganger of the 2ᵈ Harpoon was cut [but?] the first fast Harpoon drawing to a <u>wither</u>. The first

['John Dunbar **F.**   No. 9 = 8.7.' *in margin*]

however retained its hold until another was struck. Whilst the Boats towed the fish towards the Ship, two of them separated whale-hunting & succeeded in entangling another. This likewise yielded its life to the activity of the Harponeers but owing to the distance from the Ship it was not brought alongside until 4½ Pm. All hands took their dinners & began to flinch. At mid-night finished, made sail to the Nᵈ & lay too near the Ice: wind moderate. Near 50 sail of ships in sight many of them employed flinching, killing fish, or making off. A Sea-horse pursued one of our Boats for sometime.

Saturday 4ᵗʰ of June W.erly Var. S.erly
Lat. 78°14′ Lon. 4°0′E
Light winds continued during the greater part of this day, in the Evening a moderate breeze: frequent slight fog Showers. The numerous whales seen yesterday removed their quarters, we sought them amongst open patches of Ice near the main body, saw but few; proceeded then the rest of the day to the Eastward by the wind. Found the Ice lying ESE 8 or 10 miles, & then trending to the North & from thence at a great distance apparently running Eastward & then South forming a large & extensive Bight or sinuosity. At Mid-Night saw 2 or 3 scattered fish – about 40 sail in sight a few near us.

Sunday 5ᵗʰ of June Lat. 78°6′ Lon 5°40′E
S-W.erly West. Variable
Moderate breezes of wind, fine cloudy weather with heavy showers. Continued our reach ESE in clear water & at 4 am. fell in with a

['Thom*as* Welburn **F.**  No. 10 = 7. 11' *in margin*]

['John Trueman **M.** No. 11 = 8. 0' *in margin*]

great number of whales. Made a <u>loose</u> <u>fall</u>, that is we sent all the Boats in chase: at 6 am. a fish was struck & shortly afterwards a second, with the assistance of a Boat from the New Manchester that happened to be near the latter, they were both[1] by 8 am. Plyed up to the windward one[,] secured it alongside then ran down to the other & fastened it astern: clewed the Top-Sails up until we flinched – finished about 2 Pm. & made sail to the Southward. Performed Divine Service as usual in the Evening & very soon afterwards notwithstanding the fish were become scarce we succeeded in making another Capture. After

['John Trueman **M.** No. 12 = 9ᶠᵗ 6ⁱⁿ' *in margin*]

being struck the fish remained under the surface of the Water 35 Minutes, in about 20 minutes more it was killed & afterwards flinched with tollerable despatch. At Mid-Night not a piece of Ice to be seen from the deck: a few ships in sight some of them fishing successfully.

Monday 6ᵗʰ of June Lat. 78°25′ Lon. 4°55′E
WSW SW, Var.
Fresh Breezes ['of wind' *deleted*] the chief of this day, little wind in the night attended with constant Snow. Made sail to the NWᵈ & came to a body of Ice at 10 am. Saw a few fish in our course. To the windw*ar*d lay a point end, the same which we doubled in the evening of Saturday last. I considered it an object to repass it as the fish seen

---

[1] Word omitted in transcript?

seemed to proceed thither – we could not accomplish this end before the Evening & at the same time saw several Whales in pursuit of which we sent 4 Boats. Two returned about mid-night the two others rowed out of sight, for an hour & half we were in great uncertainty & anxiety about ['**Tuesday 7ᵗʰ of June** Lat. 78°28′+ Lon. 4°50′E[.] N.erly. Calms N.erly' *in margin*] them, yet one of them was eventually seen & seemed to be searching for his partner. ['The' *deleted*] A Breeze of wind springing up from the Nᵈ we steered towards the Boat manoeuvering at a distance & at 2¼ am. she was seen with the flag flying – "a fall was called" & shortly the fast Boat was distinguished through the Shower. The fish had been entangled upwards of an hour & it was not

['Thomas Welburn **M.**   No. 13 = 8. 2' *in margin*]

until its 7ᵗʰ appearance that a second harpoon was struck – very fortunately it only run 4½ lines out & never removed far from the Boat. It took 3½ lines from the 2ᵈ fast Boat. The capture was completed at 6 am, the fish taken alongside & the flinching begun at 8½ am – The weather at the same time clear & a Calm prevailed – About 20 ships in sight 3 or 4 flinching.

['John Trueman **M.**   No. 14 = 8ᶠᵗ 2ⁱⁿ bone.' *in margin*]

At noon a Breeze of wind sprang up made sail & proceeded about 20 miles to the ENEᵈ where we saw & gave chase to a single fish with success. After being struck it descended as usual & remained invisible 25 minutes, shewed itself & was killed in 10 minutes more. A calm succeeding it was towed to the Ship ['**Wednesday 8ᵗʰ of June** Lat. 78°40 Lon. 5°40′E[.] Calm Variable WSW' *in margin*] & the flinching was scarcely started when at 12¼ Pm.[1] another fish was struck. This was overcome more easily than the former, for after remaining beneath upwards of 20 minutes it yielded its life to the well aimed spears of its assailers in 7 or 8 minutes more. This was a beautiful whale – its belly was completely

['George Bulman **F.**   No. 15 + 9. 3' *in margin*]

pie-bald, the bright black making a fine contrast with the pure white. Flinched them in about 5 hours & immediately hasted in pursuit of others. From the successful fishery of the last few days it is evident that without Providence Bless our exertions we labour in vain: this is clear from a comparison of the result of our fishing in different parts of the Season – After the 5ᵗʰ of May we laboured 4 days for 1 fish where they were many times more numerous than we have seen them during our great success of late, & apparently under quite unfavourable circumstances. In the former case we perhaps fished the worst of any ship in Greenland, in the present probably the best! The John is sighted SE. In the Afternoon bore down to the John though at a considerable distance & was gratified by a letter bearing tidings of health & other blessings

---

[1] *Sic*. Probably 'Am.' intended.

from my dear M[rs] S with the well fare of our lovely Boy. Thanks be to God. The valued & gratifying epistle was dated 6th April 15 days after our Sailing.

Thursday 9th of June Lat. 78°48′ Lon. 5°0′E
WSW
My father & M[r] Jackson[1] accompanied me on board of the Esk on my return from the John & remained about 2 hours with us during which time the Ships reached by the wind under a fresh Breeze to the [N?][d] They furnished me with the pleasing news of the political world: the entrance of ['News from the John' *in margin*] the allies into Paris, the dethronement of Buonaparte by the Senate, & the flattering prospect of a speedy & lasting peace to all Europe. When my friends returned we proceed in C° to the NW[d] until we came to the Ice & happened to hit a deep Bay the western part affording considerable shelter from the Sea. Several Ships lay here: the Resolution of W*hit*by with 18 fish 150 or 160 Tons, spoke the Duncombe yesterday – we were highly pleased she had escaped from the Floes though she had not increased her Cargo. The John had been fishing of late at a field where for a while she was beset, but succeeded in turning the circumstances to a profitable account by increasing her stock of whales from one to 23 from [*blank space*] Tons to 110 Tons of Oil.

Lay too most of the Morning, in the Evening the weather being unfavourable for fishing & indeed no fish to be seen, the wind blowing a fresh Gale we plyed up to the windward Ice, reduced our Sails, lay too & cleared the after hold for making off. About 20 ships near us.

Friday 10th of June Lat. 78°50′ Lon. 5°5′E
SSW SWerly Var. NNW
Fresh Gales of wind during this day with constant small snow. Lay under a sheltering stream of Ice reaching to & fro under three close reef'd Top Sails & Jib. ['Different Ships in sight' *deleted*] ⅔ of the Crew employed making off whilst the rest alternately rest. The Vigilant spoke with 11 fish 150 tons of Oil: repaired a Rudder Gudgeon for them to replace some broken in boring out of the Ice (& seen by us) on Wednesday Inst[.] During the day several ships seen ..... at mid-night had completed 3 tiers of the after hold (except one cask) by filling 94 Casks with 137 Butts of Blubber or about 50 Tons of Oil. The Bay of the Ice in which we hitherto found shelter collapsing & [as well?] breaking upon us obliged us to suspend operations until a more convenient Season. The weather was very thick & stormy.

Saturday 11th of June Lat. 79°0 Lon. 5°15′E
SSW SWerly Var. NNW
The Stormy weather & fog continuing we found it expedient to reach out to Sea ward, passed some heavy Ice rendered dangerous by the action of a heavy South Swell. Fell in with a point of the lee Ice, had to make a tack, at noon were clear out to sea. In the afternoon the weather partly cleared & the wind abated: one ship only in

---

[1] Thomas Jackson, Scoresby's brother-in-law, and mate of the *John*. See vol. I, pp. liii–iv.

sight ..... Made sail SSE supposing the whales had betaken themselves in that direction ..... Employed Gumming Whalebone. The Augusta (the only ship in sight) sent a Boat on board of us, the Harponeer informed us that they escaped from the Fields in Cᵒ with the Gilder on the 1ˢᵗ Inst: that they had since captured 7 large fish making them a Cargo of 110 Tons of Oil & that the Gilder had been still more successful in the clear water fishery a little to the SEᵈ of us. That the two ships mentioned 17ᵗʰ of May as lying 5 miles off to the SWᵈ were the Juno & Alfred, that they left them in a very dangerous situation, the latter being crushed upon her beam ends[1] & deserted by all the Crew except the Master who betook themselves to the Juno in a situation but little better; she however at that time sustained the nip by sinking her until her hold beams were as low in the Ice & thereby served their full power in resisting its destructive force.

(Steered SSE before a fresh NNW Breeze.)

Sunday 12ᵗʰ of June Lat. 78°25′ Lon. 7°30′S
N.erly Variable NE.erly
Strong or moderate Breezes of wind Snow Showers & cloudy weather in the morning, delightful clear w*eathe*r in the Evening & night. Having proceeded to the SSE & SE until we approached the middle hook of the Foreland within 26[2] miles & seeing no whales we hauled off WNW under a Brisk sail – we found the water here of a transparent Blue Colour, which in our situation for many days past has been of a deep opaque Green. – In two hours sailing we saw a great number of <u>Razor Backs</u> & occasionally a solitary Common Whale – a White Whale was also seen. At noon the north end of Charles Isl*and* or Foreland bore NEbE about 35 miles distant, here many Razor Backs were likewise seen. Pursued some of the individuals of the Whales met with – Steered to the Wᵈ during the performance of Divine Service. The Augusta in sight. Having increased our distance from the land to about 45 miles & changed the colour of the sea to its more favourable Green, we ['saw' *deleted*] at once met with a great number of whales seen spouting in all directions. Sent six Boats in chase at 10 pm: they plied until mid n*igh*t without effect.

Monday 13ᵗʰ of June Lat. 78°23′+ Lon. 6°25′E
NE.erly Calm WSW
About half an hour after mid-night the specksioneer struck a fish 4 miles off the ship to windw*ar*d the mate at the same time temporarily entangled a large fish 4½ miles to leeward, the Harpoon did not retain its hold consequently he had a distance of near 9 miles to row to the fast boat. The fast fish ran out only 2 lines or 240 fat*hom*s remained immersed 25 minutes, appeared for 5 minutes but

['John Trueman **M.**   No. 16 = 10ᶠᵗ2ⁱⁿ' *in margin*]

---

[1] But see journal entry for 27 June 1814.
[2] Possibly '20'.

deceived the Boats & then went down 37′[,][1] on its reappearance a 2d & 3d Harpoon was struck & in 23 minutes more the capture was complete. We reached the Boats with the Ship shortly afterwards. In flinching one of the <u>specks</u>[2] was suddenly freed when by the elasticity of the extended <u>Guy</u> the tackle Block sprung up with great violence & struck William Shepperd ½ Seamen [sic] in the Forehead a most violent Blow. He was bled & put to bed very ill. John Dunbar the Boast[n] [sic] & Harponeer received a violent squeeze between the <u>Cant-fid</u> & the <u>Davit</u> from the breaking of the [rump?] rope & the fish springing

['John Trueman Robert Dowell **M.** No. 17 = 10[ft]1[in]' *in margin*]

aft whilst he leant over the Davit conveying a tackle to the flinchers.[3] This accident occurred in the last or 15th fish: he has since been off duty, but is now happily in a great measure relieved by the affects of Blisters,[4] bleeding, & quietude. When the flinching was accomplished we made sail westward soon fell in with a vast number of fish, two Boats were in pursuit near each other whenby [sic] a singular coincidence, they both struck different fish at the same moment – they were a mile from the ship & before the Boats could reach the specksioneer was obliged to slip

['Thomas Welburn **F.** No. 18 = 9.2' *in margin*]

the end of his lines 12 or 13 minutes from the striking.[5] The fish & lines were expected to be lost & all but two Boats of 7 repaired to the other fish & killed it with tolerable dispatch – at the moment that three <u>cheers</u> shewed that this was effected the other fast fish made its appearance at about a mile's distance – three Boats proceeded towards it & were so fortunate as re-entangle it, it ran out 3 lines & in 20′ was like-wise killed. The first fast lines were marvellously saved for on hauling on the 2d strik-ers line the other's Harpoon was found entangled with it, having slipped out of the

---

[1] '37″ presumably means 37 minutes, not 37 feet.

[2] *OED* s.v. 'Speck': 'The fat or blubber of a whale.' What seems to have happened was that as one of the half-ton slabs or 'specks' of blubber was being cut from the whale, it was unexpectedly detached from the carcass by the tension in the speck-tackle to which it was fixed (see diagram in vol. I, p. xlv). In *Account of the Arctic Regions*, Scoresby used the term 'slip' rather than 'speck'.

[3] This appears to have been a separate and earlier incident from the accident to Shepperd, as the next sentence in the journal indicates. In *Account of the Arctic Regions* (II, p. 296) Scoresby explained that, when flensing, 'Towards the stern of the ship the head of the fish is directed ... The smallest or posterior part of the whale's body, where the tail is united, is called the *rump*, and the extremity or anterior part of the head, the *nose*, or *nose-end*. The rump then, supported by a tackle, is drawn forward by means of a stout rope, called the *rump-rope*, and the head is drawn in an oppo-site direction by means of the "nose-tackle." Hence the body of the fish is forcibly extended.' The term 'Cant-fid' is less easily explained in this context; perhaps Scoresby meant the cant- (or kent-) purchase, the means by which the whale was rotated during flensing.

[4] Presumably the deliberate raising of blisters through the application of a vesicatory such as mustard or cantharis, in the form of a plaster or poultice.

[5] I.e. the fast boat had paid out all its lines and, with no other boat's lines at hand to connect to, had been forced to let go of the lines to avoid being towed under the sea or ice by the whale.

fish & was saved with the lines by this curious circumstance. Clewed the top sails down to flinch. The weather delightfully fine: therm. 40° Sun hot & clear. Several ships to the NW^d of us. The Middle Hook of the Foreland at EbS 40 miles Dist*ant*. Superceded John Nicholson Boatsteerer for incapacity.

The wind blowing fresh in the Evening we did not finish flinching before mid-night.

Tuesday 14ᵗʰ of June Lat. 78°40′ Lon. 6°0′E
SW, Var. SE.erly
Fresh Breezes most of this day. Delightful weather in the morning; cloudy with Snow Showers in the Evening in Night. Proceeded by the wind NW.ward until 11 am. saw then several Ships but no fish: tacked & immediately after*w*ards the wind veered more to the South & the Ship was not likely to fetch the same spot where we made sail, much less again the fishing ground which much[1] be far to windward. Hence appeared a favourable opportunity for making off; accordingly at 2 Pm. commenced operations with all hands after every man was refreshed with ['Making off' *in margin*] 8 hours rest. The Fore-hold was the scene of action where the remaining Ballast water was started, ['&' *deleted*] pumped out & filled & part of the second by mid-night.[2] The Ship meanwhile sailing to the Eastw*a*rd until 10 PM. being then near the land, tacked. About mid-night Calm. The N. end of the Foreland at EbS 15 miles distant.

Wednesday 15ᵗʰ of June Lat. 78°27′ Lon. 6°20E
Calm N.erly. Variable. ENE to ESE
Light variable winds with Calm & exceeding fine weather until ['near' *deleted*] the Evening when a fresh Breeze prevailed. After a 14 hours spell making off we set a half watch & continued the work, about 6 am. ['the' *deleted*] two tiers of the Fore hold were filled completing the same fore & aft. Proceeded then but with very reduced vigour to stow & fill the upper tier of the main hold, beginning against the after hold abreast to the pump-well.

With the N.erly Breeze of wind we steered SW with the view of finding on that course the most Eastern ['herd' *deleted*] Run[3] or herd of whales, removed from the common scene of fishing where the operation might be more successfully carried on from avoiding the intrusion of other fishers. ['a whale struck singular chase' *in margin*] We had advanced about 20 miles when we saw 2 or 3 whales & afterwards several others widely scattered around us. One appearing near the ship sent a Boat

---

[1] *Sic*: transcription error for 'must'?

[2] There may be a transcription omission or error here. The entry for the following day (15 June) suggests that Scoresby was here stating that between 2 p.m. and midnight the first tier of barrels in the forehold and part of the second tier had been filled with blubber.

[3] In the sense of 'A shoal of fish in motion, *esp*. ascending a river from the sea for spawning', the earliest citation in *OED* is from *Account of the Arctic Regions*, II, p. 214: 'The systematical movements of the whales receive additional illustration from many well known facts. Sometimes a large tribe passing from one place to another, which, under such circumstances, is denominated a "run of fish" … .'

off, whereby in a few minutes it was entangled at 7¼ O'clock Pm. All The Boats had
not left the ship before the fast fish made

['Thomas Welburn Harpoon drew' *in margin*]

its appearance running at a considerable rate, a general chase succeeded, when three
Boats coming equally near approached the game at the same time thereby so incommoding each other that none of them got fast. The fish now took to windward (Eastward) with a velocity of 3 or 4 knotts p hour some of the Boats gave chase whilst
others towed by the fast Boat. The fish now suddenly shifted its direction whilst
under water so that on its next appearance there was scarcely a Boat within a mile of
the spot. It then took a complete circuit round the fast Boat at ['a' *deleted*] nearly a
mile's distance & afterwards set off with accelerated force to windward again.
Although we continued to use every exertion under a fresh breeze of wind in getting
['**Thursday 16th of June** Lat. 78°17′ Lon. 7°30′E[.] ESE to SE *in margin*] the ship to
windward, yet the Boats were soon many miles off. The chase had been followed 6 or
7 hours when the sky suddenly overcast & for a while we were all involved in the
alarming obscurity of a thick fog, the danger of the Boats losing the ship being trebly
augmented by the existing circumstances of so singularly powerful & determined
whale.

The attenuation of the fog revived us & the pursuit was re-commenced with fresh
vigour. The Harponeers at length saw the necessity of endeavouring to fatigue the fish
by retarding as much as possible the progress of the fast Boat. At first 9 lines were
slacked out (a weight in air of 11¼ Cwt) & their inertia augmented by the resistance
of the oars of the fast Boat & others towing astern. This being found yet insufficient
['SE' *in margin*] all the Boats were applied with their sides to the fast Boats stern &
yet they were all dragged Broadside wise through the water with undiminished ['A
15¾ hours Singular chase of a whale' *in margin*] velocity. The fish however finding
ease by a change of course frequently disheartened the already languishing pursuers
by its appearance in the most unexpected places. Their continued exertions enabled
them many times to approach with[1] 12 or 14 yards but the moment the fish heard or
saw a Boat it shot from them as an arrow from a Bow. On one occasion only they got
within 8 or 9 yards & the Harpoon was hove, it wounded the game but failed to
entangle. After the pursuit had been continued without interruption for 14 hours, the
fish again turned to leeward but the Crews enervated by the present laborious exertion, their unfitness for it, many of them being sparingly wrapped in clothes drenched
in Oil, together with the hard labour to which they were previously subjected, quite
incapacitated them. The ship by this time had at length got near the fast Boat. The
wind having increased to a fresh gale the hitherto gentle lipper was [become a?]
confirmed Swell, the Boats could scarcely move in safety. As the fish now disappeared
& was never afterwards seen, it soon became certain that it must be off the hook or
dead: we had reason to believe the latter was the case. As however it was impossible
to [gain?] even the lines themselves by the Boat & equally so to haul a fish up by the

---

[1] *Sic*: 'within' presumably intended.

ship when drifting rapidly to lee-ward some contrivance was necessary to support the lines until [*illegible word deleted*] an amendment of the weather – for this purpose we slung a cask of 126 Gallons capacity, to this we ['secured' *deleted*] suspended the lines & fastened an empty Boat with a flag, both for being the better seen & to aid in supporting the lines if the cask should fail. This accomplished we called the Boats on board & all the men from the fast Boat after 15¾ hours chase, & set a watch of ⅔ Crew. The Ship under a heavy press of canvas could scarcely keep near the Boat. At this place the Middle Hook of the Foreland bore EbN about 8 or 9 Leagues distant. ['A dead fish found but from the distress of weather let loose together with a Boat nine whale lines & possibly another whale abandoned!!' *in margin*] At 2 Pm. a dead fish was seen, evidently not the one we struck, all hands were again summoned, a rope taken round the rump of the dead fish, whereby it was towed towards the Boat, but the Ship with it fell about 200 yards to lee-ward – if we remained by this fish we must drift from the Boat & probably lose it with 9 lines & it was expected another fish. It was therefore an object at least to secure the Boat & lines & one fish. For this end we made all sail to attempt to gain the Boat to secure it with the lines & then drift down to the dead fish which we placed directly to leeward. Having reached nearly an hour to the NE^d we tacked, but from the increase of swell with the wind we just fetched the same place. As the sea was already very high & was most rapidly augmenting it was deemed in vain as well as dangerous to the safety of the men in two Boats to contend, all must therefore be sacrificed, a Boat, 9 whale lines of 1080 fath. & possibly two large fish to the, chance of again finding the spot on the abatement of the Gale. The ship was laid to for taking the Boats up, they approached slowly owing to the great drift of the ship though the top-sails were lowered, & with very great danger. The Sea overlapped one of them & obliged them to her[1] Bow to windward, drop her stern first & guide her by the Oars; the other was a <u>bolder</u> and shorter Boat & scudded before the wind the oars acting as sails & rudder whereby they humoured her to the occasional Breakers with great skill. This was a most anxious time for all on board as well as in the Boats, but especially myself as I was the means of placing them in this dangerous situation, rendered dangerous by a sudden & violent increase of the wind & Sea. At length, thanks to a Benignant Providence, the [*sic*] reached us in safety & they with the Boats by the alertness of the Crew secured uninjured to our great joy. We were obliged now to treble reef the Top-Sails & to take in the Jib & after the sails were set, we reached an hour to the ENE^d & then tacked & afterwards wore every two hours, by the way of keeping as near the fish & boat as possible, at the same time that we might have some idea of their situation.

Squally weather in the night with thick snow & sleet.

Friday 17th of June Lat. 78°27′ Lon. 7°10′E
SSE, S. Var.
The wind somewhat abating in the Morning at 10 made all sail, setting Top-Gallant & stay sails amounting to as much canvass as the Masts could well bear, under which we laboured to get to windward, proceeding generally two hours on each tack, but

---

[1] *Sic*: 'turn' omitted in transcription?

occasionally accomodating [*sic*] the difference of the ship's velocity on the different reaches, at the same time taking into the account the correction necessary for the angle formed between the supposed bearing of the sought for objects & the direction of the varying wind, by increasing the time on either tack for producing the requisite effects. In the afternoon a fog prevailed so thick that no object could be discerned at more than 100 yards distance & yet we were so fortunate that at 5 Pm. when in the middle of our SE.ern reach we passed in sight of the dead fish! The Sea having considerably fallen we took it alongside. We found it so eaten of Sharks that scarcely any Blubber remained upon

['Dead fish seen by Thos Parsey Boats^r [1] & John Trueman
No. 19 about 11 feet. Afforded 6 or 8 tons of oil' *in margin*]

it but what lay on the Belly, the under part of the head, jawbones & the greatest part of the two lips – we probably got sufficient to produce 6 or 8 tons of oil. The Whalebone was decayed out, whereby from current usage it was not considered as a size or payable fish though it was ['of' *deleted*] in bulk of body sufficient to have measured 10 or 11 feet bone. The Blubber we got was in a very tollerable state, but the carcase & crang smelt nauseously from the rapid progress of the putrescence in the muscular parts. From meeting with this fish, the direction of the Boat may be estimated about SbE & the distance probably 10 miles. It is a curious circumstance that the flag left in the Boat with the lines & was seen to blow over-board soon after it was deserted, was discovered drifting round the ship's bows as we flinched & was saved.

When the decks were washed, we again made sail & proceeded as before, plying to the SbE on about 2 hours tacks, accomodating however the length of each to produce the proper direction whilst in the middle of the reach, thereby expecting to pass under the lee of the Boat every two hours. At mid-night still thick weather, blowing fresh, with Sleet or Snow at intervals.

Saturday 18th of June Lat. 78°20′ Lon. 7°25′E
SSW, SW, W. SW
The wind continued a fresh breeze & veered to the W^d. We extended our search on the Starboard tack in a corresponding geometric proportion. A premium offered for seeing & observing that Boat, produced the effect of a sharp look out. The attentuation of the fog so that objects might be seen at the distance of a mile occasionally was highly serviceable, since at 9 am. the Boat was discerned at the utmost limit of vision on the Ship's weather Bow. The fog ['Discover & save the abandoned Boat &c.' *in margin*] returned greatly incrassated;[2] by the observations made however & attending to the ship's progress &c. we passed again within sight, at a short distance under the lee of the Boat. Thus we were so fortunate as to find the lost Boat after 44 hours interval from which we were drifted by the Gale not less

---

[1] Possibly 'Boats^n'; the superscript in the transcript is almost microscopic.
[2] *OED*: 'thickened'. It is noted that the past participle, used adjectivally, is found 'esp. in *Zool.* & *Bot.*'.

than 15 miles, notwithstanding the general prevalence of the thickest fog. The Cask whereby the lines were suspended doubtless saved the boat from filling forming so excellent a <u>Breakwater</u>, that she had not leaked or shipped scarcely 50 Gallons of water during so long & tempestuous a period. All hands were summoned, lay the ship too, took the lines on board, hove them in by the Capstern, but found no fish. Thus though we failed in getting the fish we lost no actual property but rather saved such articles as amounted to a hundred pounds value.

Made all sail (4 Pm) proceeded 5 hours by the wind SSW then tacked, & continued our course larboard tacked the rest of the day.

Fine cloudy weather in the Evening. No Ships, land, Ice, or fish to see.

Sunday 19th of June Lat. 77°50′ Lon. 5°40′E
SbW

We had strong gales of wind most of this day, accompanied with thick fog, or small Rain. Thermometer 34 to 36°. Continued our westward course until we fell in with scattered pieces of Ice at 4 am. tacked & lay too. Having seen no whales in our course considered ourselves too far South. Reduced Sails therefore & remained drifting to leeward. One ship[1] seen – a Razor Back. After having performed the usual Sabbath day's duties at 6 pm. sent all hands to Bed to prepare them for the labour of <u>making off</u>, considering it a gift of time to make off, in such weather as cannot be employed in the fishery. At mid-night aroused all hands.

Monday 20th of June Lat. 78°15′ Long. 5°55′E
SbW

About 9 am. the after hold was filled with Blubber & completed. The <u>Gummed</u>-whalebone was stowed on its surface. The Main-hold was then continued & the remnant of the Blubber made off by 6 Pm. filling the hold save about 15 Casks in the upper tier around the Fore-hatch way. The amount of ['Making off' *in margin*] this day's work with those of Tuesday & Wednesday (14th & 15th Instant) was the filling of 125 Casks with 215 completed Butts of Blubber, which added to 271 before filled is 486 Butts, these according to the common proportion of 8 Butts to 3 Tons of oil should produce 182 Tons, but imagine the Casks are over-rated as our present Cargo seem to consist of probably 170 Tons.

Meanwhile the Ship lay too with a Brisk Gale of wind & continued rain. After we finished turned before the wind & steered NNW until mid-night. At that time saw a fish – sent two Boats in pursuit, they rowed over the place & scared the fish. Being exceedingly thick took the Boats up & lay too.

Tuesday 21st of June
Lat 78°30′ Lon. 5°15′E
SbW. W.erly

Very thick weather most of this day with constant Rain. Pursued a NbW course three hours @ 3 or 4 knotts & then hauled by the wind westward. In the few intervals

[1] Probably a slip of the pen: 'fish' or 'whale' intended?

which occasionally occurred wherin the fog somewhat cleared ['Thermometer all day 35" *in margin*] we saw whales – At mid-night sent 4 Boats in pursuit – at that time little wind. Many ships seen – spoke the Walker with [*blank space*] fish 220–230 Tons of oil.

Wednesday 22ᵈ of June Lat. 78°38′ Lon. 4°50′E
NW. W.erly
Light or moderate winds, thick fog for a few hours, afterwards fine cloudy weather. Saw several fish in the morning & whilst steering to speak the Sisters, one we struck – it showed itself soon after being struck & conducted itself in a great manner as the last[,] removing furiously forward but fortunately in a lee-ward direction[.] In 1¼ hours two more harpoons were struck, the 3ʳᵈ Boat that approached ['Fish staves a Boat Difficult to Capture' *in margin*] received a blow which stove & sank her – the next was violently assailed with the tail – several oars broken & some of the men slightly bruised. Two of the

[‘John Trueman F.  No. 20 = 7. 6’ *in margin*]

Sisters’ Boats now assisted in the pursuit, but the game made such rapid circuits & dashed its tail so violently around on the approach of any Boats that 2 hours transpired before another Harpoon or lance could be struck. The Sisters’ Boat at length came up to her & half an hour more completed the capture. The sunk Boat in the interim had acted as a drogue moored to the stern of a fast Boat, laid the Ship alongside of her, hooked the tackles & hoisted her up – most of the lines were turned out but the end[1] was secured – dropped the Ship down

[‘Thos Welburn M. No 21. = 3. 6 *in margin*]

to the fish took it alongside & flinched – (dimension & striker as per margin) – At the same time hauled the ravelled line on board. The Sisters only escaped 17 days ago has since procured 6 fish making her amount 18 fish 130 tons. ['Therm. 33° *in margin*] Struck & killed a little fish @ 8 & 9 Pm. during light winds & thick fog showers.

Thursday 23ᵈ of June Lat. 78°40′ Lon. 4°0′E
SSW South
The wind veered to the Southward & blew fresh – the fog cleared – made sail to the W.ᵈ – at 5 am. the John bore down to us & my Father took breakfast with us. Gave chase to two fish, a mother & its young with ship and boats before the wind, pursued about 2 hours but without success though we came exceedingly near. A single Stranger Boat mixed with ours & struck the Sucker, the wind and Sea increasing probably prevented the capture of the mother. Being near the Ice we

---

[1] Presumably the end of the whale lines, so that they could be retrieved from the sea. Note however the singular ‘line’ later in this day’s entry.

steered WNW under the lee of a patch for the pupose of watering. Procured two Boat loads of a tollerable quality from a <u>hummock</u>. The John near us with 30 Fish 170 Tons of oil. Snow, Rain, or thick fog accompanied with a strong wind alternately prevailed we reached out to Sea & proceeded to make off. Several Ships seen during the day.

Friday 24th of June Lat. 78°35′ Lon. 4°40′E
Serly W.erly
The wind abated & the fog thinned away, wore & stood to the W^d[.]

The making off was finished at 2½ am. whereby the hold was completed & ['Making off, Contents of the Hold' *in margin*] 3 Casks remained over. The contents of the hold as follows – viz. 2 Casks of 500 Gallons; 2 of 400; 37 of 300; 120, Tons;[1] 48 200's; 26, 180's; 11, 160's 43 Butts; & 12 Puncheons Whale's Blubber together with one cask of 252 Gallons

['Geo. Sinclair **M.** No. 22 = 7. 2 *in margin*]

of Seal's Blubber & one cask of Crang, amounting to 303 Casks, containing 512 Butts of Blubber & 2 Butts of Crang. By the time we finished making off we had penetrated into a Bay of the Ice where some small fish were seen. One of them we captured & flinched. The fog then recommenced & the wind shifted westward, steered to the SE & East until we cleared two Points of Ice then hauled up at Noon to the SSW^d.

Proceeded with a fresh Breeze of wind under the gloom of thick fog showers 5 hours to

['John Trueman Harpoon broke' *in margin*]

the SSW^d saw 2 or 3 whales; tacked & reached to the NW^d. At 8 Pm. fell in with the John running before the wind – at 10 the fog cleared, a fish was seen & pursued by two of the John's & two of our Boats – our Specksioneer struck it, but owing to the Breaking of the Harpoon it escaped. Several ships seen, some fishing.

Saturday 25th of June Lat. 78°28 Lon. 5°20′
South. to SW.erly
Fresh or Strong Gales during this day with much Rain Snow or sleet. Stretched off the Ice to the SE^d 4 hours[.] Saw several whales but were prevented in the pursuit by the Increase of Sea with the wind. In the evening reached amongst the Ice where lay several ships, passed amidst a considerable quantity of open Ice in various directions during 4 or 6 hours sailing. At mid night being on the exterior & unable to find any fish, lay too drifting northward.

---

[1] 'Ton' here means a barrel of 252 gallons capacity, as confirmed by the manifest (see entry for 21 July 1814).

Sunday 26ᵗʰ of June Lat 78°35′ Lon. 4°50′E
SW. SSW.
Fresh Breezes of wind – fine cloudy weather most of the day, fog or Snow Showers at intervals – Near a point end of Ice stretching far into the Sea Eastward we fell in with a considerable number of whales, made a loose fall, six Boats followed the chase 5 hours without success & were then called on board. Several Ships in Sight, of which many fished with profit.

Monday 27ᵗʰ of June Lat. 78°50′ Lon. 5°25′E
SE.erly to SSW
The weather being stormy & often foggy or thick with Rain & Sleet we could not follow several fish that were at different times seen this day. Loitered about to windward of the above mentioned promontory of Ice. Spoke the Sisters with 19 fish 135 Tons of Oil, returned their Harpoons which remained in the fish they assisted us to kill on the 22ᵈ Instant. The Sisters & accompanying Ships escaped from the Ice 13 days after us – the Augusta, Gilder, & another preceded them; the Ellen followed & the Alfred & Juno (mentioned as being left in a desperate situation by the Augusta vide 17 June) accompanied them. Thus by circumstance of peculiar Providence we escaped the first & were enabled to fish with great advantage whilst they were still detained. May the distinguishing mercies of God ever call forth our heartfelt thanksgivings! The Alfred & Juno were perhaps not so dangerously involved as represented, at least it does not seem that the Alfred was seriously stove.

Tuesday 28ᵗʰ of June Lat. 78°45′ Lon. 5.25 E
SSE SW.erly South
This day we had moderate winds thick Snow or fog showers Morning & Evening but in the interval fine cloudy weather. Saw about a dozen whales, pursued them vigorously but without success. 35 Sail of ships seen, only one of which was observed to get a fish. At night proceeded SEward into the open Sea, seeing no whales returned.

Wednesday 29ᵗʰ of June Lat 78°20′ Lon 4°0′E
South SWerly
At 10 am. approaching the verge of the Ice the fog cleared observed a Ship (the Mary & Elizabeth) flinching with ancient flying a signal of <u>full</u> ship: having previously prepared a letter for my Beloved Wife, I closed it & sent it on board – we were informed that a 74 Gun Ship & two frigates were in the Country for protecting the fishery – that one of them had communicated the expected glorious intelligence of peace with all Europe![1] The Duncombe it seems has yet but 60 or 70 Tons of Oil. Entered the Ice found it slack & pervious, worked all the day to windward under a strong press of Canvass amongst Streams & loose Ice with floes & crowded drift Ice

---

[1] It is a measure of the immediate effect of Napoleon's downfall (temporary though that was to prove) that a warship of this size could be sent to northern waters. As Steward's account for this date makes clear, the intent was presumably primarily the protection of the Archangel trade from American privateers, rather than a similar concern for the whaling fleet.

to the NW^d of us. Saw only One fish – 5 or 6 ships in C° one of which made a Capture. At mid night foggy, wind strong.

Thursday 30th of June Lat. 78°35′ Lon. 5°20′E
SSW, South, SE, E.rly
Continued plying to the SW^d with a fresh breeze of wind, during thick fog Showers, amongst open Ice, streams & occasional floes. Still finding no fish & fearing a change of wind might incommode us by preventing our return, at 8 am. altered our destination steered ENE &c and in 2 hours found ourselves at Sea with a few scattered pieces of Ice around us. From hence continued on an ENE or NE course during the prevalence of a thick fog, at the same time stowed a few Casks in the twin-decks & made off the last captured fish. At 7 the wind fell & veered E.ward & we had some difficulty in doubling the point of ['Made off last Fish, filled 10 Casks = 15 Butts' *in margin*] a floe near which we lay on the 27th & 28th Inst. The Earl Fife near us with 16 fish, 120 Tons of Oil – repaired a pump spear[1] for her.

The weather now became delightfully clear, continued under all sail by the wind NNE the rest of the day, supposing the fish must have retreated far to the N^d especially since those ['fish' *deleted*] latterly seen made a rapid progression thitherward. Different ships passed. Saw the Land.

Friday 1st July Lat 79°30′ Long. 6°0′E
E.erly, Calm SE.erly
At 3 am. met Ice ahead laying E & W – consisting externally of a close pack, internally of Floes or Fields. The weather being fine & wind light

['John Dunbar **F.**  No. 23 = 9^ft 1^in' *in margin*]

a fish seen at a considerable distance was successfully attacked – after being struck it did not attempt to fly to the adjacent Ice but decended [*sic*] obliquely downwards, made its appearance in 20 minutes, retired before a Boat reached the spot remained 20 minutes more concealed & on its next appearance a second Harpoon was struck. The Capture was effected soon afterwards. This was a most inoffensive animal: it never made the least resistance never lifting fin or tail. It was towed to the Ship during a Calm interval & flinched. Others were seen & pursued at the same time. At 8 am. the Head Land was in sight bearing East about 15 Leagues distant. 4 Ships in sight.

We had not finished flinching before rain commenced & shortly after a thick fog. The Ice appears very open to the W^d & is probably navigable 10 or 15 Leagues from hence – a promontory lies 10 miles East from us & from thence the margin trends NE.erly as marked by the blink.

Made all Sail to windward on short tacks.

In the night rigged flying Jib-boom, with the Fore & mizen Royal masts. Thick Fog.

---

[1] Smyth, *Sailor's Word Book*: 'The rod of iron to which the upper box is attached – and to the upper end of which the brake is pinned – whereby the pump is set in motion.'

Saturday 2ᵈ of July Lat. 79°25′ Lon. 5°50′E
SSW W.erly Var. SW.erly SSW.
Most of the day light winds with frequent thick fog. Under easy sail did not shift our ground many miles the first 18 hours. In a clear interval the Aimwell was seen to windward bearing down towards us – about noon Mʳ Johnstone came on board & presented us with a variety of news, chiefly relating to the uncommonly successful fishery of this Season – he however has succeeded only in part his present cargo consisting of 16 whales 125 or 130 Tons of Oil. The Perseverance one of our fellow sufferers when beset, passed us with 8 fish. In the evening the weather was clear & wind brisk made sail & began to beat to windward along the edge of the N.ern pack in a SW.erly direction amongst scattered Ice. At mid-night brisk Gales with Snow.

Sunday 3ᵈ of July Lat. 79°22′+ Lon. 5°35′E
SSW Var. W.erly
Blowing a Strong Gale most of this day with almost constant Snow, we continued beating to windward as above, but under very reduced Sails. Today we obtained a sight of the Sun at noon the first Meridian altitude we have been able to measure since the 7ᵗʰ Ult*imo*. Such has been the cloudy state of the Atmosphere, that scarcely at any time were we able to distinguish (from any external appearance) noon from mid*nigh*t.

Monday 4ᵗʰ of July Lat. 79°10′ Lon. 4°20′E
WSW W, SW
Fresh gales of wind with fog or Snow Showers, very thick in the night. At 8 am. reached amongst several streams of Ice, by noon we had beat up an opening leading to the NWᵈ amongst much Ice, afterwards found the Ice slack in that direction, made all sail & proceeded 6 hours without making a tack; having penetrated about 10 or 12 Leagues our progress was stopped by an apparent Pack of compact Ice – at the same time a thick fog overshadowing us & seeing no whale throughout the day we tacked & retraced our course amidst floes loose Ice & many patches as well as the density of the atmosphere would allow us. As we proceeded on either Course the colour of the Sea was first a Muddy Green, a pellucid blue, & then Green at the place from whence we returned. This change of colour peculiar to the Greenland Seas is permanent & by no ['Remark on the Changes of colour peculiar to the Greenland Seas.' *in margin*] means affected with the State of the Atmosphere with regard to clouds or the influence of the Sun's unclouded Rays: the blue is a sort of indigo colour, the other a kind of bottle Green. It seems not to [proceed?] from the nature of the bottom since the colour is most readily distinguished from the appearance of a deeply immersed tongue of Ice, which in the blue water appears distinct & blue whilst in the Green it partakes of this colour & ['can' *deleted*] is imperfectly seen from the want of transparency in the water. I have often noticed some particles of a yellow substance floating in the Green water which probably occasions its peculiar colour & turpidity [*sic*] & which sometimes is observed to tinge the edges of the Ice with a deep yellow hue.
   4 or 5 ships seen occasionally during the day.

Tuesday 5ᵗʰ of July Lat. 79°12′ Lon. 5°20′E
SSW.

About 4 am. we met with much loose Ice & a floe on the surface of which was collected a great quantity of water produced from the melting of the Snow & the recent Rains or moist fogs: to this we moored for the purpose of watering, sent the Casks to the Ice & filled them very readily, to the amount of 4 or 5 Tons. About 8 am. cast off on the weather clearing, worked to windward of the Floe & reached out to Sea ward.

The whales still avoiding our search I determined again to explore the more northern regions – proceeded therefore under easy sail to the E, or NEᵈ passing several open patches of Ice & many scattered pieces. In the ['Making off – Filled 23 Casks with Blubber equal to 32 Butts' *in margin*] Evening (10 Pm.) hauled under the lee of a close patch of heavy Ice to the Wᵈ for Shelter, the Sea without being heavy & wind blowing a strong Gale. Employed making off in casks stowed between the hold beams ['of' *deleted*] upon those in the hold, all the hatches of the twin-decks being removed. The Aimwell in Cᵒ.

Wednesday 6ᵗʰ of July Lat. 79°42′+ Lon. 8°0′E.
SbW SW

Very hard Gales all this day accompanied by the clearest weather we have experience [*sic*] for upwards of a month, for several hours not a cloud could be discerned – we enjoyed comfortable shelter under the lee of an isolated patch of Ice extensive at the first but rapidly diminished by the heavy Sea beating to windward & hurling considerable portions with great rapidity to lee-ward whenever the continuity was overcome. In the Evening our Range was still further limited we however still found shelter, lying too constantly under 3 close reefed T. Sail, Fore & Fr Top Stay Sails with the main yard to the Mast wearing repeatedly. Aimwell in Cᵒ.

In the morning land was discovered bearing from from E to SE & only 5 or 6 Leagues distance. At 8 pm. the Head Land ESE 4 or 5 Leagues of [*sic*]. Weather cloudy.

Thursday 7ᵗʰ of July[.] at noon. Lat 80°15′N Lon. 9°½′ E. at 5Pm. Lat 80°25′ Lon. 8°45′E. at midnight. Lat 80°7′+ Lon. 9°50′E
SWbW SW, WSW Variable

The weather was exceedingly thick & the wind violent most of this day. Fearing least the drift of the patch, beneath the lee of which we enjoyed so commodious shelter, should involve us amidst the Islands lying on the NW of Spitzbergen or beset us on the face of a Pack during the intensity of the Fog, I judged it expedient removing our quarters; having informed Mʳ Johnstone of my intention, we steered NW.ward but falling in with several close patches of Ice, agitated tremendously by a furious Sea, as we emerged from beneath the lee of the still firm patch of sheltering Ice, we had to proceed N, NNE & various other courses on a highly dangerous navigation for nearly two hours, when passing through a small opening of a Stream we met with an open space of water ['troubled' *deleted*] our sailing incommoded only by a great many small pieces of drift Ice. Proceeded then by the wind – at 5 Pm. discovered a body of Ice on our lee-bow, wore & made more sail on the other tack, setting mizen, main & mizen Stay Sails, Foresail, &c.

After this time the wind somewhat abated & the fog was dispersed – at 11¹ Pm. we were only 3 or 4 Leagues from land, struck soundings 75 Fathoms apparently mud with some rocks Hackluit's [*sic*] Head Land bearing SW Dist. 18 miles, Cloven Cliff South, 12′; Red Beach Deer Feild SE 30′. Tacked. Found our Lat. by Meridian Alti*tude* below the Pole 80°7′ & Long. according to Phipps.² 9°50′E. The Aimwell in C°.

Friday 8ᵗʰ of July Lat. 80°10′+ Lon. 8°5′E at midn: Lat. 79°55
WSW, W, WNW, NW, N NE.erly
Plying to windward with a strong Gale of wind the former part of this day – towards noon the wind veered Northward & afterwards to the NE & abated whilst charming weather prevailed for a few hours – in which time we <u>coasted</u> along the Ice accordingly as it trended steering sometimes NW.erly but commonly from W³ to WSW – the Pack appeared a close body composed of Drift Ice & Floes, abounded with deep sinuosities proceeded in a NW.erly or N.erly direction. Thus the main body of Ice ['Situation of the Main Body of Ice in Greenland at this time' *in margin*] seems to circumscribe the W.ern & Nerly parts of the land at a distance of perhaps 60 miles in Lat. 78°½⁴ consisting of an open pack: from thence converging by a very irregular line becoming more compact in 79°½ & approaching the headland within 20 miles, from thence still following the course of the Land it seems to take an E.rly direction or probably ENE leaving a large navigable space to the North of the land & possibly extending to a high northern Latitude. The space which is much more extensive in the present Season than ordinary, arises from the unprecedented prevalence of S.erly which have been so general that for nearly a month past (27 Dy.)⁵ we have not had more than 24 hours of Nerly winds the whole time.

Our endeavours to find⁶ the retreat of the Whales proving still unsuccessful it is highly probable that they have removed their quarters & have accomplishing [*sic*] their usual migration into ['quarters' *deleted*] situations to us inaccessible. Having as

---

¹ Possibly '10'.

² Scoresby was referring to longitudes recorded in C. J. Phipps, *A Voyage Towards the North Pole Undertaken by His Majesty's Command 1773*. Phipps was the second Baron Mulgrave and his descendants maintain a close connection to the Whitby Literary and Philosophical Society: the Marquis and Marchioness of Normanby are the Society's patrons, and the Dowager Marchioness is its president. The ships used on this voyage were HMS *Racehorse* and *Carcass*; Horatio Nelson was a midshipman on the *Carcass*. The places named by Scoresby are shown in *Account of the Arctic Regions*, II, Plate IV 'A Chart of Spitzbergen ...', but the longitudes on that chart, like that indicated from the Phipps account, are incorrect. If 'Cloven Cliff' was due south of the *Esk*, then the ship was close to 11°30′E. A difference of two degrees of longitude at 80°N is however only about 40 kilometres or 25 miles. The landscape and anchorages in this area were described in some detail in *Account of the Arctic Regions*, I, pp. 115–16.

³ Originally 'WNW' but 'NW' deleted.

⁴ 'Possibly 76½'.

⁵ This parenthesis was inserted above the line in the transcript, and presumably indicates that 'nearly a month' was 27 days.

⁶ 'discover' inserted above the line, though 'find' was not deleted.

Figure 4. HMS *Racehorse* and *Carcass* beset by ice in latitude 80°37′ on 7 August 1773
The engraving appeared in John Payne's *Universal Geography* (London, 1791 and later editions).

far as prudent explored the regions in the North probably 60 miles nearer the Pole than any other human beings at <u>this time in the world</u> (save the Crew of our consort the Aimwell), it now only remains for us to examine every eligable [*sic*] spot as we proceed South & if still unsuccessful we must bear away for our Dear <u>Dolce Domum</u>, Thankful to a Gracious Providence for our many mercies, & especially for our measure of success as temporal good – we have yet unemployed Casks sufficient to contain about 15 tons of Oil which we were anxious to fill – we ought however to be satisfied & thankful.

About Mid-Night foggy – light winds – Employed cleaning the Ship &c.

Saturday 9ᵗʰ of July Lat. 79°33+ Lon. 7°50′ E
E.rly Var. Calm SSW
In the morning we had most delightful weather, thermometer 43°. During a Strong breeze of wind that for a while prevailed we steered about 20 miles on a SW.erly course – at noon we had calm – a great extent of land in sight; the Head Land bearing E or EbN, King's Bay SEbS, & the Foreland SbW, the nearest land (7 Icebergs)[1] being 7 or 8 Leagues distant. Bent a spare Fore Top Sail on the main-top-sail yard during the interval in which the Main Top Sail was sent down to repair – the canvass was found worn through in several places, & the top linings [are?] very bad. Assisted Mʳ Johnstone to eat a bit of Roast Beef. In the Evening we had a brisk Gale, again from

[1] Glaciers on the west coast of Spitsbergen. See journal entry for 3 June 1812, vol. I, p. 98.

the Southward accompanied by thick fog showers. Tacked at mid night near the edge of the Ice. <u>No</u> <u>Ships</u> <u>or</u> <u>fish.</u>

Sunday 10th of July Lat. 79°27' Lon. 6°30'
SW.erly Calm
A fresh Gale with fog showers continued most of the day, under which we endeavoured to beat to windward without effect. In the Evening having passed to the S^d of several patches of Ice & floes the wind failed us. Saw two <u>White Whales (Balaena Macrocephalus Albicans)</u>[1] pursued with a Boat but could not approach sufficiently to Harpoon one of them. They very much resemble the Narwhale in the form of the body; the only apparent difference consisting in the greater length of head with larger[2] fins & tail possessed by the <u>White Whale</u> together with the uniform <u>ivory or cream</u> coloured skin. They are about equal in size & correspond in habits. The <u>Albicans</u> has no <u>horn.</u>

Monday 11th July Lat.79°10' Lon. 6°0'E
Calm NEerly Var.
Calm & cloudy the most of the night, when a Breeze of wind springing up we lay too some hours for the Aimwell – after joining C^o steered a SW.erly course – Passed thro' some considerable patchs [sic] of heavy Ice & to the W^d of some floes. No whales. Calm in the Evening with thick fog.

Tuesday 12th of July[.] at noon, Lat. 78°58' Lon. 7°50'E.
SSW
Under all sail plying to windw^d with a brisk breeze of wind amidst patches & streams of heavy Ice & considerable Floes disseminated throughout the navigable space between the land & the Main Ice. This same space 10 days ago was almost clear of Ice from whence it appears that the late Storm has ['driven' *deleted*] dispersed the westward Ice throughout the <u>Country</u>. At 3 Pm. we tacked under the lee of the NW point of Charles' Island or Foreland bearing SW scarcely a Mile distant where we sounded in 12 Fathoms foul ground consisting of exceeding sharp rocks which cut the [load?][3] like a rasp – small pieces of the rock adhering to it had a <u>corroline</u>[4] appearance, were red on the surface & white within – Tried for to Fish but without success the hooks bringing up a reddish Sea weed covered with minute rough crustaceons [sic]. The tide was running briskly to the NE^d. I readily distinguished on the shore a hut which I visited in ..... 18...[5] We here saw several sea-horses, <u>blowing like</u>

[1] In *Account of the Arctic Regions*, I, pp. 500–501, Scoresby used different Latin names, but again mentioned their similarity to the narwhale and commented that 'I have several times seen them on the coast of Spitzbergen; but never in numbers of more than three or four at a time'.
[2] Possibly 'longer'.
[3] 'Lead' presumably intended.
[4] *Sic*. See *OED* s.v. 'corraline'.
[5] In *Account of the Arctic Regions*, I, p. 118, Scoresby stated that 'My first landing in an arctic country, was on Charles' Island or Fair Foreland, at the north-west point'. See also p. 124, note 1.

narwhales, around the Ship. After laying too an hour the Aimwell joined us & we made sail westward. In our progress we fell in with several patches of Ice & floes – At 8 Pm. on the commencement of fog showers tacked near a compact stream of Ice, expended the day plying to windward.

Wednesday 13th of July Lat. 78°50′+ Lon. 7°10′E
S.erly Var. Calm SW.erly
Light winds or calms during this day. The fog cleared at 10 am. & we enjoyed an unclouded Sky for 6 or 7 hours & then a most opaque fog prevailed. On a Survey of the Ice from the mast head assisted by the indications of the blinks or atmospheric charts, we were concerned to discover that numerous compact patches with many floes were likely to impede if not arrest our navigation southward. On steering to the Wd until the land was 20 miles distant the most open space was seen lying NW.ward whilst all around from W to S. & SE seemed accumulated bodies of Ice[.]¹ to the SEd

& close by the land appeared the most eligable route. The weather being calm & clear we towed in the latter direction until the darkness of the Fog rendered it prudent to desist. The Aimwell not far distant. At noon N. end Foreland EbS 20 miles. Towards mid-night we had a light breeze SW.erly by which with the precaution of a Boat ahead ['**Thursday 14th of July** Lat. 78°40′ Lon. 8°50′E[.] S.erly Variable Calm N.erly' *in margin*] to assist the evolutions we steered amidst variety of Ice on a South to SE course until 4 am – at that time judging ourselves sufficiently near the land, (though we had no soundings in 50 Fathoms) we tacked & finding the Ice as indicated by the blink, more open we plyed directly to windward. About 6 the Fog somewhat clear & continued in showers until noon when it again recommenced with its utmost gloom. At noon the Middle Hook of the Foreland lay SE from us distant only 2 Leagues. the Aimwell being far astern we proceeded all the day under easy sail, nevertheless she did not come up. At 6 Pm. we had a calm, sent a Boat in chase of two White Whales. Discovered several

Figure 5. Scoresby's sketch of the gastropod *Clio helicina*
Scoresby's sketch of the gastropod that he identified in *An Account of the Arctic Regions* (I, p. 543) as *Clio helicina* (Transcript SCO1253, 14 July 1814). Photograph courtesy of the Whitby Museum.

¹ Suggestion of this sentence break is indicated only by the sense of the text, not by the format of the transcript.

little animals in the water, covered with a Shell somewhat like the <u>paper nautilis</u>, like it beautifully striated & of inconceivable delicacy.[1] These animals moved with considerable velocity by means of two pliable fins. They had much the appearance in the water of a large Fly with a body in size & resemblance like that of a large <u>Spider</u>. They were of a blackish brown colour. At mid-night a light Breeze from the Northward. Steered SSW.

Friday 15th of July Lat. 78°20′ Lon. 9°5′E
N.erly Very Var. Incl. Calm W.erly – SE.rly &c.
The winds this day were very light & exceedingly variable, yet they were generally fair. Continued our course SSW notwithstanding the prevalence of a thick fog – we fortunately met with very little opposition from Floes or patches of Ice, though we repeatedly heard the splashing of the water against considerable masses to the West of us. At 3 Pm. however we found ourselves involved amidst considerable masses of large drift Ice & Floes, very opportunely at the very time the fog <u>thinned</u> around us, & we discovered a passage through the midst of the obstructing masses. From this period the fog was gradually attenuated & at 5 Pm. we enjoyed a most delightful clear sky & actually <u>hot</u> sun – the thermometer in the shade rose to 48°! the tar dropped from the rigging upon deck & the Ice instead of its usual chilling appearance afforded a refreshing <u>coolness</u>! The Land was clear & formed a beautiful object, the nearest part might be 15 miles distant. The Sound of the Bugle was echoed & re-echoed at about 2 Seconds interval, the effect was curious.

As the Fog finally [left?] the horizon we had a good view of the Ice – observed many Floes & compact patches to the W^d a considerable body to the SE^d of us though in general a perfect space void of Ice extended parallel with the land to 8 or 10 miles distant from it. To the S^d & SW likewise were several Floes & scattered Ice. We likewise discovered Several Ships as we proceeded. The Aimwell was seen far astern joined by a Stranger, several ships [arose?] in the W.ern & SW.ern horizon until at length we counted 20 Sail. Some of them were made fast to Floes, several laid too, but we could not observe any Boats. After steering a variety of courses, we gained space almost clear of Ice about mid-night at the same time met a slight undulation of the Sea a sure indication of near approach to the Sea.

Saturday 16th of July Lat. 77°50 Lon. 9°E
SEerly. Variable W.erly
Whilst we had a Breeze from the SE^d it was attended by a curious refraction density[.][2] The land, though apparently clear assumed the most fantastic forms,

---

[1] Presumably the gastropod *Clio helicina*, mentioned by Phipps in his *Voyage* (p. 195) as 'Found in innumerable quantities throughout the Arctick seas'. In *Account of the Arctic Regions*, it appears as Figs. 11 and 12 of Plate XVI in volume II. In volume I, p. 543, Scoresby described it as 'Sea-snail. – An animal covered with a delicately beautiful shell, similar in form to that of the nautilus. The diameter is from two-eighths to three-eighths of an inch. It is found in immense quantities near the coast of Spitzbergen, but does not, I believe, occur out of sight of land.' See also journal entry for 16 July.
[2] Scoresby described this optical phenomenon in rather greater detail in *Account of the Arctic Regions*, I, pp. 385–6.

[aspiring?] in the form of lofty pinnacles or monuments, sometimes like Castle with spires, towers, & battlements – in a moment the figure would be changed into a noble arch or bridge, thus undergoing various metamorphoses in the space of a few minutes. The varied ['Curious effects of a SE wind & refraction' *in margin*] appearances were highly curious & amusing. A mass of Ice on the horizon appeared of the height of a cliff, & seemed to be fronted by a kind of Basaltic column, or regular columns of Ice – every object from NE to SE was more or less affected by this peculiar vapour. It may be remarked that it was preceded by a remarkable <u>hot</u> afternoon & evening with a clear sky. Nothing can be more pure than the transparency occasionally presented by the atmosphere in Greenland: cloudy weather though by far the most common is yet sometimes relieved by a brightness foreign to every other part, especially when aided by reflections from Ice or Land, the transparency is so complete that in such circumstances, with a sufficient telescope a ship's vane might be distinguished on the horizon.

The Small Animals described on Thursday were exceedingly abundant in ['<u>Sea Snails</u> surprisingly numerous' *in margin*] the water the whole of the following & part of this day. They were so numerous indeed that actually for the space of 30 or 40 miles sailing we did not observe scarcely in any place a square yard free from one or more of them to the amount of a Dozen or upwards. (They might be termed <u>Sea-Snails</u>.)

During this day we made but small progress owing to the lightness of the winds. Our course was to the SSW. At 4 am. the Middle Hook of the Foreland bore NNE¼ E & the South point E¼ N. Passed some scattered Ice & in the Evening when the Fog was thick entered a close patch of Ice, which by the aid of three Boats occasionally towing we passed in about an hour & ¼ & immediately received a great increase of swell, proving the Ice just passed to be a kind of Sea-Stream. 4 ships seen at midnight.

Sunday 17ᵗʰ of July Lat. 77°Lon. 9°16′E
NW.erly NNW North
At 5 am. we approached a stream of Ice on a SW.erly course, the wind being light & a ship near us sent a boat to enquire the news – proved to be the Sᵗ Andrew[1] with 18 fish 160 Tons of Oil – informed us the John sailed a week ago with 35 Fish, that within the last fortnight several fish have been killed between Latitudes 77° & 78°N, that the Sisters captured 3, the Duncombe 4; &c. ['From when' *deleted*] but during the last week they have seen but two whales. From whence it appears that our late excursion has been an unfortunate cruize, having never seen a single whale since July 1ˢᵗ a period of 16 days, although during that time we have explored almost the whole navigable fishing country from 80½° of Lat. to our present situation say 77°¼.

The wind now gradually increased attended with fine cloudy weather. Steered a course from South to SWbS coasting along streams & patches of Ice from the Eastern extremity of one to that of another but without meeting any cetacea except <u>Razor</u>

---

[1] According to the 1813 and 1815 contemporary lists (the Scoresby Papers in Whitby do not include a list for 1814), the *Saint Andrew* (Captain Reed) was an Aberdeen whaler.

Backs – we however continued our course conceiving it improbable finding any whales, at the same time the wind rendering a northern course impracticable, a homeward track only remained for us, whereon we might follow the trending of the Ice, so far as any possibility of fishing remains. Velocity of Ship 2 to 7 Knotts.

Monday 18ᵗʰ of July Lat 75°5′+ Lon. 10°16′E
NNE Var.
About noon the wind failed us & a calm with fine cloudy weather prevailed the most of the following part of the day. Had to haul out SEbS at 5 am for a point of Ice from thence steered SWbS. Joined Cᵒ with the Old Manchester (Adair) & Brittannia [sic], (Jacques)[1] who both desired to place themselves under our Convoy. Our people employed in trimming rigging, sails, &c.

Tuesday 19ᵗʰ of July Lat. 74°49′ Lon 10°35′E
SW.erly Variable
With a light SW.erly wind & fine cloudy weather we reached to the [WSWᵈ?] at 5 made the Ice consisting of an open patch tacked, stood off till noon, & again tacked. Messʳˢ Adair & Jacques tead[2] on board the Esk &c – the former has 135 the latter 170 Tons of Oil. They report that a fortnight ago they proceeded in a S.erly direction from the 78ᵗʰ or 79ᵗʰ ° of N. Lat. meaning to take the Ice along & go homewards that they fell in with many very large whales in 77°N. and many ships made capture – the Manchester got two & the Brittannia one – that they had seen fish almost constantly between the Ice & the land & so late as the 17ᵗʰ Instant. 4 Strange Sail were seen in the Morning. Foggy at night. No Ice.

Wednesday 20ᵗʰ of July Lat. 74°32′ Lon. 8°55′E
W.erly, NNE. NW.erly
The wind veering westerly at 5 am tacked made a course p compass about SSW. At noon it shifted to the Nᵈ & blew a brisk breeze. At the request of the masters of the two accompanying ships we handed them underlined instructions for the better keeping Company, it being their wish to sail under our convoy.

Made sail SWbW setting Royals & steering sails. At 6 pm. were obliged to bear away SSW for a point of Ice, passed a second at 10 Pm – afterwards the weather was very thick for 3 hours. A strange sail in sight steering to the SWᵈ. Velocity of ship 2 to 8 Knotts p hour.

Thursday 21st of July Lat. 72°34′+ Lon. 8°E
WNW West
Shortened sail for the Brittannia which was considerably astern & after she came up set a smart sail & steered by the wind. Made a progress of nearly 5 Knotts per hour throughout the day on a course from SW to SbW. The weather was cloudy but fine –

---

[1] The 1815 list shows the captain of the London whaler *Britannia* as 'Jacks'.
[2] *OED*'s earliest citation of 'tea' as an intransitive verb ('To drink tea; *esp.* to take the meal called tea, to have one's tea') is dated 1823.

the Sea was quite smooth until the Evening from which we judged we had emerged from beneath the lee of the Ice, proved also by the the [sic] occasional appearance of an Ice blink to the W^d. A Strange Sail seen. The people employed in sundry useful & ornamental work. The Convoy near.

Manifest
of the Cargo of the Ship Esk, British built, Burthen 354 73/94 Tons, William Scoresby Jnr Master from Greenland, of & for Whitby – To Wit,

2 Casks of 500 Gall^s	340 Casks, Containing 564	
2 — of 400	[compacted?] Butts of Blubber and	
37 — of 300	two Butts of Crang of half a	
122 — of 252	Ton each. Eight Tons of Whale	Thomas Brodrick Esqr
48 — of 200	finns and 29 Seal Skins.	
55 — of 180	The Produce of	
19 — of 160	23 Whales, and 29 Seals	
43 — of 126		
12 — of 84		William Scoresby Junr

Greenland Seas 21st day of July 1814.

Friday 22^d of July Lat. 70°57′ Lon. 8°56′E
W.erly Var. N.erly
Made but small progress this day owing to light variable winds though chiefly pretty fair – the fore part of the day steered by the wind at night a course about SWbW. Saw a number of finned whales with high pointed dorsal fins, sent a Boat in pursuit, but without success. A strange sail in sight & the Convoy in C°. Dismantled the Boats (except One) coyled the lines in two masses on the Quarter deck after washing them, stowed five Boats in the twin decks, removed two davits & performed variety of other work employing all hands for eight hours.

Saturday 23^d of July Lat. 69°46′ Lon. 7°30′E
SE
Fresher moderate winds with showers of Rain in the Evening. Steered a course SW½W with a velocity of 3 to 6½ Knotts p hour. The Convoy being far astern short-ened sail in the Morning & in the Evening lay too for the Brittannia. Weather mild – thermometer all day 46° to 52°. The Sun set at night for the first time since the 25th of April constituting a day ['⊙ Set 1st Time in 3 Mo^s' *in margin*] of upwards of 2000 hours or nearly three months. Saw some Sea Weed & Mollusca.

Sunday 24th of July Lat. 68°45′ Lon. 5°30′E
SSE S.WbS WNW Var.
The State of the Mercury in the Barometer indicated a heavy Storm, the weather was however moderate & showers of rain occurred, but in the Evening a tremendous swell arose from the SW whilst the scud had a rapid motion in the contrary direction & the wind with us intermediate with intervals of Calm: hence it was evident that a storm must have occurred during the day, not far south whilst a contending NE.erly

wind prevented its influence in the very spot in which we were placed. At 8 Pm. a strange ['Signs of Land suppose the Laffoden Islands¹ 110 miles off' *in margin*] sail in sight to the Eᵈ suppose an outward bound archangelman. At night wind for a short time blew briskly from the WNW but the force of the swell almost rivetted the ship to the spot. The Convoy near.

Monday 25ᵗʰ of July at noon Lat 67°59'+ Lon. 6°43'E
WbS SWbW
Had moderate or light winds all the day, rain the morning & a high SW.erly swell. Made a SE.erly course. At 8 pm. a strange sail was seen SW of us steering directly towards us, supposing her to be bound for Archangel & probably late from England we lay too awaiting her approach. At mid-night sent a Boat on board. She proved to be the Brig Ann of Liverpool only 3 days from Shetland & 9 from Antwerp in Ballast for Archangel. Was by account in Longitude [*blank space*]° [*blank space*]' East differing considerably from our reckoning, but from the many symptoms of approximation to Land I am inclined to believe the true place of the ship to be eastward of the Ann's reckoning & probably near a mean between the two. The Ann had experienced strong Gales of wind from the course of the Swell as we anticipated; yesterday passed three & the preceeding [*sic*] day two Greenland ships under close reefed top Sails. He afforded no political news of importance having been foreign he had no newspapers, he however confirmed the Glorious tidings of an European Peace. Having previous to this made the ['Therm*ometer* 52° to 54° Supped by candlelights!' *in margin*] signal for the convoy to close each ship sent a Boat on board the Stranger. At mid-night made sail with the Convoy in Company.

Tuesday 26ᵗʰ of July Lat. 67°12' Lon 5°30'E
S.erly SSW
Light to fresh Gales of wind, weather cloudy with Rain or Fog. Steering all the day by the wind Larboard tacked on a course from WSW to WbN & with a velocity of 1 to 5 Knotts. The Convoy in Cᵒ.

Wednesday 27ᵗʰ of July Lat. 66°34' Lon. [4?]°50'E
SW; W
The wind veering to W at 9 am. tacked & proceeded on a Course S to SSW, the Sea being considerable the ship made 1¼ lee-way. The wind blew a brisk Gale accompanied with Rain or Fog; we however set a smart sail carrying all the day single reefed Top Sails, top Gall*ant* Sails. &c. The people employed in a variety of useful & ornamental work. The Cooper preparing spare stores of Pails or Buckets &c. the Carpenter fitting my Cutter, the Sail-Maker, fitting head-cloths,² &c. &c. The Convoy in Cᵒ.

---

¹ The Lofoten Islands, off the Norwegian coast between 68° and 69°N.
² By 'Cutter', Scoresby presumably refers to his 'ship's boat used for carrying light stores or passengers' (*OED*). The *Century Dictionary and Cyclopedia*, ed. William Dwight Whitney and Benjamin E. Smith, New York, 1889–1910, s.v. head-cloth, gives 'A canvas screen for the head of a ship' as the first meaning but provides no citation.

Thursday 28ᵗʰ of July Lat 65°48′ Lon. 2°31′E

W. Calm S.erly

Light winds or Calms – thick fog sometimes, at others heavy Rain. Under all sails contending to the Southward. During a long Calm which continued all the afternoon & evening, the Sky cleared repeatedly to the northward & whilst a considerable S.erly sea prevailed a northerly swell likewise commenced, each could readily be observed at the same moment – the wind was evidently from the north at a Short distance from us, the S.erly wind however unfortunately prevailed. Saw several very large Mollusca, with [mossy?] like tips & long horizontal fibres or spines issuing from two opposite sides. The nucleus of some seemed nearly two feet in diameter. A Boy whom we took from Lerwick in the Spring for amusing the Sailors with the music of a violin, which he wielded with tollerable execution, becoming anxious least we ['Thermometer 55° to 58° *in margin*] should carry him past his <u>Dear Isle</u>, solicited to be put on board one of our Convoy that was obliged to call at Lerwick for the mustering of her Crew – according to his wish he was conveyed on board the Brittannia.

Friday 29ᵗʰ of July Lat. 64°52′ Lon. 1°20′E

S. to SE S & SSW

Fresh Gales with heavy Rain & thick fog occasionally throughout the day. Steered close hauled to the Wᵈ & Sᵈ until 8 Pm. then tacked. Fired a Gun, the fog signal for tacking, the convoy not being within Sight.

Saturday 30ᵗʰ of July Lat. 64°18′ Lon. 0°13′E

SSE, Calm, [SW?], SSE &c.

Fresh variable winds all day except an hour's Calm about meridian – with almost constant thick fog & heavy falls of Rain. The fog was so exceedingly thick in the Evening, that no object could be discerned at more than 200 feet distance, consequently the prospect was circumscribed within the space of four acres of surface![1] At 2 am. we tacked to the westward & held on a course from SSW to SWbW throughout the day. In the only clear interval which occurred we saw one of the convoy a mile astern, the other 6 or 7 miles to the Eᵈ of us. The weather so wet that no work could possibly be carried on upon deck. Hauled a curious aggregation of Shell fish on board attached to a piece of Seaweed, by means of a fishing line. It consisted of 12 or 14 of the Lepas (<u>Lepas anatifera</u> or Barnacle probably)[2] attached by a bluish Stalk to a white pearl like substance, in the centre of which lay embedded a brownish substance not unlike a nutmeg, but smaller covered with distinct deep [brown?] spots. The tentacula which each animal protruded were jointed, nearly all of a length, & amounting to about 20 in each. The Shells were marked with double reddish brown [stria?] in the form of a V on each side, in other respects smooth.

---

[1] In fact, less than 3 acres: $200 \times 200 \times 3.1416 = 125,664$ square feet $\div 43,560 = 2.88$ acres.

[2] Common name: Goose barnacle.

Sunday 31st of July Lat. 62°50′ Lon. 0°10W
Calm NW

Calm during three or four hours in the morning with thick fog & Rain. Barometer fell to 29.32 indicative of stormy or rainy weather a heavy short S.erly sea at the same time prevailed which was inclined to invade the Cabin windows. At 4 am. a NW.erly Breeze sprung up & soon increased to a Strong Gale accompanied by a heavy swell that speedily quelled the S.ern Sea. At 8 am. furled Top Gallant Sails the Ship flying with a velocity of more than 10 Knotts p hour. The Sea becoming heavy hoisted the lee-quarter Boat in – send royal yards on deck & struck Royal masts. In the Evening the wind abated, made all sail. Saw several Solan Geese, [Arctic?] Gulls, Teistas, ['&' deleted] Sea weed & Mollusca. The Manchester in Cº. The Brittannia parted Cº.

Monday 1st of August noon Lat. 61°26 Lon. 0°13′E
W.erly SEbE to S &c.

Soon after mid night the wind veered to the SEᵈ the weather was fine & cloudy – made all sail on a SSW course. At 8 am. aroused all hands, suspended the whale-lines for drying, & various other work.

At 11½ am. Latitude by double altitude of the Sun 61°27′N – at noon sun obscure. In the afternoon the wind blew very strong & the Sky was overcast & a heavy rain commenced – took the whale lines down & placed them in shelter. Removed the cables to the [Tier?] by the foremast & put the Ice-ropes in the Cable stage. Expecting ourselves near land, yet nothing able to see above a couple of miles, soundings alone could be our guide – at[1] 3 Pm therefore made the attempt & struck ground in about 80 Fathoms coarse sand, shells, & Brown specks – at 5[2] again struck soundings in 80 Fathoms shells, rocks & sand stone & at 7[3] am in 70 Fathoms hard rocks of Coral & at 9[4] in 60 Fath. fine White Sand. From these soundings I judged we[5] were to the Eᵈ of Shetland but not far distant from Land, the more E.erly soundings being constantly sand with shells, Hake's teeth, &c.[6] The Sea however was amazingly smooth which must have been owing to the continuance of a NW.erly swell & the heavy Rain. Immediately after the last Soundings were struck, the Rain abated & Land was seen bearing NW from us probably 20 miles distant: from the situation & appearance it must have been the Isle of Unst or Fetlar, likely the former. Communicated the tidings to the Manchester, which was doubtless joyfully received by the numerous host of

---

[1] '1' as a superscript cross-reference to a marginal note: 'Lat.61° 11 Lon. 18′E'. Similarly with the next three cross-references.

[2] '2' to marginal note: '... 61.0 ... 22.'.

[3] '3' to marginal note: '... 60.50 ... 21E'.

[4] '4' to marginal note: '... 60.44 ... 20E'.

[5] 'were' but with 're' deleted.

[6] Smyth, *Sailor's Word Book* : 'HAKE'S TEETH': 'A phrase applied to some part of the deep soundings in the British Channel; but it is a distinct shell-fish, being the *Dentalium*, the presence of which is a valuable guide to the Channel pilot in foggy weather.' James Cook, returning from Newfoundland in the *Grenville*, recorded on 3 December 1764, when he was south of the Cornish coast, that he 'Sounded 41 fathoms. Recovered stones as big as beans with broken shells and hake's teeth.' The absence of further comment in this journal entry suggests that Scoresby was accustomed to finding them in soundings near Shetland.

Shetlanders which throughout the day we had noticed clinging to the rigging on every mast anxiously looking out for the <u>dear, dear Isle</u>! ['Barom. 29.74 Therm. 56°, 58°' *in margin*]

The approaching darkness prevented us ascertaining our real situation, fearing to involve amongst the rocks or skerries at 10 pm. tacked. Caught several mackrell.

Tuesday 2ᵈ of August Lat. 60°19½ + Lon. 54′E
SSW to WbS. S. &c.
Fresh or light winds – cloudy or fine clear w*eathe*r at 5 am. Saw land bearing WbN 20 or 30 miles off supposed to be Whalsey (Shetland). Suspended 4 Boats lines, from spars in the Rigging, to dry – the people employed in sundry other useful work. The Manchester tacked & parted Cᵒ. – two strange sail in sight – At noon observed Lat. 60°19′½ . Long. a/c 54′.E. In the afternoon the air became damp – coyled 3 Boats lines away. at 3 Pm. tacked & steered 7 hours to the WSWʳᵈ & the rest of the day to the SEᵈ. Barometer 29.82 Therm*omete*r 56° to 60° Clouds \ am & _ ¹(Rainy) pm.

Wednesday 3ᵈ of August Lat. 59°55′+ Lon. 56′E
SW.ᵈ [*sic*] W.erly
Moderate winds all the day, cloudy with some Rain in the morning delightful weather afterwards until night, when we again had rain. The Brig Maida of London passed us within hail – did not give any news. Made a progress of 2 to 4 Knotts p hour on a SbE to SSW course. Passed a vast quantity of Mollusca & much Seaweed. Caught Several Mackrell & a Dog fish – water light green coloured. ['Bar. 29.74 Ther. 57° to 60°' *in margin*] Stretched the Quarter & waist cloths around the ship & painted one side of the paint work with the original colours, viz light Red, White & Black.

['Saw stars!!' *in margin*] Surgeon's report – "All hands in perfect health"! God be praised.

Thursday 4ᵗʰ of August Lat. 58°53′ Lon 1°42′E
W².erly SW
The weather being clear & hot, suspended the remainder of the Whalelines to dry, conisting of 24 lines. Stayed the top-masts & superior spars. Performed various other operations. Passed some fishing Boats apparently Flemish. In the afternoon coyled the whale-lines in compact parcels & stowed them in the Gun-room. At 6 Pm the wind veering to SW & ['Bar. 29.98 Therm. 58° to 64°. Clouds \ \n ∩ & _'³ *in margin*] finding ourselves considerably to the Eastward of a direct course, tacked & ['**Friday 5ᵗʰ August**[,] Lat. 58°31′+ Lon. 1°1′E[,] SW to S & SW' *in margin*] steered to the WNWᵈ until mid night. Proceeded starboard tacked 4 hours & then put about again. Wind increased to a Brisk Gale accompanied with much rain. A number of Fishing Vessels in Sight.

---

¹ Luke Howard's notation for cirrus and cirrostratus clouds. See vol. I, pp. lix–lx.
² Possibly 'N'.
³ Cirrus, cirrocumulus, cumulus and cirrostratus in the Howard notation.

The Sky cleared at Mid-day & the weather became fine, though the Sea was considerable & wind continued unabated. Made little better than a due west course, occasionally made nothing. At mid-night tacked.

Saturday 6ᵗʰ of August Lat 57°58′+ Lon. 0°22′W
W. to SW & WSW
We had light winds a few hours in the morning & then a fresh Gale from the SW hastened our progress with an accelerated velocity of 1 to 9 Knotts p hour, notwithstanding a considerable, nay a very heavy head Sea prevailed & caused the ship to plunge with vast vehemence into the opposing waves. We carried more sail than would be considered prudent at other time, but in consideration of reaching our port during the present Spring tide & thereby avoiding the expence & anxiety of waiting a week or more in an open roadstead for the influence of the change of the moon¹ affording a depth of water sufficient to admit the ship, from this consideration I say we had inducement to strain every nerve towards forwarding the course of the ship towards the attainment of the wished end. ['Bar. 29.55 Ther, 60° to 59° Clouds \, ∩ &c.' *in margin*] Sunday's Evening tide will doubtless afford sufficient depth of water & possibly Monday may not be too late. Blow propitious Breezes blow. Steered most of the day SWbW. Employed fitting top-nettings, &c &c.

In the exact situation as intimated by our reckoning, we at 8 pm. saw Land, supposed to be the hills in the vicinity of Girdleness, bearing WbN about 9 Lea*gue*s off. At night we had smooth water, & moderate wind. At 10 pm. Observed Latitude by an altitude of the Polar Star 56°40′N.

Sunday 7ᵗʰ August Lat 55°55′ Lon. 1°4′W
WSW to W & SSW or WSW
Made a course SW or SSW by the wind with diminished velocity until 6 am. the wind then veered to SW. At the same time saw land & soon discovered the Cheviot Hills bearing SW & Sᵗ Abb's Head WbS 25 miles Dis*tant*. In the Morning we had rain & squally w*eathe*r reefed top-sails & tacked at noon. At 2 pm. treble reefed top-sails, & stowed Main Sail & mizen Top Sails[.] ['Bar. 29.79 Therm 56° to 58°' *in margin*] The Jib split at 1 Pm. unbent it & replaced it by a Fore T. Stay Sail. In the Evening weather clear & more moderate. <u>Several Coasters</u>.

Dined off a Leg of mutton, the <u>last</u> of our <u>fresh Stock</u>, which though killed the 18ᵗʰ of March, has been preserved since without using any other means than an occasional dipping in the Sea. Nevertheless, that it was exposed in ['Fresh Mutton preserved 4ᵐ 20ᵈ & eat <u>delicious</u>' *in margin*] the open air to the Septical influences of uncommon rains & Fogs & the last 16 days to a temperature never below 50 but occasionally as high as 70 in the Sun's rays from which it was not shielded in the least; yet, the taste

---

¹ The term 'change of the moon' normally was used to describe a new moon, but was 'extended more or less widely to include also the attainment of "full moon", and even of intermediate phases'. (*OED*). In 1814 there was a full moon on 1 August. Scoresby needed a spring tide to enter the harbour safely; this normally occurs at Whitby for several days after new and full moons. As the journal relates, after off-loading part of the cargo on to a sloop, the *Esk* remained at sea until the day before the new moon.

was excellent, well gravied, sweet & of a delicious flavour. To an Heliogabalus[1] it would have been worth its weight of Pearls!!

Tacked 8 Pm. St Abb's Head bearing WbN distant 10 miles. Meeting a strong short head Sea made indifferent progress though the [ship lay?] up often as high as SbW. Set top-Gall*ant* Sails. At 10 Pm saw the Staples & [Fern?] Isl^d lights bearing SSW. At Mid-Night sounded in 26 Fath*om*s the lights at SWbW about 2 miles distant. Fine night.

Monday 8th of Aug*ust* Lat. 55°30′+ Lon. 1°22′W
SW WNW
We had Fresh or Strong Gales of wind throughout this day, with Showers of Rain. Reached Starboard tacked until 9 am. – then proceeded westward & on the wind veering to the WNW at 1 Pm tacked again & steered SSW. At ['Bar. 29.40 Them. 60° &c' *in margin*] 8Pm Tinmouth light bore WNW Distant 15 miles – made a progress of 6 to 7 Knotts p hour from this time till mid-night, though we shortened sail at 9 pm. At 11½ Pm. Saw the Yorkshire land & at Mid-Night Red Cliff bore SSW distant 3 or 4 miles. Soundings 28 to 26 Fath*om*s.

Tuesday 9th of August
WNW NW N.erly Calm
At 2 Am. ran into Sandsendness & lay too supported by the ebb tide. Fired Several guns & at 4¼ am. a Cobble with [4?] Pilots came off. Had the satisfaction of hearing of the welfare of all our friends particularly my nearest & dearest ties. Praised be God. The wind blowing strong with dark cloudy w*eathe*r we did not think prudent to anchor but reached off to Sea. It appears we are the third Ship much to our astonishment for we are pretty well assured that the Resolution & probably the W*illia*m & Ann left the Country before us – the Henrietta & Volunteer are the only ships arrived, the former with 18 fish 180 to 190 Tons the latter with [*blank space*] fish about 175 Tons. At 6 am. the Resolution made her appearance with a Cargo of 24 Fish 220 Tons of oil. That we reached our port before her was a circumstance affording pleasure to every person on board the Esk since, we thereby are entitled to the first turn of the Coppers,[2] whilst we expected the third. A lee-wardly tide & turbulent Sea drove us to the Sward of the Harbour as far as the North Cheek[3] of Robin Hood's Bay. On the ceasing of the flood tide we made all sail with more moderate wind & fine weather & plyed towards Sandsend ness on Short tacks near the Shore.

At 4 Pm. I landed at the Pier in my own cutter amidst a large concourse of people & soon had the happiness of ['seeing' *deleted*] observing personally the wellfare & health of my Dearest friends, particularly that of my beloved wife & lovely Boy. In the Evening the Ship brought up in Sandsend ness (7 fath*om*s water, Staiths land in

[1] Or Elagabalus, Roman emperor AD 218–222. Another way of saying that the meat was 'fit for a king'.

[2] To extract the oil from the blubber. The process was described by Scoresby in *Account of the Arctic Regions*, II, ch. VI.

[3] Shown on modern Ordnance Survey maps as 'Ness Point or North Cheek', grid reference NZ960062. Sandsend Ness is at grid reference NZ861137.

sight). Soon after the William & Ann made her appearance with 28 Fish 18 size about 190 Tons of oil. At night fine weather, Sea still considerable from the NE[d].

Unstowed the Boats & sent all but one on Shore.

Wednesday 10th of August
N.erly Calm. E.erly
Light variable winds with Calms & heavy E.erly swell all the day.

A vessel was prepared to come off to receive a lading from the Esk but from the heaviness of the swell to deliver was in feasible [*sic*].

['Whitby Roads' *in margin*] Several of the people betook themselves to Shore without leave – the transgressors were tracked & two days pay for every day's absence, agreeable ['Bar. 30.13 Therm 62° *in margin*] to the Act was proposed to be stopt off their wages & those deductions to be expended in spirits for the use of the more attentive.

Thursday 11th of August
W.erly. Var.
Light winds with fine Weather; the Easterly Swell having considerably fallen, the Oak Sloop came along side at 2 Pm. & received on board part lading of Casks ['Bar. 30.06 Therm. 60–62' *in margin*] & at 8 Pm. removed off a little & anchored near us. Many Coasters.

Friday 12th August
Werly, Var. &c.
At daylight weather still charmingly fine & wind still westerly, we renewed operations & at noon (tide time) had stowed 66 Casks of Blubber & three pairs of Jaw bone on board the Oak, furnished her with 12 or 14 Men & she proceeded to the Harbour, which she entered in Safety. The wind blew strong ['Bar. 30.06 Ther. 64° *in margin*] about noon but abated toward Evening. Many Coasters.

Saturday 13th August
SW
Boisterous weather with heavy rains at tide time, showery all the morning – as there was a chance of a sufficient tide to admit the Ship into the Harbour, she was got under weigh about noon, but finding the weather very unfavourable we brought up again near the same spot after an interval of an hour and a half. In the height of the wind I proceeded from the Harbour to the ship in my sailing Boat, a distance of about two miles in 15 minutes with an adverse tide! In the Evening more moderate.

Sunday 14th August
SE.erly
Fine weather, light variable winds. At noon the Ship was underweigh [*sic*], & had gained the entrance of the Harbour some time before the height of the tide – tacked about for an hour – the William & Ann then entered, we followed, & ['Esk moored in the Harbour' *in margin*] lastly the Resolution – all three ships got safely through

Bridge the same tide, where we moored in the Bridgeway birth. Soon afterwards the Crew was mustered by the proper Officer, when all hands but one were present & all in full health & vigour: thanks be to the beneficent Being who has thus favoured us – afforded us the needful protection, & done all things well – even to our satisfaction! The absentee ['Singular presumption of a Landsman' *in margin*] was a landsman – so anxious was he to visit the shore that he left the Ship in the Roads, the day after her arrival, but committing himself to the faithless waves – he swam lightly for near ¼ mile when his strength began rapidly to fail & had it not been for the prompt assistance of the Resolution's Boat he must have perished. He did not yet relinquish his determination of reaching the shore, but seized the first opportunity of leaving the Resolution & was not afterwards seen on board the ship[1] during her Continuance in the Roads.

[1] 'Esk' inserted above the line.

Journal of Charles Steward for 1814

Charles Steward

**Journal of a voyage, to the coasts of Spitsbergen, by Charles Steward
in capture of the Cetacea of the Northern seas: performed
during the year 1814, on the Ship Esk,
of Whitby, William Crosby[2] Jun[r] Commander –**

Kept by Charles Steward.

Nos patriae finis et dulcia linquimus arva.
Nos patriam fugimus; tu, Tityre, lentus in umbra
Formosam resonare doces Amaryllida silvas.[3]

Consedere duces, et vulgi stante corona
Surgit ad hos clipei dominus septemplicis Ajax
Utque erat impatiens arae, Sigeia torvo
Litora respexit classemque in litore vultu.[4]

In the month of February 1814 The Esk burthen 358 tons was taken by her owners
(Mess[rs] Fishburn & Brodrick) to make her second voyage to Spitsbergen, on the
Whale fishery.[5] She was but 1 year old; a very strong & handsomely built vessel, at

[1] This page is also headed 'Mar. March 4th 1810' as if the sheet had been previously intended for some earlier purpose.

[2] This is heavily written, apparently as a later 'correction', over the original text. It is not possible to determine whether that text was 'Scoresby'.

[3] This quotation is from the first of Virgil's *Eclogues*: '… we are leaving our country's bounds and sweet fields. We are outcasts from our country; you, Tityrus, at ease beneath the shade, teach the woods to re-echo "fair Amaryllis."': *Eclogues, Georgics, Aeneid I–VI*, trans. by H. Rushton Fairclough, rev. G. P. Goold, 3rd edn, Loeb Classical Library 63, Cambridge, Mass., and London, 1999, p. 25.

[4] This quotation is from Ovid's *Metamorphoses* 13. 'The chiefs took their seats, while the commons stood in a ring around them. Then up rose Ajax, lord of the sevenfold shield. With uncontrolled indignation he let his lowering gaze rest awhile on the Sigean shores and on the fleet …': *Metamorphoses*, trans. Frank Justus Miller, rev. G. P. Goold, 2nd edn, Loeb Classical Library 43, Cambridge Mass., and London, 1994, p. 229.

[5] Steward did not observe all of these activities because he did not arrive in Whitby until 2 March. (See Scoresby's journal entry for that date. Hereafter cited in these notes to Steward's journal as 'Scoresby 2 March' etc.) Every page of Steward's journal contains several brief marginal notes about the topics discussed. Unlike the similar entries in Scoresby's journals (which are far less numerous) they are not reproduced here.

present she had but her lower masts standing; having been laid[1] up since her voyage to Greenland last year. She was therefore removed from their dock directly opposite on the South side of the river (there being deeper water) and there to refit. This operation consisted of entirely rigging her; as she was rather tender[2] at sea, 12 tons of iron ballast were stowed away on each side the kelson: 3 tiers of blubber casks, each containing about 350 gallons, were stowed from the iron to the lower deck beams: the lower and some of the 2nd tier were filled with water. More casks were taken for filling blubber, but were in pieces[3] and were stowed in the gun room, or some other convenient place, in order that betwixt decks might be clear for boats and other fishing gear. The stores chiefly consisted in 7 whale boats; ice anchors; a floating anchor; 70 harpoons; a gun harpoon; 50 lances; and all sorts of flinching materials; 120 whale lines; and as many fore-gangers. She was armed with 10 guns, 8, 18lbs carronades, and 2 long 9lbs. Our provisions consisted of 6[4] months support for 50 seamen, including 5 tons of biscuit; 8 tons beef & pork. The crew consisted of the commander, surgeon; 6 harpooneers; 1 speckesioneer; 1 Skeeman;[5] 6 coxswains, or rather <u>boatsteerers</u>, (in the Greenland phrase) 6 line managers; Armourer; Boatswain; Gunner; carpenter; Blacksmith; cooper; Cook and their respective mates; the steward and seamen, making in a comp of 54.[6] Four[7] of the fishing boats were lashed between decks; all the harpoons, lances and flinching knives were kept in a chest between decks, the whale lines in the gun-room.

By Sunday the 20th of March, all was in readiness for sea; in the afternoon all hands attended tide. This was the first opportunity of getting out these spring tides. After moving about two ships lengths, the tide failed us – Efforts were renewed every high water but in vain untill,

Wednesday the 23rd March, when by the aid of[8] the evening's tide we unmoored ship, warped through bridge and got out to sea; crowds of spectators were assembled on the piers; and we were greeted with the usual honours. When out we tack'd twice to shew our owners how the ship looked at sea; the remaining pilot boat then left us, and we stood out on our intended course (NNE) for the Shetland islands. The wind was moderate with cloudy weather. The thermometer stood at 45°. At night fresh breezes of wind: the ship going about 6 or 7 knots.

---

[1] Originally 'layed' and subsequently corrected.

[2] Layton, *Dictionary*: 'Said of a vessel having a small righting moment; so being easily moved from her position of equilibrium, and slow in returning to it.'

[3] Later deleted in pencil, and 'shakes' substituted in pencil above the line.

[4] Originally '60', 'o' deleted later, in pencil.

[5] The only citation of this term in *OED* is to Scoresby's *Account of the Arctic Regions*, II, p. 306, where it is defined in a footnote as 'The officer who has the direction of operations conducted in the hold.' As Scoresby's crew list for 1814 (Scoresby 31 March) indicates, the task was, like that of the speckesioneer, additional to other duties, not a separate position as Steward implies.

[6] 'comp' is presumably an abbreviation for 'complement'. Scoresby's crew list clearly indicates a total of 52, including both Scoresby and Steward.

[7] Replacing 'Two' deleted.

[8] Originally 'aids of of'; 's of' deleted.

April [*sic*] 24th. Light winds and cloudy weather; in the morning I saw the Cheviot Hills from the mast head very distinctly, but I should not have supposed them to have been land at all, they resembled a white cloud rising from the horizon – during day several coasters were in sight, bound for their various ports; we for a far more distant land. Three gulls seen.

April [*sic*] 25th. Sudden squalls of wind and variable most of the day, but towards night a steady wind from south west. Gulls seen. [Rain?]. Thermometer at noon at 42°.

April [*sic*] 26th. In the morning fresh winds and cloudy weather. two sail in sight, to all appearances Whalers, bound on the same course as ourselves. At 3 PM. Fair isle ahead and Sumborough head on the larboard bow. At noon thermometer at 40°. In the afternoon it came on to blow very hard from S.W. ward. Obliged to take in all the small sails and close reef the topsails. at 6 abreast of the most dreary looking island (Foul). The weather was also very dark & thick; it was not thought prudent to attempt the navigation of the islands, and indeed ['all' *deleted in pencil*] commanders never attempt it at night: we therefore layed too, about half way between Foul isle and Shetland. At midnight, to our infinite surprise, we found ourselves set, evidently by some unknown current, into a bay formed of rocks; to the SW of Sumborough head. The ship was now in the most eminent danger of being lost; all hands were called; and fortunately she succeeded in [wearing?], although the sea was running very high; we then stood off to the westward, but in a few hours we were set again to the S.E ward exactly into the same place, where we had previous lyed-too; this must therefore be occationed [*sic*] by the tide; yet it is very extraordinary, as the tides on the East & south east sides of Shetland, are always accounted to be so very slack.

April [*sic*] 27th [Bore?] in for Brassa sound with fresh breezes & clear weather: we came to our anchor at 12. before our arrival there we were informed that close in with the land a tide runs NW & SE. at the rate of seven or eight knots per hour; our misfortune therefore was easily accounted for. ['We' *deleted*] cap S and I repaired almost immediately onboard the Aimwell where we were most liberally entertained by the hospitable commander: in company with D[r] Edmonstone.[1] M[r] Ross. and M[r] Sinclair gentlemen of this place. Cap*tain* Scoresby brought a newspaper containing the information of Bordeaux being captured by our generalissimo in Spain. They seemed highly gratified with it: indeed the doctor who is a very great politician was ['in extasy' *deleted*] enraptured. In the afternoon we all went onshore together: what a miserable dreary aspect it afforded! This did not much prepossess me in favour of its being quite such a pleasant place as I had heard. We travelled up a bay,[2] very much

---

[1] Presumably Laurence Edmonston, MD (1795–1879), described in the *Dictionary of National Biography* as a member of one of the oldest families in Shetland and 'for most of his long life, the only medical practitioner in the islands'.

[2] Possibly 'bog'.

encompassed with quarry stone, untill we reached the environs of the capital of the islands. On the turnpike there appeared no vestage [*sic*] of carriages of any description larger than the wheelbarrow, and of that kind there are very few, most of them being of the hand kind carried by two persons. We soon arrived in the haven of Lerwick, which presented to me a very serious but not a disagreeable appearance. The Fort was the first object which attracted my notice. This is a very well fortified place; in which are stationed a garisson [*sic*] of a few Highland soldiers under the command of Major Fortie. second in command Captain McDonald. It stands on the east side of the town, there are in it 16 guns, between which and the various compartments is a solid mass of [blue?] quarry stone forming a rock 20 feet high: The magazine and houses are therefore very well protected. From the fort we entered the town; the houses were built of the quarry stone plaistered over very clumsily[1] about two stories high. The windows very small; and the walls immensely thick. The streets are very narrow; paved with flag stone and from the quarry. in a very [dirty?] condition, although very dry clean weather. We parted with our friends and went to call on Mr Ogilvy, a particular friend of Captain Scoresby's, where we spent most of the night: I was much pleased with the unaffected hospitality with which he received us into his house; his family, his wife particularly was very well known to some ['of my' *deleted*] Norfolk people. Particularly to Sr Richard Beddingfield,[2] at a late hour we parted, and came onboard. I had now an opportunity of seeing the inside of a Shetland house. The rooms in general resembled much a partition in a castle; on account of the thickness of the walls; the smallness of the windows; the lowness of the rooms; the bareness of the walls; and the general appearance. All this day we had very fresh breezes from the southward.

March 28th. A continuance of hard gales from the southward. Captain S. had long wished for an opportunity of having his barge's sailing; he could now be gratafied [*sic*]: The boat was rigged with two [Sadée?][3] sails and manned. We [tried?] her: she sailed most delightfully. She was very stiff:[4] I do not know a more convenient & agreable piece of water for boat sailing than Brassa Sound. The land certainly rises high on each side; but not so much as in any way to cause an eddy of the wind by it. The barge's crew were composed of the best seamen in the ship: all dressed in their proper uniform viz: glazed hats[5] and blue jackets & trowsers: as we approached the shore; the people eyed us much. This evening was spent as the preceding one at Mr Ogilvy's with the greatest pleasure. During this day many Brown gulls and small birds were seen. Thermometer 44°.

[1] Originally 'clumbsily'; 'b' deleted.

[2] Presumably Sir Richard Bedingfield, a member of a prominent East Anglian Catholic family, mentioned in Rye's *Norfolk Families*, p. 37.

[3] See Scoresby 28 March. Steward's account cannot be read as Scoresby's 'Settee sails'; perhaps Steward was attempting to put in writing a term he had only heard from Scoresby.

[4] Smyth, *Sailor's Word Book*: 'Stable or steady; the opposite to *crank*; a quality by which a ship stands up to her canvas, and carries enough sail without heeling over too much.'

[5] *OED*: 'Having a smooth shining surface, produced either by a coating substance or by friction, etc.' *OED* cites 'glazed hats' in Dickens, *The Old Curiosity Shop* (1840), ch. iv.

March 29th. A continuation of strong gales from the southward all day. We took in about 100 tons more water, for ballast, as that was our chief reason of putting into Brassa.[1] Today we had the pleasure of the company of Cap*tai*n Marshall of the Sisters of Hull. Thermometer 44°.

March 30th. In the morning the Surgeon, 2nd Mate and myself, set out on an excursion on the Mainland of Shetland. The land rises very much from the sea; the tops of the mountains are almost constantly immersed in the clouds; about the time of the year at these islands, they experience a great deal of very thick weather. As I had heard from the men onboard the miserable state in which the poor of this place live, I determined to visit some of them. We accordingly entered one of their houses, without ceremony. This house was about 8 feet high; thatched with barley & oat straw well secured by lashings of thin wood from the top of the roof, to the lower part of the gable. The entrance was attended by a deal of inconvenience as the mud, mire & all sorts of filth was excessive, but thro' which it was necessary to pass previous to getting to the door. This door was 3½ feet high, the only hole of any description which could emit the smoke, and preserve some current of air in order to breathe. A fire was burning on the ground at one corner of the building, the walls were as thick with smoke as any chimney. I cannot conceive how these mortals can exist when the door is shut, for even when it was open, so much did the smoke overpower me, that I was obliged to make my exit almost as soon as I went in. There were several men and women sitting around the fire, apparently very happy. Our surgeon lighted his pipe, & very composedly joined in the conversation. Some food was preparing, of which they begged us to partake; but this I begged to be excused. In an adjoining apartment made by a few reeds; were 2 or 3 beds, but such I never should have supposed them to have been, had I not been told so: merely a piece of old board covered with a sheep skin. The house itself was built of the quarry stone, but without any kind of plaister; so that the wind rushed in between the stones very piercingly in cold weather. The inhabitants were <u>extremely</u> dirty, bare-footed; and indeed barely clothed. Altogether, it presented such a spectacle ['to' *deleted*] as I could hardly have concieved [*sic*], or any other Englishman, especially if he had been used to home. I have seen the poor houses in Russia[2] – but I really hardly think them inferior to the Shetland ones. The people conversed very readily with us concerning politics; they seemed very anxious for peace &cc. We left them & proceeded onward up a high hill from which we had a

[1] This rather oversimplifies the situation. Though the *Esk*, unlike most other whalers (Scoresby 26 & 29 March), had no need for Shetland sailors to complete the crew, the ability to take on ballast water in Lerwick made it easier for the ship to make the difficult departure from the shallow Whitby harbour. The date of that departure was determined primarily by tide levels and secondarily by local winds. By calling at Lerwick, Scoresby could then base his sailing date from that port on a different criterion: what appeared the most favourable winds for the voyage northwards. Even so, Lerwick was not an essential port of call. Scoresby's journal entry for 27 March 1815 shows that he had 'no pressing necessity' to go there, but did so mainly because the *Esk*'s non-appearance there might suggest that the ship had encountered 'some serious misadventure' at sea.

[2] Presumably at or near Archangel, with which port his father seems to have traded. See Introduction, p. xxv.

most delightful view of the town and sound, with the ships therein. We travelled NWestward: almost across the island untill we came to another harbour, but a very small one: it formed a very beautiful vale; the entrance of it had a particular grand appearance: the sea was dashing most furiously against some rocks which obstructed its passage, the hills rose to an immense height on each side. This range of hills stretches along from the N. to S.ward and is laid down in most maps and charts of the place. We arrived at the source of this river, where were standing many fishermans huts; here we got unto the road, or highway between Lerwick & Scalloway, a town on the Southwest side of the mainland; and made the best of our way, to the ship again – On going along that road, we met a great many people, men chiefly, going to join their respective ships at Lerwick; I was much surprised to see them carry their immense sea chests on their shoulders, with great facility: many of them had their wives accompanying them, who, as the men, were walking bare-footed; although this road is so uneven & rocky. This custom of walking bare-footed, I understand is also practised by the higher class of people, almost throughout the Highlands of Scotland – On Sundays they dress themselves extremely smartly viz: when they are walking about publickly. For whilst sitting in their own houses they wear but their common clothes; but when they go out, (for instance, going to kirk) they take off their stockings & shoes, carry them in their hands: when they come near the kirk, they go to some puddle of water, or any other convenient place and wash their feet which by travelling so far become thoroughly dirty; put on their stockings & shoes; and by this means cut a very reputable appearance, in that respect. This custom is practised particularly by the women. During this excursion, I saw many of their cattle. An abundance of Ponies, and of a most beautiful description. They seemed to run about perfectly wild. If I had had any convenient means, I certainly should have brought one over to England – The Sheep are small; the wool particularly fine; the mutton is not bad, in general poor: they are of different colours: white, black, lead colour; and [***] bald. These animals in winter feed chiefly on sea-weed which they gather from the sea shore at low-water. The oxen & cows are small, very beautifull in stature and colour. Their horns are short, and they are by no means wild as the ponies & sheep. The pigs are much like those of England. The poultry are in general fine, the eggs are a good size, but taste very smoky, which most likely proceeds from their dwelling with the people in their houses. The chief birds are the Wild geese wild duck: raven, brown gull; Loom;[1] An abundance of fish chiefly shell fish. Oysters here are most excellent: and tolerably cheap. There are cockells, [*** ***] and other [rock?] fish. Of the better [sort?] there are Cod, Ling, [Tusk?] and others of less note. After [***] a little about the town I returned onboard, highly gratified with what had passed. The Shetland people are in general well made men; of a middle stature; of a swarthy complexion; and active in the hour of danger though not very much so before: Self-interest & craft are the predominating features of the mind: but still they are very hospitable: they are very fond of English manufactured goods: indeed they will not take money for their common goods, but articles of England: they are sure to demand an immense deal more than the value of their goods and sometimes when they are

---

[1] The Shetland name for the guillemot.

alongside an English vessel are exceedingly troublesome and obstinate.[1] The women and girls are cheerful, lively, gay and insinuating: the children hardy and active. The general appearance of the mainland is mountainous and barren. The land near the shore is much [incoporated?] with stone but not so a little higher up it is of a black heavy nature and from the red colour of the small but numerous rills of water, and the nature of the appearance of the minerals altogether, I should be strongly inclined to think there is much iron beneath. Quantities of copper I understand have been found in the west of the country. No trees are to be seen upon this island, excepting in gardens, which are not very numerous. The chief verdure is a very rank sort of grass, a great quantity of ling grows also, and various sorts of [matter?]. Oats: Barley: Potatoes: cabages: and other vegetables are grown, but are by no means plentifull.

March 31st. Landed again on the island of Brassa, with the second mate & surgeon for the purpose of making another excursion. We intended going entirely across this island which is about 5 miles distant and if possible to cross over to the isle of Noss, to see the famous basket suspended between 2 immense high rocks for the purpose of transporting cattle &c. thither. As we passed over ['the land' *deleted*]. I had an opportunity of seeing the people till their land. This is commonly performed by the women & children, the men being too indolent. Four oxen were yoked into a curious contrivance of a plough; the two innermost and two outermost together. A lad led them and a woman officiated at the tail of the plough. More women were most labouriously engaged in turning up the ground with spades. The land on this island is much superior to that on the mainland; more of it is cultivated; and the grain carried to a greater state of perfection. Still it is very mountainous. We travelled across it, to the sea. Here we intended paying a visit to ['an' *deleted*] some old friends of my companions.[2] As we were approaching their dwelling, we were suddenly saluted by an old woman, dressed in a red Jacket, almost the only garment she had on her: quite bare footed: and even bare <u>legged</u>. She recognised us immediately; and ran towards us with joy. Although she knew nothing about me, she took me by the hand and dragged me most violently into her filthy hovel; the mate & surgeon followed. I was not exactly pleased with her <u>treatment</u> towards me; but at the same time I admired her [***], as I first thumped my head most unmercifully against the ['door?' *deleted*] top of the hole of an entrance, although I stooped as low as I could; I stumbled over sheep, pigs, dogs, cats and all sorts of animals and was nearly bitten by a cow; all of which were feeding in the parterre, into which she shewed us. This house was certainly larger than any of the Shetland poor houses I had previously seen. It was 2 stories high! Each story almost 6 feet high; at least the lower one was. I cannot say much for the upper as it was merely the gable of the building. We were most heartily welcomed by a man inside, the master of the domain I supposed. The house was horridly dark & smoky of course; in fact so dark that it [occasioned?] the afore mentioned mistake and misfortune with the animals. They brought us out something to eat, and as we were uncommonly tired, we thankfully partook of it. Luckily it was dark; I could hardly see

---

[1] Presumably this statement was learned from Scoresby; it echoes the latter's entry for 28 March.
[2] See Scoresby's journal entry for 7 April 1812.

my food or my companions of the [***] [creation?], else I should not have made so good a meal as I did. They gave us plenty of good eggs & barly & oat bread. Some of the bread I brought away with me for curiosity sake. I also bought a pair of worsted stockings, very cheap. In this manufacture the Shetland people excel; I could with facility draw these stockings thro' a finger ring, yet they were of a great size. The surgeon gave them some medicine for which they were very thankfull. I took a walk down to the sea side, with a lad to show me about. I was struck with the grandeur of the scene. The sea dashing most [***] against an immense high rock; on the summit of which stood a <u>fishermans hut.</u> This rock was upon examination very curious. At a little height from the ground were excavated several holes, which led into a cavern beneath the rock; the cavern was most [artfully?] contrived: well secured inside: it led to a great distance underground. It would appear from the native's accounts that this cavern was formed some ['time' *deleted*] centurys ago for the purpose of affording safety to those persecuted people, during the invasion of the <u>Danes.</u> On the opposite side of the water was the isle of Noss, the most fertile of this cluster; I was prevented crossing over on account of the tremendous sea which was running. I returned to the house and found our host and hostess clad in their very best garments. We took tea; and after many mutual congratulations, well wishes &c. we took leave of them. We had not got far before the old woman came running after us; she could not think of leaving us, without carrying our baskets for us; which she did the whole way over the island. She then left us and returned home. We called at many houses on comming [*sic*] home; at each I was much gratified. At one I saw the kind of mills used here for grinding corn. It merely consisted of two large flat stones between which they ground, by turning one round with their [own?] hands.

April 1st. Dr Edmonston [*sic*] Capn Munson of the Clapham and other gentlemen paid a visit to the Esk: we gave them a sail in the barge, at which they were highly gratified; whilst they were onboard great merryment was carryed on upon deck, by the sailors; dancing; music &c. In the evening went on shore and spent our time very pleasantly with Mr Ogilvy. At night we were witnesses to a bloody conflict between the Esk's spiktioneer and the spiktioneer of the Fountain of Lynn. It created a general confusion in the town: but was at last quelled by some Highland soldiers being called out. All this seemed to have been excited by the envy which the Fountain as well as many others ships in the fleet, had towards the Esk.

April 2nd. In the morning prepared for getting under weigh, but the wind comming round from the North eastward, we were obliged to give it up.[1] Went onshore and spent the rest of the day at Mr Ogilvy's.

April 3rd. In the morning being Sunday, we went onshore to <u>kirk</u> and heard a very excellent sermon from Revd — the minister. The Kirk, like most other buildings in Lerwick is of a clumsy construction; filthy in the inside; and void of light. The noisy,

---

[1] As Scoresby 2 April makes clear, the problem with a northeaster was not that it would prevent the *Esk* from sailing, but that it would make the Shetlands a lee shore after the ship headed northwards.

sleepy-headed clerk is fit to deafen one with his roaring vociferations which he gives out whilst singing, in the real scotch blarney,[1] to the ultimate satisfaction of <u>himself</u>. Spent this rainy day with Mr Ogilvy.

April 4th. In the morning light airs and clear weather; thermometer at 45°. Clapham got under weigh with three cheers from the Esk. About 9 A.M. got under sail with almost all the fleet, and proceeded up the north entry of the sound. An ugly sea running, after the late gale. At night off Balta sound. saw a ship come out; thought her to be the Henrietta of Whitby who had put to sea in the late gale of wind. At midnight lost sight of the land.

April 5th. Being now fairly at sea, we began to think about the fishery. The first job done was marking the harpoons viz: concealing the captains and ships names, in some particular part of the Instrument, so that if any other ship's crew should strike the fish, that had one of our harpoons in, we might have our claim. The fore-gangers were spliced onto the harpoons; pieces of rope about 5 or 6 fathoms long to which the whale lines are made fast: and the handles were placed into the tops of the instrument. Many Fulmars were seen – I could not distinguish any particular way of <u>direction</u> of there [sic] flying. An unfortunate <u>bullfinch</u> was seen travelling about the ship, but would not suffer itself to be taken. A <u>Norwegian Crow</u> was caught in the maintop, by one of the men. At noon the thermometer stood at 48°.

April 6th. In the morning a heavy sea & a strong gale of wind came on from the SWward. There evidently had been a strong Northerly wind blowing in this latitude, as the sea came from that quarter. Several Fulmars seen. Thermometer by a mean of observations at 46° noon.

April 7th. During all this day heavy gales of wind from the South-ward. In the last 24 hours ran nearly 200 miles. Ship generally going at the rate of 12 miles an hour. This day we made our entry into the Frigid Zone, upon which I paid the usual <u>fine</u>. We saw the same bulfinch to day, I think that we saw yesterday, but it was still too shy to be caught. It rained very hard chief of the day, the sea was running tremendously high, but our ship was in that excellent trim, that she shipped very little water. Many Fulmars seen. Thermometer at noon at 43°.

April 8th. An unabated continuance of the gale, the ship going at a great rate. Many Fulmars seen during day. Thermometer at noon at 28°.

April 9th. The gale gradually subsided untill noon; when thick weather & snow came on. A small bird was caught to day (by seamen called <u>cishel</u>[2]) I could not find its

---

[1] Not the happiest choice of word, since it is clearly associated with Ireland, not Scotland, and it means (*OED*) 'Smoothly flattering or cajoling talk.' It is, however, an earlier use of the noun (though not the verb) than the citations in *OED*.

[2] Not in *OED*, but the handwriting is very clear.

description in any book of Natural History onboard. It resembled alltogether a land bird. About the size of a sparrow, black back, and a white breast. Towards the evening the blink of some ice was just distinguishable to the Northward. A heavy sea running, and we were wishing much to make it, that we might thereby get a little shelter. Fulmars seen.

April 10th. At 6 A.M. fell in with <u>loose bay ice</u>; or pieces of round ice; of about 3, 4, & 5 feet in diameter & about 2 feet thick. There was a considerable quantity of snow on it. The pieces of ice lyed quite close one to another, but still the ship moved amongst them with a tolerable degree of facility. The cold I now began to perceive very intense, the thermometer standing at 6°. We had thus made the <u>West Ice</u>; about 40 leagues to the Eastward of the island of Jan Mayen. After reaching a few miles into it, we tacked; as our object was now to get to the Eastward, in order that we might get to the northward, up the bight, which there always is up the west side of Spitsbergen. I observed that those birds which we had constantly seen upon the passage (Fulmars) did not frequent the <u>Bay</u> ice. This description of ice is in general by the Whale fishermen called <u>pancake</u> ice, because I suppose of its resemblance to that cake. As the day was extremely clear, ['we' *deleted*] I had a pleasing opportunity of seeing the <u>Blink</u> to great perfection. This was the light reflected from the ice unto the clouds near the horizon, directly over it. It was of a very peculiar bright colour, and very strong. Today being Sunday, divine service was performed (after the forms of the Church of England), wherein I officiated as Clerk. In consequence of the cold, the men began to make an addition in their clothing; which chiefly consisted in a wig & large slouched hat; a jacket or two more; large trowsers; and [***] it was a most ridiculous sight to see many of them. it was however a true Greenland appearance. The cold ['seemed' *deleted*] at first ['to' *deleted*] had some effect on me; I could not keep myself at all tolerably warm in bed: my nose & toes were almost frozen off, although a constant roaring fire in the adjoining apartment with the door open. If I poured my tea hot from the tea pot into a saucer, it was frozen almost immediately. I therefore was forced to make the addition of an entire covering with flannell next my skin, 3 or 4 pairs of worsted stockings; 2 pair of trowsers; 2 jackets, one of them duffle; an immense pair of boots; a wig and large thick hat: and sheep-skin gloves & mittens. Had any of my relations or friends seen me ['thus?' *deleted*] in this fantastical dress, with a nose as blue as a ripe cherry, I much question whether they would have known me. The seamans duty now became quite of a different nature: every rope in the ship frozen; and in order to keep himself warm he must <u>run</u>, instead of walk the deck. As we had now reached a high northern latitude our nights became sensibly longer: indeed as we had had so much thick and bad weather they were rendered particularly so.[1]

April 11th. Thick weather came on again, with colder weather. Thermometer down to 2° – Being now in the ice no dead reckoning was kept. Continued to ply to windward, in the best way we could, and with as much expedition as possible. Two <u>snow birds</u>

[1] A strange statement, and perhaps a slip of the pen. At 70°N (Scoresby 9 April) the sun would be above the horizon more than fourteen hours each day.

seen; a great quantity of rhyme frost issuing from out the sea. This frost rhyme is somewhat similar to that seen in England, its cause I am not exactly acquainted with at present.

April 12th. In the morning the weather was extremely thick and cold: thermometer at zero. During day, different flights of Roaches, Fulmars, Looms, &c. seen. Continued working to the Eastward with the wind in ['the' *deleted*] our teeth. Got the <u>crows nest</u> to the main topmast head. This is a sort of tub, the skeleton of which is made of wood covered with leather, with which every ship is furnished on coming to Greenland, for the more easily seeing the ice at a distance, seeing whales &c. Blink of the ice very distinct and beautiful towards Northward. In the evening got clear of the ice and stood to the southward.

April 13th. At the early part of the morning it came on to blow very heavily from the E.S.E. The wind comming thus round to the southward caused a very sudden transition from the intense cold. The thermometer now standing at 32°. These changes of temperature are common in Greenland. During all this gale a very heavy sea was running. In the afternoon it abated, and subsided into a calm. 3 hours afterwards[1] it blew a hard gale from the westward directly in the opposite direction of the other. Thus in the course of 18 hours we have had two strong gales of wind, each in a contrary direction; and a variation of 32° degrees[2] of temperature in the atmosphere.

April 14th. In the morning the gale gradually subsided, untill 9 A.M. when a perfect calm, and very serene weather prevailed; during which a great number of <u>Bottle-noses</u> made their appearance. At 11 A.M. a most furious squall came on again from SE.ward, with showers of snow, and blew so hard we could ['not' *deleted*] scarcely bear any sail on the ship; this gale continued throughout the day. These gales although so very uncertain in Greenland, were predicted <u>without exception by the Barometer</u>. This Barometer which we had on board, was the one which went round the world with Captain Cook. The gales generally come on with very thick hazy weather, so that when a ship is near the ice, her situation is very dangerous as frequently it is so thick that room cannot be seen enough to [wear?][3] or stay the vessel. Each of these three last gales <u>rose and subsided in the same quarter of the compass</u>: The first in the E.S.E: The second in the W. The last in the S.E. This is a phenomena [*sic*] is[4] quite contrary to what Crantz mentions in his history of Greenland: as he says the "storms <u>rise in the South and subside in the North.</u>"[5] In <u>no gale of wind</u> have I observed this yet. Thermometer today at 34°. Fulmars seen.

[1] This is presumably what Steward intended, but 'afterwards' was added above the line and the insertion point is between '3' and 'hours'.

[2] *Sic*; both the degree sign and the word are written.

[3] The handwriting is closer to 'veer', but 'wear' seems more probable.

[4] *Sic*; 'is' was inserted above the line; what was intended was presumably '... a phenomenon that is ...'.

[5] 'The most and fiercest storms rise in the south, and take a compass round to north, where they again subside, and terminate in clear weather.' Cranz (or Crantz), *History of Greenland*, I, p. 47.

April 15th. In the morning the wind went down but in a manner rather unlike the former ones as there were frequent squalls and calms. The weather however became quite clear. Generally before these gales a screeching was heard from the birds which were constantly flying about the ship; these birds were even flying about in the midst of the storms. The Fulmars indeed appear to be particularly strong in this case; and also sometimes when ships are flinching these birds come very near to partake of the crang, The seamen will strike them most violently with boathooks, they seem however scarcely to feel their effects, as they fly a little time, then return to their prey – In the evening the blink of the ice very clear to NW^d. Thermometer at 30° –

April 16th. Weather very clear in the morning, the blink stretched from the NW.b.N to the E.S.E. As we were sailing towards it, I observed it had a greater extent in altitude the nearer we approached it. Towards the top of it, there was a thin strata [*sic*] of cloud, behind it, which gave it a very beautifull red appearance. The weather was particularly fine all day, not a single cloud to be seen, except towards the southward. where there were some of those hard white clouds mentioned by Phipps. In the afternoon made the ice, but thought ['the' *deleted*] it dangerous to enter among it, we therefore continued to stand to the North Eastward. Thermometer at 30°. Many Fulmars seen.

April 17th. Delightful fine weather throughout the day. Several sail hove in sight. Performed Divine service. Thermometer at 23°. Most of the oldest Greenland-men, seemed to think they hardly ever remember such particular fine weather on the outward passage. An abundance of Fulmars, bottlenoses, and fin-fish. These fish were of an immense size, like all the inhabitants of the polar regions; when plunging into the water, they made a very great noise, somewhat similar to that of a distant cannon firing.

April 18th. This day like the former was very serene and inclinable to calm. This was an excellent opportunity for trying the adjustments and corrections of my sextant, which I had long wish-[1] for; and untill now could not: as the weather had been in general so cold that I could not without difficulty hold the instrument. By finding the suns semidiameter and other useful adjustments it appeared to be perfectly correct; two usefull appendages were however still wanting; a double telescopic ring, ['and also' *deleted*] telescopic screens and a small screwdriver. These I must endeavour to procure on[2] my return to England – Thermometer at noon at 48°. Finners, Fulmars, bottlenoses &c. seen during the day. At 3 P.M. we fell in with a vast quantity of sludge ice. Stood more to the eastward to avoid it. In the evening fell in with pack-ice; made sail and passed close to it. At Sunset the cold became intense. Thermometer at 10°. This was caused I suppose by the ice. A fall of the thermometer during day of 38°! At midnight very cloudy and windy: it had much the appearance of a violent storm from

---

[1] *Sic*. The hyphen is at the end of the line; presumably 'wished' was intended.
[2] Originally 'one', 'e' deleted.

the Northward. During the whole time we had been amongst ice, I had observed the water to be of a <u>fine dark green colour</u>.

April 19th. Untill noon, sharp squalls of wind varying 7 or 8 points, with cloudy disagreable weather: when it cleared more up, and seemed inclinable to calm. Thermometer at 14°. No ice to be seen – Fulmars &c. seen. Towards evening a great deal of snow: the snow was of a <u>most beautifull texture</u>; but very common in Greenland I understand. It was formed like <u>a star</u>. Six radiations from one centre; each of them varigated in the most curious and interesting manner. I was particular in examining the particles with a microscope, and was struck with the evident omnipresence of a divine being in thus displaying his wondrous works when human eyes were not always to observe them. From the mast head were to be seen tens of thousands of seals, diverting themselves on the ice. [Three?] whale boats were hoisted out to go to catch some. At night they returned with 36, which they caught in the following manner. When they reached the ice, and the seals saw them, they set off for the water: the men shouted and made as much noise as they possibly could. The animals turned about stared at them with astonishment; and [dare?] proceede [*sic*] no farther. They are then to be struck at with impunity; which they do over the seals noses (for in that part they are particularly tender) with <u>seal-clubs</u> about 5 feet long and formed at one end like a common hammer. Oftentimes, as was the case once this time, the seals will spring up and strike the man in the breast and knock him over into the sea – Some difficulty was attending on getting unto [*sic*] the pieces of ice; a heavy sea was running, and they were confined on one piece an hour without being able to get off again. Four young ones were brought onboard alive. I was impressed[1] with the sensibility the creatures shewed. When the sailor took one of them up in his arms to bring it away, it seemed much distressed; it cryed like a young child, made such a <u>noise</u>; it looked up at his face to implore mercy, whilst tears ran down its face. When it was killed, I tried the <u>temperature of his blood</u>; and found it to be about 90°. This is much warmer that [*sic*] I should have supposed, as ['all' *deleted*] most amphibious animals have very cold blood; but as this one was very small and young, (for the seamen thought it had never been in the water) it might be an exception. I had not an opportunity of trying the others as they killed on the ice. The strength of animals is uncommon; they have been known to swim about after they have been flinched.

April 20th. In the morning charming fine weather: thermometer at 16°. In the afternoon made the ice again: both <u>pack</u> and <u>bay</u> ice was visible; the latter was between us and the <u>pack</u>; we were therefore much disappointed in getting some more seals. A [vast?] of Finners – Seals – Fulmars – Roaches &c. seen during the day. At night a hard gale of wind came on from N.N.E., which never varied a single point during its continuance.

April 21st. A continuance of the gale, but much interrupted by squalls and calms. Thick showers of snow &c. Thermometer at 20°. Finners, Fulmars, roaches, seals seen.

---

[1] *Sic*: the spelling error was the result of a hyphenated word at the end of page.

April 22ⁿᵈ. A continuation of yesterday's squally weather with showers of snow. This sort of weather generally presages a very heavy gale of wind, but from the favourable state of the Barometer, we were disposed to think otherwise. Thermometer at 22°. Fulmars – Roaches, Looms seen to day.

April 23ʳᵈ. Squally and variable winds, with thick showers of small round snow and unpleasant weather. We have now been a whole fortnight beating to windward of which all the crew became fairly tired. We were looking anxiously for Bear island, which we expected almost hourly to see. A very fine ice-drake seen in the wake of the ship, with fulmars & Looms. At midnight quite still and calm.

April 24ᵗʰ. In the morning light airs and clear weather. Got a lunar observation but unfortunately it proved incorrect, as some considerable mistake was made in the time. Performed Divine service. All the afternoon I was practising myself in taking the Lunar distances, the opportunity was a most excellent one; an almost perfect calm sea; the moon at a very convenient distance from the Sun (being about 60°): and the moon also to the eastward of the sun; so as the sextant was a convenient side upwards. Yet even under these circumstances I found the operation difficult[.] I felt my arm very much fatigued, by holding the sextant a long time horizontally, ['with' *deleted*] which is requisite to those commencing the practise of the contact. The inverting telescope I found a most tedious acquisition. When both objects ['are' *deleted*] were in the glass, still I could hardly bring them together; but I found by a constant motion of the Sextant round the telescope as its centre, I got it to a tolerable degree of accuracy. The longitude we made in the afternoon, by another observation was 14°26′ East. This might be supposed to be correct. These observations must be of the most exquisite use in making the ice in this part, as it is only in a certain longitude where the bight is to be found. They are attended with great convenience as not above 10 or 11 miles constitute a degree of longitude in these high northern latitudes, they may therefore be taken with an uncommon degree of accuracy. One thing is however rather disagreeable, namely the intense cold. It is a very great obstruction both to the working of the Instruments and to the hands, as one cannot have one's gloves on. Thermometer at 24°. Towards evening thick weather came on. Finners, Fulmars, roaches and ice ducks & drakes. From the great plenty in which these birds abounded all day, and also from the land blink, we suppose ourselves to be very near the island.

April 25ᵗʰ. Early in the morning the weather cleared completely up, and ice was seen stretching from E.N.E. to S.S.E. At 6 A.M. the craggy mountains of Spitzbergen became distinctly visible at about 120 miles off. The land appeared like a very bright white iland upon the horizon; the whiteness was owing to the snow – Three ships also hove insight. As the day was particularly serene, it was a good opportunity of ascertaining with precision the Longitude of the land; by an angular distance between it and the sun's centre, and the exact bearing. Also the Sun's azimuth. I tried Kelly's method for "clearing the lunar distance from Refraction and Parallax by

Projection",[1] and was very much gratified on finding it approximate very nearly. It gave the correction to 4 or 5 seconds – Got the Whale[2] lines from out the gun room and stowed them in the boats, which were hung over the quarters and beams by means of [three?] strong baulks [athwart?] the ship. In fact today all the fishing gear was got in readiness – delightfull fine weather all day. Thermometer at 24°. Towards the evening came up very much with the land, so that by 9 P.M. we were within 25 miles of it; but such is the wonderfull great deceipt with respect to the apparent distance of it, that I declare I should not have supposed us to have been more than 5 miles distant from it. This land rises to an immense height; the summits to its mountains seemed to be immersed in clouds.

April 26th. Early this morning a fresh breeze sprung up from the westward and we shaped our course rather off the land for the ice. When at a considerable distance from the land, so that it could not be seen, its blink was distinctly seen, similar to that of the ice. When near the land the water appeared of a much darker and thicker ['appear'? *deleted*] colour than before. Hazy weather most of the day. The sun never got to night for the first time; and a very long day was now [burst?] upon us, perhaps of 8 or 10 weeks duration. What a strange phenomenon; to be taking our observation on the sun at midnight! No stars are now to be seen, when they become visible again they will be as great a novelty to us again as the sun is at present. Several sail in sight. Thermometer at 22°.

April 27th. Fresh breezes and cloudy weather throughout the day. Made the ice, and continued running to windward amongst it. At noon 18 sail in sight. Two or three whales seen; lowered down boats to go in search of them, but were unsuccessful. To see whales was a long wished for sight by me. I was much deceived in their appearance by the erroneous representations of them in some plates of books on the subject. Their blowing was particularly curious, which made a great noise; it was vapour which they exhaled when on the surface of the water. In the afternoon [25?] sail hove in sight. Thermometer at [15°?] Fulmars, roaches &c. seen.

April 28th. Calm and thick weather at the early part; a breeze however sprung up and we set off working to windward; that is what is always practised in the fishery when hunting for Whales. Saw several Whales; backed the main yard; hoisted out boats, but could not succeed. The whale boats are of a peculiar construction: caulker built; rounded off on the keel fore and aft, that they may be turned round easily. Very unsteady; and furnished inside ['partic' *deleted*] expressly for their intended use. Each boat is furnished with 1 harpooneer, 1 boat steerer, 1 line coiler, who sits in the middle of the boat: the harpooneer at the bow: 6 lines, partly coiled in the middle and partly at the stern of the boat – Thermometer at 15°. Fulmars seen.

---

[1] The fourth edition of Patrick Kelly's *Practical Introduction to Spherics and Nautical Astronomy* was published in 1813.
[2] Originally 'Whales'; 's' deleted.

April 29th. Fresh breezes from the southward; anxiously waiting for ['the' *deleted*] a north-west wind, which is esteemed the best for whale fishing, as it keeps the ice open – at noon the blinks of different pieces of ice were seen, one of a field particularly: here consists the great utility of the blink as at once the blink of a field may be seen; as the <u>field</u> fishing is by all means the most plentifull (although the fish are not of so large a size as others) we made all sail for it. We came up with it in the afternoon, to which we moored. This is a very difficult operation. Great skill is required to bring the ship nicely up with the ice, at the same time not to strike her against it, as a slight percussion might be attended with dangerous consequences – A boat is generally sent forward first, to set the ice anchor in, which is done by means of proper axes &c. for the express purpose. Then the vessel is brought alongside. This ice we supposed to be about 60 or 70 feet thick. The thickness of ice is mostly ascertained by its height above water. ⅙ floats [But?] this approximation must of course be according to the age and strength of the ice. On the ice was a great depth of Snow. At this ice we remained the ['remainder' *deleted*] rest of the night. Whales, unicorns, Fulmars, roaches, looms and a <u>sparrow hawk</u> seen during day. Therm at 28°.

April 30th. Early this morning unmoored, as found that the ice to which we had moored, was <u>a floe of ice</u>, or ice seperated from a field. We stood out. No fish were seen contrary to our expectations at this ice. Heard from the Leviathan that she had not yet found her boat. This relates to a melancholy circumstance which happened on the 27 inst. As the Leviathan was beating to windward amongst some ice, she unfortunately stove herself against a piece, so as to cause a rent of 14 feet long and 9 broad, on the larboard bow. After perhaps expending most of her own materials about the necessary repair, she sent a boat to other ships near her for assistance. After having gone to some ships she came to the Esk: with sailor like liberality, she afforded her some materials of reparation. They had scarcely left us to return to their own ship, when a thick fog came on. The Leviathan lost of her boat then and was as yet not able to hear any tidings of her. Most likely by now the unfortunate men are dead with cold and hunger – Towards this afternoon the ice began to close upon us very fast, and we were under the unpleasant apprehension of being <u>beset</u>. Happily by the aid of three boats towing us out ahead (for it was perfectly calm) we succeeded in getting clear of it; after we had been out but a very short time the ice came too with a tremendous crash such as would have squeezed the ship all to pieces – Thermometer at 15°. Much rhyme frost during the day. Whales, Unicorns, Fulmars, roaches and looms seen. This being the last day in April (for tomorrow was sunday) it was a time of great merriment amongst the "jovial crew": who according to custom, made a model of the ship ['and' *deleted*] which was suspended by the two last married men on the main top gallant stay, with all sorts of fine ribbands – Blacking faces, Dancing; music: and all sorts of curious and ludicurous [*sic*] grimaces concluded the day.

May 1st. Fresh breezes which increased to a gale in the afternoon with cloudy weather: Reached from the ice to the land; which we made at the latter end of the day. This land was the Foreland, some of the highest land in Spitzbergen; Phipps measured the heigth [*sic*] of this land and found it to be upwards of a mile! It consists of several Pyramids; [towering?] to the skyes. It seems to overhang the sea. It is covered with snow, and has a truly grand and terrific appearance. Therm. 13. Fulmars seen.

May 2nd. A most violent gale of wind all day; fortunately under the lee of some ice. 1 sail in sight[.] Thermometer 15°. Fulmars and roaches seen.

May 3rd. Early in the morning the ice which afforded us such good protection yesterday, unfortunately broke up, and we were left to the mercy of such a sea as I never before saw: Running truly "mountains high". Our situation was this day particularly awfull. Our threatened [Bark?] was under very little sail of course; when in the hollow of the sea, was almost becalmed; then when she rose again on the summit of the billows every thing seemed as if it would be blown away. It was with horror we gazed on the immense masses of ice floating about against which if we had struck, we must inevitably have been lost – Thanks to the Almighty – the Esk rode the gale out as well as could be possibly expected. At night it was more moderate. During this gale we had very thick weather, after it, the horizon was covered with those "white hard clouds," mentioned by Cap. Phipps, to leeward. This gale ['is' deleted] was not like those mentioned by Crantz; it rose and subsided in the same quarter (N.N.E.) never altered one single point, and was steady throughout. Heigth of the thermometer 16°. Fulmars seen.

May 4th. Moderate weather, but the sea still running very high. Manchester of Hull made signal to speak us, we shortened sail and she came up with us. She told us, the captain was dying, and requested the assistance of our surgeon. Hove too under a floe of ice and sent him onboard. Glad to find him not so bad as we expected. Made sail again for the ice, which we came up with in the evening. The weather now became unusually fine. Therm. 20°. Fulmars and roaches seen.

May 5th. Strong breezes of wind all day. In the afternoon reached into some ice. Thermometer at 20°. Whales, unicorns, Fulmars and roaches seen. Cloudy [in?] night; wind very fresh.

May 6th. Fresh winds and moderate cloudy weather. Tried very hard to catch some fish, but still being unsuccessful. All the crew became evidently uneasy and ill-tempered at it. Thermometer 18°. Fulmars, roches, looms & [kingsmashert or kingsmarkhert?] seen.

May 7th. In the morning fresh breezes and fair, rather cloudy with a little rain. Got up to a field of ice. A vast[1] of fish seen. Stationed the boats along it. At 2 P.M. had the satisfaction of seeing a fish struck, which was indicated by the fast boat's hoisting his <u>Jack</u>. The Ship answered it immediately by hoisting hers. All the other boats which

---

[1] *OED* cites mainly poetical uses of 'vast' as a noun, but also notes its use in dialects, including East Anglia, Steward's home.

were out went to her assistance. It is a curious sight to[1] the men [running?] out of their beds when a Fall! A Fall! A Fall! is called. Some half naked, begin dressing themselves upon deck, others dress themselves in the boats. All in a great hurry. The ship was immediately directed towards some bay ice, where it was suspected the fish would come up again, And luckily a boat was dropped just in the place where <u>she did</u> come up. By that means a second harpoon was struck in – when this is done, half the job is over – This fish ran out about 3[2] miles of line. She was struck a third time and at last became so much exhausted as to come to the surface constantly for Respiration. They then began <u>lancing her</u>, running their instruments 6 or 7 feet into her. In this way she was killed. One of the boats was knocked over by the whale's tail, but no one drowned. I never was more gratified in my life than I was at seeing the death of a whale. To see the enterprising men attacking such a monster, She [rising?] her head up, and spouting blood to a great height, but was at length overpowered. Her two fins were lashed together and a lashing round the tail by which she was towed alongside, after the Ship was moored to a field. When alongside three great takles [*sic*] are made fast to her, One, the <u>winch</u> or nose takle, was made fast at the nose, another <u>the cant</u> or a [takle] made fast to the blubber about the fin, and the other the Capstern or a takle made fast about the tail; in this manner the fish is hove up a convenient heigth – The hatches are taken off the hold, and some water started from the casks. The <u>Sleman</u> takes his station here as his particular duty. The Spiketioneer and harpooners with spurs on upon the fish, and superintends its cutting up. The blubber is cut off in very large pieces and hauled upon deck. The boat-steerers cut it into small pieces, and pass it thro' a hole in the hatch into the hold, where it lies as yet. In the afternoon another fall was called, and a fine fish was struck, after running out a great quantity of line, the harpoon drew. During this day upwards of 200 whales were supposed to have been seen – Thermometer at 12°. Fulmars &c. Took a run on the ice.

May 8th. After the flinching was over, we unmoored ship from the field and made sail. Delightfull fine weather with fresh breezes. Performed Divine service. Thermometer 10°. Whales, Unicorns, Fulmars, seals, roaches, &c &c seen.

May 9th. Beautifull clear weather and almost calm. At 9 A.M. a Fall was called and after an early death she was towed alongside – This whale was much less than the other. The size of a fish is estimated by the length of the <u>whale-bone</u>. When is [*sic*] measures less than 6 feet it is not a size fish. In the afternoon Cap*tai*n S. and myself went in a boat but were unsuccessfull. Got one start but the harpoon drew. At 10 P.M. another fall was called much to our joy. This fish came up close alongside and was struck from the ship. In 55 minutes she was dead. She was towed alongside and flinched; At midnight the water was entirely covered with a thin skin of bay-ice, which had been frozen. I observed the progress of coagulation, but nothing particular occurred to me. As the weather was now particularly clear, I had an opportunity of

---

[1] 'see' omitted in error?
[2] Scoresby 9 May stated 3,200 yards (1.8 miles).

observing the variation of appearance in the sun between mid-day & midnight. I observed none, except that which must consequently arise from the difference of altitude, but I could look at him without being dazzled.[1] Martens[2] mentions his appearing like the <u>moon</u> at Mid-night. I was much deceived with respect to his altitude, which as [*sic*] about 6°. It appeared to be half as high as in the day time, although his alt is 30°.

May 10th. Calm all day; the water all around us frozen. Snow also, similar in texture to that mentioned a few days since in my journal. The ice all around us was [comming?] too very fast with most tremendous crashes, so that in the afternoon the ship was completely beset by the fields. By these violent perturbations of the ice, are attributed the cause of the <u>hummocks of ice</u>, some of them 30 & 40 feet higher than the generallity of it. We were now in a very serious plight, as we had no possible communication with the open water. Miles – and perhaps hundreds from it. Should a strong N.W. wind spring up, we may run some chance of getting loose again; if not, God knows how long we may be in this unpleasant situation. Many ships were last year confined untill ['th' *deleted*] August, before they were liberated. One[3] comfort generally arises from being beset, fine weather and calms are prevalent, which we had all this day. – – Thermometer at 16°. Whales & Unicorns seen but no birds.

May 11th. Charming fine weather; and nearly calm, it would not do however to be still, whilst we have a small fraction of water to be amongst; or rather bay ice. Got all hands on the ice and moved her a considerable distance; at least nearly to the field, where we moored, in hopes that should the ice to windward be inclined to come down upon us, we might cut a hole in the lee ice, and drive the ship in. I cannot better picture our situation now, than by referring to a plate in Phipps voyage, wherein the Racehorse and Carcass are beset in a calm. All the afternoon I amused myself running about on the ice. This is fine exercise. I almost regretted I did not bring a pair of scates with me. It is a general remark that a sailor eats 4 times as much whilst in this situation, than when in England. I am sure I found this the case, for I never am easy [few/four/five?] hours without having something to eat. Every man on board looks as healthy as possible. As a dead calm prevailed we could distinctly hear numbers of whales and unicorns blowing away, although we could not see them. Fulmars and roaches seen. Therm. 10°.

May 12th. Delightfull fine weather and calm. In the morning saw a bear comming over the ice, he however did not come close enough to get a shot at him. Today we performed an operation, in Greenland called <u>Making off</u>; or putting the blubber into the casks below. The Blubber is again passed upon deck, where it is cut into much

---

[1] Scoresby, *Account of the Arctic Regions*, I, p. 378

[2] 'There is hardly any difference of cold between night and day, yet at night, when the sun shineth, it seemeth to one that rightly considereth it, as if it was only clear moonlight, so that you may look upon the sun as well as you can upon the moon' (White, *Collection of Documents on Spitzbergen & Greenland*, p. 40).

[3] Possibly 'Our'.

smaller pieces, into a long trough, and passed thro' an [hause?][1] down below into casks. At 10 P.M. a fall was called, as boats were stationed in every little opening of the ice. Considerable trouble attended killing her,[2] as she was under the ice. However by the skill of Cap*tain* S. with his ice shoes, he succeeded, and she was got alongside and flinched. – Therm. 9°. Wales, Unicorns. Fulmars &c.

May 13th. Rather thick weather and cold[.] Therm. 8°. Continued making off. In the evening the Refraction was very great; found by my sextant it was [13′.?]. The therm. at this time was at about 9°. Gentle wind from Southward. At 10 P.M. a fall was called, and at 11 P.M. another. – Fulmars and roaches seen – ['Flinched the Whales' *deleted*]

May 14th. The fish which were struck last night being dead, all hands were employed to get them alongside. That which was struck first never came up again: she drowned herself. She was hove up by the whale line and got alongside. The <u>Sharks</u> we found had eaten above a ton of Blubber from her: this was rather mortifying, after having cost us so much labour. It is astonishing to see what gluttinous [*sic*] brutes these fish are: several were caught alongside whilst flinching. Lances and knives were thrust into them but still they seemed to eat as much as before. I cut the head off, and the tail off, one, and cut the entrails out; still he shew evident signs of life –
    The whale which was struck secondly, now engaged our attention. We almost despaired of ever getting her onboard. She was a mile from the ship: All hands were however mustered on the ice: the ice was cut thro' for some considerable distance with saws &c. and by means of ice anchors she was hove thro' for a little distance, until we came to ice of 1½ foot thick: the ice was running very fast: one piece over-lapping the other; our work [***] uncommonly: still we persisted: cut another passage; and after incredible labour effected our purpose. This ended [about?] night. All day very cold. Therm. 6° & 7° – Whales, Bears, Sea-horse, Fulmars, &c. seen.

May 15th. Fine weather, but cold. thermometer at 6°. Several bears came pretty close, but still could not get a shot at them. Performed Divine service. The crang alongside began to smell very unpleasantly; became anxious to remove the ship from it. Got about 6 yards, and were then obliged to give it up. Seahorses, bears, Whales and Fulmars seen.

May 16th. Charming fine weather; out with the boats, & cut a passage thro' the ice for the ship: this was effected, and we got into another bight of the field. No symtones [*sic*] of the ice opening; found by our observations that we were [setting?] very fast to the S.Wward. Ther. [at?] 8°. Bears, unicorns, Sharks, Fulmars &c. seen.

---

[1] What Steward was describing resembles the following passage in Scoresby, *An Account of the Arctic Regions*, II, p. 307: 'Into the square-hole in the bottom of the speck-trough, is fitted an iron-frame, to which is suspended a canvas tube or "hose", denominated a *lull*. The lull is open at both ends. Its diameter is about a foot, and its length sufficient to reach from the deck to the bottom of the hold.' However it is not possible to read Steward's manuscript as 'hose'.
    [2] Scoresby 11 May, recorded the whale as a male.

May 17th. Moored ship & made all snug. Ice as close as ever; nothing to do but eat & drink: Could not even shoot a bear, they would not come close enough. [More?] to the south westward, if we go much more we shall be down to Jan Mayen. Therm. 12°. Fulmars seen.

May 18th. Fine clear weather; got under weigh; moved about a mile from a place, we thought likely we might escape this miserable place. We would have gone father [*sic*], but it turned out very thick, and we could not see a ship's length before us. Sent a boat in pursuit of a sea horse, but could not catch it. The ugly devil frightened even the seamen.

May 19th. Thick weather and calm. Towards evening determined to move again if possible. Set a heavy press of sail: and by the aid of the boats breaking it before us, we moved about 4 miles – Moored as it was thick, near the field edge. – Therm. 16°. Fulmars & Bears seen.

May 20th. Thick disagreeable weather: the ice seemed running rapidly to the westward; nearly lost our rudder by it. In the afternoon moved the ship into a bight of the field edge. Thermom. 20°. Bears & fulmars seen.

May 21st. Got the ship under weigh, and moved her thro' some bay ice and into open water; we now had some hopes of clearing her from this place. Moored her to a field, and went onboard the Sisters Captain Marshall. Thermom. 20°. Bears & Fulmars seen.

May 22nd. Early in the morning got under weigh, as we perceived that the ice to which we had moored, was packing, and the place closing altogether. Stood to windward and at noon hove to, to perform Divine service. In the afternoon made sail again and passed thro' some pack ice to windward; with difficulty, we warped out; the weather at the latter part of the work was uncommonly thick. When clear the ship was lyed too under [brine?] ice. Thermom. 22°. Fulmars &c.

May 23rd. Light airs and hazy weather; just as badly off now as ever, although we have taken so much trouble to get clear, surrounded by bay ice. Captain Marshall with us all day.[1] Therm. 24°. Seals, Fulmars &c. seen.

May 24th. Thick weather and almost calm: all hands set to work to move the ship, towards a place which seemed to be open; ice cut thro' with saws and heaving away upon warps. Hardly stirred an inch; with the assistance of 4 ships companys (Sisters, Harmony, Duncombe, & Perseverance) comprehending about 300 hands, we succeeded in getting her thro' some very thick ice; the labour was incredible; the ice thro' which we moved was about 15 feet thick! but all consisted of several layers of bay-ice; the Sisters followed up close in our rear, but the ice closed so extremely fast,

---

[1] Scoresby did not mention this return visit in his journal.

that she was completely nipped again; when we were thro', we discharged the hands belonging to the other ships; and intended to have sent all our's to <u>their</u> assistance, but it was too late; She was so much set fast by ice, that it would not have been in the power for as many men again to have released her. It was however agreed [*sic*] that as the Esk was clear, she should [post?] away to the intended place, and if there should be any fair prospect, to hoist her <u>ensign</u>. We made sail to the S.W. passed through some more bay ice; but it was of a much looser nature. Soon we came up between two large floes of ice, and there seemed to be a passage between them, which might possibly set us free, at least into another much fairer place. On coming close to it, it appeared very dangerous, as the passage was <u>very</u> narrow, and should the ice be closing we should inevitably have been lost; but we had been so long beset, and without any favourable appearance, that it was determined on to risk her. She ran thro' it with less trouble than was apprehended: some quantity of loose ice obstructed ['it' *deleted*] her. At this exploit, a ['beam' *deleted*] ray of joy enlightened the hearts of all of us: All were interested at it. The Ensign is hoisted immediately; hoping that our worthy contacts may perceive it, and commence getting out. This place of water appeared to have been open but a very short time, perhaps yester & today. Several unicorns seen on entering; we hope from this to see some whales, as they are generally together – Therm. 22°. Fulmars, roaches &c. seen.

May 25th. Fresh breezes and cloudy weather. [***] to windward, up to the NE of the floe, where we moored. From the mast-head there seemed to be an opening into some water on the other side of the floe, which we were in hopes was the sea. Cap*tain* S. and myself went unto [*sic*] the ice to examine this place. An opening there certainly was: but the ice was setting down very fast to leeward: by the clashing of these immense bodies of ice together, hummocks of 20 & 30 feet high were raised, accompanied by a noise similar to thunder. It was a dreadfull sight to see it. If our poor ship had been between, it would have crushed her to attoms. Great quantities of this ice (hummocks) when broken appeared a reddish colour, which I cannot account for. On comming onboard again. we found some difficulty to reach the ship, as the bay ice was running at the rate of 2 & 3 knots per hour – We made sail and ran down to leeward, amongst some bay ice where we stuck fast. Got a warp & towline out, and hove away again to windward, to get clear; after 8 or 10 hours hard labour (for it was blowing hard), we reached this place, where we came from. Raw weather. Therm at 22°. Birds seen &c.

May 26th. Fresh breezes of wind and cloudy weather; At about 8 AM, the passage which examined [*sic*] rapidly opened to about 300 or 400 yards in the course of half an hour. Made sail immediately for it, and ran thro'. We now considered ourselves entirely free; made sail to windward (NE) and passed thro' a great quantity of strong pack ice. The Ship thumped very violently against some pieces, but it could not be avoided. After getting clear of it stood to the eastward, and at night came up into a fine clear place of water. Plyed more to windward and endeavoured to get fast to a floe of ice, but as it was blowing so strong, the ice anchor would not hold us. To the eastward of us the blink of the sea was visible;

and get there we must wait untill it opens more. Thermom. 16°. Fulmars and a land bird (Chesick) seen.

May 27ᵗʰ. Gales of wind and dirty weather all day: [Stretched?] to the eastward and made a stream of ice, which was now the only seperation between us and the sea: Stood to windward and at times lyed too; struck a piece of ice dangerously by the quarter, so as to set all the bells ringing and knock everything off the table. At one time thought we were beset again, but the weather clearing up a little more discovered the mistake. Therm. 22°. Fulmars, Kittywakes, & snow birds seen – a very [coarse?] night.

May 28ᵗʰ. Fresh breezes and moderate weather; saw two sail at sea; made sail, and forced thro' the sea stream into the sea; reached to the Southward about 12 miles, then tacked and stood to the Eastward: at 4 P.M. wind easing round to the Southward and 8 to S.W. ward. Steered to NNW. for the ice again: in the afternoon charming fine weather. Endeavoured to get [a?] lunar distance, but the distance was too great. Therm. 24°. Fulmars, Snow birds, Burgomasters, Dufkeys[1] and Kittiwakes seen.

May 29ᵗʰ. Gentle breezes and very cloudy. Towards the afternoon wind came more round to the westward. Two ships hove in sight, supposed them to be Hamburghers but on their coming nearer discovered one to be from Bremen. Both these ships got fast in the afternoon. In the evening 34 sail in sight; most of them amongst the ice to the westward. Reached to the Northward. At 8 P.M. a whale seen; threw all aback, and down boat after him; made sail again and kept the boat on the watch. The sea for these two last days was of a muddy green colour, which is of course the best for the fishing. This green muddy colour I observed on our first approach to the land; the blink of the land was distinctly visible to the eastward this morning. Therm. 26° at night fell to 22°. Whales, Unicorns, Sea horse, Fulmars & Duffkeys seen.

May 30ᵗʰ. Moderate weather and very cloudy; reached in amongst the ice, and amongst many sail of ships – Made sail down into a lee bight of the ice. At 11 A.M. a fish was struck, at 11ʰ 30ᵐ the second harpoon was struck: at 1 P.M. she was towed alongside and at 3ʰ 30ᵐ finished flinching. Whilst flinching shoot [sic] several birds. Made sail again from the ice to which we were moored; and worked to windward. In getting under weigh, the stern post seemed to be sprung;[2] I hope this may not prove a future danger. The carpenter was set to work to remedy it. At night passed a sea stream of ice, and worked to sea. Made all ready for making off; intending to have begun, but the night

---

[1] Probably the Black Guillemot, *Cepphus grylle*. In *Account of the Arctic Regions*, I, p. 532, Scoresby identified this bird as 'COLYMBUS *grylle*. – Tysté or Doveca' and 'dufkey' is probably a variant of the latter term. It is distinguished by its red legs and the white patches on its wings from the Common Guillemot, *Uria aalge* (Scoresby's 'COLYMBUS *Troile*. – Foolish guillemot or Loom.'). Tystie and Loom remain the Shetland names for these species (Butler, *Isle of Noss*, p. 45).

[2] Layton, *Dictionary*: 'Said of a wooden mast or spar when it is strained, or partly fractured by excessive stress.'

seemed inclined to be very coarse. – Sea of a thick green colour. Therm. 26°. Whales, Unicorn, Seals, Kittywakes, Snowbirds and Fulmars seen during day.

May 31ˢᵗ. Gale of wind with coarse snowy weather, throughout day; heavy sea running. In the afternoon it moderated a little; kept standing to windward. Towards evening as the swell was much less began to make off. Thermometer at 28°. A piece of wood seen floating in the sea, but could not tell from whence it came. Fulmars, Dufkeys, Looms, Snowbirds and Kittywakes seen –

June 1ˢᵗ. More moderate weather, with much less heavy sea on. Several sail hove in sight to leeward. Stood to windward towards the blink of the ice. Finished making off. In the afternoon very fine weather, but very cloudy. Therm. 26°. Malemokes[1] and dufkeys seen.

June 2ⁿᵈ. Gentle airs and cloudy; towards evening clear weather. Several Whales blowing, kept the boats constantly on the watch; latter part calm. Blink of the [land?] seen. Seals and birds seen. Thermometer 28°.

3rd[2] Light airs and at intervals calm. At 8 A.M. a fish was struck and in an hour after was dead. At 9 A.M. another was struck in by the ice. In the capture of the latter, they were attacked by a Sea Horse, which with difficulty they repulsed, constantly keeping in the boats wake, and diving down and comming up on each side her. Got them both towed alongside and flinched. The tail of the largest fish measured twenty feet from the one extremity to the other. At midnight made sail again to westward, as a fresh breeze sprung up. Spoke, or rather Broomed the Dee of Scotland, she had nine fish. Brooming is the general method of knowing the number of fish any ship has. That is a Broom is stuck up in some part of the ship, where the other ship can see it; She answers by lifting the broom up, and beating it down, so many time as she has fish.[3] Thermometer at 22°. Fulmars, Kittywakes, a wild Goose, and an immensity of seals seen.

June 4ᵗʰ. Light winds and fair weather, at time very cloudy. Turning to windward[4] all day. At noon amongst the ice. At night almost calm – Therm. 22°. Kittywakes &c.

---

[1] The fulmar, *Fulmarus glacialis*. See *OED*, s.v. malduck. Butler, *Isle of Noss*, p. 45, gives the current Shetland name as 'maalie'.
[2] This date omits the month, and is not indented. It suggests that Steward had begun writing the entry before remembering to date it.
[3] Scoresby did not mention this contact in his journal, and did not use the term 'brooming'. Note also that Steward did not mention the more informative contact with the *Henrietta* on the same date (Scoresby 3 June).
[4] Smyth, *Sailor's Word Book*: 'WINDWARD SAILING, OR TURNING TO WINDWARD. That mode of navigating a ship in which she endeavours to gain a position situated in the direction whence the wind is blowing'. But Steward's account differs from Scoresby 4 June, in which he says 'proceeded then the rest of the day to the Eastward by the wind.' Steward used the term 'turning to windward' again on 6 June.

June 5th. Light breezes and fair weather, standing to the Eastward. At 4[h] 30 A.M. a fish was struck; to windward: and at 5 A.M. another was struck; a long way to windward: All boats sent off to assistance. I went in one, and had the pleasure of being up at the death. This Fish was chiefly killed by the able assistance of a boat from the Manchester of Hull.[1] We got her towed alongside and ran down to leeward after the other fish. got her alongside also; and flinched them both. When finished made sail again, as we were a long way to leeward, near some ice to the Eastward. At 7 P.M. another large fish was struck but which dyed very easily; got her alongside and flinched her. After all was completed made sail. Several sail in sight, all day. Therm 28°. Burgomasters and Kittywakes seen.

June 6th. Moderate breezes of wind & thick cloudy weather with showers of small snow. Turning to windward all day. In the afternoon several Whales seen and at night sent some boats away. The weather came on particularly thick, and the boats were a long way off; at midnight became rather anxious after them – Therm 28°. Two Sea Parrots, Kittywakes, Burgomasters and Fulmars seen.

June 7th. Still intolerable thick weather, could see nothing of the boats. A 3[h] 30[m] a fall was called; the weather cleared up, and the boats were visible. After a very easy death, she was towed alongside. We then understood from the Harpooner, that he had been fast to his fish an hour and an half, but owing to the thick weather, it was not perceived by the ship. The Fish was particularly easy with him, not taking out more than 4½ lines; they had all their jackets hoisted on their oars[2] but all to no purpose. Flinched her, and made sail again. Light airs and Cloudy all day. Thermom. 26°. Kittywakes and Sea parrots seen. At 10[h] P.M. another fish was struck; towed him alongside and began flinching.

June 8th. Continued flinching the last fish, sent two boats away, and at 1[h] A.M. a fish was struck; all hands broke off, and went to the assistance of the fast boat. In 28 minutes she was dead, and began towing alongside. This fish was a great beauty, as she was <u>piebald</u>. After flinching the first, flinched her. Got every thing in order, and sent some more boats out. Calm and cloudy about noon – In the afternoon the John of Greenock hove in sight to the Eastward; bore away for her. At midnight came up her. Mr Scoresby Senior accompanied by Captain Jackson[3] came onboard the Esk, and after spending a short time with us, returned to their ship. They left with us a newspaper containing the important and gratifying intelligence of the Dethronement of Buonaparté! and by the very flattering accounts of political affairs, it appears that

---

[1] The 'New' Manchester or Manchester II, as Scoresby's account makes clear.

[2] Raising the oars was a signal that a whaleboat was running out of whale-line; the coats were presumably draped on the oars to try to make them more visible through the fog. See Account of the Arctic Regions, II, pp. 245–6.

[3] This phraseology appears to suggest that Thomas Jackson had already assumed the captaincy of the John from his father-in-law. It is more probable, however, that Steward called him 'Captain Jackson' because he had earlier commanded other merchant vessels. In My Father, pp.178–9, Scoresby clearly indicated that the transfer of captaincy took place after the John's 1814 voyage.

Europe will soon enjoy the blessings of an universal Peace. May God grant it – Therm. today at 26°. Kittywakes, Fulmars, & Looms seen.

June 9th. Strong gales of wind all day. The John is windward of us. In the afternoon began the horrid operation of Making Off. However it is a pleasant thing having a [pretty?] decent Flinch [Gut?] to deal with. Several sail insight; under the lee of [some] ice to Westward. Therm. 25°. Few birds seen.

June 10th. Blowing a hard gale of wind all day, with snow & thick weather. Continued the laborious operation of making off and by the afternoon completed filling the third tier of Casks in the aftermast hold. Broke open on the fore hold, but the weather comming on so bad, were forced to give it up, and make all sail to windward, as we were down on the sea ice. In the morning the boat of the Vigilant of London came onboard, stating the misfortune of his recently injuring his rudder: sent our Blacksmith to his reliefs. Therm. today 21°. Thousands of Malemokes in our wake.

June 11th. Less wind, and cloudy weather with snow; working to windward; no fish seen. towards the evening almost calm. Gummed [***] whale bone. Thermometer at 32°. No whales seen Fulmars & Kittywakes in abundance.

June 12th Wind came about early in the morning land in sight: British Cape bearing ['Nb' *deleted*] E.b.N. 20 miles. Bore away to the S.E. and at 9 A.M. Vogel Hook bore E.b.N. The summit of this immense high land was immersed in the clouds. A great quantity of snow seemed to have gone from it since we last saw it. Augusta of Hull in sight; her boats boarded us, thinking we were full & on our passage home.[1] They informed us of some of the ships which were beset with us. The Juno & Alfred have had some most dreadfull [jambs?] by the Ice. One of them[2] was obliged to be <u>sunk</u> with water, untill her beams were level with the ice, in order to withstand the pressure with more ease; The other by the pressure of the Ice was slewed on her beam ends. Her lower yards being on the Ice. A great number of Razor-Backs seen, lowered down boats after some whales also, after standing to the N.W. for a few miles. Stood again to the W.N.W. A white whale seen: two sail in sight, one on the weather, the other on the lee quarter: At 10 P.M. fell in with a vast of Whales; lowered down all the boats. At midnight serene weather with Gentle breezes. Therm. in morn. 34°. towards night fell to 28° –

June 13th. Serene weather with light airs of wind: boats a long way from the ship. At 1h A.M. could just discern the jack of a fast boat to windward. Made all sail for her; and by the time we reached her, the fish was dead. Got her towed alongside, and flinched. At 9 A.M. two harpooners each struck a fish at the same instant; one of

---

[1] Scoresby recorded this visit on 11 June, and that date is probably correct. Steward's version suggests that, after writing that the *Augusta* was in sight, he realized that the earlier visit had not been recorded by him.

[2] The *Juno*, according to Scoresby 11 June.

them appeared to be a very large one, as she hung a great strain on the rope. Unfortunately the other boats could not reach her before she ran away with all the lines, and was loose. The other fish was managed very well; boats got to her assistance and she was killed in a little time. The 1st Mate also got fast but his harpoon drew: this fish did not take out more than 2 fathoms of line, and therefore was but slightly fast. All the disengaged boats continued in chase of the lost fish, and at 11h 30m A.M. came up with her: they struck another harpoon in, and were thus fast again. This was very pleasing, as the loss of 7 lines would have been great. In 20 minutes she was dead. Her short time in dying must have been owing to her extreme fatigue, towing so much line after her. Beat the ship to windward and soon got her alongside. Made sail to windward again, after the other fish. At meridian charming fine weather; land in sight during all these operations – At 2 P.M. Cape Sitoe [sic] bore East dist 25 miles - Came up with the other fish and made her fast on the weather quarter. After flinching the other fish flinched her. Made sail again to the Westward. At midnight came on cloudy with a fresh of wind. Thermom. 34°. Seahorses, Fulmars &c. seen.

June 14th. Fresh breezes and cloudy thick weather in the morning. The Ship's company employed in Bending the lines onto the harpoons, coiling the ropes in the boats – Setting up Shakes Gumming Whale bone and many other jobs necessary to be done [.] By the afternoon reached within 15 miles of the land on the Starboard tack, Tacked Ship. The North End of the Foreland bearing East and the land between Hamburgh Bay & British Point N.E. In the Afternoon commenced Making Off. Started in the Fore-Hold; and by midnight, got 18 tons of blubber or so stowed away. At that time nearly calm with Cloudy weather. Got several sketches of the land; as it was tolerably clear to the Eastward. Thermometer at 32°. Looms, Kittywakes & Fulmars seen.

June 15th. Fine weather, with light breezes of wind. Continued making off, having completed the fore hold; and began starting the After Hold. At Noon the lofty land was visible above the clouds, which skirted the horizon. The Cooper employed setting up Shakes. At 8 P.M. a fish was struck to windward: immediately broke off making off. [***], and dispatched boats to the fast one & chased her till midnight when there was no appearance of getting another harpoon into her. She seemed to run very freely on all sides; at midn. a very long way to windward, but the weather was still very fine with light airs of wind. Made all sail possible towards her. Two sail in sight: One the Vigilant of London, the other the High Flyer of Hull. Therm. 31°. Looms, Fulmars, & Kittywakes seen.

June 16th. Dark clouds rising from to windward, and a very great appearance of Bad Weather: became very anxious concerning the Boats. Early in the morning the Fast Boat with 2 or 3 others alongside her, could just be seen from the masthead. But no omen of another harpoon [***] on her. At about 2 A.M. one of the boats came alongside, and gave us a very deplorable account of the rest. All 6 Boats had been lashed [***] the line; still she seemed to drag them along with as much ease as before. In fact there seemed to be no possibility of ever getting her alongside. Harpooners who had been here upwards of 20 years, said they never remembered an instance like the present! To give her the boat seemed the only thing left: A cask was conveyed to the fast boat; the crew taken out, and thus the fish had a good drogue at her back. When the men came onboard they were quite overpowered with fatigue and hunger, having been absent 15 hours, most of them pulling in the boats to windward. Many (in the [***] of a Fall being called), went away without Jackets, wigs or hats, and were thus exposed to the inclemency of Greenland weather. We now began to turn the ship up to windward as far as we could. A Dead fish, (a whale) was seen by one of the Boat-steerers; and to her we directed our course. Got a warp fast to her and towed her for some distance. Dispatched another boat to the boat which ['we' *deleted*] had been quitted, and Made sail towards her. But now a Gale of wind came on, and in a very short time a tremendous sea was risen. It was now necessary to let both dead fish, and fast one alone, therefore cut her off, and made sygnal [*sic*] for the boat to Leeward to cast off the fast boat. She obeyed it. On their comming onboard, They were in the most eminent danger; the gig was mostly full of water; up to the [thwarghts?] [***] several [***]for the other to assist her in getting thro' such a heavy sea. But thro' the Goodness of a Divine Being they both reached the ship in safety. The sails were all close reefed, and we stood to windward; Very dark and thick; with rain for the first time this year. Therm 36°. Kittywakes and Fulmars seen.

June 17th. Dark dismal weather, with a thick fog all day – early in the morning the wind came round; but still it blew very hard; with a heavy sea. At 4 P.M. fell in with the dead fish, we had yesterday abandoned. Sent away boats to get ropes fast to her; and after considerable trouble got her alongside. She was however at least half eaten away by the sharks; all the back was gone. She had now an insufferable stench attatched to her, but however the Blubber was much better to cut than was expected. Flinched her. Whilst flinching her, to our great supprise [*sic*] the fast boat's jack came floating with a few yards of the ship! This seemed marvelous: the jack had got afloat when the men quitted her for the last time, and it had come floating down to leeward during the recent gale. This clearly indicated to us the boat must be directly to windward, and thither we made sail immediately in search of her. Therm. 35°. Fulmars and Roaches seen.

June 18th. Fresh breezes of wind and cloudy weather, in general thick. Early in the morning got sight of our boat to windward. Made all sail possible, and soon came up with her. Brought the Ship up with the Floating Anchor, but it unfortunately got foul, and thereby was not very beneficial. After considerable exertion, with all hands at work, we succeeded in getting all the 9 lines on board. Fortunately the weather was very moderate during our operations, or we should [probably?] have lost lines, boat & all. Made sail again to windward (towards the Ice). We have had more Bad Weather and have been longer from the Ice this last week than any other during our being in Greenland. We began now to be rather short of Fresh Water, and it was therefore requisite we should make the ice again in order to procure some.[1] At

---

[1] Scoresby did not mention this need in his journal.

midnight a Gale of wind came on with thick Fogs. Thermometer 34°. Kittywakes, Fulmars and Roaches seen.

June 19th. Dark dismal Thick weather. The autumnal bad weather apparently comming on. Hard gale of wind all day. In the morning reached into some Brash ice to the windward. Continued all day beating to windward; at times lying too. In the afternoon sent all hands to bed for 6 hours, as we intended Making off. Under close reefed topsails. Therm. 35°. Seals, a Whale or Finner, Fulmars and Looms seen.

June 20th. Fresh gales, cloudy, thick, and rainy; at 1 A.M. started making off with all hands, and by the afternoon finished, having made off about 30 tons in the main and fore hold. At night moderate weather and winds; made more sail and stood to the Northward[.] at midnight came amongst Whales. Therm. 34°. Fulmars, Kittywakes and Seals seen.

June 21st. Thick, dirty weather, with showers of rain; Light winds. Boats away most of the day. Lying too almost all day, except running an hour or two to the N.b.W. Several sail in sight fishing: Therm. 33°. Fulmars, Kittywakes &c. seen.

June 22nd. Light winds and cloudy weather. The Sisters hove in sight a long way to leeward. Bore down for her. Lowered away a boat just before we came up to her, and at 10h the harpooner struck a Whale. This fish proved to be somewhat similar to the one we lost last week, as she was very violent. Fortunately she played her pranks to leeward, and therefore did not fatigue the boats so much. One boat on making her approach to strike in another harpoon, was stove sunk. The Crew fortunately saved from being drowned, by another boat being near her. Another boat was materially injured. It realy [sic] was an anxious sight to those onboard, as the boats were all exposed to the greatest danger. But what's danger to the Greenland Sailor! He <u>must</u> in order pursue his employment with credit to himself, risk all danger. Our hardy and undaunted Chief Mate was exposed more than the generality of them: the fish's tail many times passing over his head, like the thong of a Coachmans whip. With the salutary assistance of our worthy friend Captain Marshall, we made the capture after 5 hours. Towed her alongside and flinched her. Spoke Mr Marshall and heard that he had escaped from the place of his being beset only one week! However since that time, he had been tolerably fortunate in the fishing. Thus we left the Sisters highly grateful for the favour bestowed on us. After flinching made sail to windward. At 9h another fish was struck, on the lee quarter. He took out 6 lines and dyed easily; this fish was a <u>Sucker</u>, supposed to have left its mother but a fortnight or so. The Surgeon extracted its ears for me, which I think are rather curious. I also preserved some of the animalcula[1]

---

[1] Difficult to read in the text but the marginal note is much clearer. *OED* defines this as the plural of animalcule, 'a small or tiny animal' or 'an animal so small as to be visible only with the aid of a microscope'. *OED* also notes rather superciliously that 'By the ignorant the latter [i.e. animalcula] is sometimes made a sing*ular* with the pl*ural animalculæ*'. Even the ignorant, it seems, are assumed to know the declension of Latin nouns!

which are found on the skin. Those I put into Spirits of Wine. Got flinching done, and all clear. Made sail again. Therm 31°. Sea of a light, thick Green colour. Burgomasters, Kittywakes, and Fulmars and Ducks seen.

June 23rd. Fresh breezes, which increased to a gale of wind at midday with cloudy and thick weather. Early in the morning John of Greenock close to us. Mr Scoresby Senior came on board the Esk and spent much of the morning with us. After his leaving us, we got sight of an old Whale and its young one, which we chased for [1½?] hour. They ran rapidly to leeward for a considerable distance, then turned directly in the winds eye. The Jane of Aberdeen pursued them also, and at last got fast to the young one. A Gale comming on, we were obliged to give up the chase, and run into some pack ice to the Westward, where we remained for some time. In the Afternoon came out and began to make off our blubber. At midnight the wind was moderate but cloudy. Therm. 31°. Fulmars seen. Sea of a light clear blue color [sic].

June 24th. Moderate breezes of wind, and clearer weather. Finished making off at 2h A.M., which completed the hold, and a cask or two extra. On completing the hold, the crew gave three Huzars. At 3h 30m a fish was struck, and quite unexpectedly too: in an hour and an half she was killed[,] towed her alongside: ['and deleted] flinched her. About this time very light airs, and at times thick. Made sail again and about noon ran to leeward round a point of shear ice. Hauled our wind again round the Sea Stream of ice, and beat to windward. Thick weather with fresh breezes of wind. At 10h 40m A Large fish was struck to leeward. Turned the ship up to windward. In half an hour we pereceived to our great mortification she was loose: occasioned by the breaking of the harpoon. Got our boats on board again by midnight. Gale of wind comming rapidly on. Therm. 30°. Fulmars & Kittywakes seen. Sea suddenly turned of a beautiful green colour.

June 25th. Strong gales of wind; reached out to sea. Thick weather with snow & rain. In the afternoon more moderate. Made sail to the westward, and came up with some pack ice. Many sail in sight, tacked to windward. Ran to Eastward for some distance, then hauled up north. [Continued?] so all night. Therm. 34°. Fulmars & roaches seen.

June 26th. Moderate weather and breezes; cloudy. Ice to Leeward. Working to windward and lying too all day. Several Whales seen. Had a Loose Fall for most of the day, but were very unsuccessful. Many ships on both sides struck fish. Thick with snow [***] [***]. Therm. 31°. Fulmars seen.

June 27th. Strong gale of wind, with thick weather, and rain & snow. Spoke the Sisters, and got some intelligence of the unfortunate fate of some ships which were beset with us. All of which seem to be badly fished. Lying too most of the day and working to windward. Ice to leeward. Whales, Fulmars & Kittwakes seen. Therm. 31°.

June 28th. Pleasant weather. Light breezes and cloudy for the most part of the day clear, no fog. Many whales seen. Boats down for much of the day but extremely unsuccessful; Most of these fish seemed to be [stragglers?] running very fast to wind-ward. John of Greenock in sight amongst the ice about [***] miles distant. At midnight [***] to windward, ice being to the westward. Therm. 35°. Fulmars, Kitty-wakes, and Looms seen.

June 29th. Fresh breezes with cloudy weather. In the morning [***] to windward. The Mary[1] of Hull hove in sight in the S.S.W., with her ensign for going home. At 12 came up with her; put letters on board, and received some very gratifying news, namely Peace with all nations, excepting America! Imprisonment of Buonopartè! and that a Ship of the line[2] and two Frigates were cruising in Greenland, in order to repulse the Americans, should they attack the trading ships. After this made all sail to the West-ward, as there appeared to be Whales there. Continued all day with an heavy press of canvass set, endeavouring to get to the westward. Passed thro' many streams of Ice. At midnight going at the rate of 6 or 7 knots on the bowline. Several sail in sight. Therm. 31°. Seals and Fulmars seen.

June 30th. Fresh breezes and cloudy with thick weather. Got some of the Guns from the 'twixt decks in order to make off,[3] which we commenced at the meridian. Steered E.N.E. for the [Headland?]. At 4 P.M. finished making off: the weather cleared up and we discovered 18 sail of ships; Land on the beam, and a floe of ice to leeward. Spoke the Earl of Fife of Shields, who gave us a vast of news &c. The weather all at once became particularly serene: it fell nearly calm, and we are in danger of drifting on the lee ice. However with the assistance of two boats towing ahead, we succeeded in getting round the point. Steered now N.N.E. None of these ships seemed to be fish-ing. In fact the season seems to be drawing to a close very rapidly. At midnight sailing on the wind (N.N.E.) at about the rate of 4 knots. Seals, Fulmars, Burgomasters &c. seen.

July 1st. Light airs of wind and cloudy. Bore away. At 4h A.M. a fish was struck to windward: that was to all a very joyful circumstance, as we almost despaired of killing any more. All the boats were despatched immediately, and in a very short time she was dead. From the mast head, the Head Land was very visible: I could also distinguish the ice stretching from that land; to the southwestward. The outside of this ice was packed; the rest was the solid Barrier of Ice which extends to the North Pole. Thus it would appear that we could penetrate but 12 miles or so, farther N. It would be impossible to proceede more to the N. this year. When Lord Mulgrave was on his voyage of discovery toward the North Pole,[4] he advanced about 50 or 60 miles farther; but this was under much more favourable circumstances. From this it must

[1] *Mary and Elizabeth*, see Scoresby 29 June.
[2] I.e. a naval vessel carrying 74 or more guns.
[3] As Scoresby's account (30 June) makes clear, the *Esk* was running out of space in which to store casks of blubber.
[4] The Phipps voyage of 1773 with the *Racehorse* and *Carcass*, which reached 80°48′N, or 78 nautical miles north of the *Esk*'s latitude of 79°30′ on 1 July.

appear that the ice varies its direction very much in different years. This change of direction is entirely owing to the winds. Heavy Southerly gales after Winter must render the extremity of the ice packed: the wind then comming from the NorthWestward will force this packed ice from the Solid Ice and in this manner, opens the country more or less, according to the prevalency and strength of these winds. A N.W. wind therefore must render the ice more accessible on account in the first place, of the direction of it being NE. & SW, [also?]; this ice at its extremity being packed, by SE. wind will [drift?] off to the S.E.ward. Last night there appeared to be some streams of packed ice between our ship and Charles's Island, from the North Foreland to Cape Sitoe; NW. wind must therefore have prevailed here whilst we had them from the S.S.E. & SW. I picked up a piece of wood today. It would appear that this wood must come floating from Archangel or Siberia, It was rendered very hard, excepting the outside, which of course must be soft on account of its being in the water so long. It was about 3 feet long; ½ foot in circumference; and had never been chopped or cut. At 8 A.M. got the fish alongside when it fell calm. She appeared to be an old one, and had been struck before. Her blubber cut excellently well. Flinched her, and got all right again. Made sail. Backed down into the lee ice, & tacked again: stood to the southward. It now came on intollerably thick and continued so throughout the rest of the day. At midnight it fell calm – In the morning the sea was of a dark sky blue, and by night had turned to a muddy light green. Therm. 39°. Seals weddings[1] in abundance. Fulmars, Duffkeys and Looms seen.

July 2nd. A continuance of uncommon thick weather, with light breezes of wind. Commenced getting up some of our flying sails. At about 7 A.M. it cleared up more and we discovered the Aimwell of Whitby bearing up for us: upon which we hove too. It however soon came on impenetrably thick again; fired two of the [great?] guns, in order for her to know where we were. At 11 A.M. as it cleared up, she found us and ran down to our weather quarter. Captain Johnston came on board, (Malemoking as called in Greenland), and gave us plenty of news. From him we understood that two American Frigates were in Greenland! Most likely these Frigates are mistaken; there being two English here. At noon bore away round a point of ice, and hauled our wind again. At 8 P.M. a heavy gale of wind came on, which set the pack ice driving to the Eastward. the usual thick weather accompanied the gale[.] Made all snug. Water changed its colour today from Blue to Green. Therm. 30°. Rigging all frozen. Fulmars seen. Several sail in sight. Clapham & Perseverance amongst them.

July 3rd. A continuance of the gale all day, with snow; but in general tolerably clear. Extreme clear weather seems to be peculiar in Greenland. When clear at all, it is very clear, so that ships are visible on the horizon, until just the tops of their masts are seen, a distance of 25 miles or so. Several ships beating to windward with us, to the Westward, standing about 2 hours on each tack, but making the longest reaches to the southward. Being Sunday performed Divine Service. No whales seen. Sea of a dark sky blue colour. Therm. 35°. Fulmars seen.

---

[1] Apparently a euphemism for 'mating'. The word is clearly written.

July 4th. Fresh breezes and very cloudy weather. Worked about 40 miles in amongst packed ice to the NWestward.¹ The Aimwell & Perseverance kept company with us for a considerable distance but by a thick fog then lost sight of us. The wind was very unsteady, varying 4 points. At 9 P.M. on comming (As we supposed) in the extremity of this very deep bight, being [***] rank small pacted [Folows?] of ice, we stood again to the Eastward; the wind came round to the S.S.E. For these last several days the wind has constantly gone round to the Southward at night. Quite moderate winds & weather at latter part of the day. Therm. 32°. Fulmars seen. Sea of a clear light green colour.

July 5th. Fresh breezes and moderate weather. Continued our course for the clear water: at 9 A.M. considered ourselves entirely out from the ice, and therefore bore away N.N.E. At 6 hauled our wind, round a [flow?] of ice to the Northward; and when clear wore and stood on the larboard tack, to get shelter; as a strong gale of wind had every appearance of comming on. Made off the last fish which filled 24 casks; being almost 13 tons. Therm 33°. Fulmars seen.

July 6th. Hard gale of wind, and very serene weather. When the fog cleared up, [it?] discovered the land to us, much nearer than we supposed. This land we had some difficulty of ascertaining. The charts of this land certainly are <u>erroneous</u>. We had an excellent observation on the Sun, which gave us our Latitude with the greatest precision; and then by reference to the charts; it would appear that we were to the Northward of Magdelena Bay.² The contrary was evidently the fact. The Bay was visible to the Northward. It was the most rugged and [curious?] [***] seen immense deep vales almost filled up with snow[.]*³ Thousands of eminences very rocky and rugged above and on the mountains, which seemed towering to the skies. The North end bore East due. At [8?] A.M. The Aimwell [***] was in co. with us, split his main topsail. Still under the lee of the Flow of ice, but it seemed breaking up. It now blew tremendously hard. The ice (4 P.M.) was driving round to the N.E. ward very rapidly; made more sail. At 8 P.M. it came on very thick. Ran down under the lee of another stream of ice, which was part of the ice-stream we just had left. Kept dodging under it. The Aimwell was then out of sight, owing to the thick weather. Blowing very heavy. Therm. 33°. Fulmars seen.

July 7th. Blowing tremendously hard, with an impenetrable thick fog. The ice to windward breaking up fast but the ice ahead still kept massy. Determined to stay yet under it. However at 9 P.M. as we feared very much we must be driving in amongst the north west islands & rocks which were, as I may justly say, hardly explored

¹ The 'N' was inserted above the line, apparently as an afterthought.
² This passage raises difficulties. Scoresby's noon latitude of 79°42′N has a '+' sign attached to it, indicating his belief in its precision, but the aeronautical chart of Spitsbergen shows Magdalene-fjorden at 79°35′N, which is close to where it is shown on Scoresby's own chart of 1820 (*Account of the Arctic Regions*, II, plate IV).
³ Footnote in original: '*These vales which were now visible filled up with snow, or ice, as I suspect, are those Ice bergs mentioned by Lord Mulgrave in Lat. 79. 44. Long. 9 [E?].'

['amongst' *deleted*] enough for a ship to seek relief under in such a gale as this. It was therefore determined on to run to the Westward as well as we could. After passing thro' many streams and Brash ice having bore away with difficulty; and on account of the thick weather which rendered our situation particularly awful & dangerous, we hauled up to the westward and lost sight of the Aimwell – She fired guns which we respectively answered, in order to keep company. After beating about one hour on this tack, with an immense high sea; it blinked up, & we saw a vast of loose washed ice. A stream of packed ice to leeward; the Aimwell on the weather quarter; and the land. This intermission of clear weather was very gratefull to us. At once we knew our situation. We were not so near the islands as we had supposed: But we were on a lee patch of ice, and in amongst brash ice. We had clear weather for the rest of the day, excepting now and then a little thick. ['The' *deleted*] We tacked and stood well in with the land. Being so completely thrown out of all reconning [*sic*], we were at a loss to know which these islands were. On comming closer we made them out. Hackluit's H^dland bore S.W. and the extremity of Rein Deer land bore S.E. by an observation of ⊙ at midnight we found ourselves correct. This land is like the generality of Spitsbergen immensely high. As we came very close to it several beautiful Icebergs were visible, which were Valies filled up with ice. A great quantity of snow had left the mountains, being the latter end of the season; altogether it formed a most picturesque scene. On comming closer, we had less wind & that of the land. At midnight tacked.*¹ Therm. 34°[.] Fulmars & Burgomasters seen.

July 8th. The gale now moderated, and tolerable clear weather ensued. The wind came fair, and we were again satisfied. After standing in with the land until meridian, Tack'd: Cloven cliff bore SW.b.S We had a [***] view of the land from Hackluit's h^d to Cloven cliff, and from thence to the N.E ward land was distinguishable, which I supposed was <u>Deer Field</u>. Worked to windward at some heavy ice stretching NW & SE. About 2 P.M. Cap*tain* Johnstone of the Aimwell came onboard. <u>Malemoking</u> and staid the rest of the day. Delightful fine clear weather. At midnight a thick fog under the land: but still the summit was distinctly visible. From our getting so very far North this time, the ice must have been much broken up since the 1st inst, when we were in Lat. 79°50'. The ice was at that time clearly seen stretching from Hackluit's H^d to the W.S.W., and then again to the S.W. From our being able to penetrate so far north, we naturally suppose that navigation might this year be carried on to an immense distance towards the North Pole. We have been within about 10 miles as far as Lord Mulgrave went,² and when we were there, no ice to the Northward was to be seen; not even the blink; except a small pack just to leeward of us, which had drifted from the Southward. What a pleasure would it have been for us to gone as far as the ice would have permitted us! Had it not been irrevalant [*sic*] to our orders we would have performed it. We now intend if possible to take along the ice for a long way to the S.W. At midnight got an observation. Therm. 36°. Fulmars and a Seahorse seen.

---

¹ Footnote in original: '*Got soundings in 70 fathoms. Soft clay & rocks. Our highest lat. 81°N.'
² Scoresby 7 July recorded a latitude of 80°25' at midnight, 23 nautical miles south of Phipps' farthest north.

July 9th. Charming fine weather. At 3 A.M. it came on to blow very heavy but by 9^h it entirely subsided and almost fell calm. We had now a beautiful view of the land; The N. Foreland. Hakluits h^d & the seven Icebergs all distinctly to be seen. The Aimwell in company. Standing to the S.W.ward. At 3 P.M. went aboard the Aimwell, where we continued until night; when a fresh breeze sprung up: but this wind was a foul one. Stood in for the ice. Therm. at noon 46, at night 35°. Kittywakes, Dufkeys & fulmars seen.

July 10th. Fresh breezes and cloudy weather, but no fog. At 5 A.M. fell in with a sea stream of ice. [***] and stood out &c. Performed divine service; After which less wind, which was succeeded by a calm near midnight. In the afternoon had considerable trouble in working to windward of a pack of ice. Our Ship on account of the unsteadyness of the wind, made more lee way, than otherwise. Our Compasses were in a most terrible state for travelling: often differing 8 points or so. Indeed this variation of compasses is in general the case in so high a northern latitude: The magnetic dip being about 80°. A large extent of land still in sight. The Icebergs &c. At midnight calm, and in great hopes it would bring about a change of wind. Sent a boat in search of a White Whale which was seen, which was pursued 4 hours: but ineffectually. Therm. 35°. Fulmars, Kittywakes and Looms seen. Sea of a light green colour.

July 11th. Light airs and cloudy weather: a thick Fog which continued throughout the day. Wind came about, and we stood to the S.W. met with some pieces of packed ice, upon which we sometimes were obliged to haul more to the eastward. Ship going in general at about the rate of 3 knots per hour, Towards midnight calm. Aimwell not in sight, owing to the Fog. Therm. 33°. Fulmars & roaches seen.

July 12th. Early in the morning a fresh breeze sprung up from the N.W. It is extrordinary [sic] what an immense number of winds from the Southward we have had: it is rather an unfortunate thing as we are so far North and want to get along the ice. Having stood a considerable distance to the westward amongst the ice, we tacked and stood in towards land. A vast many streams of ice obstructed our passage thither but however it was clear and therefore not much danger was to be apprehended. At 2 P.M. we had come in with the land untill we were not more or rather less than a mile from Vogel Hook. A great quantity of packed ice seemed to have been driven out from Foreland Fiord to sea. Having come in untill we [sounded?] 12 fathoms on the [rocks?], we hove aback. We had suddenly showed our water from 17 fms to 12. The bottom appeared to be sharp pointed coral rock. The lead was very much cut, and a vast quantity of of red rock was brought up. We threw our fishing lines out, but caught nothing; a quantity of seaweed was brought up, some of which I have preserved. Being now so near the land I had a good opportunity seeing it well. The summit of this land which is about a mile in heigth, ['as we' deleted] was immersed in clouds. Directly opposite us is one of the most extraordinary natural phenomena that Spitsbergen ['produces' deleted] exhibits – Namely a pyramidal mountain. This mountain gradually tapers untill it reaches the top, in regular steps. It has a fine view of the Seven hills whose tops [***] I could not see, on account of clouds &c. Cap*tai*n Scoresby some years was on shore here: he then discovered a large huts [*sic*], which had been built by some Russians, who had been transported here for some misdemeanour. In it he found some flour, meal and other necessaries. The men were all dead. Today we saw the [very?] same hut, apparently in good condition! It was a square one; we could distinctly discern the court yard, & chimney. It stood on a small eminence under the most [huge?] of the land. However <u>we did not land; we could not I suppose; but for what reason I know not. A better opportunity, we could not have had.</u>[1] The water over these rocks was of a beautiful green colour – Several large Seahorses came up close to the ship. A strong tide was setting to the North Eastward. In about an hour the Aimwell came up with us. He threw all aback and sounded, and we both made sail to the westward again. It then came on thick. At midnight perfectly calm. Therm. 35°. Burgomasters. Kittywakes, Looms, Dufkeys, and a Land bird seen.

July 13th. A light fair breeze[2] sprung up and we shaped our course to the South Westward but ice was now completely between us & the Southward; & for what we were able to see, we must be in a very disagreeable situation. Cannot get to the Southward. How and when shall we reach dear England? An immense distance from it as yet – and no apparent chance of getting clear. The season is advanced, and no ships in company with us but the Aimwell. Never mind – sailors must never be down hearted. We shall get clear one time or other. – At meridian a great quantity of heavy ice all around us; [put?] boats and towed: the Middle Hook in sight bearing S.E. It continued calm, with a few intermissions of light airs from all points of the Compass untill midnight. In the evening it came on, with the thickest weather, I think, I have ever seen in Greenland; and in consequence of it ran foul of a Flow of ice; however no injury was sustained; and with aid of boats towing we weathered it. We fired guns as usual for the Aimwell to keep company and also blew the Bugle Horn. I was surprised to hear what an enormous echo there was; this I suppose was owing to the Fog. Therm. today at 36°. Looms, Roches & Fulmars seen.

July 14th. Early in the morning a fresh breeze sprung up. But as [usual?] a foul one. Stood in for Cape Sitoe, which we made in about 4 hours. Then kept standing about an hour on each tack, untill it fell calm in the afternoon. Here we met with an immense number of a sort of Sea fly: evidently a small shell fish; of a most peculiar & delicate texture; being of a beautifull purple [about?] its fins – and its body of a [***] colour. It was very small, and of a round figure. The water was here of a fine light blue colour. At midnight we had a light air from the Northward. Therm 33°. Very

---

[1] This account, evidently told by Scoresby to Steward, can easily be confused with that which appears in *Account of the Arctic Regions*, I, pp. 118–35; both for example include mention of visiting living huts and finding the bodies or skeletons of Russians. However, the visit described in *Account of the Arctic Regions* is clearly dated late July 1818 and was 'on the north side of King's Bay' on the mainland of Spitsbergen (Kongsfjorden, 78°58′N 12°5′E). What Steward recorded was a description of an earlier landing by Scoresby on Prins Karls Forland; this was mentioned in the *Account*, I, p. 118, and in more detail on p. 141, where the year of the landing is given as 1809.

[2] Originally 'breezes'; 's' deleted.

cold. Rigging of the ship all frozen. Two immense Seals seen two white whales[1] & Dufkeys.

July 15th. Light airs and thick fog. [Passed?] a vast of heavy [land?] ice to the westward. Very warm. Ther*mome*ter being at 45°. A [***] flying from the SW and every appearance of a wind from that quarter. At 3 P.M. it cleared up for about ¼ hour; and Cape Sitoe bore N.N.E. distant 7 leagues. Passed some flows of ice. The Ship going about the rate of 1 or 2 knots per hour – Lost sight of the Aimwell. Towards evening it cleared up, & fell calm: and an hour or two afterwards a gentle breeze sprung up off the land. Seventeen sail now in sight: one of them we supposed to be a ship of war, standing on the other tack. Continued our [rout?][2] the land and at midnight began to [dip?] the N. Foreland: the S. end of Prince Charles's island nearing E.b.S dist. 8 leagues. Charming fine weather. My chief amusement now was catching Mice. The whole ship was swarmed with these troublesome vermin. Also rats. Indeed I could not sleep at night, without having these creatures running all over me. My face & every where else. At midnight the wind seemed inclined to Southering. Seahorses – Dufkeys, Looms Seals & Fulmars seen.

July 16th. Delightful weather. Quite clear; and not much ice to intercept us. Wind came round to the southward, & from thence to the westward. At Meridian thick & calm. Towards night [***] 2 boats & towed thro' some very rank packed ice. This ice when it was blowing at all was [joined?] into a sea-stream: but on its falling calm is parted and the different pieces laid very much [askew?]. It would appear that all this ice possessed electricity; and by the positive & negative electricity action on one another they form a pack. When it blows, loose brash Ice combines and forms Streams &c. but when it falls calm, if the ice is at liberty, the electricity of the same [nature?] coming into contact, they mutually part and thus render the ice rank and brash[.] – Towards the latter end of the day, we had for the most part light airs and clear weather. Two[3] sail hove in sight; each on the larboard tack. Therm 44°. Seals, Seahorses, Roaches, Duffkeys, Loons & Fulmars seen.

July 17th. A fresh breeze springing up in the morning, and quite fair, we bore away for England. How pleasant the thought! after having been confined in a dreary place like this. May prosperous winds attend our back and waft us speedily to our homes. Spoke the St. Andrew, who gave us a great deal of news concerning the departure of some of our friends to Britain &c. I observed a Fog. sucker, as it is called, or an appearance during the fog similar to a rain bow.[4] The Britania & Manchester in

[1] Previous three words inserted above the line.
[2] *OED* cites this variation of 'route' up to the 19th century.
[3] Possibly 'Five'.
[4] Evidently what *OED* and Smyth, *Sailor's Word Book* , identify as a fog-bow. Smyth's description is 'A beautiful natural phenomenon incidental to high latitudes. It appears opposite to the sun, and is usually broad and white, but sometimes assumes the prismatic colours. Indicative of clearing off of mists. (See FOG-EATER.)' Smyth also includes the similar 'fog-dogs.'

company with us all day. Passed through a stream or two of washed ice. We continued our course along the edge of the ice to the S.S.W.. At midnight blowing fresh. Ship going at the rate of 6 or 7 knots per hour. Therm. 35°. Finners, Burgomasters & Fulmars seen.

July 18th. Fresh breezes and cloudy, but delightful weather. At 4 A.M. two strange sail hove in sight, which we supposed to be Men of War – They were hauling in to the eastward – Manchester & Britania still in company about 3 miles to the Eastward of us. At 8 A.M. called all hands and set to work to take down the Crows nest. Rig steering sail & staysails and perform many similar jobs necessary. At meridian it fell nearly calm & remained so for the rest of the day. Spoke the Manchester & Britania: they gave us some news concerning the Fishing – The former said he had not seen fish for 10 days, and knew of no ship which has. The latter stated his having been amongst multitudes of Whales – the master himself was in pursuit of one on Sunday last (yesterday). According to his account, the Whales were running very fast to the westward, towards the ice. He mentioned the various ships which have gone home. All the ships seem to be uncommonly well fished. Therm. 36°. Finners & Fulmars seen.

July 19th. A breeze sprung up directly contrary. Began [***] to windward. Pleasant cloudy weather, Manchester & Britania in co. In the afternoon the captains of the two ships came on board the Esk, and remained most of the day. At midnight rain and light breezes of wind. Tackd and stood in to the westward. Therm 40°. Arctic gulls, Finners & Fulmars seen. Sea of a clear green colour.

July 20th. Light breezes of wind and rainy weather. Continued standing to the westward, untill she fell off to N.W. when we tack'd. No ice was then in sight. At meridian a fresh breeze sprung up quite fair for us, and we crouded [sic] all the sail we could. Today we delivered our instructions to the Manchester and Britania: they having placed themselves under our convoy. Shaped our course S.W. and [carried] the blink of the ice on the starboard beam. At 7 P.M. we passed thro' a loose stream of ice. A strange sail hove in sight to leeward, apparently a whaler. At 9 P.M. passed thro' another stream of loose [breaking?] ice: I hope this will be the last ice we shall fall in with on the passage. For the rest of the day we had fresh breezes and fair weather; The ship going at the rate of about 7 or 8 knots per hour. Therm. 40°. Fulmars, Finners & Arctic gulls (by Linnaeus called Boatswains[1]) seen.

July 21st. Fresh breezes and cloudy weather. the wind seemed much inclined to westering. Continued our course SW. The Britania & Manchester in company. Wind freshened but eastered, therefore took in studdingsails. When close hauled our companions beat us. Nothing particular occurred during the remainder of this day. Therm. 42°. Fulmars and Arctic Gulls seen.

---

[1] It seems improbable that Linnaeus used that term, but 'boatswain', and 'parasitic jaeger' are alternative names for what Scoresby, *Account of the Arctic Regions*, I, p. 534 described as 'LARUS *parasiticus*. Arctic gull' and is now known usually as the Arctic skua, *Stercorarius parasiticus*.

July 22nd. Fresh breezes and cloudy weather: the wind [***][***]. Steered S.S.W close hauled. At meridian fine clear weather, but cloudy. Manchester and Britania in company. At 4 P.M. a strange sail hove in sight: we supposed this strange sail to be the ship, we saw on the 20th inst to leeward: she then appeared to be [stoped?] for the stream of ice. We continued in sight of this Vessel for the rest of the day. Just after meridian it fell calm or nearly so. In the evening we fell in with a great number of large fish, with immense fin on their backs of 6 or 8 feet along, which come to the surface of the water to take breath. ['These fish' *deleted*] No one onboard knew the name of them. Some said they were sword fish. Towards midnight a gentle air sprung up ['from' *deleted*] Set the steering sails &c. Therm. 44°. Fulmars and Arctic Gulls seen.

July 23rd. Fresh breezes and cloudy. All the sails set we can spread. As we were now going free; the Manchester & Britania went [far?] astern, so that at 9 A.M. we were obliged to sail with the Mizen topsail aback: Mainsail up: and no studdingsails set. Yet these are two of the best sailers in Greenland. At meridian a fine wind: Manchester came up: and running away home, at the rate of 7 or 8 knots an hour – The strange sail still in sight, on the same course as ourselves (S.W) – Towards night the wind [***] very much & it came on thick. Passed some sea weed. Sun set to night after a day to us of about 4 months: the sun having been above the horizon all that time. A heavy swell comming from the S.Westward Luffoden island bore E.b.S. by [chart?] dist 120 miles. Ther. 48°. Fulmars, Arctic Gulls & [skates?] seen.

July 24th. Gentle breezes of wind & moderate weather. Our course SW.b.W. Manchester and Britannia in company. Wind seemed inclined to come from the westward; a swell seeming to come from that quarter. Performed divine service. At meridian the ship broke off to NW. Clear weather and the wind freshening. Tacked and stood to the southward. At 8 P.M. a strange sail hove in sight; she seemed running directly before the wind and we supposed her to be bound for Archangel. At night we [were?] flattered by a light air from the Northward, but it was of very short duration. A heavy sea was running most of the day from the Southward and from it there appears to have been a very heavy gale of wind from the Southward. At midnight gentle breezes of wind and cloudy. Therm. 52°. Fulmars and Sea Gulls seen.

July 25th. Gentle breezes and cloudy weather. Still a vey [*sic*] heavy swell on, which continued throughout the day. Fleet in Company, but the Britannia a long distance astern. Our course about South making 2 points leeward. At meridian serene weather. We now suppose ourselves to be not far distant from that dreadfull [rocks?] Maelstrom:[1] and from our longitude we must be not far from the Luffoden Islands. At noon moderate winds & weather. At 6 P.M. a strange sail hove in sight about 10 miles to windward: he was running before the wind with a heavy press of canvass on.

---

[1] Like the Sumburgh Röst, a sea area known for centuries because of its danger to ships. Located at 67°48′N, 12°50′E, its characteristics were modelled in a 1997 paper by B. Gjevik, H. Moe and A. Ommundsen: 'Strong Topographic Enhancement of Tidal Currents: Tales of the Maelstrom.'

On his first perceiving us, he shortened sail, and hoisted his ensignia. We hove too to speak him. As the wind lessened, he was a considerable time comming down: we could not distinguish his flag untill he was close to us, We took him at different times for a Batavian, Russian and Englishman. However, not being ['able to' *deleted*] certain of him, we made signal for the convoy to close. At 11 P.M. he came up, and with a gun from the Esk, we brought him too. Sent a boat onboard him. He furnished us with little news. He was light. From Antwerp bound for Archangel. Belonged to Liverpool his name was the Ann. He had left the Shetland islands but 3 days. He informed us of Monsieur[1] being in France, and expecting to be crowned king of that Nation: that trade was already carrying on between us & the French. Buonaparté was in some island in the Mediterranean. He did not know whether our good Old King was alive or not: so we will still continue to pray for him. An American Frigate had been captured by the English: what their names were, he could not tell.[2] An English sloop of war had been captured by the Americans; but he was also in ignorance concerning their names.[3] Our troops were going on well in America. That [terms?] were to be concluded on, at the end of this month. &c. &c. &c. He had passed several Greenland ships homeward bound. Some so lately as yesterday morning: but it was blowing a hard gale of wind, as was expected, and therefore he could not speak them. After getting our boats onboard, we made sail again, with gentle breezes of wind. Therm. today at 56°. Fulmars seen. A piece of wood seen & some sea weed seen. Sea of a bluish green colour.

July 26th. Gentle breezes and cloudy. At 4 A.M. as the ship broke off very much; we tacked: and the[4] layed W.S.W. good. The wind seemed inclined to freshen. At meridian clear weather with fair breezes of wind. Towards the evening we had thick weather and rain. A heavy sea on. Manchester and Britannia in company. At 8 P.M. the Manchester made signal of a strange sail being in sight: but we could not distinguish her: perhaps owing to the thick weather. At midnight fresh squalls of wind. Reefed topsails &c. Therm 56°. Fulmars and Mother Carey's chickens[5] seen. Piece of wood & sea weed seen.

July 27th. Fresh breezes of wind, and thick disagreeable weather. At 9 A.M. as the ship lyed no higher than W.N.W. We tack'd. A heavy head sea on, which continued throughout the day. At meridian more wind with less thick weather. Convoy in company. Britannia some distance astern. During these last 24 hours we have got well

---

[1] The name by which Louis XVIII was widely known for much of his life.

[2] This may refer to the capture of USS *Frolic* by HMS *Shelbourne* and *Orpheus* on 28 April 1814. This is often referred to as taking place in the 'Florida Passage'. That term, however, now refers to 'A portion of the Atlantic Intracoastal Waterway between Bryan County and Ossabaw Sound' in the state of Georgia (Krakow, *Georgia Place-Names*). The naval incident presumably took place in what is now the Florida Strait, between that state and Cuba.

[3] This latter event was probably the encounter between USS *Wasp* and HMS *Reindeer* in the Western Approaches (48°36′N, 11°15′W) on 28 June 1814.

[4] *Sic*; 'then' presumably intended.

[5] 'Sailor's name for stormy petrels' (*Brewer's Dictionary*, p. 759.)

to the westward, and therefore can now well afford a westerly wind. In the afternoon, took in another reef of the main topsail &c. For the remainder of the day, we had much foggy weather; and rather less wind at midnight. Therm. 54° <u>Fulmars</u>, Sea Gulls & Kittywakes seen. Also a quantity of sea weed seen.

July 28th. Light breezes of wind which subsided into a Calm at 9 A.M. Fogs for the most part. A heavy swell on. At meridian calm [also?] with very thick weather. In the evening a breeze of wind sprung up from S.W. At this time a swell came on from the northward: it came on several times thick from the leeward quarter &c. From this I rather suspected a fair wind – At midnight a steady breeze: rather better. Therm. 56°. Fulmars seen.

July 29th. Fresh and pretty fair gales of wind, with dirty weather. But our fair wind lasted no longer than untill meridian, when it came almost [***] an end. During 9 and 10 o'clock this morning we we¹ going 8 or 9 miles on the bowline.² Manchester & Britannia in comp*any*. In the afternoon it came on immoderately thick & We lost sight of the convoy. The wind comming round to the westward, or towards it, we tack'd ship at 9 P.M. From the badness of the weather we think it probable we have lost of [*sic*] convoy. Therm. 55°. Fulmars seen.

July 30th. Light & variable winds. At 2 A.M. tack'd. Still a continuance of uncommon thick weather. The Britannia in the morning was seen at a considerable distance to windward. Surely they must have seen the Esk: but they never bore down for us. At meridian a fresh breeze sprung up and was tollerably fair for one hour or so, when it scanted us. In the evening we had the thickest weather, we have had during the whole voyage; being scarcely able to see twice the length of the ship. Therm. 57°. Fulmars, Arctic Gulls, and [Young?] gulls seen. Sea of a *light* blue colour.

July 31st. Moderate breezes of wind with rain and thick weather. At 2 A.M. it fell calm, and at 3 A.M. a breeze sprung up, quite fair, it increased to a gale by 5 A.M. when we reefed topsails. At this time the ship was going 12 knots per hour. Our fine wind did not last long: as by 4 P.M. we rigged our royals yards again, out reefs, set steering sails &c. In the evening charming weather: cloudy and moderate breezes of wind. Therm. 52°. Finners, Fulmars, Solan geese, Arctic Gulls, Young Gulls – Brown Gulls – Dufkeys & Mollusca seen. Sea weed seen.

August 1st. Gentle winds and clear weather. In the morning the wind came round. At meridian wind variable, weather and inclinable to rain. At 4 P.M. threw all aback, and got soundings in 80 fms; shells, white and brown specks. Wind came on very strong. In small sails and reefed. Two hours after got soundings again in 80 fms.

---

¹ *Sic*: 'were' presumably intended.
² Smyth, *Sailor's Word Book*: 'A rope ... used to keep the weather-edge of the sail tight forward and steady when the ship is close hauled to the wind; and which, indeed, being hauled taut, enables the ship to come nearer to the wind.'

Coral rock, and fine sand. An hour after that sounding again in 70 fms. Fine sand. Spoke the Manchester, who thought we were on the east side of the Shetland islands, as did ourselves. Soon after She got sounding in 60 fms. Shells &c. At 9 P.M. some land ['hove' *deleted*] in sight, in the N.W. distant about 7 leag. Made more sail; the wind having moderated. This land we supposed to have been the mountains between Haroldswick & Norwick. The wind rather scanting as we tack'd. It now blew hard with a heavy swell on. Manchester tack'd also. At midnight very dark, with heavy thick weather. Therm. 57°. Fulmars, Solan Geese, Dufkeys, Hillocks and small Gulls seen. Sea, where the Sound*ings* were of a light blue colour.[1]

August 2nd. Strong winds and cloudy weather. At day break 5 sail hove in sight. Two in the Northward. Manchester left us and made the best of her way for Brassa Sound. At 5 A.M. some land which we supposed to be the island of Fetlar, bore W.N.W. distant about 7 leagues. Continued our reach to the southward. At meridian fine clear weather, with fresh breezes of wind. At 3 P.M. finding the ship to break off[2] to S.E. we tacked at [*sic*] stood to the westward. The wind came now almost an end; we tacked at 10 P.M. Rainy weather, with fresh breezes of wind. Therm 58° young gulls seen, and Makarell caught. Much sea weed seen. Some mollusca seen.

August 3rd. Rainy weather and the winds rather variable: continued working to windward about an hour on each tack. At meridian fine serene weather. A Brig hove in sight, running down to leeward. Spoke her but she gave us not a word of news. All the rest of this day was particularly beautifull, with light breezes of wind, which towards midnight became tollerably fair with showers of rain. Therm. 60°. Young Gulls seen. Dog Fish & Makerell caught. Abundance of all sorts of sea weed seen.

August 4th. Fresh breezes of wind and clouds, with some rain, early in the morning. As the Sun got higher the wind seemed inclined to Souther: but at meridian it still kept about [West?] At this time we had most charming weather, with light breezes of wind: the ship going about 4 knots. In the afternoon, a strange sail hove in sight, apparently bound for Archangel. We fell in with 18 sail of fishing smacks; but the wind scanting us, at 6 P.M. we tacked, and stood in for the Scotish [*sic*] coast. The wind for the rest of the day was variable – At midnight we tack'd again – Wind inclined to freshen. Therm. 60°. Solan Geese, Young Gulls, Porpoises, and Makarell seen. Much sea weed seen.

August 5th. Strong breezes of wind, with rain. At 3 A.M. tack'd. Towards mid-day it cleared up. In the afternoon we fell in with the Flemish Fishing boats. One of them passed directly under our lee. We waved him, which he answered. In the evening charming fine weather: still blowing very fresh, but much less sea on. Caught an astonishing number of Makerell. At night we observed these fishermen casting their

[1] Steward presumably meant that the sea colour, at the place where the soundings mentioned earlier had been made, was light blue.

[2] Smyth, *Sailor's Word Book*: '"She breaks off from her course", applied only when the wind will not allow of keeping the course; applies only to "close-hauled" or "on a wind".'

nets; this we hope to be a sign of more moderate wind. At midnight tack'd ship. Wind inclined to the Northward. Therm. 59°. Solan Geese and Young Gulls seen.

August 6ᵗʰ. A beautifull fresh fair wind rose with the sun which we hope to turn to good advantage. We became now particularly anxious, as the Esk would have her last opportunity for getting into the harbour on Sunday night. Should this prosperous breeze attend us, a day or two, no doubt, but we shall reach Whitby roads in that time. At 3 A.M. a schooner hove in sight to windward: she ran down to us, and we spoke him. He was a Scotchman from Gothenburg bound for – –. Loaden with deals. Had no news with him. Enquired concerning [some?] Whalers [&c.?] – parted – Made all the sail we could. A Brig to Leeward on the same tack as ourselves. At meridian fresh breezes of wind with some rain. Peterhead bore W¼N dist 49 miles. Made sail down into the Firth of Forth. All the afternoon most charming fine weather. At 6 P.M. saw the land, which we supposed to be about Aberdeen. At night saw some stars – for the first we had seen on the passage. No doubt but stars were to have been seen before, but on account of the dismall weather which we have had almost all our passage home. However I am sure that they are quite a strange phenomena to us, who have not seen any for some months. We found our latitude by the Polar one as marked in the margin.¹ The night was beautifully serene: and the pleasantest we have spent for some time having a fair wind. The ocean was luminous, but not in a great degree. At midnight less wind. Therm 59°. Solan Geese and Young Gulls seen.

August 7ᵗʰ. A Foul wind come again, and I fear we shall not reach home these <u>springs</u>. Several coasters in sight. At 6 A.M. Land was seen. The Cheviot Hills and St. Abbs Hᵈ bearing NW dist about 25 miles. Continued our stretch to the Eastward untill noon when we tackt. A most furious Gale then came on, which [***] us to reduce our sails &c. But as we were on a ['lee' *deleted*] weather shore, we did not feel a very heavy sea. Towards the evening the wind subsided, and charming weather prevailed. We reached into Berwick Bay, untill we found the wind scanted us: we then tackd. We did not find our land breeze quite so favourable tonight as we had wished for; the ship scarcely lying South. A fair wind was at this time particularly desirable, as we were on a very dangerous coast. The Staple and Fern islands prevented us comming so near the shore, as to gain the best of the breeze: We were obliged to give the islands a wide berth, as reefs of rocks lay off each island. We did not come within 6 miles of the lights, which were intermitting; shewing themselves but once or twice in a minute. At midnight it was inclinable to calm. Ship going about 4 knots. Today for the first time no fire was lighted in the cabin. Fires were obliged to be kept burning, on account of the twixt decks being so very damp. Therm. 59°. Solan Geese and Hillocks seen.

August 8ᵗʰ. Gentle breezes of wind and clear weather. At 4 A.M. the Staples and Fern lighthouses [dipped?] at [N.N.W.?]² Continued standing out towards sea. Our ship

---

¹ Note in margin: 'Lat. By alt of Polar star = 56°41′N'.
² Possibly 'W.N.W.'

now sailed rather badly owing to the loss of the jib. On that account therefore we were obliged to take in the mizen topsail &c. in order to balance the small quantity of sail ahead. This considerably reduced our progress. At 9 A.M. we tack'd, and stood to the westward. At noon we saw the Coquet islands; and at 2 P.M. as she fell off considerably we tack'd. She then layed SbW good. The land which we now saw was very bright, and seemed covered with verdure. What a difference between ['the' deleted] its appearance, and that of the bleak, barren Spitzbergen! But the latter most likely I shall never revisit again, so I will not complain. I have been most thoroughly pleased with my voyage; although it may be [in?] ['most' deleted] many people's eyes one that would not have been undertaken by a person who expects to immediately set out for the East Indies. – – All the afternoon we had fresh breezes of wind, but a disagreable head sea on. At night she saild faster: at about 8 P.M. we saw Tinmouth lighthouse; bearing W.N.W. dist 15 miles. Continued standing to the SSW.ward. A [***] charming night. At midnight saw the Yorkshire land, which we supposed to be [Skintley Foot ?].¹ Therm. 58°. Land birds seen.

August 9ᵗʰ. Fresh breezes and serene weather. Got soundings in 26 fms – as we were now close in with the land, and had not far to run before we should arrive at Whitby, we saild under easy sail (Three Topsails and jib), that we might not reach the roads before day break. Continued sounding all the way. At 1 A.M. we arrived in Sandsend roads. We were under the necessity of keeping a continual fire of the great guns, in order to raise our [dilatory?] Pilots. At 3 A.M. they came onboard. At noon we had fresh breezes of wind with rain. As we had now drifted considerably to the south-ward, thro' Whitby roads, by the flood tide, we tacked her up to windward, into Sandsend roads and brought her up. Landed in Whitby.

Nothing particular occured onboard untill the 13 Inst. when we got under weigh with the flood tide, and came into the harbour. Thus ends my journal of a Greenland Voyage, with thanks to Almighty God for his continual protection, thro' all ['my' deleted] the perils and dangers during these last five months; after having supposed ourselves to have run over about 20,000 miles. Amen.

£

The Esk boiled 193 tons of oil, selling at 32 per ton.

[The following page is the cover page of an 'Appendix to the forgoing Journal of a voyage to Spitzbergen In the Ship Esk of Whitby. Performed in the year 1814. Charles Steward.'. The appendix was evidently intended to be, as the heading on the following two pages states, a 'Meteorological Journal, kept onboard the Ship Esk of Whitby, on a Greenland Whale Fishing Voyage. 1814.'. However, only the first page was completed, covering the period 23 March to 30 April, in columns headed by date, lati-tude, longitude, temperature, wind direction and strength, precipitation or state of the atmosphere ['Aqueous Meteors', e.g. 'Cloudy', 'Rain', 'Thick'], sea colour, birds and animals seen, and 'Remarks'.

¹ There is no such current place name on the Yorkshire coast. However, there is the village of Skinningrove, which would be consistent with the *Esk*'s arrival in Sandsend Roads an hour later.

The final page of the manuscript is an inscription. apparently in Steward's normal handwriting, that repeats part of the quotation from Virgil's first Eclogue with which the journal began. 'Mr Solomon Charles Steward. Nos patria fines et dulcia linquimus arva[.] This forgoing line is Dedicated to Mr Solomon Steward by permission of the Honble Mr Deudney.']

Journal for 1815

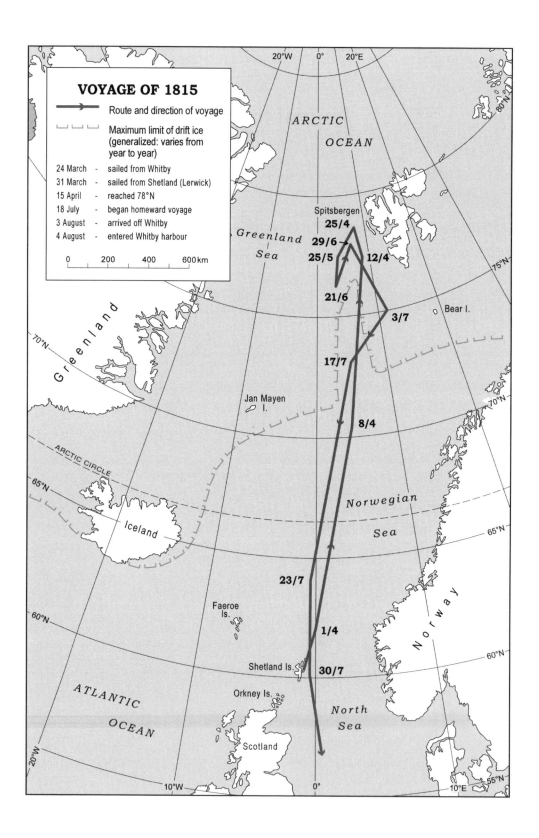

VOYAGE OF 1815

→ Route and direction of voyage

⌐ ⌐ ⌐ Maximum limit of drift ice
(generalized: varies from
year to year)

24 March - sailed from Whitby
31 March - sailed from Shetland (Lerwick)
15 April - reached 78°N
18 July - began homeward voyage
3 August - arrived off Whitby
4 August - entered Whitby harbour

0   200   400   600km

ARCTIC
OCEAN

Spitsbergen
25/4
29/6
25/5   **12/4**

Greenland
Sea

21/6

Bear I.

3/7

17/7

Greenland

70°N

Jan Mayen
I.

8/4

ARCTIC CIRCLE

65°N

Norwegian
Sea

Iceland

65°N

23/7

Norway

Faeroe
Is.

60°N

1/4

60°N

Shetland Is.   **30/7**

Orkney Is.

ATLANTIC
OCEAN

North
Sea

Scotland

20°W   0°   20°E

80°N

75°N

70°N

55°N

10°W   0°   10°E

Journal of the Third Greenland or Whale Fishing Voyage under Divine Providence of the Ship Esk of Whitby by William Scoresby Junr Commander. 1815

On Saturday the 11th of February, unmoored the ship. In the afternoon withdrew her about a hundred yards from her winter birth, but were prevented from getting her out of the Bell <u>gate</u>[1] on account of obstructions received from the Resolution and Volunteer.

On the morning of the 12th attended tide, the ship however did not float. Attended again in the afternoon and by prompt exertions, were enabled to heave out into the stream and moved opposite Brown's quay alongside of two transports.

During the week the mate, specksioneer, second mate, & boys were employed rigging the ship and stowing the casks in the hold.

On the 22^d took on board seven chaldrons of coals.

23^d. Received 7½ Casks of beef containing 5 tons 3 cwt 2 qrs 19 lb, and 4½ casks of pork containing 3 tons 2 cwt 2 qrs 23 lb, from the Store.

24th. The two ships which hitherto lay within us having hauled away we moved alongside of the quay. Received on board 11 Casks or 5½ Tons of Beer from Mr Stonehouse.

25. Received 10 casks, containing five tons of beer from Clarks.

28.[2] Filled 3300 gallons of fresh water in eleven casks.

On the 1st of March received 2½ tons of bread from S. Nettleship, which excepting 2 cwt was stowed in three lockers.

2^d. Took on board two tons of bread from I. Hamilton, which filled 7 casks of 180–200 gallons capacity each, with a surplus of four hundred weight.

March the 3^d. Eight sacks containing one ton of flour, received from Mr Anderson, was packed in two casks.

5th. Received 80 bushels of potatoes from M^r. I. Mead.

[1] *Sic*. Correctly 'gote': see the similar opening statement in the 1814 *Journal*. Here it appears that the text was initially written as 'gote' and later altered to 'gate'.
[2] Possibly '6', though the 26th was a Sunday.

9th. 4 Barrels of ale from Mr G. Stonehouse and the same quantity from Mr C. Clark.

13th. Received a cask of fine ale, a present from T. Fishburn Esqr. to be distributed to the crew in the progress of the fishery, if favoured with success. S. Henderson furnished 40 stones of oatmeal.

15.[1] Took the guns on board, consisting of 8, 18 pounders carronades, and 2 long nines,[2] together with a quantity of small arms & pistols. The same day the news of the ratification of the peace with the Americans on the part of the president, reached us[3] – but from the unsettled state of Europe ['made' *deleted*] owing to the attack made on France by Bonaparte,[4] induced us to retain all our engines of defence.

16. Took the crew on board, [cooked?] provisions for them, and entered into general pay. Set the rigging up, &c.

17 Bent sails, and received sundry small stores on board.

18 Paid hand money, month's advances and harbour pay to the officers and seamen, in the presence of Messrs Fishburn & Brodrick & other gentlemen, according to the usual rates in the port of Whitby, viz. To Harponeers 7 guineas hand-money – to the second mate one guinea extra, mate two guineas extra, gunner ½ a guinea extra, as[5] month's advance & to the specksioneer one guinea extra as hand money. To boat-steerers, in addition to harbour pay 3£; to linemanagers 2.17/6, to Seamen 2.15/- and to landmen 2.5/- to 2.10/-[.] To the Surgeon 3..15/- to the carpenter [*blank space*]; to the cooper [*blank space*]; armourer [*blank space*]; &c. The amount paid was [*blank space*].

Monday the 20th of March a party consisting of 15 gentlemen dined on board. Sundry others received.

21. Nine half barrels of gun powder stored in the fort magazine[6] were received on board.

22d. Various work performed and variety of stores received. A party of 25 ladies and gentlemen tead on board, &c.

---

[1] The *Memoirs* of the Wernerian Natural History Society record that Scoresby's lengthy paper 'On the Greenland or Polar Ice' was read to the Society in Edinburgh on this date, evidently without Scoresby being present.

[2] A nine-pounder gun.

[3] The Treaty of Ghent, ending the War of 1812, had been signed on 24 December 1814. However, it did not take effect until it had been ratified by the US Senate and President Madison in mid-February 1815.

[4] Napoleon landed in France from his exile in Elba on 1 March 1815, and reached Paris on 20 March. See also journal entry for 29 March.

[5] Possibly 'a'.

[6] Presumably the battery at Scotch Head. See footnote to journal entry for 21 March 1812, vol. I, p. 66.

Distribution of the Esk's Crew into Watches & Boats' Crews. 1815[1]

Mates Watch		Specksioneer's Watch		Captain's Watch	
John Dunbar	Thos. Wilburn	Robt Dowell	W. Welburn	John King	Thos Fell
R^d Francis	T. Scorfield	J.[2] Webster	J. Carthew	J. Davies	W. Ward (1)
Sam. Jopling	H Brown	J. Hutcheson	R. Simpkin	T. Anderson	J. [Swiser?]
J. Wilson	W. Hustler	W^m [Rennox?]	J. Oxley	W. Stringer	T. Shippy
J. Watkins	J. [Nevill?]	H. Coates	J. White	F. Brown	W. Lorne
W. Shepherd	W. Lawrence	J. Unwin	J. Pennock	W. Jolley	J. Midford
J. Stamp	J. Hebden	W. Bigelon	Geo. Sair	W. Ward (2^d)	Geo. Boyes
Extras		Extras		Extras	
Anderson Graham (Cook)		R^d Sleightholm		D. Robinson	
T. Wells [Shp?]		[N. Corner?]		– Wilson	
– Welburn		R. Dowell		R. Elder	

March 23^d Prepared for Sea. Received on board One and a half Bullocks weighing [blank space] cwt [blank space] qr [blank space] lb; the Legs, chines, and finer parts of which were retained in large pieces for <u>fresh Stores</u>; the coarser parts were cut into 8 or 10 lb pieces and corned for present use. This makes the amount of our Provision in Beef and Pork, Nine Tons, 0 cwts, 3 quarters, 13 lb.

At Tide time unmoored and hove the Ship down the Harbour about two thirds the distance of the Bridge, where she grounded; meanwhile the Volunteer, Lively, Resolution, William & Ann, Aimwell, and Valiant sailed to Sea with a favourable Gale of wind. In the night the wind blew tremendously from the west to north-west, and much rain fell.

March 24th Good Friday. Immediately on the Ship's floating in the Morning, hove her to a birth opposite the Two Dolphins, a little from the Bridge and a direct fair way.*[3] At 2 Pm. she again floated, the wind was favourable and weather fine. Hauled through Bridge, set the Sails, and at 3 Pm. passed the W. Pier end to Sea-ward, amidst the loud huzzas and greetings of the numerous spectators there assembled.[4] A heavy squall from off the Land, accompanied with Rain, obliged us to furl the Top Gall^t Sails & reef Top. Sailes; after however making two or three tacks the weather cleared and the wind abated. At 4½ Pm. we reached close to the Pier Head, tacked and quitted the Pilot, and all our shore friends. On mustering the Crew, we found, all hands, (amounting to 55 persons) on board and <u>all sober</u>!

Made Sail, and steered to the NEbN to NNE accompanied by ['with' deleted] the Henrietta – with moderate variable winds. Much Rain.

[1] This table was on a sheet of paper that had been tipped in to the transcript. It was followed by a blank page.

[2] All the initial 'J's could equally well be 'I', but are identical to the 'J' of 'John Dunbar'.

[3] Footnote in original: '*Received a Bushel of Pease on Board, and a similar quantity for the Resolution, she having sailed without them.' See also entry for 23 April 1815.

[4] Scoresby had also sailed from Whitby on Good Friday in 1812 (27 March). On both occasions the advantages of fair winds and a spring tide at full moon seem to have outweighed the superstition against setting sail on a Friday.

[Journal now adopts the normal three-column format.]

Saturday 25th March Lat. 56°10+ Lon. 10'W.
WSW, NW, Var, W.
Fine cloudy weather the fore part of the day, wind a Brisk Gale; squally with Rain in the Evening. Pursued a NbE to NNE course with a velocity of 4 to 7 knotts p hour. A Strange Sail in sight to the W^d steering a parallel course; the Henrietta in Company. The Sea [commoded?] by various swells.

Sunday 26th March Lat. 58°24'+ Long. 42'W.
W. SW. SSW.
Fresh to hard Gales of wind with dark cloudy weather, and towards night a high Sea. In the Morning saw a ship at a distance which it seemed had suffered the loss of Foremast and Bowsprit – she did not however shew any signal for the purpose of requesting assistance, we therefore continued our course. At [1?] Pm. furled Top-Gall^t Sails, main-sail, mizen, & Jibb & at 4 reefed Top sails and sent down Top Gall^t yards. At 7½ pm. the weather was very tempestuous and dark, [finding?] ourselves nearly in the Parallel of Fair Island, we hauled by the wind to the E^d under three close reefed top sails. Parted C° with the Henrietta.

Monday 27th March
SSW SbE to SW
During the night the wind increased to a ['[dismal?]' *deleted*] Hard Gale & the weather was dark and hazy. At day break (4 AM.) the wind had veered to SbE bore away to the NNW under the Top-sails & Fore T.M.StaySail. The Storm now increased and was rendered far more dismal by the obscurity of heavens occasioned by constant Rain. The uncertainty of the ['direction' *deleted*] position of the Land, the nature of the Storm, which was not only very severe, but prevailed in a dangerous direction for the East Coast of Zetland, rendered the search for the Land a very hazardous and anxious undertaking. We should have persevered direct to the fishing stations, having no pressing necessity to call by the way, but, knowing that our friends would not doubt of receiving communications from us, and that consequently they would be racked in the uncertainty of our safety & would naturally attribute the failure of intelligence to some serious misadventure. These considerations induced us to use every exertion to attain a harbour. At 10 Am. saw Land which Providentially proved to be the very spot at which we aimed: for sometime ['however' *deleted*] we were racked with uncertainty with regard to its situation – the haziness of the weather prevented us from seeing it distinctly though not more than two or 3 miles distant. We had to haul up WNW to double Brassa Island. At 10¾ AM. steered up the channel and at 11½ came to an Anchor in Brassa Sound & safely <u>brought up</u>. Many ships being in the Harbour we took a situation <u>without</u> the [fleets?], and were moored ere the Pilot could board the Ship.

The men having dined, the Afterhold was opened out and the casks removed for the purpose of filling the 2^d tier with water as ballast, which had been intentionally omitted that the Ship might not be brought to too great a draught of water for the harbour.[1]

Squally weather with rain during the Afternoon and Evening. The William & Ann, and the Aimwell prove to be the only Whitby Ships which have taken this Harbour, the rest must have passed from their not being able to <u>fetch</u> the coast or from their unwillingness to hazard the <u>making</u> of the Land so untoward & appaling [*sic*]. Men are very plentiful here in consequence of most of the Ships being supplied from their own ports.[2]

Tuesday 28th March
SW to WbN

Excessive hard Gales with Showers of Rain & Hail. Came in one vessel. Employed filling water in the hold, preparing fishing apparatus, and fitting Greenland Sails & Rigging. Rode during the day by the best bower anchor with 75 fathoms of Cable. This anchor weighs near 20 cwt which is 4 cwt larger than the common proportion for Tonnage – it proves imminently serviceable in this Harbour where the ground is loose & bad for riding, and where storms are so exceedingly prevalent at this Season.

Wednesday 29th March
NW, W, SW, SSE, West.

We had fresh Gales of wind with hard squalls throughout this day – accompanied occasionally by heavy Rain. Several ships sailed for the Greenland Fishery – two arrived from England, which brought very gloomy news with regard to the affairs of Europe – such as, that Buonaparte had actually reached & entered Paris without opposition & that the King & Royal Family had retreated into England for Protection – &c – &c.

In the Afternoon I visited my Friends on shore – in the Evening a terrible squall of wind and Rain prevailed – and I found my barge's crew were chiefly inebriated. As I did[3] consider it prudent to trust my life with such men, I accepted the offer of a bed on shore for the night.

The prosperity of Lerwick being considerably dependent on the assistance it affords, in men, to the Whale fisheries, it is likely to suffer a serious privation on the present occasion. Last season the Shetlands Islands are said to have supplied 1400 Men, which men received on an average £15 each for their services ['[who?]' *deleted*] or the whole £21,000 add to this the Agents' commissions of 5[4] p Cent or 1050£, and perhaps a sum of £500 expended by the Masters and English Seamen of the fleet gives a total of the Sum of 22550£ – ['all' *deleted*] most of which is the price of labour & consequently does not require any of the prosperity of the Country in return. [Now?] of this Sum it appears that ⅔ is in the first

---

[1] This refers to Whitby harbour, not Lerwick.
[2] See entry for 29 March 1814.
[3] 'not' presumably omitted in error.
[4] This and other values were inserted in pencil.

instance expended in Lerwick & eventually the greater part of the remainder flows into the Coffers of the Merchants or Agents – upon which they have their profits of Trade and their Commissions as clear gain. At a moderate estimation this may amount to 3000 pounds Sterling p annum! In the present year it is supposed that the Greenland Fleet will not require above ⅓ of the number of the last and some preceding years, and as those are at lower wages in consequence of the decrease in the demand, the money added to the Stores of the Country will probably not exceed 5650£ which is but one fourth part of that of some former years. Here we have a striking effect of war – where the contention of nations becomes the Interest of a Country – whereby war is preferred and Peace dreaded as an Evil!! To do the people justice however, I must not omit to mention that the respectable inhabitants are in general very loyal subjects and notwithstanding the influence of interest, they do justice to national feeling by their tenacity for the honour of Britain in the Glory of her Arms – in the propriety of her politics and in the integrity of her Senators.

Thursday 30th March
W. SWbW

Fresh gales – cloudy fine weather. Several Ships sailed to Sea – four sail arrived from the Thames. Arrived also a King's Cutter[1] with orders to all the Men of War on the Northern Stations to proceed immediately to the Downs,[2] to be more completely under command.

Friday 31st March
SWbS

Fresh Breezes with fine clear weather. All our work being now performed, such as filling 90 Ton Casks with water, preparing fishing utensils, fitting sails & masts for the Northern Gales, procuring two Casks of Sand, eggs, fowls, &c. &c. made preparations for sailing. At Noon weighed anchor, proceeded out of the North Channel to Sea where the Pilot left us at 2 Pm. Steered EbS until we gained a fair birth of the Land, NE until we passed the skerries at 6 pm. and then shaped our course for the Arctic Circle p Compass NEbN. In the Evening distributed the Crew into three watches, arranged two Boat's Crews in each watch, lotted for the Boats, &c. &c. At 8 pm. the northernmost part of Shetland bore NbW about 3 Leagues distant. The Aimwell in company.

[1] I am grateful to Michael Phillips for the following comment: 'The King's Cutters were the vessels of the Excise Board and, between 1785 and 1845, were the fastest vessels afloat. They were distinguished by a sliding bowsprit which could be extended to four-fifths the length of the hull. By a law of 1785 civilian cutters could only have bowsprits that were bolted to the hull and that did not exceed two-thirds the hull length, on penalty of forfeiture to the Crown.'

[2] Smyth, *Sailor's Word Book*: 'DOWNS. ... The name is also applied to the anchorage or sea-space between the eastern coast of Kent and the Goodwin Sands, the well-known roadstead for ships, stretching from the South to the North Foreland, where both outward and homeward-bound ships frequently make some stay, and squadrons of men-of-war rendezvous in time of war.'

Saturday 1ˢᵗ April at noon Lat. 61°52′+ Lon. 0°7′W
SWbS. SE.erly
This was a charming day though almost too mild for the Season. The thermometer was constantly above 50°in the shade – at noon as high as 55 or 56°! The wind was light inclining to Calm. Continue to steer NEbN. Exposed the best bower cable to dry. Aimwell in Cᵒ.

Sunday 2ᵈ April Lat. 62°58′ Lon. 0°14′E.
SE. S. SW. S.
Dark [hazy?] weather – wind light & variable – Sea peculiarly turbulent. It appears that Strong Gales of wind must prevail both to Nᵈ & Sᵈ of us, as heavy swells are particularly evident from each point. Course p Compass NEbN. Aimwell in Cᵒ....¹

Monday 3ᵈ April Lat 64°32′ 0°39′E
SW. var. NE.
During this day we had Calm & Storm – haze & Rain & turbulent Sea. The competition between opposite currents of wind has rarely been more apparent. Since we left Shetland ['the' *deleted*] we had no wind stronger than a Royal breeze² & yet the whole distance the Sea has been in a singular state of agitation. Sometimes swells from the ['Peculiar effect of contending winds' *in margin*] N. S. and E. have been strikingly evident within a few minutes & sometimes the whole might be distinguished at one time. The Barometer at Noon on the 1ˢᵗ Instᵗ was 29.80 – on the 2ᵈ 29.50 & on the present 29.06. These circumstances rendered the fact evident that the S.erly & N.erly winds were struggling for the pre-eminence & that we happened to be at the point of competition where their forces mutually balanced each other, or rather where the S.erly stream had somewhat superior momentum. It therefore amounted to a certainty that storms prevailed both before & behind us at the same time from the opposite points whilst we partook of the disadvantages of neither, except so much as arose from the strange agitation of the Sea. At 6 Pm. we had a few minutes of variable wind & then a fresh Gale from the NEᵈ fell at once [into?] the Sails. The top gallᵗ sails were immediately furled & the Top-Sails were Double reefed. It however continued on the increase accompanied by Rain & a prodigious <u>cross Sea</u>; so that by 9 Pm. our sails were reduced to close reefed top-sails reefed fore sail – fore top Stay-Sail & mizen Stay-Sail[.] Steered to the NWᵈ. Aimwell in Cᵒ[.] At 10 Pm. the Bar. had risen ¼ of an Inch indicating that ['the' *deleted*] a remnant of the Storm had alone reached us. And so it proved ['**Tuesday 4ᵗʰ April** Lat. 66°52′ Lon. 1°6′E[.] NEerly Calm.' *in margin*] for very early in the Morning the wind fell to near calm. Wore to the Eᵈ at 4 A.M. At 8 A.M. the sky was clear and the day very fine – a strange sail appeared to the North of us. Aroused all hands, exposed the cables to the Sun, cleared the cable stage & placed the Cables therein, placed all the Ice ropes in an orderly manner and distinctly [*illegible word*

---

¹ Ellipsis points in transcript.
² The term 'royal breeze' cannot be traced. Scoresby may have meant a wind in which the light sail termed a 'royal' or 'top-gallant royal' could be used; according to Smyth, *Sailor's Word Book*, s.v. ROYAL, this 'is never used but in fine weather'.

deleted] accessible in the cable tier. Aired sails. Sent up T. Gall^t Yards and performed sundry other operations suitable to the favourable Season and necessary for our situation. In the afternoon a fresh ['SE.erly (7pm. Much lightning and some thunder!!()]' *in margin*] SE.erly breeze sprung which at night had increased to a brisk Gale. Proceeded under a smart sail to the NE. p compass / Aimwell in C°[.]

Wednesday 5th April. Lat. 66°52′ Lon. 1°6′E
SE. SEbE
At day-light several strange Sail were in sight, to the amount of 5 or 6. The weather Showery, wind a brisk Gale – on the whole tollerably fine. Continued steering on a NE course with a velocity of 5 to 7 knots p hour. A Ship, supposed ['(Aurora Borealis seen.)' *in margin*] to be the Mary & Elizabeth of Hull crossed us steering about NNE. Aimwell C°[.]

Thursday 6th April Lat. 69°14′+ Lon. 3°12′E
SEbE ESE. E to NNE
Fresh Gales of wind – occasional Snow Showers – fine weather. Proceeded to the NE so long as the direction of the wind would permit; in the afternoon the wind had veered to the E or ENE & our course in consequence was deflected to the NNE or N. and eventually to NW when we tacked, about 11½ Pm. The Aimwell in C°[.] One strange sail in sight.

   This being the anniversary of the nativity of Mrs S. it was celebrated by the Crew uniting "to splice the main-brace"[1] – whilst the Harponeers joined with myself & the rest of the Cabin in-mates – in the commemoration of the event, in ['the' *deleted*] feasting off a lump of Roast Beef & Plum-pudding – the solidity of which was attempered by the enjoyment of a moderate ['plentiful' *above the line*] supply of Aque Vitæ[2] and other favourite beverages.

Friday 7th April Lat. 70°9′ Lon. 4°22′E
NNE. N
Strong gales to light breezes of wind – weather fine; cloudy, with some Snow Showers; Sea high from the Eastward; insomuch that the Ship made a slow advance to the Eastward. The afternoon & Evening were charmingly fine. The Sun set clear at 7h [*blank space*] m. Pm. bearing p. Compass ['Therm. 8 pm. 30" *in margin*] N45°W which gives the variation 24°51′ W.[3] Aimwell in C°[.]
   In the night the Aurora Borealis was visible & very brilliant. No wind.

Saturday 8th April Lat. 71°16′ Lon. 5°36′E
SW.erly SSW.
Soon after mid-night a breeze of wind sprung up from the SW^d which increased very gradual throughout the whole. In the Evening it had attained the force of a Severe

---

[1] To issue an extra ration of rum.
[2] Correctly (*OED*): Aqua-vitæ, i.e. strong spirits such as brandy and whisky.
[3] See Appendix, p. 295.

Storm, and much small Rain accompanied it. We proceeded with an accelerated velocity until the log indicated near 10 knotts, at which time (2 pm.) we took in Studding Sails and top-gallant sails. At 4 Pm. double reefed top-sails & at 8 close reefed those sails. The Sun being now set – the weather thick – and our path dark – having already reached a Situation in which Ice very frequently occurs in formidable aggregations – we hauled by the wind to the SE^d under three top-sails & fore-t.m. stay sail. The night proved dismally tempestuous, the Sea ran high, and the Ship laboured considerably. Parted C^o with the Aimwell.

Sunday 9th April Lat 72°37′+ Lon. 8.31E
SWbW to WbN. SSW & W.
At day-light (3½ A.M.) the wind abated but the atmosphere still continued heavy & dark. At 8 AM. made sail & steered to the NE or NEbN the rest of the day under a brisk Gale of wind. Three ships in sight. In the Evening we had several thick showers of prismatic snow. The twilight scarcely deserted the sky throughout the night.[1] Twice during this day, Divine Service was performed (as usual) consisting of the form used by the Church of England & followed by ['Thermometer 36° to 34°.' *in margin*] one of Burder's or Kidd's Village Sermons,[2] to as many of the crew as could crowd into the Cabin. The Men all attended with great propriety.

Monday 10th April Lat 74°56′ Lon. 10°14′E
WNW
The wind increased during the night, and continued blowing a strong Gale all the day – accompanied by Snow showers and a considerable lowering of temperature. We proceeded under a heavy press of Sail on a course about due North with a general velocity of 7 or 8 knotts p hour. Our sails consisted of main-sail & foresail (unreefed) – doubled reefed Top sails, Jib – fore-top-stay sail & mizen. My intention in thus forcing the ship forward with such a pressure of canvass, was for the purpose of informing the very favourable direction of the wind, in advancing without risk into the country should it be open or making the Ice in the event of a close season. A beam or side wind, is of all others the safest for this purpose – because should Ice appear in the most unfavourable posture and at the most unexpected time, yet the wind admits of the Ship's returning on the same line whereby it advanced. This is of great importance in dark heavy weather, as on the present occasion, where the atmosphere was never free from Snow showers. [With?] S.erly winds the country can rarely be entered without some risk – they in general blow hard, & are accompanied by a heavy Sea & thick weather. Now when scudding under such circumstances, should the Ship fall into any deep bay of the Ice, it might readily occasion its loss – for the Ice then meeting her on each tack, and the turbulent Sea preventing her working out to windward, she must

---

[1] At this latitude and date, there is continuous astronomical twilight (sun's centre less than 18° below horizon), but not yet continuous civil twilight (sun's centre less than 6° below horizon).

[2] In his journal entry for 25 April 1813, Scoresby had mentioned his use of Burder's *Village Sermons*. Thornhill Kidd's *Sermons. Designed chiefly for the use of villages and families* was published in 1812 and in several later editions.

fall upon the Ice; whence a wreck is the probable consequence. The fall of the thermometer was very considerable this day. At 7 AM. the temp. was 17° being a decrease
of 17° in 12 hours! At 11 AM. the temp was 15°. So much water assailed the deck in
the course of the day the Ship was literally covered with Ice, in some places to an
amazing thickness. The excessive cold & forcible wind, called forth all the ante-gelid[1]
habiliments of the Crew ['Greenlandmen's costume' *in margin*] in the most ridiculous
form, and the most tasteless ['mode of [apparition?]' *deleted*] arrangement imagin-
able. In addition to the usual articles of dress ['were' *deleted*] are displayed in great
profusion, large Boots, mitts, and upper jackets, sashes for the waist, comforters for
the neck and immense cow hair wigs for the head & ears, decorated with prodigious
tails covering the shoulders & extending half way down the back. In addition to
these, some of the Crew wore waterproof seal skin jackets, trousers, and mitts – thus
all together forming one of the most grotesque groups that can readily be imagined.
Notwithstanding this ridiculous appearance of the Greenland Seamens' costume, it
must be observed that few of the articles therein employed can possibly be dispensed
with. The intenseness of the cold, rendered more offensive by the necessary exposure
to the wind, and[2] flying spray from the Sea becomes so oppressive and painful that it
required every precaution of warm clothing & considerable action to resist ['their
combined effects.' *deleted*] its morbid tendency.[3]

In the Evening the wind abated in some degree. 5 Ships in sight.

Tuesday 11th April Lat.76°.33' Lon 10°.20'E
NW. Calm. SEbE to East
We had several hours of Calm weather, attended with much small Snow in the
Morning. Having attained a fishing latitude, summoned all hands to prepare for
active operations. Took out two of the four Boats in the Twin-decks, and after
placing all the Davits suspended them at the quarters, along with two others from
the deck. ['Put' *deleted*] Displaced four of the Guns, two of which we stowed in the
Galley and the other two under the Bowsprit on the Forecastle, leaving six 18[In.?]
Carronades in their places on the deck. It was our intention, to coyl the whale-lines
in the Boats, but thick Snow was unfavourable for the operation, therefore the design
was abandoned. Placed the <u>Guy</u> and lashed up <u>Cant Blocks</u>, together with other
preparatory work. At 2 Pm. a fresh Gale sprung up at SEbE, which rapidly increased.
Put the Ship under a snug sail & steered NEbN. In the Evening the ['density' *deleted*]
Snowing in a measure ceased & the ['Therm^r 10° to 16°' *in margin*] atmosphere was
considerably attentuated. Saw land (some part of Spitzbergen) bearing East supposed
to be 15 or 20 Leagues distant. Made sail in the night. Five ships occasionally in
sight.

---

[1] Not in *OED* as such, but the latter cites Scoresby's use of 'gelid' in *Account of the Arctic Regions*, I, p. 298.

[2] At this point the words 'powerful intrusion of seawater, which is no sooner cast upon the deck than it is converted into Ice – the concurrence of these things, at the same time, is' are deleted in pencil in favour of the rendering that follows, also in pencil, as far as 'so oppressive ...'.

[3] The deletion, and the three words that replaced it, are in pencil.

Wednesday 12th April Lat 77°.21′ Lon. 8°.27′E.

E.rly. Var. Calm. NNE Variable.

Made some small progress to the N^d during the night. At 7 AM. had a Calm. The Snow then dispersing we again saw the Land (suppose between Bell Sound & Ice Sound) bearing E. p compass about 20 leagues – this gives our longitude 8°15′E, whilst my longitude by account at the same time showed 8°3′E. a degree of accuracy too striking to be esteemed more than a fortunate coincidence.[1] A breeze sprung up from the N^d at 9 AM. made all sail to the W^d (by the wind) in search of Ice & whales. The weather was cloudy with little showers [' Made Ice in Lat. 77.25 Lon. 6°2′E' *in margin*] of small snow. At noon prepared to coyl the lines in the Boats and by 4 pm. [six?][2] Boats were fitted for active service.

At 7 pm. passed two or three small pieces of Ice, at 8 passed through a stream of young Ice – at 9 many streams of Ice appearing ['Frost rime' *in margin*] to the W^d we tacked. The therm*ometer* fell to 7°[.] 5 sail in sight.

At Mid-Night tacked & stood towards the Ice.

Thursday 13th April At noon Lat. 77°.32′ Lon. 7°40′E.

NE. NW. Very var.

Fresh breezes with strong squalls. Atmosphere clear above, but obscured near the horizon by <u>frost rime</u>. Worked to windward during the night (which it may be noticed was ['not' *deleted*] in no way dark) ['but' *deleted*] at 7 Am. we tacked near a stream of young Ice & steered to the E^d we unexpectedly met with a large quantity of Ice on our reach consisting of large patches & Streams of pancake bay ice intermixed with many large lumps – to the N^d appeared a solid body, under the lee of which were laying too 8 sail of ships, amongst them we distinguished the Everthorpe, Sisters, Clapham &c. This Ice was unbroken to the horizon and consisted, apparently, of bay and heavy ice indiscriminately mixed. As the frost was very intense, I deemed it imprudent to rest here, ['and accordin' *deleted*] lest on the abating of the wind we should be <u>frozen up</u>, ['accordingl' *deleted*] therefore, to prevent casualties we proceeded eastward, winding through the channels between the streams and numerous scattered pieces of Ice. At 1½ p.m. we regained the open sea which seemed to admit of a free navigation to the NE^d[.] Two of the ships inside followed us, the rest so long as we could perceive them, continued at rest. Four sail to the NE^d of us. The appearances of the Ice where the [fleet?] were lying too, suggested a continuance of it throughout the country to the N^d of the 77½° of N. Lat. this was another inducement to persevere to the eastward, being the most probable course of succeeding, even had the ice proved to be generally dispersed throughout the N.ern part of the country. The remainder of the day we ['Ther^m 6° to 10°' *in margin*] worked to windward near the exterior streams of ice.

In the Evening 13 sail were in sight. Very squally w^r.

---

[1] Scoresby's noon latitude of 77°21′ suggests that he was seeing Jarlsberg Land, south of the entrance to Van Mijenfjorden and Van Keulenfjorden (Scoresby's 'Bell Sound'), and not the coast to the north of these fjords as he supposed.

[2] A 'five' appears to have been altered to 'six', but neither is definite.

Friday 14th April Lat 77°.58′ Lon 7°.10′E
NE. to E. very var.
Hard squalls in the morning with thick frost rime & disagreeable short sea. At 4 Am. tacked near the Ice & stood to seaward until 8 the wind then veering to the eastward & the weather becoming fine proceeded starboard tacked until 2 Pm. Penetrated several streams of heavyish ice – when we tacked, we were on the borders of a vast agregation [*sic*] of considerable [***] open water to the NW^d & SE^d but a body of ice apparently from ['to' *deleted*] the North to the East.

At Noon the land was visible for a great extent: the Middle hook of Charles Island bore NE p compass 15 or 20 Leagues distant. Spoke the Sisters of Hull (J. Rose) – made the Ice the 3^d inst^t in 72° lat & 4°W Long. could not gain the main ice for bay ice – saw few seals – observed 5 foreigners sealing – saw 2 whales in lat. 76° out of sight of ice, &c. At 2 PM. tacked near some heavy patches of Ice which appeared close & compact to the N^d & E. but open to the NW^d proceeded under the lee of an open pack about 15 miles to the SSE, the ice then trended about south & appeared solid to the land; this idea is also corrobarated [*sic*] by the closeness of the atmosphere over the land all the day, whilst in other direction, showers & clouds continually prevailed. Thus finding no passage northward on the east of this ice we returned the same way & entered the NWern channel, at 8 pm. steered about NNW until 11 when falling in with much ice tacked & worked up to the NE^d[.] Saw one ship flinching a whale not far distant & another apparently in pursuit – we however, could not meet with a single individual. In the night the wind blew strong, accompanied by thick Snow Showers & frost rime. The twilight was scarcely evident.

Saturday 15th April Lat. 78°.1′+ Lon. 5°.25′E
NE. NNE variable
Worked to the NW^d amidst large streams & patches of ice until 4 am. having then gained the extremity of an opening lay too. At 9. made sail returned to windward & perceiving a vast opening to the NE proceeded that way. At noon we saw the <u>blast</u> (or breathing) of some cetaceous animal which we took for a whale and sent a boat in pursuit of it. As the sea was considerably agitated by the wind, and the boatsteerer inexperienced they chased with effect & struck, unwittingly, a razor back. In the space of about one minute it had withdrawn 400 yards of line from the boat, being a velocity of above 15 English miles or 14 nautical miles in an hour. The velocity being so immense the harpooner was unable to check the line in the least degree by turns around the <u>bollard</u>, after he ['was' *deleted*] did effect this, the boat flew along the surface of the water with amazing velocity. Upwards of – of the lines were now expended & no boat within 200 yards to afford a replenish, in two minutes more he must have parted with the end and put up with the loss of 720 fathoms of whale lines. Fortunately however at this juncture the line broke, within 30 or 40 yards of the harpoon. The razor back is an animal of amazing size, it exceeds considerably in length the common whale, but is much more slender. It affords a very small supply of blubber & of an inferior quality. It is remarkable for its speed when frighted. It is less timid than the whale of a bluish black colour, and acquires the name of

['Wᵐ¹ Welburn   Razor back lost.' *in margin*]

razor-back, by fishermen on account of the angular form of the back.

The harponeer who struck this animal declared he never saw it, but only observed it under water & perceived its blowing – he remarked that the harpoon ['struck' *deleted*] penetrated with particular² difficulty – that it resembled striking against a piece of ice rather than against a whale.

Having hauled the lines in, and hoisted the boats up we made sail to the eastward, after two ships (the Clapham & Duncombe) which now preceded us. Found much water and likewise many very compact aggregations of young & old Ice intermixed. Had some difficult sailing occasionally to effect our intentions. By 5 Pm. we had made an ENE course since 9 Am. a distance of about 35 miles: the land was now extensively in sight, the Middle Hook of the Foreland at ENE about 10 leagues off. At this period we had come to the edge of a large compact stream, through which the Duncombe was in the act of attempting to bore, but without effect – the Clapham had passed it at a more favourable time, and had sailed 10 miles to the eastward and was then observed to lay too as if at the extremity of the opening. As the Ice here, as well as yesterday, appeared most solid to the eastward; & the clearness of the atmosphere in that direction was a striking indication that this was the case; as the period in the fishing season was yet too little advanced, so that during the intensity of the frost besetment must be inevitable in close ice by the intervention of new ice; & as by the showery weather to the westwᵈ we had an indication of water and actually found the most room in that direction; the considerations induced me to forego the <u>accustomed track</u>, and to return to a more roomy and less hazardous situation. We had advanced so far before I made this determination, that we had but just room to wear round, by striking two or three pieces of ice, & with some difficulty returned by the same channels on which we advanced. By 7 pm. we had retreated about 8 miles of the course, when I observed a whale at a great distance, with a pocket telescope: it continued at the surface almost without motion (except the rising & falling occasioned by breathing) for at least half an hour: when we had come pretty near the place I sent a boat towards the spot; the fish soon re-appeared, and was speedily <u>struck</u>. Three boats were sent to the assistance of the one which was <u>fast</u>, whilst the two in the twin-decks were withdrawn. The killing of this whale was attended

['Thomas Fell **M.**   Nᵒ 1 = 10ᶠᵗ4ⁱⁿ' *in margin*]³

with a great deal of trouble – being struck near a stream of ice it made its appearance in half an hour at the edge & then penetrated into the midst of it – the boats had to row above a mile to come near the place, and then they pursued across the ice, leaping from

---

¹ Possibly 'Mr'.

² Originally 'particularly;' the final letters deleted.

³ This and the following tail sketches show a small number (in this case '2') between the '**M**' and the tail.

piece to piece, and frequently getting wet – at length a second harpoon was struck: The fish immediately ran off to windward & before another boat could reach it, sheltered in a more formidable stream. It was again pursued over the ice & two more harpoons struck. These were followed up with lances, and about 11½ pm. the whale was killed. We had to force through the stream of ice to get to windward of it, and after gaining a situation nearest the fish, we put the ship again into the stream & forced to the place where the fish just floated quite erect with the head upwards. There was great difficulty in affixing a whale line to it, as a harpoon would not penetrate the head, a hole however was at length cut in the <u>nose end,</u> and the fish thereby gently dragged to lee-ward, until the lines were all disentangled & the ship & fish clear of the ice. We then secured it alongside & made sail to the W^d to gain sufficient drift to flinch, as however the wind was very much abated the ship could not clear a stream which lay to leeward – entered the narrowest part, bored through and began to flinch. 37 ships in sight!

Sunday 16th April Lat. 77°50′ Lon. 6°50′E
var. SW.erly N. var.
The wind was slight whilst we flinched, which operation finished a breeze from the SW^d sprung up. The ice having accumulated considerably around us, we steered to the S^d several miles winding amongst the numerous pieces, then worked to the SW^d into an extensive opening apparently communicating with the sea. Performed the usual Sabbath day service in the afternoon. 41 Sail in sight. At 9 pm. the wind suddenly veered to the N^d and at the same time a strong Serly swell assailed us. At 11 two boats went in ['**Monday 17 April** Lat.77°50′ Long 5°50′E[.] N.erly' *in margin*] pursuit of a whale and one of them succeeded in striking it. The

['Thomas Welburn F. 6  N° 2 = 10^{ft}8^{in}' *in margin*]

fish run out 12 lines and penetrated the Ice to the eastw^d the boats were led wide of its track and it was not until 2 AM. that we approached it with the ship after having for some time sought its retreat. By means of signals the windward boats were brought near the place, whilst a boat which had remained on board proceeded in pursuit. Twice that the fish arose to the surface, it avoided the boats by their pursuing a wrong direction; at length I was enabled to place them agreeable to my own opinions & fortunately, the prey arose within 20 yards of one of the boats. Three more harpoons were soon struck, yet the capture was not affected before 5 AM. in a place amongst much ice, 5 or 6 miles distant from the spot where it was first entangled. About six got the fish alongside & secured – immediately made sail to the westward until we had sufficient drift to flinch, we then clewed the sails up and commenced [operations?] by removing several casks out of the hold for the formation of a <u>flinch gut</u>. The wind now blew a fresh gale – snow showers were frequent and a considerable swell prevailed – these hindrances very much retarded the flinching in as much that the operation was not finished before 3½ Pm. Two boats were yet absent, for the safety of which I was under great anxiety – I feared they must have missed the ship as she had drifted away from them 8 or 10 miles.
    We however lost no time in making sail and tacking to the [***] on which course having advanced 2 or 3 miles I perceived a ship 4 or 5 SE from us bearing a flag – the

purpose it was suggested to my mind as being addressed to us on account of our boats – we therefore bore down and were rejoiced to find the strayed men all safe. The vessel proved the Vigilant – Peal of London – the boats having pursued a course too much to the S^d fell in near her and hoisted their jacks – Mr Peal imagining they were entangled with a fish, kindly sent two boats towards them, but presently they were undeceived & took charge of them, and took upon himself to search for the Esk. It was indeed a Providential circumstance that the boats gained & were seen by the Vigilant, for few ships being in the same direction, their safety was in some hazard. Mr Peal took Tea with me – he informed me that so early as 30th March the Vigilant was in Greenland that there was no Ice near the land at that time, except bay ice, and that one ship advanced to the lat. of 80° without interruption – that he thinks the ice which now lays near the land, has drifted from the E^d of the Head land – that he saw a great many fish near the Foreland – & that he captured one of about 20 tons of Oil!

After Mr Peal returned to his ship steered to the SSE, fearful lest the ice which now lay to the eastward should involve and beset us: at the same time with the hope of meeting with Whales.

Tuesday 18th April Lat 77°37′ Lon. 8°E
E.rly. Calm Var. Amazingly Variable. S.erly. E.erly. N. &c. &c.
The morning of this day was most charmingly fine, the atmosphere was without a cloud, the wind was light, the sun shone with particular effulgence and warmth. We entered a Bay formed by large patches of ice, extending 10 or 12 miles to the NE^d at the extremity of which lay several ships whilst others had penetrated farther in a Northern direction. The wind calmed at 9 Am. The land was then visible from the SE. to the NNE – Ice-Sound¹ bore east about 10 leagues distant; Bell Sound SEbE; and the Middle Hook of the Foreland NEbN. Whilst we lay almost surrounded with ice, at the distance of scarcely a furlong, the temperature of the sea at the surface and to a depth of 2 or 3 feet was 38°, or nearly 10° above ['the' *deleted*] its freezing point. Now such a temp. is certainly very remarkable where the mean temp. of the year does not exceed [*blank space*]° and especially amidst large collections of ice. The fact confirms an opinion which I have long entertained, that an under current sets along the W. coast of Spitzbergen to the N^d whilst an upper current conveys the ice in a southwestern direction from the high Polar regions.²

¹ There is a dot above 'sound', suggesting an 'i', but otherwise 'Ice-Sound' appears to be the correct reading, and is broadly consistent with its location on Scoresby's 'Chart of Spitzbergen …', Plate IV in *Account of the Arctic Regions*, II. It is nowadays Isfjorden.

² 'Fram Strait lies between Greenland and the Svalbard group of islands, the largest of which is Spitsbergen. As the only deep-water connection between the Arctic Ocean and the world ocean, Fram Strait is an important site for the exchange of mass, heat, and salt. The warm West Spitsbergen Current (WSC) and the ice-infested East Greenland Current (EGC) are the two major currents in Fram Strait. While the WSC carries warm Atlantic waters north into the Arctic Ocean, the EGC transports cold, fresh water and sea ice south out of the Arctic basin. In this manner, the currents work together to make Fram Strait the northernmost permanently ice-free ocean area in the world.

'The WSC is the northernmost extension of the Norwegian Atlantic Current. It flows

At 11 am. the sky was rapidly obscured with clouds and snow showers resulted. Partial breezes sprung up in various directions at short distances. SE.erly winds however being most prevalent where we lay we ran the ship through some streams of ice to the NW^d and gained the open sea. In the evening we had thick snow and fresh gales from two or three quarters with intervals of calms in the space of half an hour. N.erly, E.erly, & S.erly winds alternately prevailed with the force of a fresh gale in rapid but irregular succession during several hours. The appearance was most uncommonly singular to any one unacquainted with these seas, and to the most experienced it could not fail particularly to interest.[1]

Wednesday 19th April Lat. 77°42′ Lon. 7°20′E
SEbS. SSE

About mid-night however a strong gale arose at SEbS which soon gained the supremacy and afterwards prevailed without interruption. Tacked about during the day under an easy sail on the exterior of the ice. The weather cleared in the afternoon, but the wind continued a strong gale – saw several ships at different times, chiefly to leeward of us.

Thursday 20th April Lat. 77°50 Lon. 7°54E

The wind abated in the morning – snow showers for a while continued to fall, but at length the day became charmingly fine. At 9 am. reached in with the ice and pene-trated some small streams – at 10 o/c saw three whales which we pursued with three boats, for a long time, but without success. At Noon the middle Hook of the Foreland bore NE distant 15 leag*ues*. The atmosphere was constantly clear over the land but cloudy & showery elsewhere. Examined the ice which lay packed between us & the land, seeing none of the objects of our search hauled off NW under a light air of wind. The Vigilant near us. Three other ships seen at noon.

At 3^h 42′50″ Pm. apparent time, the mean of 8 sets of observations gave the Vari-ation of the Compass 15°37′W. The opportunity was excellent ['Var. Compass 15°37′E [*sic*]' *in margin*] and a small compass with a very light card which I had provided for the purpose acted admirably.[2] At the time of observation the lat. of the ship was 77°50′ and long. 7°54′E. The middle hook of the Foreland bore NE¾N distant 48′; South end Foreland E¾N = 38′;[3] Ice Sound E½ S; and Bell Sound ESE½ S.

---

poleward through eastern Fram Strait along the western coast of Spitsbergen … It is about 100 km wide and is confined over the continental slope, where it reaches its maximum current speed of 24 to 35 cm s^{-1} at the surface. Because it transports relatively warm (6 to 8°C) and salty (35.1 to 35.3) Atlantic Water, the WSC keeps this area free of ice' (Gyory, Mariano and Ryan, 'The Spitsbergen Current'). The website text from which this quotation was taken (http://oceancurrents.rsmas.miami.edu/atlantic/spitsbergen.html) contains many citations to source material, which have been omitted from the quotation.

[1] In *Account of the Arctic Regions*, I, p. 403, Scoresby used the events of this day as an example of 'intermitting gales'.

[2] See Appendix, p. 292.

[3] Because the symbol ′ is the standard abbreviation for minutes of latitude and longitude, and one nautical mile is equivalent to a minute of latitude, it is understandable that Scoresby used it as an abbreviation for 'miles'.

Friday 21st April Lat. 78°[0?]'N Lon. 7°30′E
Very Var. NW.erly W.erly
Light winds all the day, with constant snow, until 6 pm. when it ceased. The wind blew from every quarter and almost every point of the compass, in the morning, but after 8 am became a steady breeze. Plyed to windward on the exterior of all ice, during the obscurity of the sky, but on its clearing entered several streams and open patches of brash ice. Saw four whales at different times of the evening, in pursuit of

['Thos Welburn **15. F** No 3 = 10 ″ 0′ *in margin*]

which, at one time, was four boats. At 11 Pm. one of them was entangled, though very slightly by a heave & as it never descended many fathoms under the surface afterwards, it was soon secured by 4 other harpoons. It did not yield its life to the lances of its ['NB. The Sun would be on the horizon at midnt but not visible'[1] *in margin*] assailants until ['about' *deleted*] somewhat past mid-night. At 2 am. ['**Saturday 22d April** Lat. 78°15′ Lon 6°59′E. SWbW SW' *in margin*] commenced flinching, having cleued all the sails up with the top-sails at the mast-head. At 7 finished, made sail to ply to windward the ship being not far distant from the lee-ice, which on the wind veering to the SWd drifted directly towards the land. Several ships seen, but none of them were observed to fish with success. The remainder of the day plying to windward amongst streams of ice. In the evening, blowing a strong gale of wind, reached into a turbulent sea to the eastward.

Sunday 23d April Lat. 78°0′ Lon. 5°50′E
WSW W. WNW.
Continued under a strong gale of wind, working to windward frequently near streams of ice. At 1 pm. the Resolution approached us from to windward & received from us a supply of pease & sundry other articles which they left behind them in Whitby. The Resolution it appears having drifted past Shetland in the Gale in which we entered Brassa Sound, returned soon after we left and remained until the 10th or 11th instt she but made the ice yesterday and has seen only one fish. At 2 Pm. she proceeded to the NEd whilst we lay too under the shelter of some streams of ice.

At noon 14 sail in sight. Fine cloudy weather.

In the evening the wind lessened, much water appeared to the [Nrd?] made sail and entered amongst crowded pieces of scattered ice and formidable patches – at 10 Pm. reached a large opening of ice in which we worked to ['**Monday 24th April** Lat 78°16′N Lon. 6°20′E[.] NW. Var. N.erly' *in margin*] windward during 5 hours. At 4 am. being at the extremity of the opening, the weather amazingly fine, and no fish seen, were inducements to seek a richer situation – 5 Ships were in Co & 3 in sight 15′ to the Nd.

Returned by a Similar track on which we entered and at 9 am regained the open Sea. ['again' *deleted*] The wind now had fallen nearly to calm – prepared to make off by reefing top sails and clearing the after hold of 100 packed casks, 13 Beer Casks, 6

---

[1] Scoresby was correct: at 78°N the sun remains above the horizon from 20 April until 25 August.

or 7 Bread casks, a flour cask, and a number of empty casks – this laborious operation together with starting an immense quantity of water and making all ready for
commencing filling with blubber, was performed by all hands in the most cheerful &
active style in somewhat less than four hours! The remainder of the day was calm,
and most serenely fine – the thermometer stood at 30° – several narwhales were seen
and ['NB. The Sun was above the horizon & visible at midnight' *in margin*] one
whale several of the ships in sight sent boats to a great distance in pursuit of fish but
without any success.

Tuesday 25ᵗʰ April Lat. 78°25′ Lon. 8°30′E
NE.erly
About 2 am. a breeze sprung up from the NEᵈ steered ['star' *deleted*] laboard [*sic*]
tacked towards the land. At 4 all hands having wrought with a great alacrity and
unanimity for 20 hours, set¹ half of them to bed & continued a half watch. At 11 am.
the ship approached the land ice which now appeared a solid pack, concentrated to a²
breadth of about 15 miles – when we tacked the middle Hook of the Foreland bore
EbN Dist. 5 Leagues[.] Several ships were seen during the day, which again passed
almost without clouds. About 9 Pm. the Making off was brought to a close and casks
as p margin filled with blubber. Cleared the decks.

Wednesday 26ᵗʰ April Lat. 78°30′ Lon. 7°0′E
NE NNE Calm. S.erly
Fresh to light breezes of wind most of the day – weather most delightfully fine. The
Remarkable continuance of fine and mild weather is at this season of the year
almost without precedent – June or July rarely affords opportunity so favourable
for the objects of the fishery. The ice to the NWestward [proved?] as hitherto an
open pack of light ice – to the northward navigable to an unseen extent – as we
played to windward we saw several whales and had some good opportunities of
capture but all failed. At Noon we had penetrated a considerable distance and no
fish were to be seen – steered to the eastward & then to the southwest. At this time
4 ships were seen amongst the ice to the [W?]ᵈ 15 miles distant – and the land
(Middle of Foreland) at East 9 leagues dist*an*t. Calm in the afternoon – a fresh
breeze of wind from the Southward in the evening – plying to windward on the
exterior of the ice.

---

¹ *Sic.* Possibly a transcript error for 'sent'.
² There is marginal note at this point, in the following form:
'6 of 300 G. ⎫
26 of 252 ⎪
16 of 200 ⎪
11 of 180 ⎬
4 of 160 ⎪
12 of 126 ⎪
2 of 84 ⎭
87 Casks [*blank space*] Butts'.

Thursday 27ᵗʰ April Lat. 78°20′ Lon. 8°30′E
SSE. S. SW. WSW
The breeze which now prevailed proved the incipient of a most dreadful storm – furious in itself, it was rendered singularly awful by the dangerous circumstances under which we navigated. It progressively increased as the day advanced and at 2 Pm. seemed to have gained its acme. Meanwhile the ship being surrounded by ice in every point except from SbE to SW, and in no part at more than a few miles distant, we worked to windward with all assiduity under a heavy pressure of sail, that in the event of such a storm as we apprehended from the indications of the barometer, we might gain room to drift, when we should be unable to resist the violence of the gale. During about two hours we lay sheltered by a projection from the land ice into the sea on the west. About 1 pm. the swell broke through the ice from the southwestward and rendered our stay highly dangerous amongst drifting labouring pieces. Reached as far to the eastward as we could get, tacked, and lay too until we sent down topgallant yards, took the waist boats upon deck, and lashed the four quarter boats with their bow rings even with the upper part of the davits, and secured their other ends by lashing them to their respective davits as they hung, we then essayed forth, but did not escape without danger from a number of heavy pieces of ice which opposed our passage; one of them we struck with a considerable force on the weather bow, and could not possibly avoid some of the smaller pieces. The wind was now south, as we proceeded to the Wᵈ it veered to SW. At 7 Pm we fell in with scattered pieces of the western ice – wore and stood to the SSE. The wind now blew furiously, the sea was tremendous, whilst thick weather ['increased' *deleted*] added to the awfulness of the scene. About 8 Pm the wind veered to WSW – ['Bar. at Mid-Nᵗ 28.79! Thermometer 30°–28° *in margin*] reached two hours to the SEᵈ then wore apprehensive of its westering more. About mid-night again met with ice which obliged us to put about.

Friday 28ᵗʰ April Lat. 78°10′ Lon. 9°35′E
W. WSW Var. W. WNW. Variable
Our situation was now highly alarming – a dreadful storm blowing from the west, a lee pack of ice only a few miles distant, and a rocky lee shore not more than 5 or 6 leagues off; the sails reduced to three close reefed top sails, fore, foretop, and main stay sails, each of which seemed ready to blow away. About this time the cross jack yard[1] broke in two near the slings. At 3 am. wore and stood 2 or 3 hours to the NNW then wore again and proceeded on a course [scarcely?] SSW which with 2½ [or?] 3 points leeway and 1½ points variation only left a due course of SEbS ['whilst' *deleted*] where the trending of the land is about SSE. At 5 am. the weather cleared – saw the land under our lee, apparently not more than 10 miles distant, but fortunately no ice was near; it must have drifted to the northward of us. Finding our ['Dreadful storm.' *in margin*] situation almost desperate, though the wind was somewhat lessened, set the fore sail and troy sail and let a reef out of each ['of' *deleted*] topsail. The ship plunged with alarming violence from the very mountainous character of the sea. The

---

[1] Smyth, *Sailor's Word Book*: 'CROSSJACK-YARD (pronounced *crojeck-yard*). The lower yard on the mizen-mast, to the arms of which the clues of the mizen top-sail are extended.'

wind at noon veered to the WSW, wore, set mizen & reefed jib whilst the ship advanced to the NW^d in the hollow (or trough) of the sea: on the direction of the gale veering again to the W^d returned again after 2 or 3 hours. These frequent variations of the wind proved a providential relief for having improved every change we found ourselves very sensibly advantaged. In the evening the weather was worse, the land was still near us under our lee, the Sea was prodigiously increased and met the ship nearly ahead, being deflected from the direction of the wind by the margin of the ice. Four or five ships were seen in different directions, carrying a similar sail with ourselves. About 4 pm. the ship passed over a mountainous sea, and buried her bowsprit and appendages many [yards?] beneath the following surge, which most unfortunately came threatening with its summit uplifted as high as the fore yard, and breaking hurled its mass of waters upon the bowsprit & bow of the ship, literally burying them for several moments. The concussion was dreadful – ['Dreadful Sea. Sprung the Bowsprit &c.' *in margin*] the quivering bowsprit received a serious fracture and but just supported the shock – the fore top stay sail was torn completely out of the bolt rope, was seperated from the stay in almost every <u>hank</u> and remained suspended by a single corner – the ship partook of the horrid tremor – rebounding with dreadful violence the stern was nearly immersed in the same surge – several squares of the cabin windows were broken and the cabin almost deluged with the influx of the water. The effects of the shock were in other respects striking. The helmsman was projected over the wheel & terribly bruised – various articles were displaced and hurled to a distance – a large deal box which stood on the level part of the cabin lockers was thrown forward & after making a complete revolution fell on its base on the table at a distance of three yards from the place – the <u>cant fall</u>[1] was also thrown out of the main top and fell into one of the boats. – The altogether [*sic*] beggars description – it was in fact <u>horridly sublime</u>.[2]

All hands were instantly summoned to relieve the enfeebled bowsprit and to secure the unstable foremast. The sails were first reduced – a hawser was then taken out of the hawse hole, clinched round the fore top mast upon the cap on the foremasthead and hove ['very' *deleted*] so tight by the windlass that the force of the forestay was not felt by the bowsprit. Some sailors now at the hazard of their lives, cut the slings and other entanglements of the sprit sail yard, and sent it upon deck; eased the jib-boom <u>in</u>, parallel with the bowsprit; and replaced the lanyard of one of the bob-stays which was broken by the springing of the bowsprit. Having performed these operations made sail as before abating the fore top, and main stay sails. In the evening the ['NWbW' *in margin*] weather again darkened & became exceedingly tempestuous, but the wind having veered to NWbW, we took

[1] Smyth, *Sailor's Word Book*: 'SPIKE TACKLE AND CANT-FALLS. The ropes and blocks used in whalers to sling their prey to the side of the ship.'

[2] Not an oxymoron in the context of 18th and 19th century notions of the sublime. Both Edmund Burke (*Philosophical Enquiry into the Origin of our Ideas of the Sublime and Beautiful*, 1757) and Immanuel Kant (*Critique of Judgement*, 1790) included frightening events in their definitions of the sublime; both agreed that 'the crux of the sublime is a certain degree of detachment' (McKinsey, *Niagara Falls*, p. 34). Gripping though Scoresby's description is, the detachment is still evident.

in the mizen and fore sail, nevertheless the ship continued to plunge very heavy and made four points of lee way. At 8 pm. the South end of the Foreland bore EbS. distant 3 or 4 leagues.

Saturday 29th April Lat.77°29′+ Lon. 9°40′E
NWbW Variable

In the morning the weather began to amend – the Barometer had risen to 30.00 inches. The sea soon fell and ere noon we made sail setting single reefed top-sail with main top gallant sail, &c. The people employed repairing the wreck of the gale. Carpenters repairing boats which were damaged & preparing <u>fishes</u>[1] for the bowsprit – boatswain fitting bowsprit shrouds – armourer making hooks, ring bolts and thimbles for affixing them to the bows, &c. &c. &c. At noon tacked to the northward. 2 ships in sight. Before night we had fixed a pair of Bowsprit shrouds of 6 inch rope extending from the extremity of the bowsprit to ring bolts beneath the cat heads on each bow – to which bolts was also affixed the jib boom [guys?]. The fishes were got into a state of forwardness. Fell in with streams of brash ice ['before' *deleted*] about mid-night – tacked and worked up to the NWd. Foreland in sight.

Sunday 30th April Lat. 78°10′ Lon. 6°20′E
NW.erly W. SW. Variable W.erly

Fine weather – wind moderate. Having entered amidst disseminated ice and loose patches, several miles, we saw a number of fish, and though the Sabbath day the prospect of success was so enticing that we could not resist the temptation of pursuing with several boats. One of the boats was so near as about five yards of two fine whales – by an unfortunate blunder they escaped him. At 2 Pm. called the boats on board and lay the ship too until we performed the usual Sabbath duties. In the evening plyed to windward amongst small ice, streams and patches. Several ships in sight. Middle Hook Foreland ENE.

Monday 1st May Lat. 78°25 Lon. 7°30′E
W.erly NNE

The entrance of the month of May was celebrated by the crew with the accustomed sports and ludicrous ceremonies attending the suspension of a garland, clad with ribbons on the main top gallant stay. The music consisted of Drum, tambourine, kettles & frying pans, tin pots, &c, &c. and the blackened faces of the men, their preposterous costume, and their awkward dances was calculated to relax the muscles of the most grave countenance. After they exhausted their humour & scheme of sports, and exhaled the stimulus of a course of drams, they all retired to rest but the watch. The garland besides the clothing of ribbands had a very appropriate appendage. On the top was placed on a spindle the figure of a whale, a harpoon in its

---

[1] Smyth, *Sailor's Word Book*: 'FISH, OR FISH-PIECE. A long piece of hard wood, convex on one side and concave on the other; two are bound opposite to each other to strengthen the lower masts or the yards when they are sprung, to effect which they are well secured by bolts and hoops, or stout rope called woolding.'

back and a boat laying by the line with the [esks?] distinguishing fishing jack displayed at its stern.

Worked to windward all night under a fresh gale of wind – the streams amidst which we navigated extended nearly to the land, and joined the western pack. About 10 am. we emerged from amongst them into a sea lying to the northward. The wind increasing to a very strong gale, the weather being very thick with frost rime & considerable swell, we were obliged to reduce sail and dodged under two treble reefed top sail, fore-top staysail & troy sail. Encountered much drift ice as we reached to the eastward and passed thro' ['Therm. 17° to 12° Bar 30.13' *in margin*] an open patch wherin we could not avoid all the pieces of ice. In the evening had a pretty clear navigation.

Tuesday May 2ᵈ Lat. 78°15' Lon. 6°40'E
NNE
Fresh or strong gales with some snow showers and frost rime. The weather was bitter[1] in the morning, made sail and reached to the northwestᵈ about 35' before we came to the ice, which formed a loosish pack. Joined Cᵒ with the John, received a visit from Mʳ Jackson[2] who gave the following information[.] They were employed making off, having captured one large whale & picked up a dead one within the week past. That, 50 or 60 sail of ships were to the [N?]ᵈ of us and near 40 sail in sight. That, the Henrietta has 3 fish, Aimwell one, Wᵐ & Ann, & Resolution clean. That, the ice is now pervious northward nearly to the headland, but they have seen no fish to the Nᵈ of our present situation, &c. Reached tow*a*rds the land, weather stormy – at noon the Middle Hook of the Foreland bore EbN distant about 12 leagues. At 9 pm. tacked near the land ice consisting of close patches of very heavy ice. Blowing hard all night ['**Wednesday May 3ᵈ Lat. 78°0+ Lon. 6°35'E**[.] North NNW' *in margin*] steered off to the Wᵈ under a low sail. About 5 am. approached the western ice, wore and dodged under easy sail.

The day proved very fine – the sky was almost without a cloud – and the Barometer at 30.55 – yet the gale continued with little abatement with intense frost. The John in Cᵒ. [Upwards?] of 20 sail in sight.

In the evening perceiving an opening of the ice leading to the wᵈ we entered it, and proceeded 15 or 20 miles about WbN between two compact patches of heavy ice accreted together by bay & pancake ice. Saw several whales – as the sea was here smooth we pursued, but without any success. Worked to windward during the night, in the ['**Thursday 4ᵗʰ May Lat. 77°45 Lon. 5°10'E**[.] NW to N' *in margin*] most considerable openings of the ice – at 6 am. were at the extremity – found whales scarce, <u>razor backs</u> occupying their places. At 10 am. perceiving no prospect of bene-fit and fearing the intensity of the frost should [arrest?] us we returned by the way we entered and during the remainder of the day plyed to windward on the exterior of the ice. Several ships. In the evening saw several whales – pursued without success. The

---

[1] *Sic*. Transcription error for 'better'?

[2] Thomas Jackson, Scoresby's brother-in-law, now commanding the *John* of Greenock, in place of William Scoresby Senior.

Clapham succeeded better having struck & killed a fish close by us. – Strong gales, cloudy.

Friday 5th May Lat. 77°50' Lon. 6°20E
N. NNE Variable.
Strong gales most of this day with thick snow showers – worked to wind*ward* with little effect until noon, amidst streams & patches of ice – then lay too under the lee of a compact stream. Several ships near us. <u>Teaed</u> on board the Egginton – this ship & the Thornton, the master of which joined us, are both <u>clean</u>. At 8 Pm. the weather was somewhat better, reached out from beneath the stream to the E^d & found ourselves in the land water – made sail and stood off the ice. The John in C°... Saw three or four whales during the day.

Saturday 6th May Lat. 78°15' Lon. 5°30'E
NE. Var. N.erly Variable – Incl. Calm E.rly – SSE
This was a fine day, though dull and showery.[1] In the morning entered the ice, and persevered several hours to the NW^d amongst compact patches and streams, consolidated by bay ice. About noon had reached a circular opening in which we saw some whales – boats were sent in pursuit of each, but we did not see them again, although they waited upwards of an hour. The wind fell to nearly calm in the afternoon – as the water was freezing and the prospect not very enticing we directed our efforts to returning to the eastward by a different route from that in which we entered. Assisted the progress of the ship by towing with one or two boats whilst we had a light air of wind from the NNE. Eleven sail of ships were seen to the w^d of us at noon – apparently in the way of fishing, but without any appearance of success. As the afternoon was mild & ['Bowsprit fished' *in margin*] more favourable than any period which has occurred since the bowsprit was sprung, we set about strengthening it by the application of <u>fishes</u>. A 2½ inch oak plank 12 feet in length was laid on the flat of the upper surface & spiked to the bowsprit. The two pieces of the broken cross jack yard, together with a similar spare piece of a spar were connected together in the form of an arch, having the curvature of bowsprit, and bevelled so as to rest [firm?] and closely against each other – one surface was then fitted to the bowsprit and the other rounded so as to form a neat and strong fish of 15 feet for the lower part of the bowsprit – this was also attatched by spike pointed bolts and the whole braced and secured by 4 stout clasp hoops which were made and applied in a perfect manner as if they had been prepared on shore. The preventer forestay was then withdrawn, and the bowsprit considered more secure in its present state than it was before the accident. At the same time rigged a new cross jack yard made out of a small spar, which we brought for a troy sail boom, but never applied.

[1] Another statement that would appear contradictory, except to the British. As Susan Coolidge wrote of her American principal character on her first day in London (*What Katy Did Next*, 1886), 'Afterwards, when she understood better the peculiarities of the English climate, she too learned to call days not absolutely rainy 'fine', and to be grateful for them.'

We had light variable winds with showers of snow until 9 Pm. when a SSEerly breeze sprung up – whereby we were enabled by a ['(NB. Found two varieties of mollusca in the water.)' *in margin*] circuitous route to escape from amidst the ice into the vicinity of the sea. At mid-night reefed topsails and lay too. John in Cᵒ.

During the calm of the evening I visited several pieces of heavy ice and fractured portions from the edges of each at a depth of some feet below the surface where it was solid & firm – when examined ['Sea ice, all fresh, of old formation.' *in margin*] every one of the pieces proved perfectly fresh. The ice was all cloudy – but transparent in this [*sic*] pieces, and evidently a vast quantity of air globules [crowded?] throughout the masses.

Sunday 7ᵗʰ of May Lat. 78°20 Lon. 6°25′E
SEbS WSW
In the morning a fresh gale of wind in the evening a light breeze. A heavy fall of snow occurred whilst the wind continued at SEbS & for some time afterwards. At 2 Pm. it veered instantaneously to the Wᵈ and shortly abated to a light breeze. Made sail to Nᵈ steering from point to point of the streams of ice on various courses from N. to SE. The sky cleared towards mid-night – a vast accumulation of ice appeared in every direction except to the Sᵈ & Eᵈ – hauled by the wind and plyed to the SWᵈ. Upwards of 50 sail of ships in sight.

Monday 8ᵗʰ May Lat 78°13′+ Lon. 6°30′E
W. NW. N.
Light breezes to fresh gales with snow showers. This morning two or three plans of proceeding presented themselves. To run to the Southwestᵈ[,] to ply into the ice to the NWᵈ[,] or to endeavour to gain a more Northeasterly situation. To stay where between 50 & 60 ships were cruizing was out of the question. Against going to the southᵈ there was the probability that the whales heretofore seen had entered the ice in about our present parallel. And against searching them to the NWᵈ I considered that in our former essays that way we had met with them in very small numbers, and that as 20 to 30 ships had already taken that course, of which we were the most leewardly, I had no hope of making any advantage of it. The north eastward then remaining to be considered. Should we be able to gain that lat. of 79° in a tollerable offing from the land we might hope for whales. This way there fore we proceeded, though we were anticipated by three or four ships to the northward of us. After working north until about 1 pm. we reached to the ENE about 6 hours, passing many streams & compact bodies of ice to the northward & scattered patches all round us, we then tacked within about 5 miles of the land – supposed to be the Middle Hook of the Foreland but could not ascertain precisely from its summit being concealed in clouds.

Tuesday 9ᵗʰ of May Lat. 78°35′ Lon. 9°E
North very var. 3 or 4 pts.
A lane or channel of water clear of ice & several miles broad presented itself here in and annexed to which we plyed under a brisk sail to the northward. We continued

our exertions in getting to the northward along shore all the day under a brisk sail and with squally winds. At noon we were within 3 miles of the <u>Devil's thumb</u>[1] – at 5 Pm. tacked very near the north end of the Foreland close by the land ice, where was an ice berg about 50 feet in height above the surface of the water, but not very large in circumference – it was composed of very compact ice. Saw several sea-horses near the shore. Several ships in sight plying to the northward. John in Cᵒ.

Wednesday 10ᵗʰ of May Lat. 78°45′+ Lon. 7°45′E
The wind being light and exceedingly variable we made very small progress. In the afternoon were much incommoded by the formation of bay ice. At noon observed in lat. 78°44′46″N – the north end of the Foreland bearing due east distant about 6 leagues. 32 sail were seen in the morning most of them to the northward of us. In the evening worked to the westward amongst patches of heavy ice & bay ice with floes at a distance to the northward. Saw a white whale (Balæna albicans).[2] No mysticeti.

Thursday 11ᵗʰ of May Lat. 78°32′ Lon. 6°46′E
NNE NNW
The ships which had penetrated 15 or 20 miles in different directions north of us, all returned – seeing at the same time no probability of finding whales, we began to return to the SWᵈ winding amongst patches & streams of old ice intermixed with small & bay ice. At first we steered 15 or 20 miles to the SSEᵈ and hauled up to the NWᵈ by the wind – on which course finding a convenient channel to the south of a body of slack ice, we advanced about 20 miles and then came to ['an' *deleted*] a ['open' *deleted*] pack too compact to be easily navigable. Still seeing no whales, though the ships in sight were all working to the Nᵈ the amount of 15 or 16 sail, yet considering it a hopeless direction under the existing appearances & circumstances, we bore up and steered to the Southward & were eventually followed by most of the fleet. Our first course as directed by the ice was SSE about 10 miles then southwesterly about 15 miles amongst a vast quantity of ['crowded' *deleted*] young ice, crowded together in a variety of aggregations. Here we saw a cetaceous animal which we pursued but never came sufficiently near to determine whether it was a common whale or a razor back. Saw an immense number of roches[3] collected into flocks containing several thousands of individuals each: the sea where they occurred was of a deep olive green colour – containing some substance which it deposited on the edges of the ice & tinged it of an orange yellow colour. The wind blew a brisk breeze most of the day accompanied by thick showers of snow – the atmosphere was [amazingly?]

---

[1] 'On Charles' Island is a curious peak, which juts into the sea. It is crooked, perfectly naked, being equally destitute of snow and verdure, and, from its black appearance or pointed figure, has been denominated the *Devil's Thumb*. Its height may be about 1500 or 2000 feet' (*Account of the Arctic Regions*, I, p. 97). Although not identified as such, this may be the dark peak shown in volume II of the same, Plate III, no. 3.

[2] Now *Delphinapterus leucas*.

[3] Presumably the Little Auk, or Dovekie, *Alle alle*. In *Account of the Arctic Regions*, I, p. 528, Scoresby described 'The Little Auk or Roach'.

gloomy, even at mid-day. Passed several foreigners in the afternoon – About 20 ships in sight at mid-night. The John in C°.

Friday 12th of May Lat. 77°50′ Lon. 5°50′E
NNW. NW. Var North
Blowing strong all night with almost constant small snow – lay too amongst open ice and drifted to the SE^d Many ships worked to windward past us. At 9 am. made sail and steered to the SW^d during 6 hours amongst very open ice & scattered patches. In the afternoon hauled up to the WNW by the wind, penetrated a loose stream and soon after saw two or three whales – pursued them with 2 to 4 boats, but without success. In the evening reached to the westward to the edge of ['Thermometer 12° to 10°. At Mid-n^t Lat. 77°32″ *in margin*] compact patches forming by their aggregation a pervious pack. Saw a ship inside flinching, but perceiving no fish returned & steered to the SE^d. 20 to 30 sail of ships in sight. The John in C°. At mid n^t light winds.

Saturday 13th of May Lat. 77°15′ Lon. 4°0′E
N. NNW. Variable NNE
We had light winds the whole of this day, with fine cloudy weather. Searched the sea around for whales – saw several at intervals – reached far to the eastward & in the evening returned & entered a loose patch of ice where 4 or 5 whales were seen, one of which we had the fortune to entangle. It sunk on being struck – run rapidly to the w^d

['Thos Welburn F   N° 4 11^{ft}2ⁱⁿ [bone?]]' *in margin*]

reappeared in about five minutes – presently disappeared & returned to the surface again in about 20 minutes. In an hour & 10′ from the time of being struck yielded its life to the lances of its assailants. At Mid-N^t began to flinch. Three ships laying to the W^d in a mass with sails cleued ['Got a Seal' *in margin*] up appeared as if two of them were assisting the other in repairing some damage.

Sunday 14th May Lat. 77 7+ Lon 4°30′E
Nerly to NEbN. Var
We had light or moderate winds all this day: the morning was clear & charmingly fine; in the afternoon & evening [was?] a considerable fall of snow. Explored some ice to the eastward & then returned 20 miles to the westward saw only two whales. Several ships in sight, none of them to appearance fishing.

Monday 15th of May
N. Variab. NW. W. SW. very variable
Light winds and fine cloudy weather. Yesterday we had some intimation of the Clapham having been destroyed by an accidental fire. Passing the Zephyr in the morning we were told that her late Commander Mr Munroe (a very worthy & superior man) was then on board that ship together with a boat's crew of his men. I visited him for the purpose of comisserating [*sic*] with him on the distressing event, found him uncommon affected & depressed & much in the need of consolation. From

himself & Capt. Bell of the Zephyr I received the following particulars of the affecting[1] catastrophe. The ship was amongst fish – had the success of three large whales – was in the lat. of 78°22' all well & the crew in high spirits. Dinner was just over & Mr Munroe resting himself in the cabin, when the second mate (a thoughtless ['Destruction of the Clapham by fire.' *in margin*] but active young man) entered with a candle and lighted it at the fire – the master asked him where was going with – he replied "into the gun room to get a rope for to lash a pair of jaw-bones with" – he was told that he must either procure a lanthern or go without a light – he preferred the latter & got what he needed & retired. Mr Munroe now ascended the <u>crows nest</u>, had descried a fish at a distance & pursued the direction with the ship. Meanwhile the 2^d mate, had returned again to the cabin for more rope – he was proceeding with a naked candle as before, when the mate observing him, desired him to pay attention to the master's orders & put the candle in a lanthern; at the same time calling for one the candle was placed in it & the man with an assistant descended. The gun room was crowded with the cables, sails, and spare whale lines – it was lined with Russia mats[2] for defending the whale lines from friction, ['and' *deleted*] the sides were filled with oakam:[3] & immediately beneath was the magazine containing 16 barrels of gunpowder, but rendered inaccessible ['by' *deleted*] [from?] the hatch being covered by the cables and other stores. The men not readily finding what they required, the 2^d mate took the candle out of the lanthern & attached it to the exterior of the lanthern – presently it fell upon some oakam, but was not observed by them until some part of it was on fire. They immediately attempted ['the' *deleted*] to extinguish it by throwing upon it a bundle of Russia mats, ['which' *deleted*] these firing also added to the flame ['and' *deleted*] which immediately ['the blaze' *deleted*] communicating to the lining of mats & the oakam in the [wings?] the whole was in a blaze before the fellows attempted to cry of assistance & then, showed their alarm by roaring "water water"! To the master's inquiries of the cause of the confusion he was answered "the ship's on fire." He slid down the backstay & in half a minute was in the midst of the flames. Water was now handed down – all was consternation – the flames prevailed and increased notwithstanding their utmost efforts. The cabin deck was scuttled – but chief seat of the fire, in the oakam could not be reached. Perceiving their efforts unavailing & dreading the explosion of the gun-powder the crew quitted their posts and prepared to quit the ship – the [affecting?] ['Clapham burnt' *in margin*] solicitations of the master & his frenzied ['conduct' *deleted*] solicitude recalled them to their duty & they declared they would return if they were blown up, with redoubled efforts they now passed down water in immense quantities – when now the Rum cask burst with an explosion like a cannon and [trebled?] the blaze. The master yet remained in the gun-room – when the deck above the magazine

[1] Possibly 'aflicting'.

[2] *OED* has an 1875 citation: '*Russia-matting*: matting manufactured in Russia from the inner bark of the linden.' The 1987 Supplement has an 1839 citation from J. J. Audubon.

[3] *Sic*. This spelling is consistent in the transcript; *OED* gives it as an obsolete (to 18th century) variation of 'oakum'. Layton's *Dictionary* defines oakum as 'Rope that has been unlaid and the yarns teased out. Used for caulking seams, filling fenders, and other purposes.'

was observed on fire and the oakam burning in the seams the dread of an explosion again drove the men from their stations, whilst two who attended on Mr Munroe, forced him from the place of danger. He had just reached the windlass when the magazine exploded – tearing away the starboard quarter, stern & much of the deck & setting fire to the ship from one extremity to the other, together with the sails on the main mast. The shock was so tremendous that for a few moments those upon the deck scarcely believed they existed – on recovering their recollection however they all leaped into the sea & were taken into the boats. In a few hours the conflagration had destroyed the ship to the water's edge. The crew rowed in board the Zephyr where they were hospitably taken care of & afterwards distributed by boat's crews into different ships. Thus by an act of presumptive carelessness was destroyed the finest ship that ever ['Entered' *deleted*] engaged in the whale fishing trade. The Esk was her nearest counterpart – but was exceeded by the Clapham by her sailing which was superior in a remarkable degree. The Clapham was fit in the most liberal style – was the pride of the owners, on her third voyage only, and had previously been very successful.

I remained about three hours on board the Zephyr & then returned to my ship, after having seen Mr Munroe in somewhat better spirits. I endeavour to console him by a view of his case compared with what it might have been. First it was under circumstances wherein a shadow of censure could not be passed upon him since he had used peculiar precautions – Second, that he was indebted to Gracious Providence for having escaped with his life – for a minute longer tarrying would have been his destruction, and Thirdly in a Religious point of view the distressing occurrence must eventually prove to his advantage.

> "In ... erring Reason's spite,
> one truth is clear – whatever is, is Right."[1]

Mr Bell informed me of another disaster in the loss of the master of the Middleton. Navigating the ship in the storm in which ['we sprung' *deleted*] the Esk's bowsprit was sprung, elevated on a cross plank laid over the deck for the purpose of directing the ship to more advantage. Whilst he appears to have been guiding the ship thro' betwixt two pieces of ice & passing suddenly to leeward – a lurch of the ship hurled him over the ships quarter. They had some shelter from the ice, so that they were enabled ['Proceeded 30' NE saw no fish' *in margin*] to lower two boats, but their efforts to get to windward to him were unavailing and had like to have been attended with the loss of one of the boats & crew.

Tuesday 16th May Lat 77°40′ Lon. 5°10′E
SW.erly
W. NW. very var.
We steered about 15 miles to the ESE with the wind from the SWd where amidst some patches of ice, we saw several whales. Had 2 to 4 boats in chase for several hours –

---

[1] Scoresby had previous quoted, at greater length, this extract from Pope's 'Essay on Man' in his journal for 12 June 1813.

some of them had very near chances, but all eventually failed. The John was more successful, having got her fourth fish. During the day we passed over a great space of [surface?] on a great variety of courses – saw some whales. 19 sail were in sight 5 or 6 of which were seen to make captures.

The weather was very fine all the day – towards evening nearly calm.

The sea here is of a deep olive green colour seems thick & muddy.[1] This appearance of the ocean is probably peculiar to Greenland. Where ['Colour of the Sea.' *in margin*] the sea is so deep that the rays of light appear not to penetrate to the bottom & where the water is pure or transparent, the colour is generally if not always a fine Ultramarine Blue. Where the depth is not great the true colour of the water is affected by the quality of the bottom. Thus fine white sand affords a light green – dark land a light blackish green – rocks a blackish ['blue or brown' *deleted*] colour, – while loose sand in a tide way ['causes' *deleted*] produces a muddy ['whiteish' *deleted*] greyish colour. Large rivers give the sea a tinge of brown, and fresh water in general is brown, tho' it partakes considerably of the colour of the substances over which it passes. It may be observed that the colour of the sea is liable to much deception in observation, and can only be correctly ascertained by looking downwards through a long tube reaching nearly to its surface & where some of the external light is shielded by some means from the eye ['Causes of the green colour of the Greenland Seas ascertained' *in margin*] during the observation. The trunk of the rudder may be used for this purpose and answers tollerably well. If then the sea is thus examined its colour is neither effected by sun nor clouds. A strong light from the sun merely enlightens the water & renders the shade of colour less [dark?] but has no effect on its constituent. If however the sea be viewed from an exposed position and at a distance, its colour will seem to vary with every passing cloud. The Sea in Greenland (where perfectly transparent) is of an ultramarine blue colour, but in many places it becomes of a blackish olive green. This is its colour here. The ice ['immersed' *deleted*] floating in this peculiar water appears yellow on its edges, from the deposition of some substance which also gives the peculiarity of shade to the water. For the purpose of ascertaining its nature & submitting it to a future chemical analysis I preserved a quantity of snow from the surface of a piece of ice which had been washed by the sea and which was & is

---

[1] In the margin opposite this line is the pencilled note 'See 12 May 1817'. This evidently refers to a lengthy passage in Scoresby's journal for that date, which itself has the marginal note 'Observation of the <u>Colour of the Sea</u> in various situations'. The passage is as follows: 'When near the land in shallow water, the colour of the sea was apple green, varying according to the nature of the ground: white sand producing pale green, dark yellow deep green, rocks brownish, &c. In all deep seas remote from land which I have yet visited, I have invariably found the colour of the sea ultramarine blues (deep shade) or more blue or a slight tinge of greenish blue, the Greenland seas only excepted. Hence in deep seas the colour is nearly that of the [azure?] atmosphere and probably arising from the same cause. Near the mouths of large rivers the sea is coloured with the mud of fresh water from the rivers with the various substances was shed from its supplying mountains which is held in suspension in the water – in strong tides & shallow water we see sometimes a grey [streamed?] milky coloured sea or of other shades according to the nature of substances removed from the bottom & the colour of the ground itself – near shore in still water or in all still shallow seas the native colour of the sea commixed with that of the bottom of the sea constitutes all the varieties of colour & intensity which we observe.' See also journal entry for 19 May 1815.

coloured to a brownish shade – this snow was still wet with sea water. On dissolving a portion in a wine glass it appeared perfectly nebulous throughout from a number of small semi-transparent spherical substances, and a vast quantity of small pieces of fine hair, like a child's hair chopped small.[1] On examining these substances with a microscope I was enabled to make the following observations. The globular looking substances appeared to be molluscous & of about $\frac{1}{20}$ to $\frac{1}{30}$ of an inch in diameter, they were variously marked by faint dashes with with [sic] no determinate order. The fibrous or filiform substances were far more interesting & the examination more satisfactory. They varied in length from a point to $\frac{1}{10}$ of an inch, and when highly magnified were beautifully & regularly <u>moniliform</u>.[2] In the larger masses the number of beadlike articulations amounted to about 30 hence their diameter seems to be ['Examination of substances which occasion the olive green colour of the Sea' *in margin*] about the $\frac{1}{450}$ part of an inch. Some of the larger ones were observed to become extended when [curved?] and to vary their forms when imperfectly extended, but whether they possesed [sic] loco-motive power I could not perceive[3] though I conceived from analogy that they must; and I fancied I could discern some collateral [silky?] fibres issuing from the moniliformes [sic] which might be their organs of loco-motion. They all had the property of decomposing light into the colours of the spectrum, which in some positions were very vivid & beautiful & every colour perceptible. The size of the articulations seemed nearly equal in all & their length only differed with the number of articulations. It is not improbable but that the very little appearance of life which I observed might be occasioned by the animalcule being injured by being deposited on the ice. When the water containing them was heated it emitted a very disagreeable odour – in some respects resembling the smell of oysters but so strong as to be offensive.

Hence it is very evident that these substances give the peculiarity of colour to the sea in these parts, and from their appearance & great profusion are evidently sufficient to occasion the great diminution of transparency which always accompanies the colour. The contrast of the blue or common colour of the Sea & this olive green, is so striking that every fisherman is familiar with it & always [prefers?] the opaque or green kind because in it the whales do not so readily take the alarm by a boat approaching them from the cloudiness it must occasion in distant vision. The line of seperation of the two shades is also so striking that altho' you may not perceive the very line yet, you can sometimes distinguish the change in five minutes sailing. On Saturday, Sunday, and most of yesterday we had the blue coloured transparent water.

Hudson remarked this difference of colour, but drew a conclusion from cursory observation which happened to be erroneous – he remarked that the sea was blue

---

[1] It seems probable that what Scoresby was observing were the two principal foods of the bowhead whale. The 'globular looking substances' were probably copopods (mainly *Calanus* species) and the 'fibrous or filiform substances' were euphausiids or 'krill'.

[2] *OED*: 'Of the form of or resembling a necklace; necklace-shaped; having contractions at regular intervals; consisting of or characterized by a series of globular or oval protuberances suggesting a string of beads.'

[3] Originally 'perceived', but the final letter deleted.

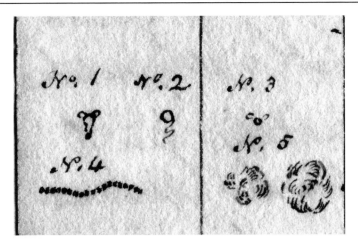

Figure 6. Scoresby's sketches of microscopic plankton
(Transcripts SCO1254, 17 May 1815). Photograph courtesy of the Whitby Museum.

where he met with ice, and green where it was free from ice.[1] This probably might happen to be the case at the period he made the observation, but from the cause of its colour it must evidently be erroneous. Capt[n] Phipps seemed not to have met with ['or at least noticed' *deleted*] any of the green colour.

Wednesday 17th of May Lat. 77°30′ Lon. 6°10′E
W.erly. Calm. Serly SWerly. var. Incl. Calm S.erly
Light winds inclinable to calm all this day – fine cloudy weather. Advanced about 15 miles to the SE[d] until we found ourselves at sea, with a few scattered pieces of ice only in sight. At noon a large extent of land in sight – the S. end of Foreland about EbN – 15 leagues dist[t].

In the afternoon (2 Pm) tacked and, as fast as the wind would allow, proceeded about west. Saw several White Whales, but no Mysteceti. The John in C[o] 2 or 3 other ships in sight.

['Examination of the Sea Water pursued' *in margin*] On renewing the investigation of the green sea water, this day, I was enabled to make some further discoveries. I procured a quantity of the seawater and on minutely examining it I observed several ['other [***]' *deleted*] animalculæ besides the substances before seen. I could not possitively [*sic*] speak as to the vitality of both the matters before examined but of these

---

[1] In the account of Hudson's first voyage, in 1607 to the Greenland Sea, the changes in sea colour are mentioned several times after reaching latitude 77°30′N on 6 July. The passage to which Scoresby referred was later that month: 'The *fourteenth*, in the morning, was calme with fogge. At nine, the wind at east, a small gale with thick fogge; we steered south-east and by east, and running this course we found our greene sea againe, which by proofe we found to be freest from ice, and our azure blue sea to be our icie sea. At this time we had more birds than we usually found' (Asher, *Henry Hudson the Navigator*, p. 13). Note that Asher (p. vi) believed that 'it would seem most likely that the whole account of the voyage was written by Playse, but owes the greater part of its value to the notes which Playse derived from Hudson's journal'. John Playse was a member of the crew on the 1607 voyage.

newly discovered I could not be ['at' *deleted*] for a moment at a loss. I distinctly found three species, neither none[1] of which was visible with the naked eye.[2] Through a double microscope the largest species [N° 1][3] appeared about the size of a grain of what is considered, rather coarse sand, is[4] seemed of a brownish colour – it moved in the fluid with a regular motion & nearly in a direct line. N°2 appeared globular with a dark coloured appendage – ['it appeared' *deleted*] about half the size of the former & advanced with a curious zig zag motion. N°3 was so small as to be just discernible – it was of a paler colour than the others & moved with amazing rapidity by sudden starts, between each of which it was for a moment perfectly stationary – the direction of its movement was always varied. The number of these animaliculæ did not appear so large as those of the former ones observed. The number of the molluscous kind (N°5) was truly immense: I am persuaded that the[5] individuals were not more than ¼ of an inch [asunder?]. ['Calculation of the number of these animals occurring in a cubical mile.' *in margin*] At this estimate a cubic inch appears to contain about 64; a cubic foot 110,592; a cubic fathom 23,997,872, and a cubic mile about 23,888,000,000,000,000. From soundings made in this situation it is probable the sea is upwards of a mile in depth, but whether these substances occupy the whole region is uncertain. However, provided the depth to which they extend is but 250 fathoms[6] the above immense number of one species may occur in a space of 2 miles square. Suppose it were required to count the number of the molluscæ in such an extent, allowing that a person could count a million in a week (which would be scarcely possible) then it would require that 80,000 persons should have commenced at the creation of the world to complete the enumeration at the present time! What a stupendous idea does this give of the works of the creation & of the profusion of Divine Providence in those works ([7]of these animals[8] so numerous – whose economy is unknown – which have remained unnoticed for 6000 years[9] – we are lost in wonder in the contemplation.

If ['Though' *deleted*] the number of these animals appear immense in the small space here considered what must be the amount required to produce the discoloration of some hundreds, nay of many thousands of square miles, which bears the same character and doubtless owes its peculiar colour to the same cause? Were the

---

[1] 'none' was inserted above the line, but 'neither' was not deleted.

[2] Five very small numbered sketches were inserted here in the margin (see Fig. 6). Below them is a pencilled note: 'See 30 May 1817'. This refers to another examination of such plankton, described in the journal entry for that date.

[3] Brackets in transcript, not an editorial insertion.

[4] Transcription error: 'it' intended?

[5] Originally 'they', but last letter deleted.

[6] Scoresby's vertical extrapolations were unrealistic. 'The vertical distribution of mesozooplankton in the 0–200 metre water column of the fjords and coastal waters shows that over 60% of the biomass is situated in the top 50 metres of the upper layer in summer' (Węsławski et al., 'Greenland Whales and Walruses in the Svalbard Food Web before and after Exploitation', p. 44).

[7] The parenthesis is opened but not closed.

[8] Originally 'animalculæ' but amended.

[9] Despite his exposure to the Huttonian-Wernerian debate at Edinburgh University (see vol. I, pp. xxxi–ii), Scoresby evidently still accepted Bishop Ussher's 17th-century calculation that the world had been created in 4004 BC.

water transparent it might owe some part of its peculiarity appearance[1] to the quality of the bottom, but its opacity proves that it is the suspension of some material substance which occasions the phenomena.

It is remarkable that the water containing all these substances is of less specific gravity than any hitherto examined during the voyage – though the number of trials amounts to 11 or 12.

Thursday 18ᵗʰ of May Lat. 77°20 Lon. 5°45′E
S.erly Var. North. NNE.
In the morning fine clear moderate weather – fell in with 3 or 4 whales on our reach to the westward, one of which the Boatswain struck, by

['Wᵐ Welburn.  Harpoon drew' *in margin*]

reason of the harpoon drawing however it[2] unfortunately ['lost it' *deleted*] escaped us. Made sail – at 8 am. the wind veered suddenly to the Nᵈ proceeded to the NWbW 6 hours about 25 to 30 miles – In the afternoon blowing a strong gale, with snow showers and no whales to see broke out the main hold, started the water and made off the fish captured Saturday last. Meanwhile we steered the ship through much ice to the SSEᵈ a a distance of about 10 miles – then falling into the margin of the sea, lay too. A strong S.erly swell. Several ships seen. The John parted Cᵒ.

Spoke the Lively of W*hit*by. Mʳ Wilson the master & Mʳ [Craig?] passenger supped with me. They have 2 fish & about 55 Butts of blubber saved from the wreck of the Clapham – makes them about 50 tons of oil.

Friday 19ᵗʰ of May Lat. 76°40′ Lon. 4°20′E
NNE, NbW. Var. NEbE &c.
Most of this day a strong gale of wind prevailed, accompanied with thick showers of snow. Lay too until noon. Finished making off at 2 am. after a spell of somewhat less than 10 hours wherein 45 butts of blubber were stored in 25 casks, whereof 19 were tons and the remaining 6 hundred gallons each.

At Mid-day the colour of the sea was changed to a <u>bluish green</u>, ['Greenish Blue water – remarks on'[3] *in margin*] a deeper colour than Sime's[4] but tollerably bright.

---

[1] 'peculiarity' inserted above the line, but 'appearance' not deleted.
[2] Originally apparently 'we', but 'it' overwritten.
[3] Unusually, there is a right-facing brace enclosing this marginal note.
[4] Despite the variant spelling, this is clearly a reference to the author of a book published in Edinburgh in 1814: Patrick Syme's *Werner's Nomenclature of Colours, with Additions, Arranged so as to render it highly useful to the Arts and Sciences …* . Werner was Abraham Gottlob Werner, Robert Jameson's teacher in Freiburg (see vol. I, p. xxxi) and Syme described himself on the titlepage as 'painter to the Wernerian and Horticultural Societies of Edinburgh'. This is therefore an example of Jameson's continuing influence on Scoresby's development as a scientist. For the significance of this work by Syme, see Paclt, 'A Chronology of Color Charts and Color Terminology for Naturalists', pp. 393–405, and Dolan, 'Pedagogy through Print: James Sowerby, John Mawe and the Problem of Colour in Early Nineteenth-century Natural History Illustration', pp. 275–304.

On examining the water I found the molluscous animals much less numerous, than in the olive green water, and the moniliformes very scarce. Animalculæ N° 2 was present but I did not observe the other species, though I confess I did not examine the water so minutely as on the former occasion. On proceeding to the westward the Sea became perfectly blue, and to the eastward olive green – therefore it is probable that the bluish green colour was occasioned by the admixture of the two varieties. The paucity of the animal substances therein [is?] some support to this conclusion.

In the afternoon reached under a brisk sail 8 or 10 miles to the w^d amongst several patches of ice and many scattered pieces. Seeing no whales returned – as we proceeded passing under the lee of a large piece of ice, the helmsman unobserved luffed the ship towards it. Providentially I at the moment [mounted?] the rufftree rail to ascertain whether the ship was perfectly clear of the piece, and barely in time for the preservation of the ship – for altho' the helm was instantly weathered the piece of ice grazed the larboard side near the main chains with a forcible crash. If the ice had been struck more directly, it must have been of the most serious consequence, as it was large, and the velocity of the ship not less than 7 or 8 knots.

We had hard squalls in the afternoon, but in the evening the sky cleared and the wind abated. Made sail to seaward.

Saturday 20th of May Lat. 77°21′+ Lon. 4°55′E
N. NNE, &c. Var.
Moderate to fresh gales of wind – weather fine & clear. In the morning entered the ice & explored to the westward, as far as we could with safety navigate – no fish seen returned. The John joined us and accompanied us to the eastward – passed thro' much ice on a reach of 30 miles after which worked directly to windward with a large quantity of ice to the northward of us. One ship killed a fish near us – we saw one. [Left?] 15 sail laid too in whole of water to the westward. At night 6 or 8 sail in sight.

Sunday 21st of May Lat. 77°30′ Lon. 6°25′E
North. Var.
The wind lessened in the morning and the day became charmingly fine towards noon. Lay too at the extremity of a bay of the ice with close ice all round, except to the S & E^d. After performed Divine Service in the forenoon, we made sail, having seen but one fish here, and passed thro' very crowded ice on an ENE course a distance of 10 or 12 miles – by the edge of a close patch saw a whale – sent a boat to the spot, which succeeded in entangling it by a heave. Though the fish took in[1] a ['close' *deleted*] compact patch the rest of the boats hunted it

['Tho. Welburn M.  N° 5 = 11.0 to Tail 21½ f^t broad' *in margin*]

---

[1] Possible omission in the transcript: '... took refuge in ...'?

so well that it yielded its life in about an hour. Meanwhile we manœuvred the ship to the best advantage, gained a windward situation more clear of ice, where we took the fish along side & flinched it, plying to windward most of the while.

In the night the wind was very light and atmosphere perfectly free from clouds. Several ships around us. 2 or 3 fish seen. Aimwell near with one fish.

Monday 22ᵈ May Lat 77°36′ Lon. 6°54′E
N.erly Calm. E.erly
Most of this day passed without wind or clouds. In the evening a light air arose from the Eᵈ and clouds were in the southeast quarter. I spent the afternoon, together with Mʳ Jackson on board the Aimwell. Our crew employed themselves in gumming the last fishes [sic] bone – unbending top sail & rebending the older sails – clearing decks, &c. &c. Thermometer exposed in a wooden case to the Sun [arose?] to 50° at 1 Pm. The whale bone of the fish caught yesterday had several of the [longest?] laminæ on one side seperated across about 2 feet from the gum as if occasioned by disease. The extremitys of the stumps were covered with short hair – some of the laminæ were partly seperated & yet remained suspended by a small part. The little progress which the ship made was towards the NE. Several ships.

Tuesday 23ᵈ of May Lat. 77 48 Lon. 7°10′E
NW.erly Nerly Var. Calm.
Charming weather – atmosphere clear – sun hot wind very light. Advanced about 20 miles to the NEᵈ amongst crowded ice in general, but towards evening navigated in a large expanse of water. Saw but two whales – both of them running with great velocity to the NWᵈ. Amused the sailors by igniting their pipes with a lens made of transparent ice, which to their amazement performed the concentration without any loss to its own substance.[1] Several ships near – all at loss to know where to look for fish.

Wednesday 24ᵗʰ May Lat. 78°0′ Lon. 6°56′E
E.erly Var. Calm W.erly. &c.
This day like the two preceding was clear – mild & calm. The sea was like a sheet of glass – a perfect calm subsisted for several hours though we could observe ships to

[1] 'Fresh-water ice is fragile, but hard; the edges of a fractured part, are frequently so keen, as to inflict a wound like glass. The homogeneous and most transparent pieces, are capable of concentrating the rays of the sun, so as to produce a considerable intensity of heat. With a lump of ice, of by no means regular convexity, I have frequently burnt wood, fired gunpowder, melted lead, and lit the sailors' pipes, to their great astonishment; all of whom, who could procure the needful articles, eagerly flocked around me, for the satisfaction of smoking a pipe ignited by such extraordinary means. Their astonishment was increased, on observing, that the ice remained firm and pellucid, whilst the solar rays emerging therefrom, were so hot, that the hand could not be kept longer in the focus, than for the space of a few seconds. In the formation of these lenses, I roughed them with a small axe, which cut the ice tolerably smooth; I then scraped them with a knife, and polished them merely by the warmth of the hand, supporting them during the operation in a woollen glove. I once procured a piece, of the purest ice, so large, that a lens of sixteen inches diameter was obtained out of it; unfortunately, however, the sun became obscured before it was completed, and never made its appearance again for a fortnight, during which time, the air being mild, the lens was spoiled' (Scoresby, 'On the Greenland or Polar Ice', pp. 270–71).

the eastward with an easterly breeze & others to the westward with an opposite wind. Saw several narwhales. ['[Middle Foreland at east.]' *in margin*] About 20 sail of ships to the N^d amongst crowded drift ice & floes. Fitted a boat with ['Gun' *deleted*] Harpoon Gun &c. & exercised the Officers. In the evening employed making off. S.erly swell.

Thursday 25th of May Lat. 78°10′ Lon. 5°40′E
NW.erly N. NE. Var.
 Delightful weather – winds very light – temperature of the air 32° in the shade and 50° exposed to the sun. We finished making off very early in the morning having filled with blubber 11 casks of 252 gallons each and 6 of 300 gallons or 35 butts. These casks were partly in the second tier in the main hatch way and partly in the 3rd tier against the after hold. At noon we had worked to the NW^d ['for' *deleted*] to a considerable extent and found ourselves amongst very heavy drift ice and some floes. 26 sail of ships appeared to the N^d & NW^d of which 15 or 16 made sail towards us. Spoke the Duncombe with 4 fish 64 tons oil – she had been 30 miles to the NW^d amongst floes and much bay ice without seeing a single fish. Retaining no hope of succeeding to the N^d when so many had returned without success, we bore up and again made sail to the S^d. Most of the fleet steered to the SW but we steered SSE with the intention of visited [*sic*] Point Look Out if the wind allowed and perhaps of doubling that promontory in search of whales, which have now retired from their usual haunts and cannot be found.[1] At mid night were in very open ice.

Friday 26th of May Lat. 77°26′ Lon 9°40′E
NNE. Var Calm. S.erly
Continued our course SSE with a moderate breeze of wind until noon when we were becalmed – the land about 10 leagues distance – point look out at SEbS. Passing through some loose ice we killed a sea-horse. He was shot whilst basking on a piece of ice and then retreated to the water – as he remained about the surface he was attacked with lances and a harpoon – whenever the boat came near he always faced about and two or three times laid his tusks in the boat's gunwale. We took him on board – made some careful measurements & then flinched him leaving the head & paws attatched to the skin that it might be stuffed if required. The skin, [&c.?] after being well salted was packed in ale cask which required an immense weight to get the head of the cask in. The extreme length of the animal was 12^ft 4^in and the greatest circumference 8^ft 5^in. The animal seemed to be old – the inside of the paws was covered ¼ of an inch with a rough horny substance; yet the tusks only measured 12 inches in length & 7 in circumference – they were very white & appeared to have been renewed. The skin was regularly an inch in thickness and generally covered with very short brownish coloured hair. The fore paws measured 2ft 2in. in length & 12 inches in breadth. The stomach was found filled with the remains of seals – amongst which the skin & blubber was very apparent.

---

[1] Scoresby's 'Point Look Out' is the southern tip of Spitsbergen, 76°30′N 16°30′E. It would be very unusual for Scoresby to go east of this point in search of whales.

In the evenings [*sic*] we had a fresh breeze from the westward which quite discomposed our plans. I had intended to have visited Point Look out but a lee wind and its exposed situation rendered the adventure imprudent. Hauled by the wind to the SW^d and tacked at mid-night in lat. 77°0'N. Point Look Out bearing SE distant about 15 leagues. 2 Ships in sight.

Saturday 27th of May Lat. 77°25' Lon. 7°0'E
W. Var.
Steered all day (excepting 4 hours) by the wind to the NNW or NW^d. In the evening we had again a calm. The weather was cloudy with some showers of snow and the wind light or fresh breeze. Two ships only in sight. No fish. Our whole progress was not above 40 miles on a NW course. Saw very little ice.

Sunday 28th of May Lt. 77°25' Lon. 5°10'E
Variable NbE
We had a fresh breeze of wind the whole of this day with fine clear weather. Sailed by the wind to the NW^d [1] with obstinate perseverance through the midst of very compact heavy ice winding occasionally on different courses to avoid such places as were impenetrable. At 8 pm. saw a large opening of water to the NW^d into which after some critically hazardous sailing we entered. Here we saw several ships – including a number which accompanied or followed us amounted to upwards of 20 sail.

Monday 29th of May Lat. 77°27'+ Lon. 3°16'E
W.erly Var.
Fresh breeze of wind with fog showers. Persevered on a NWerly course plying to windward when the wind veered to the W. which was at 2 AM. Fell in with several floes and much bay ice – worked up between two large sheets of heavy ice a distance of about 15 miles when we reached the extremity of the opening, consisting of floes and bay ice – the former principally generated by the cementation of the pieces of a pack by bay ice. Some few whales were seen by the ships around us – we saw but one. In the afternoon near 40 sail were collected within sight – no one of them had above 4 fish and several were yet clean. A large break appeared to the N^d amongst the floes into which we forced a passage thro' some broken ice and soon met with several whales – six boats were sent in chase and some good opportunities offered but unfortunately we were not successful. We saw at least a dozen individuals – mostly large fish. The John ['closely' *deleted*] (which joined us about noon) closely followed us and ten sail shortly afterwards, the united boats of which, amounting to about 70 soon dispersed the whales & without any one making a capture. In the evening we observed the place where we entered the opening was enlarged to a ['sailable [***]' *deleted*] navigable channel. Worked up towards it, but before we attained it, a thick fog commenced. When I left the deck in ['**Tuesday 30th May** Lat 77°32' Lon. 3°15'E[.] variable SW.erly' *in margin*] the night I left orders that the ship should be worked out of this opening into the adjoining water. Some negligence of one of the

---

[1] Originally 'NWbW', but amended.

officers however caused them to mistake the direction and when I arose instead of the ship being [extracted?] I found her in the farthest & opposite extremity at least 5 miles from the place of entrance. Lowered all the boats, as the wind came Southerly, and endeavoured to tow the ship head to wind, to accomplish our regress least the change of wind should be the means of besetting us. The fog continued thick all the day. At 2 Pm. the wind being freshened we ['Saw one whale & several narwhales'¹ *in margin*] desisted towing & worked to windward according to the best estimation which I could make of our situation. At 10 the fog cleared & we had passed the narrows.

Wednesday 31ˢᵗ May Lat. 77°23' Lon. 3°35'E
S. SSE
Moderate breezes – fog showers or cloudy weather. All night we worked to windward under all sails and at 7 am. arrived at a barrier of drift ice which had formed by the edge of the floes since we entered the same channel on Monday morning. Slack ice appeared at a distance to wind ward and a communication was nearly formed by the dividing of the conglomerate floe about 9 am. I was determined to escape from here if possible both on account of the scarcity of whales and the abundance of ships 37 sail being in sight. We therefore worked up an [uncommon?] narrow channel in many places not more than 120 yards broad and still crowded with ice. Moored to the floe for a few minutes but on observing the opening before alluded to sufficiently large to be navigable we cast off & forced through the midst of some opposing pieces of ice & [wound?] along the channel – at 2 Pm. we were amongst [sailing?] drift ice – proceeded by the wind to the ESE under all sails with the intention of taking advantage of the Southerly wind for once more exploring the more northern regions. About 5 Pm. we entered a vast body of slack ice in penetrating which we had a great deal of difficult sailing, having to wind amongst the pieces on every point of the compass between ESE and North – once we were obliged to make a tack and afterwards to bore through a narrow stream composed of very heavy ice. The ship fell with considerable force against one of the pieces without the possibility of prevention. At mid-night we ['**Thursday 1ˢᵗ of June** Lat. 79°0' Lon. 6°35'E[.] South SSW' *in margin*] saw open water to the southward and southeastward – but to the ENE the direction that we followed was yet a great profusion of ice. In the morning we entered the land water – steered to the NEᵈ under all the usual sails ['and' *deleted*] with topmast & lower studding sails in addition. The breeze being fresh we made rapid progress. At Noon the north end of the Foreland bore ESE about 20 miles distant – a few scattered streams of were² only to be seen, whilst the blink indicated a compact body of ice to the W NWᵈ & Nᵈ but to the NE clear water along the shores of the land. As we steered north we passed a great number of ships in the ice, probably we saw on the whole 50 or 60 sail. At 1 Pm. the breeze had increased to a fresh gale – the barometer indicated a further increase, hauled up therefore to the WNW and in two hours approximated a body of floes – contained some considerable interstices – yet however we did not consider it prudent to force amongst them, therefore lay too.

¹ There is again a right-facing brace around this marginal note.
² *Sic*: 'ice' presumably omitted by mistake when transcribed.

In the evening hazy disagreeable weather. The John in C° a few other ships occasionally in sight.

Friday 2ᵈ of June Lat. 79°10 Lon. 6°45′E
SSW – SW. Var. North
Most of this day we passed dodging under easy sail nearly in the same place with regard to the ice. The wind blew a hard gale in the morning accompanied by snow and sleet, but at noon it began to abate. In the evening we had little wind – made sail reached to the ice to the wᵈ and found it consisted (as far as we could see at least) of an aggregation of floes consolidated into a pack. About 7 Pm. the wind suddenly veered to the north and afterwards the breeze increased. Worked up into the extremity of a sinuosity and lay too. 2 Ships near us. Heavy weather at mid-night.

Saturday 3ᵈ of June Lat. 79°15′+ Lon. 6°45′E
North
A brisk gale of wind with clear weather and keen frost occurred this day. Lay too the fore part of the day: dined on board the Dexterity of Peter Head. The Dexterity has three fish 35 tons of oil: the Enterprise in C° 5 fish 75 to 80 tons: the Leviathan 3 fish; &c. &c. At noon the north end of the Foreland bore ESE distant 10 or 12 leagues. In the afternoon perceiving no chance of penetrating the floes in this place, which were aggregated into a compact body, ['and' *deleted*] seeing no fish, but observing an appearance of open ice to the west and SWᵈ we made sail and ran to the southward on various courses accordingly as the margin of the floes trended. Penetrated every sinuosity but without seeing a single whale – at 10 PM. hauled by the wind WNW under the lee of some large floes and proceeded about 20 miles along an opening which led us ['**Sunday 4ᵗʰ of June** Lat. 78°53′+ Lon. 6°E[.] North' *in margin*] within sight of nearly 60 sail of ships. In the morning the wind fell, but not before we had worked some distance to windward & nearly gained the edge of a floe where we saw 3 or 4 small whales. One of the fleet caught one of them.

Having spoken some of the ships we gained the following intelligence. That the Royal George had returned to Hull in distress from whence she set out again for Greenland on the first of May.[1] That, at that time, the Lord Barham Straits fishing ship had arrived in a Scotch port totally dismasted.[*2] That all the Allied Powers of Europe were rapidly concentrating their forces to attack the destroyer of ['its' *deleted*] their countries' peace. The Success of the ships still continuing very poor and the prospect very [***] indeed. The Resolution & Volunteer of Whitby together with over 15 other ships are yet clean. A great many others have only one fish each. It appears two foreigners have gone home full of seals having caught several thousands each. Many Dutch and Hamburghers are in Greenland but few of them fished. We are told one now in sight has a fish and 3500 seals and only wants another fish to complete his cruise.

[1] 'Another ship which had to put back was the *Royal George* of the Davis Straits contingent. When within 200 miles of Cape Farewell on April 6, she lost her foremast and bowsprit in a gale of wind, reaching Hull on April 20, a quick passage for a lame duck. After being refitted, she sailed for the Greenland seas' (Lubbock, *Arctic Whalers*, p.199).
[2] Asterisked note in margin: '*This report appears to me to be without foundation.'

In the afternoon having a gentle breeze of wind we plied up a narrow channel on the west margin of a very heavy & extensive floe or probably field – here we met with several small whales and notwithstanding it was the Sabbath day, the great scarcity of these objects of our voyage, induced us to send three or four boats in pursuit of them. Before mid-n[t] I imagine we saw nearly 20 individuals yet we could not entangle one. The John made one capture and the Enterprise of Lynn two in the course of the day. 10 or 15 sail of ships in sight in an opening of the floes west from us – as many near us – and upwards of 20 more to the SW[d] of us. Moored to a point of ice projecting from the east side of large floe and ['The John' deleted] placed two boats on watch. The John made fast ['**Monday 5**[th] **June** SWbW W. NW. N. NE N. NNW.'[1] *in margin*] near us – as likewise did the Aimwell which worked up in the morning. Mr Johnston gave me to [sic] pleasing intelligence that I might anticipate a letter which was on board the …[2] from my affectionate wife. He had received an epistle by the same vessel which left Hull about the middle of April. Mr Johnston told us likewise that the *William & Ann* had captured four large fish with one of which they had the misfortune to lose a man [drowned?] and with another a man killed. In the latter instance the fish was never approached without its making a most tremendous display of its strength by the amazing force of its fins and tail on the water. One of the boats was dashed to pieces in which the man was killed, at the same an harponeer and another of the crew were seriously hurt. It appears the fish at length destroyed itself by the violence of action after being entangled about . . hours.

About 6 am. the wind veered progressively from SWbW to W – NW. and North. The Esk then lay against the ice – unmoored set the sails aback & she went astern clear of the point of the ice – the wind then however veered to NE and freshened so that there was not room to back[3] her off the ice. A line was taken to the ['bay' deleted] ice adjoining the point – the sails at the same time adjusted for the evolution & the ship was very efficiently tacked about. The Aimwell meanwhile lay in a deep sinuosity of the ice directly into which the wind now blew. They laboured for 2 or 3 hours with very little effect in endeavouring to warp out. As it appeared we could assist them we [***] the Esk before the wind to within 50 yards of the Aimwell, sent them the end of a towline which when fast, we made all sail and dragged the Aimwell a distance of 400 yards like about and all in the space of 15 minutes – the Esk just cleared the point of ice, so that the smallest hindrance would have either entangled her or prevented further assistance.

It is worthy of remark that the fish taken yesterday by the John had broken its jawbone against the bottom when at the perpendicular ['Sea 600 fathoms deep in

---

[1] The usual geographical coordinates are absent, but see the marginal note on sea depth during this day's entry.

[2] The transcript shows only ellipsis points, but from the journal entry for 8 July 1815, the ship in question appears to have been the *Cyrus*. According to Lubbock, *Arctic Whalers*, p. 199, the *Cyrus*, a new vessel, was the last of the Hull fleet to leave port, on 10 April. 'She immediately ran into bad weather, lost a man overboard and received such damage that she put back to the river for repairs on April 19.'

[3] Possibly 'tack'.

Lat 78°53 Long. 5°56′E' *in margin*] depth of 600 fathoms. We expended most of this day in exploring the sinuosities of the neighbouring fields and floes in which however we failed in finding any whales. At 2 Pm. ran before the wind 4 or 5 miles then hauled up into a very narrow channel between two heavy floes leading into much water to the westward. Penetrated a few miles, but observing several ships making all speed out and not perceiving any fishing, we returned. At 9 Pm. again made sail to the SE^d until 11 when we found ourselves almost surrounded by ice ['at' *deleted*] near the bottom of a deep bay which the prevalence of thick snow showers prevented us from examining therefore hauled out, ['and' *deleted*] worked a little to windward and lay too. The wind then blowing a very fresh gale. Aimwell & John in C°.

Tuesday 6th of June Lat 78°27′+ Lon. 6°50′E
NNW North. NNE
At 10 am. the weather was clearer and wind more moderate made sail and manœvered amongst a vast number of floes and pieces of heavy ice, towards the southeast and south. Supposing ourselves, at 2 Pm, about 20 miles south of our situation of Sunday we again hauled by the wind to the NW^d under the lee of a chain of floes, in a channel of water bounded by another chain of floes on the SW parallel to that to the windward of us. We continued our search with some variation of direction & without making but one short tack until 9 Pm. Then wind was then light so that we worked slowly to windward toward the edge of a field where 5 foreigners lay moored – one of them with his Jack flying, a signal of a fish being struck. Two boats preceded the ship as we worked up, but did not see any whales. Saw a number of narwhales. Several sail of ships in sight. Spoke the Margaret of London with 3 fish.

Wednesday 7th of June Lat. 78°36 Lon. 5°10′E
N. NNE
Light winds with fog showers. This day was expended in circumnavigating after laying to the SW of the field. In running to the southward I ['had' *deleted*] expected to have been able to penetrate farther westward as also to gain a more retired situation for about 20 sail of ships had accumulated around us within the distance of 2 or 3 miles. Saw but one fish all the day which the Aimwell captured. The John likewise caught one. We had some trouble in getting round the floe from the formation of bay ice. It is remarkable at this season for to see new bay ice, yet we have observed its formation in considerable sheet for several days past. The mean temperature of the atmosphere for the last five days is not more than 21° therefore the formation of ice is not to wondered at.[1]

At Mid night saw upwards of 30[2] sail of ships: 9 or 10 lay NW from us, 12 or 15 miles distant all but one made fast, but apparently not fishing. The Refraction of the atmosphere caused them to assume a peculiar shape. Their masts appeared to be only

[1] *Sic*: 'to be wondered at' presumably intended.
[2] Possibly '20'.

about half their real length compared with the size of the hull, hence the viewed [*sic*] in perspective they appeared singularly inclined.

Saw a number of narwhales and two bears.

Thursday 8ᵗʰ of June Lat 78°34′ Lon. 5°15′E
NE.erly N. NW. W. &c. WSW
This day passed like many of the preceding with light winds, fog showers, on the whole fine weather but no whales. This paucity of whales is truly distressing and singular. In situations and under circumstances the most favourable according to common experience, not a fish is now to be seen. The ships scour about the country in the utmost disorder – the oldest commanders are at their wits' end. We continued near the field before mentioned within sight of about 30 ships. Fields and floes all round us, veins of water amidst them, and adventurous fishermen penetrating every fissure. Saw the John with two other ships enter a narrow channel on the NW of the field. In the Evening began to work to the southwest. Replaced the mizzen with a larger sail and rigged flying jib boom. At Mid Night fine cloudy weather, free from fog or snow Therm*omete*r 20°.

Friday 9ᵗʰ of June SW. S SSE. var. S. Lat. 78°25′ Lon. 5°10′E
SW. S SSE. Var. S.
At 10 am. blowing a brisk breeze of wind, having attained the extremity of an extensive opening of the floes where there was no egress, we ran two miles north and then worked through a narrow channel into a greater expanse of water to the westward followed by several of the fleet. Here under all sail we worked to the [southward?] – in the evening ['came' *deleted*] navigated amongst heavy drift ice as well as floes and bay ice. The master of the Royal George came on board to require of our Armourer to repair for him the sweevel[1] of an harpoon gun. He informed me that several fish had recently been killed to the southward of us, a few leagues and that many had been seen by some ships in the present fleet. About mid night our progress was arrested by a chain of floes which lay directly across our path assimilating with crowded drift ice on either hand, so as to prevent our access into an opening expanding to a great extent to the southward of us and apparently communicating with the sea. Lay too. A great number of ships to leeward working up.

Saturday 10ᵗʰ of June
Lat 78°22′ Lon. 5°30′E
S. to WSW & SW.
Moderate or light winds very fine cloudy weather. We soon found the ice closing around us and with such rapidity that ere we could make our escape by the way we advanced the passage was blocked up and we had to bore through amidst several small pieces of drift ice. Steered to the Eᵈ & Nᵈ with a view of making our passage to the seaward side of the ice lying to the eastward of us and then of working round it a

---

[1] *OED* gives 'sweevil' as a Scottish spelling of 'swivel'.

few leagues more to the southward. We were foiled in this attempt however by not being able to discover any passage to the sea, within about 15 miles of the place from when we commenced the search in a NEerly direction, and nothing but a formidable barrier all round to the S^d SE^d & E^d. As we reached to the westward at 2 Pm a fish was discovered; the second only that we have seen since Sunday last – sent two boats which had the good fortune to harpoon it on its second appearance –

['Thos Welburn **M**  N° 6 = 8. 6 [NB?] a wounded fish' *in margin*]

In 65 minutes it was killed – made the ship fast to a large piece of ice – & flinched it. Nearly 50 sail of ships have now accumulated within sight of us – none of which have the appearance of fishing. At 9 Pm therefore, having observed several strangers accomplish an entrance from the sea by a channel about 10 miles to the northward of us, we cast off and made sail for the place, and about mid-night proceeded through it.

Sunday 11th of June Lat. 78°35' Lon. 7°50'E
SSW. S SE. S. SSW. S. variable
As the wind was a light or moderate breeze we reached to the SE^d E^d ENE^d &c. close by the wind, passed several floes, and after 8 am. navigated solely amongst loose ice. At 2 pm. the drift ice was become widely scattered and we had approximated within 30 miles of the land, which we could discern through the clouds near the horizon: we then tacked. Unfortunately the wind immediately veered to the SW so that after proceeding 4 hours to the WNW we found ourselves at or to leeward of our situation at 6 am. From hence we began to work to windward under a brisk sail though the wind increased to a fresh gale. We could see within the floes (at 7 pm) about 20 of the ships which we left yesterday bearing about west from us, at the the [*sic*] distance of 15 or 17 miles. 5 other ships at a lesser distance on the exterior of the floes.

Monday 12th of June Lat. 78°25' Lon. 6°0'E
S. SSW. S SSE. S. SW Var. Calm. W.erly
The wind increased about 4 am. to a very strong gale accompanied with thick showers of snow – lay too during 3 or 4 hours of its excess & on its ['abating' *deleted*] subsiding about 8 am. made sail. Reached to the eastward & met a strong swell which rendered our navigation dangerous & difficult, we then returned to the westward. Passed several streams of ice & scattered pieces, and at noon were ['at' *deleted*] near the edge of several floes. The afternoon was calm & foggy. 6 or 8 ships occasionally seen. The *Willia*m & Ann & Aimwell 3 miles SW from us.

Tuesday 13th of June Lat. 78°23'+ Lon. 5°40'E
Calm W.erly Var. N.
We had no wind in the night and but a very light breeze until evening, it then increased. The weather was foggy during the calm & afterwards cloudy with some showers of snow. We made an attempt to proceed westward but after entering the ice almost 10 miles we found the floes and drift ice so closely approximated as to render the mass impervious to ships. Lay too.

M^essrs Johnstone & Stephens dined with me, and in the afternoon Mr Sadler of the Aurora joined us. The Aimwell has 2 fish; Wm Ann 4 large; Aurora 1. I had intended proceeding further south and then penetrating the ice as far as possible, but Mr Sadler induced me to change my intention by his confident assurance [*sic*] that the ice was no where pervious between the lat. of 77½° (from whence had just come) and our present situation. That, it consists of large fractions of floes and so closely aggregated as to render the sea unnavigable amongst ['them' *deleted*] it. The W*illia*m & Ann has been very recently as far south as 76° of lat. but never saw a fish.

On the increase of the breeze, we all made sail in C° first to the eastward into the land water and then to windward. Several ships passed us on their way before the wind, steering to the S^d. Several others seen within the ice. Therm^r 39° to 34°. N. end Foreland EbN 40′.

The sea about noon was very nearly <u>blue</u>. On examining the ['Blue sea water contains some of the minute <u>molluscæ</u>.' *in margin*] water I was disappointed in my expectation – for I found it still contained some of the minute molluscæ but in by no means the profusion with which they abound in the olive green water. I could not discover however either the <u>moniliformes</u> or the <u>animalculæ</u>. Therefore the theory before advanced (17th May) may still be correct. The colour of this water was between the Verditter[1] & ultramarine blues.

Wednesday 14th of June Lat. 78°33′ Lon. 6°25′E
NbE Variable
The wind blowing a moderate or fresh breeze we plyed to windward all night and in the morning (10 am) made a reach to the westward amongst loose ice and streams until 3 pm. when we arrived at the exterior of the floes which we left on Saturday. In the interior we saw near 50 sail of ships and not one fishing, several running to the S^d but the greater proportion working to the northward. Not conceiving the probability of advantage to be derived from again entering amongst the floes, we returned into the land water and made sail along the edge of the ice to the southward, with the intention of penetrating the ice, if possible near the lat. of 78°0′. Several ships seen pursuing the same direction. The Aimwell accompanied us and the Lion of Liverpool with one fish joined us in the night. At Mid-Nt Middle hook of the Foreland at EbS 30′ dist*an*t.

Thursday 15th of June Lat. 77°57′+ Lon. 6°E.
NNE NEbN. Var.
At 11 am. imagining the ship far enough to the south and at the same time observing the ice to be slack we hauled by the wind to the NW^d. At 1 Pm. tacked at the edge of a chain of floes. The wind blowing fresh, we soon worked to windward and gained a channel which led us about 8 miles further to the NW^d. Then by some very critical sailing amongst crowded drift ice lying between two floes, after making several tacks we gained another opening which conducted us about 8 miles further to the NW^d and then we reached a compact barrier formed of floes and heavy ['drift' *deleted*] packed

---

[1] *OED*, s.v. 'verditer': 'A kind of pigment of a green, bluish green or (more freq.) light blue colour …'. *OED* lists several alternative spellings, but not Scoresby's.

ice. The ice appearing slacker to windward we (after laying too a little while) again made sail and had some very hazardous and difficult sailing to work through the midst of several pieces of heavy ice: we made two tacks in a channel not more than 100 yards broad. ['Firm'[?] *deleted*] In the evening the wind increased to a fresh gale, but the weather continued tollerably clear. From 9 Pm. to 2 Am. we navigated amongst very rank drift ice inter- ['**Friday 16ᵗʰ of June** Lat. 78°11′+ Lon. 4°30′E[.] NNE. N. NW. W.' *in margin*] mixed with floes: During which space we advanced about 6 miles more to the north. We then fell into comfortable sailing – worked 6 miles more to the north & then sailed about 10 miles to the WNW and then worked into a very extensive opening amidst large floes and loose ice, wherin were several ships, but as usual no whales.

At Noon the Middle hook of the Foreland bore EbN or ENE about 60 miles distant. Nearly 20 ships in sight steering every variety of courses.

Perceiving an opening leading a considerable distance to the westward, we worked therein a distance of about 10 miles amidst ragged floes and crowded drift ice. At the extremity was a narrow communication towards another opening in the same direction which we should have penetrated had we not observed a ship running out of it. Lay too, and sent a boat on board. She proved the Middleton, the master of which was drowned in the beginning of the season. They saw five small fish Sunday last, but none since. They have now 3 = 40 Tons of oil. They observed the John a great distance to the NWᵈ completely encircled by ice, but apparently fishing occasionally.

We now steered to the eastward, gained a large opening and then proceeded about ENE the rest of the day.

Saturday 17ᵗʰ of June Lat. 78°30′ Lon. 6°10′E
W.erly Calm. E.erly
We had a calm most of this day. Made off the last captured fish in the forehold, which filled 18 casks = 26 butts. Mʳ Bennett master of the ['Middleton' *deleted*] Venerable dined with me: his success is [*blank space*] fish 55 tons. He informed me that a few small fish had been captured amongst these floes during the past week.

Hearing that the master of the Valiant of Whitby, George Sinclair was much distressed in a fracture of the jawbone by the extraction of[1] a tooth, and the wound dangerous I sent our Surgeon with offers of advice and assistance. This man was last year my mate and though he had been treated with the greatest kindness and respect,

[1] At this point there is a marginal table:
'Making off.
4 casks = 252
3 " = 200
3 " = 180
3 " = 160
2 " = 126
3 " = 84
3 " part full.'
The table is completed by a right-facing brace indicating that the contents of the casks amount to '26 Butts'.

notwithstanding I had evinced myself his particular friend and instructed him in every of the most critical cases of seamanship and nautical astronomy – yet notwithstanding these kindnesses he was so ungrateful on his being offered the command of the Valiant to make proposals to almost all my officers to sail with him, as an inducement to which he promised superior stations. A few consented but the greater part refused. This baseness obliged me to view him with contempt. Nevertheless on hearing he was serious ['Sinclair's ingratitude' *in margin*] ill I sent him assistance – which however proved unnecessary as his grievance had been exaggerated. Baseness was still more than ever evinced in his conduct – for Thomas Welburn taking charge of the boat was first pressed to stay beyond his orders, then intoxicated, & lastly offered an advanced station in the Valiant the next fishing season which it seems he acceded to. This man it may be noticed has been the striker of 5 of the 6 fish which we have captured – hence they covet his services,*[1] and have been so barefaced as to endeavour to seduce him from us when on a message of kindness and charity! Good God how are such men debased – surely they must have attained the climax of ingratitude!!

In the evening we had a light breeze from the eastward. Lay too.

Sunday 18th of June Lat. 78°34 Lon. 6°10′E
Variable N.erly
Light variable winds or calm. Lay too until noon then steered to seaward amongst loose ice, on a southeasterly course. Some small showers of prismatic or filiform snow fell in the evening. At 9 Pm. we gained the exterior of the ice, where a southeast swell prevailed.

The Aimwell in Company. 10 or 12 sail in sight. The Foreland 40′ off.

Monday 19th of June Lat. 77°23′+ Lon. 5°40′E
N.erly NNE
Having now persevered for a considerable time in the usual fishing latitudes with very trifling success during the month I wished to try the more southern latitudes: accordingly taking advantage of a fresh breeze of wind we steered along the edge of the ice from point to point on various courses between SSE and WSW making during the day an advance of about 120 miles SWbS. Spoke the Enterprise with 7 fish. The Aimwell & Valiant following us together with a ship unknown.

We had delightful fine clear weather throughout the day.

Tuesday 20th of June Lat. 75°59+ Lon. 3°50′E
N. NbE
At 4 Am. when at the distance of 2 or 3 miles from a point of the main ice, our optics were gladdened by the sight of a whale, being the only individual of the species seen in 10 days. Two boats were instantly lowered down and the fish lay until the mate struck a harpoon whilst his boat [watched?] its back. It remained underwater

---

[1] Marginal note in transcript: '*T. Welburn declared that Sinclair offered him a situation but this was found to be false …'.

['John Dunbar F. Nº 7 = 11..2 Cant 28 f' *in margin*]

only 4 or 5 minutes and then [***] about in various directions with great velocity. In about 20 minutes it made towards a very compact part of the ice, but diminishing its speed four harpoons were struck before it reached the shelter and ['the whale' *deleted*] then being assailed with lances vigorously applied it yielded its life very soon after 5 am. Took it alongside and flinched it in 3 hours. Whilst we were clearing the decks and paring the jaw-bones two other whales made their appearance, they were pursued without success for two hours. At Noon 6 sail were within sight.

The ice here trends with a sinuous edge about SWbS. The sinuses[1] are very deep and extensive and the points narrow and very compact. Indeed the ice is only pervious in a few distinct[2] places – and these seem to afford but a difficult navigation.

In the afternoon gave chase with ship and boats to 3 or 4 different whales which we saw – they led us 10 or 12 miles to the SSE^d. the sea was however so turbulent that the boats plied with difficulty and without success.

Wednesday 21st of June Lat 75°53′+ Lon. 3°0′E.
NbW NW. W to NNE
In the night made two or three tacks to the eastward to weather a point of ice & then reached a considerable distance into an opening of the ice extending several leagues to the NW^d & terminating in an open pack of heavy ice. Saw several whales had occasionally 5 boats in pursuit. At 3 Pm. we had reached to the ice on the NE. side of the opening whilst two of the boats chased a whale to the NW^d and succeeded in striking a harpoon. They ['ship' *deleted*][3] were at that time full 8 miles from the ship, we immediately proceeded towards the place under a moderate breeze of wind whilst the rest of the boats

['John Dunbar F  Nº 8 = 11..1' *in margin*]

preceeded [*sic*] us. The accompanying boat with the striker having bent on his lines they were mortified on the reappearance of the fish, by not being able to make any further progress in the capture. The Perseverance of Lynn lying two miles to windward very kindly & opportunely sent two boats & also ran the ship down to our boats – they succeeded in striking a second harpoon on the fishe's' [*sic*] third appearance at the surface of the Sea. Shortly afterwards our boats arrived at the place and completed the capture in about a quarter of an hour afterwards. The weather had hitherto been most delightfully fine, but as we were about taking the fish alongside at

---

[1] *OED* lists as obsolete a definition of 'sinus' as 'A bay, gulf, or arm of the sea'. The latest citation in *OED* is 1789: 'The great number of friths, sinuses, or arms of the sea.'

[2] Possibly 'distant'.

[3] The sentence initially appears to have begun 'The ship ...' and 'y' was added to the first word when 'ship' was deleted.

8 pm. a thick fog which had threatened us for some time in [*sic*] the windward horizon suddenly enveloped us – Lay too and flinched.

Ere we had finished flinching the fog dispersed and thick snow showers occurred. During the day we saw 12 sail of ships – 7 or 8 of them must have preceded us hither, the remainder accompaning.

Thursday 22ᵈ of June Lat. 75°56′+ Long. 3°15′E
NNE. Variable

Light winds – inclinable to calm. Thick snow showers.
Worked a little to the Nᵈ and in an open patch of ice saw 4 or 5 whales; sent 4 boats in pursuit – the mate ['came' *deleted*] got very near one of them, but it escaped. 10 ships to windward under all sail plying to the Nᵈ. The Aimwell struck a fish. In the evening penetrated a quantity of open ice in an easterly direction and at mid-night gained the seastream.

Friday 23ᵈ of June Lat. 75°48′ Long 2°55′E
NNW. NW. NNE. Var.

Sailed about 6 miles SW along the interior edge of the sea-stream, saw no fish, hauled by the wind and reached to the westward until we came to the edge of an open pack. Inside we saw 6 ships, three of them made fast & apparently making off – attempted to penetrate the ice towards them but the wind being very light and the ice crowded, we found the attempt difficult. Tacked therefore, ['&' *deleted*] steered into the open water to the eastward, reduced sails and set all hands to make off in the forehold. We called all hands at Noon ['am.' *deleted*]. At 3 pm. the hold was completely cleared and all the water started which was filled for ballast. At 3..40¹ pm all hands having dined commenced filling the casks with blubber and at 5 am. the operation was completed. Thus 53 casks containing by estimation 96 Butts of Blubber, but probably more correctly 90 butts, were filled in 13ʰ 20′ at the rate of about 7 butts p hour.

The state of the hold after this <u>making off</u> is as follows. The <u>ground</u> & <u>second</u> tiers completely filled fore and aft together with the <u>third</u> tier of wingers likewise complete, excepting 4 casks, and 7 casks in the 3ᵈ tier.

At Mid-night the ship passed the sea stream. Steered by the wind to the NEᵈ. Weather foggy – wind very light.

¹ At this point there is again a marginal table:
'Casks filled with Blubber
      G.
16 of 300
20 of 252
6 ″ 200
2 ″ 180
3 ″ 84
3 ″ 252 filled up.'
The table is completed by a right-facing brace, enclosing the first five rows of the table indicating that the contents of these casks amount to '96 Butts'. The main text, however, suggests that the brace should have been included to include the final row, which presumably refers to the three casks that were indicated on 17 June as 'part full'.

Saturday 24th of June Lat. 76°0' Lon. 4°20'E
N. NW. W. WSW. SW.

The fog cleared away about 9 am. and the weather became charmingly fine. A fish arose very near the ship at 7 am. so near indeed that it seemed to take the alarm, for it was not seen again.

Under a very light air of wind we followed the course of the ice from E to N. About noon, the breeze increased; entered an open patch of ice & penetrated a loose pack the distance of several miles. Seeing no fish & the ice becoming more crowded returned by the wind to the Sd. The wind increasing to a strong breeze, reached 6 hours to the SbE then tacked, and returned by the wind to the WNW. Saw three Cetaceous animals, gave chase to one of them, but found it to be a Razor Back.

During the day we saw 15 or 16 sail of ships the whole or greater part of which steered under all sails to the northwestward along the edge of the ice.

Sunday 25th of June Lat. 75 47+ Lon. 5°E
SW. WSW

Strong to fresh gales of wind snow or hazy weather. In the afternoon we scudded 5 hours to the NEd hauled under the lee of a point of ice & lay too. 10 sail of ships in sight some laying too others running to the Nd. No fish.

Monday 26th of June Lat. 76°20 Lon. 5°50'E
WbN. Calm NE.erly. SE.erly. var.

The wind abated in the night. Light airs prevailed in the morning. A boat from the Hope of Peterhead boarded us. The harponeer gave the following news. Viz. That a vast number of fish had been lately seen and many caught between the latitude of 73½° and 76°. The following is the success of some of the ships. Eliza 11; Margaret of Hull, 10; Diamond, 9; Elbe 10 = 80 tons; Hope 5, 80 tons; Union 5, 80 tons; &c. We afterwards spoke the London with 5 fish = 60 tons; and Brothers 4 fish.

Procured about three tons of fresh water ice. The ship then laying near a stream of ice the wind veered to the Ed and the ship fell against the ice. In passing through it the agitation of the swell occasioned some severe blows from the pieces. At Noon made sail and steered once more along the edge of the ice to the southward under a very light breeze of wind.

Passing a point of ice we saw some thousands of seals basking on the pieces: sent two boats which however being preceeded by others from the ['Killed a Seal. No 2.' *in margin*] Hope, killed but one seal. 9 sail in sight.

Tuesday 27th of June Lat. 75°55°[*sic*] Lon. 4°30'E
South SSE. SSW.

Wind light during the night accompanied by fog or rain. Working to the southward. About Noon entered the ice amidst several patches of drift ice fell into a large hole of water where navigated three ships: supposing them to be part of the six sail within the ice mentioned on Friday last we sent a boat to windward whilst we worked that way with the ship. From the master of the Middleton (new¹), they learnt that no fish had been seen by them since Monday 19ᵗʰ, that on the preceding day was a large <u>run</u> and many were killed. The Middleton has 8 fish which with about 20 tons of the Clapham's blubber makes about 80 tons of oil. The accompanying ships are the Diamond with [*blank space*] fish [*blank space*] tons, and the Elbe with 10 fish = 140 tons.

The wind now increased to a strong gale accompanied by much Rain – the sea was considerable & we had some difficulty in finding our way out to sea again – which however we accomplished about 4 Pm.

From the accounts which we have received from different ships, it would appear that the very successful fishing which occurred lately in the <u>southern latitudes</u> was first followed in the 74ᵗʰ–75ᵗʰ degree; about the day following the ships in the 76ᵗʰ & 77ᵗʰ degrees began to fish, and that after the [run] no fish was to be seen from lat. 76° to our present situation. The fish likewise appeared to advance in a northern direction. Supposing therefore they might again make their appearance in still more northern situations, under the gale which now prevailed, although the weather was very thick and disagreeable, we steered along the exterior of the ice on a NE to NNE course according to its known trending.

Wednesday 28ᵗʰ of June Lat. 77°50' Lon. 5°50'E
S. SSE. SE. E.erly Var. NE &c.
The wind was of very variable in intensity and direction. It continued however a brisk gale accompanied with haze or rain until about noon and then considerably subsided. Meanwhile we had made a rapid advance towards the north and in the afternoon saw the Foreland obscurely through the fog. In the evening the wind was very light tacked and sent a boat on board the Industry to enquire the state of the northern fishery – we likewise communicated with the Eggington, Volunteer, Royal George & Sisters. The sum of the intelligence is comprised in the following remarks. The loose ice has, it seems, enclosed the floes and set down upon them so that the Royal George and others had great difficulty in making their escape. Several ships which could not [follow?] were left astern. None of the ships has seen a fish of from 15 to 25 days and had heard of no captures. The Volunteer when at the navigable ['Greenland news. State of the N.ern fishery' *in margin*] [***] westward amongst the floes saw 13 sail enclosed in the ice without a present means of egress, further west was the John & the Henrietta. One ship of the 13 was seen with an ancient in the main top mast rigging supposed to be a signal of distress. No ship could approach very near her. There are it seems yet 10 to 15 clean ships or upwards, and 20–30 which will not each exceed 20 tons. The Volunteer has but 3 tons of oil from 2 fish the Resolution is yet clean, together with the Eggington, Zephyr, Friendship, Equestries, &c. The Industry has 1 fish = 15 tons; Royal Bounty 3 = 20 tons; Sisters, 2; Royal George 2; &c. &c.

At Mid-night calm weather, sea very turbulent, atmosphere dark and heavy. The middle hook of the Foreland bearing EbN 10–15 leˢ. Lat. 78°8' Long. 6°E. Saw two Razor backs. Saw about 20 ships during the day, several of them Foreigners.

¹ This parenthesis presumably is to emphasize that Scoresby meant the person who had taken over after the death of the Middleton's previous captain during the voyage. See journal entry for 15 May 1815.

Thursday 29th of June Lat. 78°0′ Lon. 6°50E
NE.erly E.erly.
Showers of rain with very light winds prevailed most of the day. About 10 am. made all sail and steered to the SE^d. At 9½ Pm. the Middle Hook of the Foreland bore due North distant 56 miles. Steered from hence SSE in a direct line for the land which appeared in sight farthest to the south. At Mid-night delightful clear weather. ['mid night. Lat. 77°42′40+' *in margin*] Sea turbulent, distinct waves flowing evidently from both the SSW and North. No ships within sight. At Mid. Ob^d Lat. 77°42′40″. Surveyed the coast as we advanced.

Friday 30th of June Lat. 77°19′22″+ Lon.[1]
ENE. Var. Calm. NNW
Light winds all night charming clear weather, scarcely a cloud seen throughout the day. In the afternoon we had a moderate breeze of wind and in the night a considerable increase.

The weather being so favourable and the opportunity unexceptionable I took angles of the capes, bays, mountains, &c. as we sailed along the coast. These angles were taken by means of an azimuth compass ['Survey of the Coast of Spitzbergen begun.' *in margin*] the distances measured by the log.[2] The compass I employed was fitted up from my own plan for to suit these latitudes. The card is small and light, the bar is set on its edge, the magnetism thereby more concentrated. It was found to act charmingly when kept in the same situation, but when removed to any other part of the ship there was a strange anomaly observed.[3] On the larboard side of the main deck (the place where all the bearing of the land were observed) the Sun at Mid-Night bore N35°E. At noon the bearing was S38°W and at mid-night following N35°E the mean of which is S36°W.[4] From this mean as the variation of the compass the bearings taken were all referred. The ['Anomaly in the Compass attraction of the Ship' *in margin*] anomaly alluded to when the compass was removed, though it does not affect the observations in question, is too remarkable to be overlooked: it is a subject which has heretofore engaged my attention, but as some new facts were disclosed they may be here noticed. At noon I have observed the Sun's bearing was S38°W but when the compass was removed to the opposite side of the deck the bearing was only S7°W. a difference of 31°. This anomaly being so considerable I repeated the experiment a few minutes afterwards – On the larboard side of the deck the bearing was S.45′W [*sic*] and on the starboard side S 14°W the difference 31° as before, which proves the

---

[1] There is no longitude value in ink in the transcript. However, '12° 15′E' has been inserted in pencil, presumably by another hand at a later date.

[2] A footnote in *Account of the Arctic Regions*, I, p. 113 states that 'In the map of Spitzbergen, an extent of coast of above 200 miles, between Point-look-out and Hackluyt's Headland, is laid down from an original survey. In several particular situations I found an error of 10 miles of latitude and 2 or 3 degrees of longitude, in our most approved charts.' The map he refers to appears as Plate IV in volume II of the same.

[3] See Appendix, p. 292.

[4] I.e. the sun at noon would be expected to be at an azimuth of 216° according to the magnetic compass, equivalent to 180° true.

accuracy of the observations and the dependance to be placed on the motions of the card. When the compass was removed to the centre of the deck in front of the companion the sun bore S21°W at noon which differs only 1½° from the mean of the former observations: hence the real variation of the compass would appear to be about 22°W. ['Variation of Compass.' *in margin*] On some other parts of the deck the anomaly was much less, and the greater bearing was in one case on the starboard side of the deck: this however might be affected by the attraction of a quantity of iron [which?] was very near the spot. Where the anomaly was greatest; viz. on the main deck there was no iron longer than a nail or a bolt within 15 feet of the place, therefore it must be the attraction of the body of the ship which occasions the anomaly.[1]

At noon the sun's altitude was 35°44' (lower li.)[2] whence the true latitude 77°19'22"N. At this time a variety of intersecting bearings were determined from which the distance of the land and the height of two mountains were determined. A remarkable mountain on the coast in latitude .... N. subtended an angle of 1°58' at the distance of 15 miles – height of the eye 15 feet, hence the height 3306 feet. And the more remarkable mountain in lat. 76°57'30"N. subtended an angle of 2°53' at the distance of 14 miles when the height of the eye was 15 feet. Hence,

To Angle subtended by [Horn?] Mount   2°53' 0"
Add complement of dip 15^{ft}   <u>89 56 18</u>
                                   92 49 18   Sine–log = 9.999473
             + Distance of Mount   <u>14 0</u>
                                   93 3 18
                              <u>180 0 0</u>
                                   86 56 42   Sine. Arith. Co. = 0.000619
Log. semi-diameter of the earth + height of the eye = 6966387 = <u>6.843007</u>
                 logarithm of 6967855   =   <u>6.843099</u>
      Sub. semi-di. of earth   =   <u>6966382</u>
      Height of Horn Mount ...   <u>1473</u> ['height in' *deleted*] yards.

But by another set of observations wherin the ∠ subtended was 2°32' at the distance of 16 miles the altitude seems to be 1457 yards, the mean of the two which will probably be nearest the truth gives the altitude of Horn Mount 4395 feet.[3]

A little to the north of Horn Sound on the front of the coast rests ['Icebergs described' *in margin*] an immense ice-berg:[4] it extends eleven miles in length, its

---

[1] This passage indicates the very early stage of Scoresby's thinking on what was to be a lifelong concern. Here he appears to be thinking primarily of horizontal influences on the compass, and he did not identify such items as the cannon and iron ballast that could be expected to have a significant effect on the compass deviation. See Appendix, p. 292.

[2] Lower limb, i.e. the altitude of the lowest point on the sun's circumference. See Appendix, p. 293.

[3] Scoresby was evidently sighting on Hornsundtind, by a substantial amount the highest peak in southern Spitsbergen. Given the circumstances of the survey, Scoresby's values are of good quality. Modern maps indicate an altitude of 4,690 feet (1,430 m), in latitude 76°54'15". This very distinctive mountain is illustrated in *Account of the Arctic Regions*, II, Plate III, No. 4.

[4] The term here means a glacier or icefield descending from a high altitude to sea-level.

[***] climbs the back mountains above 1000 feet, and the edge next the sea, which is in many places perpendicular subtended an angle of 10′ when at the distance of 15 miles: hence its perpendicular [front] by the ['Iceberg height of the perpendicular edge.' *in margin*] preceding formula appears in some parts to reach the height of 402 feet. Its surface presented a most beautifully smooth inclined plane of snow, its edge appeared uneven, but the distance was too great to distinguish its colour, it most resembled a cliff of white marble. Near the Southern Cape lays another iceberg nearly as extensive as the former – it rests in space between two large groups of mountains and reaches to the summit of the hills against which it rests. Several smaller icebergs were seen in passing along – they however presented nothing very remarkable.

After mid-day we steered on a due course S44°E with an ['Survey pursued' *in margin*] accelerated velocity of 2½ to 5 knots p hour. Every 4 or 6 miles I took bearings of remarkable facts of the coast. At mid-night we had approximated the coast within about 10½ miles observed the sea breaking on different ['Rocks on the Coast' *in margin*] groups of rocks at the distance of 6 to 10 miles from us, some of which lay 4 or 5 miles from shore. The meridian altitude of ['mid n^t Lat. 76°47′2″+' *in margin*] the sun below the pole was 9°52′30″ whence the latitude 76°47′2″[.] Horn Mount bearing E48°N and South Cape S62°E (due) the former 13½ the latter 21 miles distant.

Saturday July 1st Lat. 76°15 Lon. 14°40′E
NNW. NW.
Continued our course until 1¾ am. when observing the reef or low land which extends from South Cape, ahead of us we hauled out due south and at 3 am. South Cape bore E20°N. 12′ whence its latitude = 76°39′N.[1] having sailed from mid night S44°E 8′; and S5°E = 6½′ due courses with which the bearing and distance of South Cape affords a difference of lat. of 8′S and which applied to the mid-night latitude determines the situation of S. Cape as above.

Passed a considerable ice berg afloat in the sea – its upper ['Floating iceberg' *in margin*] surface was covered with a brown soil or rubbish and its edge had the appearance of white marble with grey veins. Saw a razor back and many thousands of Fulmars in the water but no mysticeti. At 3 am. not meeting with the objects of our search, having obtained a tollerable survey of the coast, and fearing the wind should <u>wester</u>, we hauled off shore WbS under all sails with a fresh gale of wind.

The weather became cloudy in the forenoon and foggy as the day advanced – the wind veered to the NW directly adverse for our attaining the edge of the ice. At Mid-night wind a moderate breeze.

John Hebden, Cook's mate, who has for some time been indisposed, is now seriously ill of a kind of paralysis. All the rest of the crew are ['Therm^r 30 to 40°. Bar. 30.02' *in margin*] blessed with the best[2] health. Saw some Razor backs.

---

[1] The lowland on the mainland extends further south, to about 76°34′N. If, however, by 'South Cape' Scoresby meant the southern summit of Kistefjellet, that is at 76°36′N.
[2] It appears that the transcript originally used a different (but not decipherable) phrase, for which 'the best' was substituted.

Sunday 2ᵈ July Lat. 75°13′+ Lon. 12°37′E
NW to WNW. Var.
Wind very light & variable all the day, attended with fine weather. Made very little progress and that not in the required direction – we made a course about WSW which is less than three points of the trending of the ice. ['Therm. 30 to 40 Bar. 30.08' *in margin*] Saw several razor backs.

Monday 3ᵈ July Lat. 74°53′+ Lon. 10°50′E
NNW. N. Var. NW. NNE to W.
Light variable winds most of this day – our approximation towards the ice was still very slow and indirect. Passed two pieces of ice and a <u>crang</u>. Saw several razor backs.

In the evening – thick fog showers occurred – the wind was variable 6 or 8 points. At 8 pm. saw an open patch of ice – at 11 ['Therm. 31 = 39 Bar. 30.10' *in margin*] tacked near it made a board to windward & then reached along the [***]² ['**Tuesday 4ᵗʰ July** Lat. 74°30 Lon.8½°E[.] Variable NE' *in margin*] side of an extensive stream, on which lay a great number of seals killed 30 of them. The fog dispersed as the day advanced, and [three?] vessels were discovered under <u>a light sail</u> steering towards us on a SW.erly course – lay too sent a boat on board a Brig which proved to be the Hope of Peterhead the London & the Calypso all on their way homeward meaning to run along the borders of the ice as far as John Mayne Island.³ Having previously prepared a letter to Mess F. & B.⁴ & one to Mʳˢ S. I now wrote a third to my Father, and sent them on board the Hope. Those vessels have been near the ice between this place & lat. 76° ever since we left them on the 25 ulto. without seeing

['Dead Fish seen by Thoˢ Schofield  Nº 9 = 11.0' *in margin*]⁵

a single whale, and now despairing of seeing any more, they have concluded on moving homewards. The London has 7 fish, 5 large & 2 small; the Calypso 5, 3 large & 2 small; & the Hope 5 large[.]

In the afternoon we had a confirmed steady breeze of wind and tollerably clear weather – Reaching to the NWᵈ amongst loose ice at 7 Pm we got sight of a dead fish which we immediately secured & flinched. It was much [swoln?] & smelt horridly, nevertheless the blubber proved pretty good though all the back part was eaten of sharks. We got about 22 butts from off it, the jawbones and [¾?] ['Therm. 38°=30°⁶ Bar 30.5' *in margin*] of the whalebone; half of one side was lost.

---

¹ Perhaps meaning 3 p.m.
² This is an abbreviation for a direction, but it is not decipherable.
³ I.e. Jan Mayen.
⁴ Fishburn and Brodrick, builders and owners of the *Esk*. See vol. I, p. 131.
⁵ Presumably in order to distinguish this as a dead whale, in the sketch in the margin the horizontal parts of the tail are in black, but the vertical part is only in outline.
⁶ Possibly '38°=3 pm'.

Wednesday 5ᵗʰ of July Lat. 74°35 Lon. 7°30′E
NE.erly N.erly
The wind blew fresh in the morning accompanied by fog showers. As the blubber was constantly losing much oil and as the ship was in most greasy predicament we immediately began to make it off, that¹ the flinching &c. was finished. At noon we finished, but the rest of the day was spent in gumming & <u>cleaning</u> the whalebone, making off seals and cleaning the ship. Meanwhile we reached under easy sail to seaward of the ice. Spoke a foreigner without fish or seals! ['Thermometer 30 to 37° Bar 29.96.' *in margin*] In the evening tacked and returned towards the ice. Wind moderate, a considerable sea, dark gloomy weather. 2 foreign ships in sight.

Thursday 6ᵗʰ of July Lat. 74°45′ Long. 6°30′E
NNW. N. var.
Moderate breezes of wind accompanied with fog showers. Proceeded under a brisk sail by the wind – found the ice trending to the NWᵈ. In the afternoon we entered the ice – had comfortable navigation amidst streams and scattered drift ice. Tacked at 7 pm. Took on board a lump of pure ice weighing about 2 tons as ['for' *deleted*] a stock of fresh water. At 11 pm. we repassed the sea stream, ['and' *deleted*] advanced all the night to the NEbN & in [**Friday 7ᵗʰ of July** Lat. 74°55′ Lon. 4°45′E[.] NW to NNE' *in margin*] a very short time, no ice was to be seen – Saw several ships at intervals. At 8 am. blowing strong, tacked and steered by the wind to the NW. which veered as we ['turned?' *deleted*] performed the evolution, from NW to NNE. Employed the people in cleaning the ship, scouring sides, sending up top gall*ant* cross trees, &c. At noon a strong gale prevailed with rain & very dark weather – reduced sails. In the evening the wind fell the atmosphere cleared & we had presently a charming night. 2 or 3 ships within sight. At mid nᵗ the ice was not within sight to the NWᵈ.

Saturday 8ᵗʰ of July Lat. 75°10′+ Lon 3°10′E
NE.erly. E.erly
The course of the ice still trends to the NWᵈ most of the preceeding & part of this day we continued our course to the NNW or NW without interruption whilst much ice appeared to the SWᵈ at no great distance. We had very little wind all the day – very fine weather. Tacked near a stream of ice at 8 Pm. soon afterwards the masters of the Elbe & Neptune of [*blank space*]² came on board the Esk. The Elbe has 10 fish

¹ Marginal table inserted at this point, similar to those summarizing previous making offs:
'made off.
8 Casks of 252 G.
4 .... of 200
1 (Seals) .. 126'
These three rows were enclosed by a right-facing brace indicating that the total amounted to '23 Butts'.
² The contemporary printed list for 1815 includes the *Elbe* (Captain Young) of Aberdeen and two whalers named *Neptune*: from Aberdeen (Captain Drysdale) and from London (Captain Robinson). From the context and sentence structure of the journal, it seems probable that Captain Drysdale was Scoresby's visitor.

140–150 tons & the Neptune 14 =135–140 T. They were both on their way home-wards. The Neptune has fished entirely in the place we left on the 31st of May in lat. 77°11' to 79°30'.[1] She was mostly alone, saw the last fish 29th June, and only left the situation two or three days ago.

One of these ships as she approached hoisted her ancient, mistaking the Elbe for the Diamond[2] – we imagined (she being afar off) it might be the Cyrus[.] I flattered myself with the receipt of the long expected epistle from my dearest partner in life, but alas! I was miserably disappointed.

Sunday 9th of July Lat. 75°27'+ Long. 3°0'E
E.rly NE.erly
John Hebden seems to be rapidly approaching that bourne from whence there is no return.[3] His nervous energy seems almost destroyed. He has not uttered a rational sentence of several days past – for two days he has not spoken a syllable, neither has he taken the least subsistence. He lays in a wholesome airy bed, is excellently attended upon by his master the Cook, and appears to overcome the hours of time without pain or unconsciousness. Hitherto he has had but little fever: in the night of this day however there was a considerable increase. That fatal symptom the ruttling[4] in the throat began in the afternoon.

This day like the preceding was delightfully fine & clear with very light winds. Made but small progress in working to the northward along the exterior of the ice. Several ships seen during the day.

Monday 10th July Lat. 75°31'+ Lon. 3°10'E
NNW to NWbW. variable
Charming weather, light winds. Such amazing clear weather at this season of the year is in Greenland a very rare circumstance. Fogs in general are now almost constant yet we have scarcely had a thick foggy day since we entered the country. Had whales been[5] in any moderate quantity and remained accessible ['Remarks on the clearness of the weather.' *in margin*] to the fishermen to this period most of the ships might have been filled whereas it is probable there is not a full ship in the country, at least we have not heard of any one. Several have gone home, but not one of those near full. We have not now seen a living whale since the 23d of June.

[1] Because of overwritten corrections, there is some doubt about both the values of degrees (but not the minutes).

[2] Also from Aberdeen (Captain Moffatt).

[3] An allusion to *Hamlet*, iii, 1: 'Death,/ the undiscover'd country, from whose bourne/ No trav-eller returns.'

[4] One would expect 'rattling' but the spelling is fairly clear both here and in the journal entry for 10 July. *OED* lists 'ruttle' as both a verb and noun, the latter as 'A rattling noise in the throat', and indicates that this form is dialect, especially in eastern England. Robinson's *Whitby Glossary* defines 'ruttle' as 'to gurgle like water pressing through a pipe', and has a separate entry for 'death-ruttle'.

[5] Originally 'being' and then corrected.

About noon we passed the seastream of the ice and reached to the westward until 3 Pm. Saw 7 ships bearing NW the farthest distant of which could not be less than 20 miles off. Not being able to make any progress in that direction where the ice appeared slack on account of the wind we kept our reach to the northward within a quantity of loose ice and streams. Sent two boats after a number of seals which lay on a point of ice – they did not get one.

John Hebden continues much in the state in which he passed the preceeding day, yet with an increase of fever and toward night a great increase of the ruttling in the throat: For the first time however these 3 or 4 days he was presented with a quantity of wine at intervals amounting to near half a pint, which he swallowed.[1] I occasioned his place to be ventilated by the admission of ['all the' *deleted*] air, ['that could' *deleted*] in removing the hatches.

Tuesday 11th July Lat.76°16′ Lon. 3°30′E
NW to NNW
Light or moderate winds, dark cloudy weather with fog showers or small snow – SW.erly swell. Continued our reach all this day to the NNE or NE^d had occasionally to bear away for ice passed much scattered drift ice and streams. At 8 pm. took on board about 1½ tons of fresh water ice in [a mass.?] No ships in sight.

John Hebden continues without apparent alteration, except that his fever is somewhat abated. His eyes were generally open & wandering about but how far he was sensible of objects around him could not be ascertained. He took about ⅓ of a pint of wine during the 24 hours …

Wednesday 12th July Lat. 76°40′ Lon. 4°25′E
NNW to North. Var. NNE.
The wind was moderate at the fore part of this day but towards evening it increased to a fresh gale accompanied with thick showers of snow. We sailed under a brisk canvass, working to windward, sometimes in the open sea at others amongst streams and scattered pieces of drift ice. Today our dinner consisted of [a pie?] made in part of a [bowl?], the last of our stock, which was killed in Shetland and has since been preserved fresh by the antisceptic powers of the frost when suspended in the open air beneath the mizen top.

In the evening a great change was observed in the sick man. He was unable to swallow any wine – his pulse merely consisted of a kind of fluttering scarcely perceptible – he was seized with strong shaking paroxisms and his respiration[2] became irregular and disturbed. ['**Thursday 13**th **of July** Lat. 76°57′+ Lon. 4°0′E[.] NNE NNE to NbW' *in margin*] The Surgeon sat by him as well as others of the crew. At 2 am. he gently breathed his last and assigned his soul into the hands of his Maker without a struggle or any appearance of pain. Thus died a man of honest industrious character leaving a widow with one or two children to deplore his loss. The nature of his

---

[1] For a comprehensive review of the medical use of wine in this period, and earlier, see Paul, *Bacchic Medicine*.
[2] This word replaces one that was deleted and illegible.

complaint prevented me from ascertaining the state of his mind with regard to ['The death of J. Hebden.' *in margin*] the [best?] things: he was never perfectly rational from the first attack of the paralysis, and his mental powers failed more rapidly than his bodily functions. – His body was now removed from the cabin in which he lay and soon afterwards shrouded in his bed rug, and laid in decent state until a ['[favourable?]' *deleted*] convenient opportunity should offer of committing the corpse with due ceremony to the deep.

Blowing strong all night with thick snow showers we reached into the sea to the eastward and met a considerable swell. At noon entered the [bordre?][1] of the ice but perceiving four ships running before the wind we steered in such a ['way' *deleted*] course as to waylay them: Sent ['Greenland news.' *in margin*] a boat on the board [*sic*] the Elizabeth she has 7 fish = 70 tons oil & is accompanied by the New Manchester with 1 fish; the Mary Francis with 2[2] fish; and the Perseverance of Hull 1 fish, all four of them [bound?] homewards having seen no fish of three weeks. During the day other 9 vessels passed us the only one of which we spoke was the Sisters with 2 fish, had just left the floes in lat. 78½° where eleven sail together with the Henrietta & the John were at a recent period still beset. The master considered the fishery as concluded and was on his way home together with several of the ships accompanying him. In consequence of the information thus derived, at 8 Pm. we bore up and steered to the SSW with the intention, Deo Volentè,[3] of visiting the ice in the vicinity of John Mayne island as a last effort & hope of success the present season.

Friday 14th July Lat. 75°15′+ Lon. 4°25′E
NbW to NWbW

Fresh breezes of wind. The morning was cold (therm. 28°) & thick showers of fili-form snow fell; The afternoon was clearer & the evening was charmingly fine. The therm*omete*r rose to 40°.

Cruised along the edge of the ice all the morning – occasionally passing within streams and disseminated pieces of drift ice. At Noon steering SbW we left the ice & did not see it again until night though we hauled up SWbS^d. Three ships which preceeded us about 8 miles, & which we overtook hauled in towards the ice and disappeared. One of their partners followed us. Saw some razor backs.

At 11 am. we summoned all hands upon deck, laid the ship too, and after reading the beautiful & solemn ordinance of the "burial of the dead", the corpse of the deceased John Hebden was committed to the ocean, and instantly sank, having a bag of sand attached to the feet. The seamen were all pleasingly attentive and many of them showed to be much impressed. May the Great God in whose hand is the breath of life sanctify this his Providence to his shipmates who are witness of his dissolution.

---

[1] *OED* lists 'bordre' as a 17th-century variant of 'border', but in this case it is probably only a slip of the pen.

[2] Possibly '7'.

[3] The grave accent is clearly written, but inappropriate.

Saturday 15th of July Lat. 73°35′+ Lon. 5°55′E
NW to W.erly Variable
Light winds all night and in the morning attended with delightful clear weather. Found the extension of the loose ice trending from the SW to S. along which we steered, passing occasionally within several streams & at one time a large aggregation of ice was seen to the eastward which could not be overlooked. At noon we were in the open sea, working to the SW^d under all sails. 3 Foreign & 2 English ships in sight. One of the latter, the Mary & Elizabeth, seemed inclined to keep C° with us, we however outsailed her and did not see after 6 pm. when a thick fog commenced which terminated in a great fall of rain.

Sunday 16th of July Lat. 73°06′+ Lon. 5°20′E
W.erly WSW
Blowing strong with thick damp disagreeable weather, most of this day. Followed the course of the ice which now trended SW.erly by plying to windward. A considerable swell prevailed.

Monday 17th of July Lat. 73°5′ Lon. 4°50′E
WSW. Var. NW.erly Calm. &c.
Light variable winds to calm, attended with thick fog or rain. From 8 am. we reached to the N^d until 4 Pm. before we saw ice. A stream then appeared to the SE^d of us & another to the W^d. From the direction of the swell it appears that the margin of the ice now trends more westerly than it has hitherto done. A very light air of wind prevailed from the eastward in the night but scarcely sufficient to enable the ship to steer the Sea.

Tuesday 18th of July Lat. 72°45′ Lon. 2°40′E
E.erly ESE
The breeze increased as the day advanced, but until 6 am. the fog was so amazingly dense, that objects could scarcely be distinguished more than two ship's lengths off. Steered SWbW or WSW until 8 am. the atmosphere then clearing and no ice being seen we bore up WNW and set lower & top mast studding sails. Though we made a progress of 3½ to 4 knotts p hour and steered NWbW in the afternoon we did not see ice until 8 Pm. when the fog, which for several hours had been amazingly dense, became rather attentuated and a stream was discerned extending from E. to North. Heavy weather all night, steered along [**'Wednesday 19th of July** Lat. 72°6′ Lon. 2°0′W [*sic*] ESE to ENE' *in margin*] the edge of the ice which trending WNW, W. to WSW. In the morning the fog ['[then?]' *deleted*] being occasionally very dense we twice embayed ourselves in the ice and had to haul out by the wind to the southward. At noon as we reached to sea-ward we perceived the ice at a short distance to lee-ward during 15 miles sailing. The wind now increasing to a very brisk gale, the sea rolling in high swells from the SE^d & the atmosphere being impervious to vision at a greater distance than 100 yards – these concurrent considerations rendered the design of exploring the ice further in these situations perfectly incompatible with prudence, therefore it remained for me merely to ['Left the ice.' *in margin*] decide whether we

should await the conclusion of the gale & a favourable opportunity or avail ourselves of its furthering influences by commencing a homeward passage. After some reflection knowing that the time of the general termination of the fishery was past, ['and' *deleted*] that ['under' *deleted*] the fishery for the present season did apparently close with the month of June, and that the prospect here is as hopeless as may be imagined – I determined on the latter. ['[namely?]' *deleted*] Accordingly at 1 Pm. we made all sail and left the ice on a SSW course, after having expended 28 days on fishing stations without seeing a living whale. Called all hands and removed 5 pairs of jaw-bones from the forecastle & bows and stowed them in the hold upon the blubber casks, struck the crow's nest and sent up two royal-masts.

In the evening somewhat clearer weather – sea very cross and turbulent. Continued to steer SSW with a velocity of 7 to 7½ knotts.

Thursday 20ᵗʰ July Lat. 69°12′ Lon. 2°0′E
NEbE E.erly
The wind continued to blow a fresh gale until the afternoon, when it gradually subsided to a light breeze. Under its influence we steered SSW and at noon had run a distance of 174 miles since the preceeding day at noon. At night the velocity was diminished from 7½ to 8 knotts to 3. Much rain fell in the morning which on the subsiding of the wind terminated in a fog so thick ['Remarkably dense fog' *in margin*] that the circle of vision was contracted to a radius not exceeding 50 yards! The fog was really so dense that it passed by the eyes like smoke, and was not transparent half the length of the ship.

The agitation of the swell cause [*sic*] the water which had long lain amongst the timbers of the ship (bilge water) to emit such ['Bilge water' *in margin*] powerful gaseous fumes, as to tarnish the brass and copper utensils of the cabin with a variety of prismatic colours. The copper was greyish black & such of the wood work as was damp assumed the colour and metallic lustre of <u>black lead</u>. Silver and even gold suffered a change receiving a tinge of brownish black. I never knew the hydrogenous vapour so powerful except when starting or emptying the ballast water out of the blubber casks.

The day being favourable for cleaning the ship, whilst every article was soft and wet, we employed the watch in scouring the decks and [paint?] work with urine and sand which removes the grease and dirt with surprising celerity.

Friday 21ˢᵗ July[1]
E.erly Calm. NE.erly
Light winds all this day, fog in the morning, cloudy in the evening. Still steering SSW (which course however on account of the attraction of the ship appears to be really SbW½ W) generally with a velocity of 2 to 4 knotts p hour. At 8 am. called all hands, dismantled all the whale boats scrubbed them and stowed four of them in the twin-decks. All the lines we washed and and placed in two coyls upon the quarter deck. Sent royal masts aloft & fitted a new mizen top gall*ant* mast & royal mast, the old ones being too short. At 7 pm. discovered a strange sail to the

---

[1] No geographical coordinates are shown for this date.

westward steering by the wind starboard tacked. She proved to be a brig, suppose bound for Archangel.

Manifest of the cargo of the ship Esk, British built, burthen 354 73/94 tons, William Scoresby Junr Master from Greenland of and for Whitby. To wit,

30 Casks of 300 gall^s	)	213 casks containing	(	
91 " " 252 "		345 butts of blubber of		
35 " " 200 "		half a ton each. Also		Thomas Brodrick Esqr
16 " " 180 "	}	one cask containing	{	
7 " " 160 "		30 seal skins		
15 " " 126 "		Four tons of Whale finns.		
11 " " 84 "	)			

The produce of nine Whales and thirty Seals.

Greenland Seas 21st day of July 1815.   William Scoresby Junr.

Saturday 22^d July Lat. 66°8′ Lon. 0°43′W
N. NbW NW.
Variable light airs of wind or fresh breezes towards the close of the day. Weather dark and cloudy. Steering SSW to SWbS under all sails with a velocity of 3 to 6 knotts p hour. The people employed in various needful and ornamental work.

Sunday 23^d of July Lat. 64°6′ Lon. 0°46′W
NW.erly Var. W.erly
We had a fresh breeze of wind in the morning which fell to a light air in the after-noon, occasionally calm. Weather cloudy. Made a course about SSW p compass. Saw several bottle-noses. Mollusca seen floating ['Thermometer 47 to 51° *in margin*] in the water. The evening was fine & serene: the western horizon free from clouds.

Monday 24th of July Lat. 63°38′+ Lon. 52′W.
Calm var.
Calm or very light airs of wind all the day. Made little or no progress. Early in the morning the weather being serene & fair we suspended five boats' lines upon [booms?] betwixt the mizen & main masts, for to dry. At 3½ Pm. they were suffi-ciently dry, took them down & coyled them in seperate parcels of a line or 120 fathoms each. Scrubbed ['Saw several bottlenoses' *in margin*] the ship's sides again. Performed various necessary work.

Tuesday 25th July Lat. 63°20′ Lon. 0°55′W
SWerly. NWerly Very Var.
The sun rose clear about [*blank space*] am.[1] & soon afterwards some stars were seen, which were now considered as much a phenomenon as the sight of the sun at mid-night when we first entered Greenland. This day was charmingly fine & clear until 8

---

[1] At this date and position in 1815, sunrise would have been at approximately 2.50 GMT.

Pm. A light breeze of wind prevailed from the SW^d. At 6 Pm. the atmosphere became dark in the western horizon & soon afterwards a small western sea was perceptible – this circumstance together with the motion of the scud, which was from WSW to ENE, indicated wind from the W^d at no great distance. To meet it the sooner therefore we tacked at 7 Pm. entered beneath the canopy of dense cloud at 8 and presently had a heavy rain. Towards mid-night lightening [*sic*] was seen to the westward & at 11 pm. ['Ther^m 53° to 56°.' *in margin*] wind veered to NW.

Wednesday 26th July Lat. 62°43′+ Lon. 1°W.
WbN NW. [Var.?]
Rain in the morning – cloudy weather with light winds the remainder of the day. Steered SSW½ W p compass with a velocity of 1 to 2½ knots. In the evening saw several solon geese, & mollusca. Caught a dog-fish. Had a very heavy swell from the NWbW increasing until noon & decreasing towards night.

Thursday 27th July Lat 61°45′+ Lon. 1°0′W ['Correct^d?'] long 0°45′E
W.erly Variable SWerly
Light airs, of wind, charming clear weather. Proceeded on on [*sic*] SSW½ W course the fore part of the day; in the afternoon the wind veering SW.erly advanced close hauled. At 10 am. lat. 61°50′ long. by account 1°W.[1] tried for soundings but found no bottom with a perpendicular line of 120 fathoms. Picked up a log of fir wood 20 feet in length by 14 inches square it was perfectly sound. A ship crossed our stern steering to the eastward, supposed for Dronthem[2] or some of the neighbouring Norway ports. At night another vessel was seen a great distance to the westward. Employed painting the ship, matting the rigging, &c. &c. &c.

At 8 pm. lat. ['by' *deleted*] 61°30′ long. by a/c 0°45′W[3] Shetland bearing [*blank space*] distant [*blank space*] miles (as ascertained by subsequent observations) struck soundings in 105 fathoms water, fine white sand.

Observed several Solon geese. Caught some Dog-fish. Mollusca also seen.

Friday 28th July Lat. 61°15′ Long. a/c 0°3′E Long. corrected 1°48E
SWbS variable
Fresh winds – cloudy weather. Reached by the wind starboard tacked until 6 am, then tacked, stood two hours westerly then tacked again. At noon struck soundings in [8?]6 fathoms fine light grey sand with small white or yellowish specks. At 2 Pm. tacked & stood to the westward all the night. ['Soundings.' *in margin*] At 6 pm lat. 61°12′ long. corrected by subsequent observations 1°35′E sounded in 86[4] fathoms

---

[1] Beneath this longitude there is an insertion: 'Corrected 0°45′E+', accompanied by a marginal note: 'NB. These are the true longitudes considering Hangcliff as laying in 0°56′W & [Lambaness?] in 0°37′W.' Lambaness is in fact at 60°49′N 0°45′W.

[2] Trondheim, Norway, 63°36′N 10°23′E.

[3] Here there is a similar insertion, linked to the text above by a right-facing brace: 'corrected = 1° 0′E'.

[4] Possibly '56'.

water fine yellowish grey sand. and at 9 pm. lat. 61°12′ long. corrected 1°17′E struck soundings in 95 fathoms fine yellowish gray sand with smooth shells & small whitish specks.

Caught a great many mackrell probably nearly 200 so that all hands had a treat of fresh fish.

From the profusion of mackrell & quality of soundings, notwithstanding we deepened our water in sailing [westward?], I concluded we must be to the eastward of ['our reckoning' *deleted*] Shetland, consequently to the eastward of our reckoning.

Observed a ship steering to the NEward, probably an Archangelman.

Saturday 29th of July Lat 61°7 Long. a/c 0°37′W. Long. corrected = 1°8′E
SWbS Var. SbW Calm.
Fresh breezes to calm – dark hazy weather. We continued our reach to the westward in the hope of seeing the land – but at day break being hazy & having deepened our water to 105 fathoms we tacked.

The want of a survey of soundings around the Shetland islands occasions great inconvenience & waste of time to the ships employed in the Greenland & Archangel trades. It is a desideratum of manifest importance. We find the approach to the English British[1] channel as well known with regard to depth of water & quality of soundings as that of our most accustomed harbours whilst the charts of the northern approach do not contain any soundings to the northward of Shetland & the few which are noticed between Shetland and Norway are not much to be depended upon. It would appear by the charts that there are no soundings to the westward or northward of Shetland & yet I have found ground in fathoms at the distance of ['Remarks on the deficiency of soundings and the imperfection of the Surveys of the Shetland islands.' *in margin*] 70 miles in the parallel of 60° & there are likewise soundings to the NW, N & NE of Lambaness to a considerable extent. It is likewise somewhat remarkable that islands attatched to the interests of Great Britain ['and' *deleted*] so nearly situated & abounding with fine harbours should not be deemed worthy of a formal survey. The charts extant are replete with errors and omissions. Rocks of the most dangerous description are unnoticed & places of importance erroneously figured & the whole more evidently incomplete from the almost total deficiency of soundings. Besides the dangers around these islands are not generally ['Dangers in the approach to the Shetland islands.' *in margin*] sufficiently considered – thick weather being very prevalent the making of the land is attended with particular hazard on either side. On the west lie the Ve Skerries 5 or 6 miles from the nearest land and the [Havre de grind?] an assemblage of sunk rocks 4 or 5 miles from Foul island and at a much greater distance from the main. On the east side are several blind rocks particularly one lying at a considerable distance off [***] & another called the Soulden near Brassa. The Skerries also being low & rocky & lying far from the main form a danger in which it is very easy for a Ship to get inextricably involved. Now much of the ['danger' *deleted*] hazard arising from these dangers might be obliterated

---

[1] 'the English' is inserted above the line, apparently to replace 'British', but the latter word was not deleted.

by a careful survey & minute soundings. The quality of the soundings are in many parts so particular that they would afford a sure indication of the situation of a ship in thick weather.[1]

All this day we had a heavy swell from the west which occasioned a disagreeable motion in the ship on the abatement of the wind.

At 11 am. we tacked and soon afterwards we had a calm. Several fishing lines being let down to the bottom we caught a great many coal fish,[2] & some Cod. Our lat. was 61°8 & long <u>corrected</u> 0°51′E. soundings 92 fathoms, fine yellowish gray sand. Heavy damp weather in the night. At 10 PM. a breeze of wind sprang up from the NNW steered SWbS until mid-night. Two [land?] birds flew on board the ship.

Sunday 30ᵗʰ July Lat 60°15′28″+ Long. a/c 2°10′W True longitude = 0 25 W Error of long. 1 45
NNW to NNE
The colour of the Sea which has been Green of different tinges most of the way from Greenland changed on our entrance into sandy soundings to <u>Verditter blue</u>. This is what I did not expect, I should rather have supposed the contrary would have been the case.

The breeze increased the weather was obscure with ['[dark?]' *deleted*] haze and rain and altogether disagreeable as the day opened. Having steered SbW until 4 am. that we might pass on the east side of the land, we then having sounded in 92 fathoms water (lat. 60.53 long. corrected 1°0′E) yellowish gray sand with brown & white specks of shells which indicated an eastern position of the ship, we hauled to the WNW with the view of making the land to the northward of the Skerries as ['Soundings' *in margin*] the weather was peculiarly untoward. At 6 struck soundings in 80 fathoms coarser sand somewhat of a darker gray with larger specks – lat. 60°50 long. corrected 0°34′E. The weather now clearing that we could see several miles we bore away WSW under all sails with a velocity of 8 knots. The western swell which was very heavy yesterday was this morning at 4 am deflected from its direction to NW.erly – at 6 it assailed us from the NNW began to subside & at 7 disappeared. This ['was a' *deleted*] I considered certain indication of our approximation to the coast & so it proved for at 9 am. we descried land (Halswick[3] isle of Unst) bearing NNW½ W and soon afterwards traced the coast further to the west.[4] At noon Hangcliff[5] bore W½ N

---

[1] In *Account of the Arctic Regions*, II, p. 373, Scoresby returned to the need for 'an accurate survey of the Shetland Islands' and 'the soundings around them'. He also urged 'the erection of Light-houses on two or three of the most dangerous and prominent parts of the coast'. That statement carried a footnote mentioning that 'My friend Mr Stevenson, the distinguished Engineer to the Commissioners for Northern Light-houses' had told him that lighthouse construction was about to begin, commencing with Sumburgh Head, which was first lit in 1821. See Bathurst, *The Lighthouse Stevensons*. The Scoresby Papers in Whitby do not appear to include any correspondence between Scoresby and Robert Stevenson.

[2] *Pollachius virens*; also known as the saithe or coley.

[3] Haroldswick, 60°47′N 50′W.

[4] In the margin at this point is a longitude correction, indicating an 'Error of longitude' of 1°45′ between the noon determination of 2°10′W and the 'true longitude' of 0°25′W.

[5] Scoresby's 'Hangcliff' appears to be the cliffs on the east side of the Isle of Noss, the highest point being Noss Head (see vol. I, p. 77, note 1).

our lat. observed was 60°15′20″N the lat of Hangcliff 60°9 – with which diff. of lat. of 6½ miles & course of W½ N or WSW corrected of variation, we have 17 miles for the distance of Hangcliff & 31 miles for the difference of long. between it & the ship. Now the long of Hangcliff appears to be about 0°56′W[1] from which deduction 31′[2] we have 0°25′W for the true long. of the ship, but the long by account is 2°10W the difference of 1°45′ shows the error of the reckoning. The lat. by a/c agreed with the observation to half a mile therefore the latitudes of the preceeding soundings will probably be correct.

At noon changed our course to SWbS. At 6 Pm. Hangcliff bore North 35′ distant & Sumbro Head NW 26 miles. Saw 3 ships to the westward, steering to the SW[d] and a brig by the wind standing to the Eastward. At 8 pm. saw Fair island. Fine clear weather in the evening; made good progress.

Monday 31st of July Lat. 58°6′ Lon. 1°6′W.
NbE. N.
Charming weather – wind a fresh breeze and favourable. Advanced on a course SW½S – SWbS with a velocity of 7 to 4 knotts p hour. In the morning removed the cables from out of the cable stage into the tier, and bent them to the anchors. Coyled the ice ropes in the cable stage, &c. &c. At 11 am. Saw land, and at noon [Mormount?] (near Buchaness) bore WbS and Kinnaird's Head W¾S distant 38 miles. At 4 Pm. [Mormount?][3] bore NW. Before night we had advanced considerably along the coast. All sails set. A ship of war chased us for some time in the evening – but on nearing us, and making us out, she hauled by the wind to the eastward. Several coasters seen.

Tuesday 1st August Lat. 56°7 Lon. 1°40′W
NNE to NW. S.erly. SW.erly E.erly
Summer weather, light winds. We held an undeviating course to the SWbS with a velocity of 5 to 1¼ knotts, until 2 Pm. when a partial calm occurred. About 9 am. descried the land on the south side of the Firth of Forth bearing SWbS. At noon spoke a smack from the Orkney bound to London with a cargo of fish, which gave us the gratifying intelligence that peace was once more returned to Europe, through the gallantry of our British troops with most splendid honours & that the pest of the world, the violator of treaties and oaths was again taken captive or has delivered himself up.[4] This intelligence so grateful to the feelings of all our crew was received

[1] Scoresby's values for the latitude and longitude appear to be very accurate. Noss Head is at 60°8′N 1°0′W, grid reference HU553398.

[2] It would be easy to read this value as '21' but this would be erroneous in context.

[3] Although it is unlikely that this chart was available to Scoresby, 'Mormount Hill' is clearly indicated on the 'Carte particulière de la côte occidentale d'Escosse, depuis St Abb's Head jusqu'à Duncansby Head' (Paris, Depôt Général de la Marine, 1803), suggesting that it was a standard navigational aid in that period. The French chart is displayed online at www.nls.uk/digitallibrary/map/early.coasts.cfm?id=858. Now known as Mormound Hill, the landmark lies about 10 km (6 miles) south of the coast at Peterhead, and rises to 234 m, (768 feet); 57°36′N, 2°2′W, grid reference NJ009570.

[4] The Battle of Waterloo had taken place on 18 June, and Napoleon's abdication followed four days later.

with three cheers & returned by [the?] smack with loyal heartiness. These pleasurable feelings were ['[very?]' *deleted*] enhanced by the distinguished [share?] which the idol of our country, the brave & judicious Wellington bore in the unequal contest.

At 5 Pm. a S.erly breeze sprang up – reached towards the ['Therm. 58° to 61°' *in margin*] land & tacked at 7. St Abb's Head bearing WNW 5 or 6 miles distant.

In the evening a strong easterly swell arose, but as the day had been fine & wind light we expected a land breeze in the night, in this however we were disappointed for at 9 Pm. the wind veered to the east and blew fresh. At 11 pm. as we only made a leewardly course & the Staples lay near our track we tacked. At 11½ PM. saw Fern Island & Staples lights bearing about South 15 or 16 miles distant.

Wednesday 2^d August Lat. 55°50′ Lon. 1°50′W
E. NE. E. SE. S. SW. Var. S. NW.
At 2 am. the wind fell & veered to the northeastward – tacked. Calm most of the forenoon & light variable winds in the afternoon – At 11 am. Berwick bore WbN[1] distant 10 miles. Bamburgh Castle SSW. Staples light house SbW. Many coasters seen.

Saw a large Razor back! Sounded at 2 Pm. 42 fathoms. ['Saw a Razor back!' *in margin*] In the evening we had a light breeze of wind southerly – stood towards the land in expectation of a westerly wind in which we were not disappointed for at 9 pm. the wind veered to NW. Steered south until the breeze was confirmed then SEbS, SE, or SSE to avoid the dangers of the Staples. Had the lights in one bearing WSW at 11 pm. the wind blowing a 6 knot ['Sea beautifully luminous' *in margin*] breeze. The night was dark & cloudy – the sea beautifully luminous. The ship's track ['was' *deleted*] appeared a Sea of liquid fire, whilst the water disturbed by the bows was equally beautiful. It appeared that wherever a bubble was produced in the water, the [luminousness?] was a consequence.

Thursday 3^d August
NW. Calm. E.erly. Calm. W.erly
We retained the breeze all night – the morning was cloudy & land obscure, steered South ½ E until day light and then SSW with a velocity occasionally of 7 knotts p hour. About 6 am. the atmosphere cleared and the wind immediately began to abate – we were then near the mouth of the Tees – Hartlepool bearing WSW – the Yorkshire land within Sight from SbE to SWbS. Above 60 coasters around us. At 10 got sight of Whitby Abbey bearing SbE. Set outer studding sail with the hope of saving tide into Whitby – which on account of the north westerly wind and and approach of the spring we expected sufficient water over the bar for the ship; her draught being only about 13 feet. ['At noon. off Huntcliff.' *in margin*] In this however we were disappointed for the wind fast abated so that at noon we were becalmed off Huntcliff with about 60 sail of coasters all without us. Early in the afternoon a light breeze from the eastward sprang up under which we reached towards Whitby. At 5 we received news from the shore by a pilot cobble, as the ship passed opposite to Sandsend, and were rejoiced to find good news from all friends. For my own part I had particular cause of

---

[1] Originally 'SWbN', but 'S' deleted.

thankfulness in hearing of the health of my affectionate wife and son as well as parents and other kindred.

   We found ourselves the first ship – news however had been received of the Aimwell and Valiant, which worked into the ice within sight of us on the 22^d of June, having met with a vast quantity of fish and made a successful fishery. The rest of the news of the port was uninteresting. At 6 pm. the wind ['fell' *deleted*] subsided and the swell from the sea urged the ship towards the shore and obliged us to anchor in Sandsend Ness in about 10 fathoms water. In the evening the land breeze commenced and we rode secure with the wind at west.

Friday 4th August
WSW
Wind strong with cloudy weather and showers of rain. In the morning I went on shore and had the happiness of confirming the report of the pilots in the health of those friends in whom my affections are almost entirely absorbed. Returned to the ship accompanied by my Father and Mr Fishburn [Jn^r?] at noon. At 1 Pm. got under weigh and immediately that the signal was displayed, indicating a sufficient water for the ship we bore away for the harbour under a strong press of sail. The great velocity of the ship impelled her, head to wind, a considerable way up the harbour, the sails were speedily withdrawn, warps taken out and vigorously applied to windlass and capstern, whereby we were enabled to heave through the bridge and immediately grounded. Unbent sails.

[Narrative now reverts to the full width of the page, as at the beginning.]

Saturday the 5th. In the morning tide hauled the ship into a birth and moored. On Monday 7th Paid the seamen's wages comprising monthly wages, fishing [cutting?], and striking money, 5/- p month advance on first month's pay, and oil money for 100 tons, leaving the remainder to be settled when the precise quantity should be ascertained. The Valiant arrived this day with 14 fish about 190 tons of oil.

Tuesday 8th we began to boil. **On the 17th** the Aimwell arrived with 11 fish about 140 tons of oil; Both the Aimwell & Valiant commenced their passage under the same wind which we took advantage of! **On the 18th** the William & Ann arrived with 4 fish; the same day Resolution clean; & Volunteer 2 fish = 3 tons.

On the 20th of August we received news from Captain Jackson stating the safe arrival of the John at Greenock with 20 fish = 140 tons of oil. Great anxiety had been entertained respecting the safety of the John, Henrietta, and a number of other ships which ['had' *deleted*] got beset about the same time. It appears they were frequently endangered and that some of the ships received some severe presses from the ice: the Henrietta received some damage. Many of these ships were ill rewarded for the[1] anxiety of themselves and their friends having only succeeded in capturing a very few

---

[1] Originally 'their'.

small fish. The John, Henrietta & Margaret of London were perhaps the only ships of upwards of 20 that made a tollerable fishery. They did not see any fish after we did, and only made their escape at the beginning of August.

On the 21ˢᵗ the Henrietta arrived with 24 fish about 140 tons of oil. And, on the 22ᵈ the Lively completed the fishermen of this port in her arrival with 3 fish and 20 tons of the Clapham's deserted blubber about 60 tons of oil.

On the [*blank space*] **September** the boiling of the Esk's cargo was completed which on being gauged amounted to 135 tons [*blank space*] galls of oil and 6 tons [*blank space*] cwt. of whale fins.

Journal for 1816

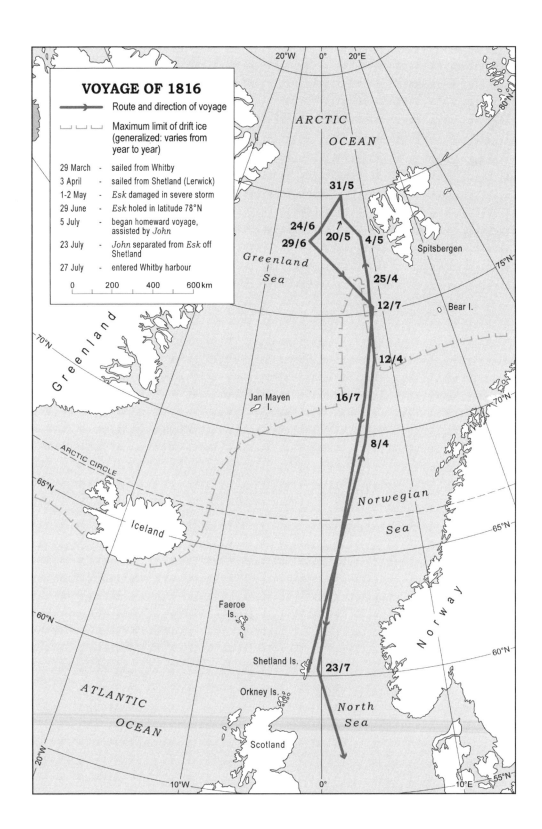

VOYAGE OF 1816

→ Route and direction of voyage

⌐ ⌐ ⌐ Maximum limit of drift ice
(generalized: varies from
year to year)

29 March	-	sailed from Whitby
3 April	-	sailed from Shetland (Lerwick)
1-2 May	-	*Esk* damaged in severe storm
29 June	-	*Esk* holed in latitude 78°N
5 July	-	began homeward voyage, assisted by *John*
23 July	-	*John* separated from *Esk* off Shetland
27 July	-	entered Whitby harbour

0   200   400   600 km

ARCTIC
OCEAN

31/5

24/6   20/5   4/5
29/6   Spitsbergen

Greenland   25/4
Sea   12/7   Bear I.

70°N   12/4
Greenland
Jan Mayen   16/7
I.
8/4

Norwegian

Iceland   *Sea*

Faeroe
Is.

Shetland Is.   23/7

Orkney Is.
North
Sea
ATLANTIC

OCEAN   Scotland

N o r w a y

Wednesday March 27th 1816[1]

S.erly

Being all ready for sea, made preparations for sailing. At high water the Esk wanted near a foot & a half of water of her floating line, consequently it was in vain to attempt to remove. The Henrietta hauled into the Bridge way, but grounded & was obliged to return to her moorings. Some of the other ships floated.

Thursday March 28

SE.erly

The tide in the afternoon rose about 6 inches higher than on the preceding day – the Henrietta got to sea. The Resolution, Aimwell, and William & Ann removed but none of them could pass the Bridge. None of the other ships floated notwithstanding the people of the Valiant emptied a considerable quantity of their ballast water.

Friday March 29

S. Var. SE. &c.

['Fine' *deleted*] Still weather – but cool and cloudy. Attended tide in the morning: the water however did not reach the height it attained the Evening before by 5 or 6 inches. All the fleet were in consequence detained. In the course of the day we emptied 18 casks of <u>fresh</u> and <u>ballast</u> water and trimmed the ship nearly on a level by removing a quantity of shaked casks from the after hold to the bows. The afternoon tide was [favoured?]; the first four of the fleet got to sea with ease, but the Mars[2] & the Esk being the last, the tide began to subside before the former passed the bridge – she grounded on the point of a Sand near the bar so that we were obliged to take a towline to the Pier and await her removal – in a few minutes she was hauled off and we instantly followed and got to sea in safety at 5 Pm. with all hands on board and all

---

[1] Unlike the transcripts of all previous journals since Scoresby took command in 1811, this has no title-page and, unlike these and later voyages, has no preliminary pages devoted to the preparations for the voyage. It adopts the three column format ('Dates', 'Winds', 'Occurrences, Remarks, Observations &c') from the beginning. However, there are several blank pages in the transcript between the 1815 and 1816 journals, and the two recto pages before the 1816 journal are marked in pencil 'Title page' and 'Introduction', suggesting that Scoresby intended to provide an opening similar to those of other journal transcripts.

[2] Captained by Scoresby's father, who had left the Greenock Whale-fishing Company after the 1814 voyage (the *John* of Greenock was subsequently captained by Thomas Jackson, who had married the younger Scoresby's sister, Arabella, and was previously the mate on the *John*). 'My Father … was content, for the first time during a period of above thirty years service, to remain for a season (that of the year 1815) unemployed. But, ill at ease in a condition of entire idleness, he undertook, for a couple of voyages, to sail out of Whitby (without engagement of property in the adventure) in charge of the *Mars*, a new ship of 343 tons, belonging to his old and steady friends, Messrs. Fishburn and Brodrick' (Scoresby, *My Father*, p. 179).

in a state of sobriety! The pilot left us at six Pm. and we made sail on a NNE course Whitby Abbey bearing SSW – 1½ miles distant.

Saturday 30ᵗʰ March Lat 55°38′14″ Long. 47′W.
SE. S. SW. W. SW. W.

Light variable winds, charming weather, At day light steered North to join the Mars which was at a considerable distance on the larboard quarter. The Resolution & Aimwell were descryed far astern carrying every sail – the ['Bar. 30.33. Therm. 44° *in margin*] William & Ann & Valiant likewise astern under studding sails & the former with royals, whilst we proceeded under an easy sail. Lay too nearly two hours about noon, until the Mars came up. Steered afterwards NNE. In the night light variable winds.

Sunday 31ˢᵗ March Lat 56°54′ Lon. 56′W.
W. SW. SSW. Var.

Continued on a NNE course in company with the Mars with the velocity of 3 to 5½ knotts p hour. The air was cool – atmosphere dense, – wind moderate and fair. At noon my Father sent a boat on board requesting ['Bar. 30.36 Therm. 40° *in margin*] a few bibles, the quantity allotted him by the Whitby Marine Bible Association[1] not being sent. I returned by the Boat four of my [parcel?] together with some other articles which he wanted. The rest of the Whitby fleet are out of sight. Performed Divine Service twice during the day. 45 of the Crew attended in the morning.

Monday 1ˢᵗ April Lat. 59°10′, Long. 2°W.
South

The weather was dark & chill during this day – wind progressively increasing until evening when the ship attained a velocity of 9 knots p hour. At 2[2] Pm. we descryed Fair Island bearing NNW – 5 or 6 leagues distant. The tide being against it we passed it slowly. As there was a prospect of reaching Brassa Sound before dark we made all possible sail, steering along the land. At 5 pm. passed Sumbro head & at 7 passed Mousa Island. As we approached the entrance of the Sound the evening closed & the night was very dark. A pilot boat met us at some distance from the anchoring, so that we brought up with safety & convenience. [Found?] the William & Ann and the

---

[1] 'The *Whitby Auxiliary Bible Society* was instituted in 1812. It annually sends £100, or upwards, to the British and Foreign Bible Society, besides a larger sum for the purchase of bibles and testaments, to supply the vicinity. In the course of last year [1816?] 558 bibles and 230 testaments were issued from the depository; most of which went to supply the kindred institutions that have arisen out of this society. These institutions are, the *Whitby Bible Association*, and the *Sandsend and Lyth Bible Association*, both formed in 1813; the *Pickering Branch Bible Society*, begun in 1815; and the *Whitby Marine Bible Association*, begun in 1816' (Young, *History of Whitby*, II, p. 631). A footnote to this quotation states, *inter alia*, that the officers of the Marine Bible Association were 'Rob. Campion. Esq. president and treasurer; Mr. Wm Scoresby, jun and Mr. Robt. Wilson, secretaries; and a committee of 12. To the funds of this association, Mr. Wm. Scoresby, senr. gave a donation of 50 guineas.'

[2] Possibly corrected to '1'.

Valiant had preceeded us & lay at anchor in the <u>bight</u>. A few ships only were in the harbour, the [***]¹ part of the fleet having sailed for Greenland. Hail showers.

Tuesday 2ᵈ April
S. SSE.
Fresh gales with showers of hail or sleet. Disagreeable weather. At day break all hands were called to fill water in the casks for ballast. In the course of the morning we had taken in 40 or 50 tons. Set the top-mast rigging up and various useful work. The Valiant sailed.

Wednesday 3ᵈ April
SSE S.
Fired a signal gun at day light & prepared for sea: the Mars however not being ready, (my Father having taken 6 or 7 extra men in consequence of the ship being extremely leaky) we remained unmoved the whole of the morning & forenoon. The men here are exceedingly plentiful and may be engaged at very low wages. The profusion of ['men' *deleted*] sailors to be found in every port at this time, renders these Islands somewhat neglected. Some ships however have yet taken a considerable number of Shetlanders, preferring the best of these men to the English ordinary seamen. The best wages given to experienced hands, competent to do all seaman's duty, is 40/- or 2 gui*nea*s p month & 10/6 p size fish, which with an average voyage is scarcely more than ½ of what we pay. Good men who have had but little experience in the fishing engage for 28/- to 30/p mo. & 5/- p size fish – and indifferent hands much lower. At 1 Pm. my Father not yet being on board his ship & the day advancing fast, we hove up the anchor, made sail & proceeded to sea; where we arrived in safety at 2½ Pm. The wind being somewhat easterly, we carried a brisk sail to clear the Skerries. Two sail preceeded us & the *Willi*am & Ann and the Mars followed in the course of an hour. Having reached well to the eastward we shortened sail until the Mars came up. At 6 Pm. bore away Hangcliff bearing SW dist*ant* 14 miles. Passed the Skerries about 8 pm. & then steered NEbN during the night.

Thursday 4ᵗʰ April Lat. 61°23′ Lon.10′W
SW.erly Var. SbW.
At day light the North end of Shetland bore WSW. As we sailed faster than the Mars we shortened sail. We had dark weather all the day, with frequent showers of hail or sleet. Steered NNE with a velocity of 4 to 7 knots p hour. The Mars in Company. Unbent cables.

Friday 5 April Lat. 63°59′26″+ Lon.32°.30″E²
SSW. Var. to SSE
Fresh gales of wind. The weather being now clear we hauled the wet part of the cables on deck to dry & in the afternoon coyled them in the Cable Stage – having first removed the Provisions – ropes, and other <u>lumber</u>. At 9ʰ 15′ 50″ am. app*arent* time at

---

¹ This appears to be 'princi-' with the hyphen ('principal'?) uncompleted on the next line.
² *Sic.* Presumably a transcription error for '32′30″E'.

the ship found the time by the chronometer 9ʰ 16′ 27″ from which deducting 2′ 47″ the equation of time makes a difference of 2′ 10″ in time or 32′ 30″ of long. easterly.[1]

In the evening we had some strong showers of large hail with strong squalls of variable winds. Took the top-gallant sails in, and reefed top-sails. Scudded under reefed top sail & fore top mast stay sail the Mars being astern.

Saturday 6ᵗʰ April Lat. 66°54′ Lon. 2°18′E
SSE. Variable. SEerly.
Heavy squalls in the morning with much rain. Proceeded on a NE course under easy sail, occasionally with a velocity of 9½ knotts p hour. Towards noon the wind began to subside & in the afternoon we had pleasant weather. This being the anniversary of my beloved wife's natal day, the crew were supplied with an extra mess-bottle[2] to drink her health & commemorate the occasion.

Sunday 7ᵗʰ April Lat.67°54′42″ Lon 3°2′E
After performing Divine Service to as many of the crew as could crowd into the Cabin, which indeed amounted to ⁹/₁₀ of the whole, I mentioned to them the bibles and testaments which were committed to my charge for dispersal among them, by the Committee of the Whitby Marine Bible Association, and that as I was at liberty to set any price on them I thought proper, the[3] seamen should have them for one half of the cost price, but from harponeers I should expect something more. It afforded a particular pleasure to observe the eagerness with which the greater part of the crew flocked round the steward when I desired to take the names of those who wished to become purchasers of bibles – in a few minutes he produced a list of at least three times the number that we were able to supply. As far as they went I therefore distributed them, beginning at the top of the list and proceeding regularly downwards. This desire in seamen for possessing copies of the scriptures, it were too sanguine to attribute entirely to the principle of religious feelings – nevertheless it was pleasing inasmuch as it evidenced a wish to become the possessor of this sacred treasure and that desire was sufficiently strong to induce them to contribute their money for procuring it. By the way of supplying the rest of the crew I shall attempt on some future opportunity D.V. to establish a Marine Bible Association on board the Ship – which may the great author of all Good bless and prosper.

We had light variable winds, during most of this day from the SE & E – towards night accompanied by showers of rain & strong squalls. Our progress was in consequence variable, our direction however was in general towards the NE.

Monday 8ᵗʰ April Lat. 69°30 Lon. 5°0′E.
SE.erly Var. Calm
Light winds or calm. Fine weather. Some showers of sleet in the morning, afterwards dry but cloudy. Cut a [boom?] main-sail & [boom?] cross jack, also a fore & aft foresail,

---

[1] See Appendix, p. 296.
[2] Not in Smyth, Layton or *OED*.
[3] Possibly originally 'they', with the last letter deleted.

out of three old sails brought from home with us. Received from the Mars a spare guy which she had on board – our's being insufficient. Sent on board the Mars various articles which were needed & which we could spare without inconvenience. Calm in the evening. Spanned harpoons.

Tuesday 9th April Lat. 69°50′ Lon. 5°32′E
Calm. NW.erly. NNW Variable
Calm during several hours in the morning – a NW.erly breeze then sprung up which increased by reiterated squalls to fresh gale attended with frequent showers of snow. Hitherto the thermometer since we sailed had only in one instance been observed below 40°, it now however began to sink apace, and in the course of the evening the air was sensibly chill. The thermometer at 8 Pm. stood at about the freezing point. The ['Many herrings seen' *in margin*] passage thus far as [*sic*] been singularly favourable & moderate, we have not yet experienced so much wind as to make our abode at sea, the least uncomfortable. In the morning a vast quantity of herrings were observed shewing themselves in large shoals at the surface of the water and leaving a greasy track behind them. Steered by the wind to the NE^d under a brisk sail. Sail-maker employed finishing boom sails, &c.

Wednesday 10 April Lat. 71°24′+ Lon. 9°10′E
NNW. NW. Var.
The thermometer at 24°–20° called forth a display of wigs, comforters, [sashes?], & mitts among the crew & induced them to levy the usual tax of Cape [Bottles?] on those of their number who had never before sailed to the northward of the North Cape. Spirits not being sold to the men they levy the contribution in coffee & sugar and then enjoy themselves for a few days thereon.

   The sea being considerable & wind a fresh gale, the Mars exhibited an advantage over us in the point of sailing – we however kept company by setting top gall*ant* sails & even passed ahead of her.

   Squally weather – cloudy – particles of finely crystallized snow constantly appeared in the air & sometimes a shower would occur.

Thursday 11 April Lat 73°4′ Lon. 9°34′E
SE. Var. NW. W.erly Calm. NE.erly
About mid-night the wind suddenly veered to the SE and blew a strong gale during the space of 3 or 4 hours and then as suddenly shifting to the W^d subsided. Snow showers occurred throughout the day in frequent succession. In the Evening a large fall of flaky snow took place. The wind then calmed. The Barometer being low (29.38) a sudden storm was expected – furled top gall*ant* sails. About 10 pm. a breeze from the NE sprung and rapidly increased to a gale. The snow being then granular & very small, yet so profuse as to prevent us seeing above 60 or 80 yards we had nearly run foul of the Mars which tacked unseen by us and came so unexpectedly and close upon us that it was with the greatest difficulty we passed clear of each other. We now treble reef'd the top sails sent down top gall*ant* yards and reached under a snug sail to the NW^d.

It is worthy of remark that the Mars has proceeded thus far, at least 1200 miles from her port & until this night was <u>never once tacked</u>. Being new ship this was the first occasion on which she was tacked![1]

Though the snow was frequently very profuse, yet the twilight never disappeared. By a blink to the NNW^d expect there is ice in that direction at no great distance. Temp. of the air 34° to 29°.

Friday 12 April Lat. 73°5′ Lon. 7°2′E
NNE N.
Blowing very hard all this day with frequent snow showers. The temperature of the air became very much reduced – this with the smoky state of the cabin & the turbulence of the sea rendered our lodgings extremely uncomfortable. The thermometer stood at 12° in the evening. A stream of air of this ['Uncomfortable Lodgings' *in margin*] temperature was requisite to be introduced into the cabin by the way of keeping any fire at all. At 7 pm. wore and stood to the E^d. Parted C^o with the Mars.

Saturday 13 April Lat 72°45 Lon. 8°2′E
N. to NE. & N.
Blowing very hard in the morning with heavy squalls[.] we stowed the foresail & reduced sail to close reef'd fore & main top sails & fore top stay sail. Snow showers occurred the whole day. On the wind veering to NE wore at 7 am. & reached the rest of the day to the NW or WNW. In the afternoon the wind abated considerably began to make sail. At 8 Pm. sent up top gall*ant* yards & set all sails. Passed a piece of ice.

Sunday 14 April Lat. 72°54′ Lon. 5°0′E
N. [NNW?]. Variable
Light variable winds most of the day. Tacked at 6 am. Had almost constant snow. In the morning after reading prayers & a sermon to as many of the crew as could get into the Cabin – I proposed the formation of a Bible Association on the [*sic*] board the ship for the purpose of furnishing those with bibles at any easy rate, who ['plan of a Bible Association proposed & adopted by the Crew' *in margin*] wished to possess a copy of the Scriptures. Being a member of the British & Foreign Bible Society I engaged to avail myself of the privilege of purchasing bibles at subscriber's prices, which are about [20 p c^t?] below prime cost and thus furnish every one who wished to be a subscriber of a penny p week or 4/4 at once, with a minion[2] bible for the same, myself making up whatever deficiency might occur in the subscriptions for paying the subscriber's prices. To this they readily assented as appeared by 12 of them immediately offering themselves as subscribers. [Thus?] much being done I distributed several copies of a printed address adapted for the purpose, and reserved the remainder of the proceedings for another occasion.

---

[1] Scoresby made a similar remark in his journal on 7 April 1813, after the *Esk* had travelled over 700 miles on her maiden voyage.

[2] The pocket-sized British and Foreign Bible Society minion 12mo Bible was published in 1814. Minion is an old type size approximating to 7pt.

In the evening the prognostics & phenomena attendant on sudden storms, were exhibited in their most striking characters. First we marked the descent of the mercury in the barometer in a rapid manner ['SE' *in margin*] & to a considerable extent, – 2^d a strong SE swell arose – 3^d The appearance of an ice blink was presented ['Prognostics of a sudden & violent gale' *in margin*] in the SE quarter where there was no ice[1] – 4th the snow which was almost constant during the afternoon in crystallized flakes – now became granular & so profuse that we could not see an hundred yards – 5th the wind whilst blowing a fresh gale progressively veered from NNW to NE or E – & 6th clearing away of the snow to leeward when to windward it was uncommonly dense was the immediate forerunner; so that, in an instant a dense storm took the sails back & threw all into confusion. Every sail was relaxed – halyards & sheets let fly and it was a length of time before the sails were secured though all hands were instantly summoned, owing to the great heel of ['Sudden Storm' *in margin*] the ship & the slippery state of the decks. With all those signs it would appear we might have avoided this confusion and risk of the sails. My anxiety to get to the eastward of the ice, with which we were quite surrounded at 6 Pm. induced me to press every sail in an ENE course and latterly to the ESE by the wind. At 7 pm. we passed to the northward of streams of ice laying as far to the S^d of us as we could discern from the mast head.

The wind coming to SE obliges us to carry all the sail possible to gain an offing of the ice. We therefore set reef'd main sail & fore sail – treble reef'd main & fore top sails – mizen – & fore top-stay-sail. Under which we made considerable progress. The rapid rise of a turbulent sea was truly astonishing. Steered ENE.

Monday 15th April Lat. 73°55′ Lon. 7°20′E
SE to East.

A very hard gale all this day with tremendous sea & sleet, snow, or [haze?]. The wind having veered to E. at 9 am. and meeting with a piece of ice we wore & reduced sail. On the northern reach we ['experienced' *deleted*] made a progress of 5 knotts p hour & the lee-way was not so much as 2 points. On the S.ern tack after furling the mainsail, fore-sail, & mizen, the velocity did not exceed 2½ miles p hour & lee-way increased to 4 points. The ship did not labour as much as might have been expected in so mountainous a sea.

Tuesday 16 April Lat. 73°30′ Lon. 6°30′E
E.

At 7 in the morning we wore again the weather during two hours being more agreeable – the barometer however shewed no signs of amendment, but ['on' *deleted*] rather the contrary: accordingly the gale recommenced at 9 am. with additional force – nevertheless we set fore & main courses by the way of keeping as much to the N^d &

---

[1] In *Account of the Arctic Regions*, I, pp. 398–402, Scoresby described, and quoted examples of, such 'sudden storms', including (p. 398) the statement that 'If the [falling] snow clears away, the gale is often at hand, whilst a luminousness on the horizon, resembling the ice-blink, sometimes points out its direction …'.

E^d as possible. We now experienced most of the disagreeable attendant on a gale of wind at sea, amongst which the smoke of the cabin fire was not the least considerable.

In the course of the day several of the helmsmen were projected over the wheel – one man received a cut in his cheek from a blow by the wheel – another was cast over it & fell upon the roughtree, but happily fell on deck.

At 8 Pm. fearing to meet with ice we wore the ship & immediately reduced the sails & rendered her less laborious.

Wednesday 17 April Lat. 73 23 Lon. 5°46′
E. to NE.
['Until' *deleted*] No amendment of the weather being perceptible we stood to the S^d & SE until noon & again wore to the N^d. In the course of the evening the sea & wind were somewhat fallen – set reef'd jib & mizen & proceeded all the night to the northward. No ice to see.

Thursday 18th April Lat. 74.13+ Lon. 1°30′E
NE. Variable NNE
In the morning we enjoyed better weather. Saw scattered pieces of ice at 3 am. notwithstanding which we reached to the NW or NNW until 11 am. meeting then with much loose ice & streams of brash ice[,] we tacked. Saw a few seals in ['Long. Chron^r 9 am 2°0′30″E' *in margin*] the water & two upon the ice. A ship was seen in the [***] which appeared to be the *William & Ann* of Whitby. The thermometer among the ice fell to 16° at sea in the evening it was 22°.

Set Gaff foresail, in the Evening. Sent up top gallant yards, &c.

Friday 19 April Lat 74°40′ Lon. 3°4′E
NE. to E. Variable
Made different tacks in the course of the night and day, pressing with all sail to get to the northward. Found the course of the loose ice to lay about NE and SW, with the wind at east we lay NNE – a short tack now and then enabled us to make a little progress to the N^d. In the course of the afternoon & night a very heavy swell prevailed rolling from the SSW towards the NNE. The wind beginning to blow hard at the same time from the E. the ship plunged & so heavy in standing to the southward that we were obliged to stow the jib and main sail. All the day we had almost constant snow.

Saturday 20 April Lat. 75°17′ Lon.3°47′E
E.erly.
Continued plying under all sail to the NE^d when the wind was in some degree subsided, which took place in the forenoon. In reaching to the NNE we met with much scattered brash ice and some streams which obliged us occasionally to tack. The *William & Ann* which parted with us yesterday joined C^o again at night. We had light wind, with snow showers in the afternoon: in the night thick snow with a fresh gale. Reached out to sea, from 8 o'clock Pm. to midnight. Then tacked. Strong S. swell.

Sunday 21 April Lat. 75°35′ Lon. 4°41′E
S.erly Calm. Werly
Thick snow in the morning with light variable winds or calm. Steered to the ENE on the winds coming to the south. Calm for some hours & afterwards a light ['Lat. 75°37′ Lon. 4°41′′ *in margin*] air from the westward. In the afternoon a boat came on board from the Mars, which appeared in sight in the morning, brought no news. A thick fog immediately ensued, but by means of a bugle horn tho' the ship was three miles distant we were enabled to coalesce. This fog was ['Remarkable fog for the season' *in margin*] particularly remarkable at this season, as it perfectly resembled in density & appearance the fogs of July. The temp. of the air was about 32°. At 6 Pm. the temp. was 30°[1] & the moisture of the fog adhered to the rigging & formed a transparent ice. The temp. of the wood &c. on which ice was forming was 30° of the air 29½ on deck & at the mast head 20°. I had expected that this ice formed in consequence of radiation but could not certify the idea. Meeting with small streams of brash ice & scattered pieces of ice we steered an easterly course all the ['night' *deleted*] evening & night. About mid night ['**Monday 22^d April** Lat 75°50′ Lon. 7°44′E[.] Variable NNE. Calm. S.erly SE' *in margin*] curious [buffs?][2] of wind occurred from various quarters whilst a strong swell prevailed from the SSW. At length the wind [fixed?] at NNE. ['& then veered the' *deleted*] Continued steering easterly. We had partly calm weather most of the day, and a breeze of wind from the S^d or SE in the evening.

The weather being mild & favourable we roused the hands at 9 am. & fitted 5 boats for the fishery – two we removed from the twin decks & suspended by the davits on the exterior of the ship. The Mars in C° steering NEbN in the evening. Towards mid-night the wind began to blow strong, attended with thick snow showers; falling in with ['ice' *deleted*] a great number of detached pieces of ice we tacked at 11 Pm. after steering to the NE–ENE – 30 or 40 miles.

Tuesday 23 April Lat. 76°14′ Lon. 9°40
SE
All this day we had a hard gale of wind, with heavy squalls in the evening – attended with thick fog, [haze?], or snow. Worked a considerable distance the eastward among loose ice & streams, until the ice became crowded & the gale very heavy then reduced sails to two close reefd top-sails under which we reached to & fro, sheltered from the principal part of the swell by a body of ice lying the SE^d of us. Being annoyed with much drift ice, our navigation was very dangerous. The Mars in C°. A Dutch vessel near us.

Wednesday 24th April Lat. 76°59′+ Long 9°E
SE. Calm. SW.erly S.erly
The wind began to subside early in the morning – at 4 am. began to ply to windward & at 8 under all sails we entered the ice and pushed forward, winding in and out on various courses from this time to 3 Pm. We had then reached an opening of the ice,

---

[1] '3' seems to have been written over '4'; a temperature of 40°F is unlikely in the conditions described.

[2] Perhaps a transcription error: 'puffs' intended?

when the wind failed us. We saw two or three whales – none of them near. The Mars sent 5 boats in chase, but without success. Some narwhales and seals were also seen.

The weather which was thick all the fore part of the day became clear in the evening. We then discovered a compact body of ice lying from SE to NE of us – ice somewhat more open from NE to NbW, and from NbW to WSW navigable ice. 13 or 14 ships were also seen to the N & W of us.

The fear of getting beset, as the water began to freeze induced us to reach into more open ice to the W^d on the commencement of a SWerly breeze at 8 Pm. The Mars in C°. Lay too & plied about in a convenient opening all night, if we can call that night which is light. The sun does not set at ['mid-night' *deleted*] this time, though as yet we have not seen it at mid-night.

Thursday 25 April Lat. 77°0′ Lon. 8°30′E
SE. E NE. N
Fresh gales of wind – cloudy fine weather – strong southerly swell. Whilst we were employed bending a boom foresail in the morn*i*ng, I had the good fortune to espy a whale at a short distance from the ship – Two boats instantly set off in pursuit and the mate [rowed?] upon the back of his prey before it was aware of any danger. A harpoon was of course struck & the usual alarm of a "<u>fall</u>" followed with all the confusion, joy ['noise' *deleted*] and distraction attendant in general upon these events. Two boats with lines were yet in the twin decks and one more in the chocks upon deck, it was therefore above half an hour before an adequate force was despatched. The fish

'John Dunbar F.   No. 1 = 9^{ft} 9^{in} bone' *in margin*]

ran briskly under water to the NW^d for a few minutes & then descended nearly perpendicularly downwards the depth of 750 fathoms. After 35 minutes she rose to the surface nearly exhausted & <u>blowing blood</u>, in 5 min more a second harpoon was struck & after other 15[1] minutes it yielded its life to the lances of our harponeers. After the fish was to all appearances lifeless the harponeers proceeded as usual to cut holes in the fins for lashing them together & in the tail for securing it to the bow of a boat. Both these operations were nearly complete and all the lines but the mate's cut off when to their great astonishment the fish revived – pushed some distance forward & dashed its tail amongst the boats with alarming violence. The second or real death however then succeeded.

Having worked the ship pretty well to windward we lay too and clewed the sails up and flinched the fish whilst we drifted down an opening to leeward. We could not avoid falling against some pieces of ice – one of which owing to the viol. of the swell struck the ship with great force. We succeeded in flinching in <u>four</u> hours, which was excellent work as a beginning. As we finished the ship had reached the leeward ice notwithstanding our care and despatch and was with a little difficulty got clear by working to windw*a*rd.

After flinching we worked to windward amidst a vast collection of detatched pieces of drift ice interspersed with streams and patches of the same, under a brisk sail &

---

[1] A correction written over '20'.

joined the Mars in good opening in the course of the night; after which ['**Friday 26 April** Lat. 76°55' Lon. 8°35'E[.] N. NNW' *in margin*] we worked a little to the NE^d and then lay too. All the ships which on the 24th were seen to the NW^d of us are now at the NE, some of them not far distant.

During the day we cruised about in various directions in search of fish, but saw none. Bent <u>boom</u> main sail, continued blowing a fresh gale accompanied with snow showers. The southerly swell has not yet subsided.

Saturday 27 April Lat. 76°45' Lon 8°40'E
NNW
A fresh gale of wind with a constant fall of crystallized snow prevailed until Evening. Cruised about, searched various places for fish but saw none. Two were seen in the course of the day by neighbouring ships. Three ships arrived from the sea. Spoke the Vigilant of London which left the Thames only 9th inst*ant* brings some little national news, and informs us that the Earl Fife[1] of [Banf?] was wrecked in getting out of the harbour.

Some peculiar phenomena were observed in the evening preceding a shift of wind. Whilst reaching to the NE^d under a fresh gale of wind and <u>thick granular</u> snow, we suddenly ran into a calm, the sails trembled, the water was curiously agitated and in less than a minute, the wind veered to the E^d. The water then beginning to freeze & a light breeze succeeding, for fear of getting frozen in, we made all sail to attempt to get to sea. The Mars accompanied us and 12 sail of ships followed – five ships which were 10 or 15 miles to the NE^d alone remained behind. We encountered a vast quantity of loose ice and patches, among which we navigated on a course from SSE to W. the whole of the evening & morning.

Sunday 28 April Lat 76°30' Lon. 8°30'E
N.erly Var. Calm. S.erly
Light winds continuing, we pursued our course to the SSW^d among crowded ice until 11 Am. when it fell calm. We perceived that the SE. ice has drifted round us and enclosed us, as already we had returned farther than we first entered and yet the exterior is not discernible from the mast head. A whale was seen at noon which very narrowly escaped the Mars' boat. Lay too the rest of the day being nearly calm.

Monday 29 April Lat. 76°26'+ Lon. 8°9'14+
NNE. N.
Early in the morning a breeze sprung up – drifted and reached to the westw*ard* into an open space amidst considerable patches & streams of ice. Several ships around us, but none of them fished, nor do any we have yet spoke know of any being taken. In the afternoon a fish appeared near the ['Enterprise' *deleted*] Superior[2] and was struck & killed by her people.

---

[1] *Earl of Fife* (Captain Wilson) in the contemporary printed list.
[2] Of Peterhead (Captain Hutchison).

Tuesday 30 April[1] Lat. 76°20′ Lon. 8°10′E

N. Calm SE.erly SSE

We enjoyed most agreeable weather until the Evening the wind was light, sky clear and sun effulgent & powerful. We plyed about in an opening of the ice without seeing any whales. The narwhales were seen in considerable numbers. Being calm at 6 Pm. prepared for making off, and soon afterwards commenced the operation in the fore hold. A fresh breeze of wind springing up from the SE[d] invited us to push forward to the northeast*ward*. Proceeded under a [less?] sail, until 2 am. that we finished making off, on our E to NE course – in [**Wednesday 1 May** Lat. 77°4′ Lon. 10°30′E SSE' *in margin*][pursuing?] which we passed through a vast accumulation of drift ice. Being annoyed at the same time with a heavy fall of snow, the navigation became exceedingly difficult, and all the powers of the mind were kept in perpetual action in securing the ship from danger as we advanced, among patches and detatched pieces of drift ice of various magnitude. At 3 Am. the snow became attenuated when we perceived we had encountered the greatest difficulties[2] during the interval of obscurity occasioned by the snow. We now made sail, and steered under a very fresh gale of wind ENE to NNE. The openings gradually became more extensive until 5[3] am. when we discerned a space of water beyond the ice, having the appearance of the sea. After passing through several difficulties, enduring two or three blows from the ice, whilst we advanced 6 or 7 miles, we reached the <u>sea</u>. Here the wind blew a strong gale, whilst we were assailed with a considerable swell & thick snow showers. Close reef'd the top sails and furled all other sails and reached to the E.ward under these. Met with a great quantity of brash ice and some patches. We were not able to determined [*sic*] where the sea here be the <u>Land Water</u> or it be the continuation of the ocean

---

[1] In *Account of the Arctic Regions*, II, the seventh and final chapter (pp. 438–88) is entitled 'Narrative of Proceedings on board the Ship Esk, during a Whale-Fishing Voyage to the coast of Spitzbergen, performed in the year 1816; particularly relating to the preservation of the ship under circumstances of peculiar danger.' The events of the voyage prior to 30 April are however summarized in a very brief opening paragraph. In the next paragraph, which opens 'On the 30th April we forced into the ice …', Scoresby commented that 'In the course of fourteen voyages, in which I had before visited this inhospitable country, I passed through many dangers wherein my own life, together with those of my companions, had been threatened; but the present case, where our lives seemed to be at stake for a length of time exceeding twelve hours, far surpassed in awfulness, as well as actual hazard, any thing that I had before witnessed.' He repeated this statement in his autobiography, adding that 'Whilst the wind howled through the rigging with tempestuous roar, the sea was mountains high, the weather thick with snow, and a vast body of dangerous masses of ice close beneath our lee.'

[2] At this point there is a marginal note:

'Making off.

Casks filled with the blubber.

  3 of 300 Gallons

15 ″ 200

  2 ″ 180

  2 ″ 126

  <u>7 ″ 84</u>

   29   Casks = 40 butts'

[3] Overwritten on '6'.

unimpeded by ice in a direction more easterly than that in which we attempted to penetrate. Owing to the unfavourable state of the weather & the full employment of the crew, the garland[1] was not suspended until after the usual time.

At 2 Pm. we fell in with a compact patch or body of ice – we wore and on our return the wind having increased to hard gale, we were much incommoded and endangered by the numerous lumps of ice that intercepted our course: which were rendered particularly ungrateful by the constant fall of small snow and heavy swell. Sent down top-gall*ant* yards, [hoisted?] the waist boats in, and lashed the rest up to the davits.

As the day advanced the weather became more dreadful and as the ship fell to leeward our situation became more alarming. At 7 pm. the lumps of ice around us had become so numerous that the yards were in constant motion in our efforts to avoid them. At 9 we were obliged to pass through a stream of brash ice & at 10 we fell in with a heavy patch of ice which the ship could not clear it we lay too with the hope finding shelter from the swell under the lee of a point of the patch which just discern through the obscurity occasioned by a constant fall of small snow. In this hope however we were disappointed for no shelter was to be afforded by the ice except where were collected a vast number of large masses of ice, in violent agitation. We then wore and soon discovered a still ['The situation of the ship becomes dangerous' *in margin*] more alarming appearance, ice was seen ahead and too [*sic*] leeward so that we were completely embayed. The ship must ['therefore' *deleted*] inevitably drift into the ice; all that we could do therefore was to direct her as far as possible against the smallest pieces. Our situation was now singularly awful. The storm raged with an excess of violence; the swell was so prodigious that the Mars at the distance of 200 yards was frequently invisible from ['Severe Storm' *in margin*] our deck, the whole of her hull & even her masts being intercepted by the mountainous sea; the atmosphere at the same time was so obscure that we could not see above half a mile; while the ice towards which we rapidly approached was plunging and [labouring?] ['with the' *deleted*] in a most violent degree. One ship a little to leeward fell towards the ice on the larboard tack; we approached on the other tack ['The ship forced into the ice during the prevalence of tremendous swell' *in margin*] in the hope of finding greater shelter that way. Perceiving a narrow part of a stream with the appearance of water to leeward we directed the ship that way, and after enduring some violent concussions, notwithstanding we avoided all the larger pieces, we gained a slackish place [here we?] wore[2] to drift in the opening towards the NW which afterwards seemed to extend a considerable way to the North. After drifting as far as convenient we attempted to wear the ship, but most unfortunately it happened that the <u>trim</u> of the ship had been unexpectedly injured by our recent making off, so that although we had twice the space that would have been required in ordinary circumstances, yet with all our efforts and the employment of every art suggested by experienced navigators, the ship could not possibly [be?] weared. To

[1] The Mayday garland: see the journal entries for 1 May in other years. See also the journal entry for 4 May 1816.
[2] Possibly 'were'.

prevent the danger of a heavy blow against the opposing ice we backed all the sails and with the helm a lee[1] we were necessitated to forgo the advantage of the favourable appearance of the ice to the NE^d of us and to allow the ship to fall into the midst of a patch of ice that showed no termination. The Mars which closely followed in the opening we had made in drifting through the stream was more successful, as likewise was a strange ship which appeared at this time: both of them obtained the situation to the NE^d which for the distance of half a mile at least appeared encumbered only with slack ice.

Thursday 2^d of May Lat 77°30' Lon. 9°10'E
SSE
We now approached the patch of ice; all hands stood at the braces, whilst the violence of the swell and the consequent agitation of the heavy ice to leeward, impressed us with the most alarming apprehension of a disastrous result. During seven[2] successive hours I never left the mast head, as from that elevated situation I could best appreciate the magnitude & relative position of the pieces of ice we [***], and during the same period the yards were scarcely for five minutes together at rest. The whole of the energies of ['Dangerous situation of the ship' *in margin*] my mind were in a state of the most active employment in my endeavours to avoid the most dangerous pieces of ice, during this period, and the state of anxiety occasioned by perceiving the evils of our situation constantly accumulating, is not easily describable. These feelings were increased by the prospect which had appeared so favourable to the NE and by our constantly to the [most compact?] situation whilst another attempt which made to wear was alike with the former unsuccessful.[3] The ship was the most endangered by the ice which she approached on the quarters. As she rolled very tremendously occasionally, the shock produced by falling against pieces of ice under the counter was most prodigious. We however endeavoured as far as possible to receive where it was unavoidable the most weighty blows on or near the bows, the ship being as strong as possible in those places – whilst the quarters and stern from the nature of their construction are essential weak in comparison. The rudder is likewise much exposed and of the most serious importance in the prosperity of our future navigation. It may suffice to say further, that notwithstanding all our care, the use of fenders made of junk and whale's tail, the prompt management of the yards, we were yet unable, to prevent severe blows in every part of the lee or ['Damage sustained' *in margin*] starboard side of the ship on[4] of which broke the upper ['gudgeon' *deleted*] pinion of the rudder and started the second gudgeon – others fractured the boats skids and [tore?] off the [gansery/gunnery?] steps, slightly bruised the quarter piece and the upper edge of the doubling in one or

---

[1] Smyth, *Sailor's Word Book*: 'A-LEE: The contrary of *a-weather*: the position of the helm when its tiller is borne over to the lee-side of a ship, in order to go about or put her head to windward ... . *Helm's a lee!* the word of command given on putting the helm down, and causing the head-sails to shake in the wind.'
[2] 'eight' in *Account of the Arctic Regions*, II, p. 441.
[3] From the sense of the text, words appear to have been omitted in the transcript.
[4] *Sic*; 'one' presumably intended.

two places – nevertheless we were providentially enabled to avoid every one of the largest pieces, indeed all our care was directed to this effort and with the most happy issue. One of the largest pieces which we encountered was a little before our extrication into a small opening of clear water. This piece however was by far the smallest of near twenty which completely blockaded our drift – we received it under the fore chains, on its ['straight flat side' *deleted*] ['Violent concussion of the ice' *in margin*] straight windward side, which met the ship's side in a parallel direction. As the ship unfortunately was in the act of a violent rolling she [met it?] two or three most tremendous blows. The evenness of its side however together with the strength of the ship where the blow was encountered, probable preserved her from destruction, or at least from being <u>staved</u>.[1]

It was near 7 am. when we gained the first respite ['Fall into an opening of the ice and gain a respite.' *in margin*] falling then into a tollerable opening with the exertion of every energy we were enabled to wear the ship round when reaching to the eastern extremity of the opening we lay too whilst we made preparations for spending a little time in the hope of a speedy change of the weather. Finding the ship not to be trusted in wearing, as on another attempt she ran foul of a large piece of ice which was at a great distance from the place where the commencement of the evolution was attempted, we made the necessary arrangements; and set the needful sails to enable her to tack on either side of the opening. As the wind was somewhat less, and the sea a little resisted by the ice, we set jib, mizen, troy sail, & foresail under which we worked with comparative safety. The <u>boom</u>*[2] of the boom foresail having broken we were obliged to bend the square foresail. In the mean time having secured the rudder head by a tackle connected with the mizen mast, and the fractured part of the broken pinion by a <u>wedged</u> lashing; we began to remove all the lumber and weighty articles from the fore part to the mid-ships of the ship, which we found had a good effect in improving the trim. By working to the windward side of the opening we were enabled to lay too from 10 to 15 minutes and then again work to windward. In this way, alternately laying too and plying we spent 6 or 8 hours.[#3]

The sky having cleared about noon, the Mars was seen about two miles distant to leeward with a jack hoisted at the mizen mast head. Considering it as a signal of congratulation, we answered it by jack at the main. At 4 pm. the weather was clear and wind a little more moderate, perceiving a passage through the boundaries of the water in which we lay leading to a large opening to the E^d we stretched that way and

---

[1] 'On examining the ship, we found our only apparent damage to consist in the destruction of most of our rudder works, a few slight bruises on the sides, and a cut on the lower part of the stem of the ship.' (*Account of the Arctic Regions*, II, p. 441.)

[2] *Marginal note in transcript*: 'NB. The boom fore sail is a sail fixed to the foreyard with a narrowish post, which is stretched when aboom & which boom is fixed by its center to a tackle connected with deck whereon it swings in a very convenient manner without the annoyance of either tack or sheet whenever any evolution is performed.'

[3] *Marginal note in transcript*: '#In trying the pump we were afraid that a leak had been produced by the blows received from the ice; but in that we were happily disappointed, as it proved to have been merely the water which was started when we made off that occasioned a depth of near [3?] feet in sounding the pump.'

lay too therein. Unbent the main top-sail to repair, and in bending it again set it at the mast head by the way of careening. I examined both sides of the ship in a heeling position but could not discover any unevenness or any apparent damage more than what has been enumerated. We now stretched into a still more eastern opening, and lay too therin. At 10 pm. saw land bearing NEbE & apparently 40 miles distant. Could not however recognize the exact place. The sea was likewise visible to windward of a compact body of ice, defending us now almost entirely from its undulations. The Mars and several more ships remained in their original situation but this time were to the westward of us. The ice does not appear very compact, but suppose with a favourable occasion, it might be penetrated for a considerable distance at least either in an eastern or northern direction.

Friday 3ᵈ of May Lat. 77°40′ Long. 9°5′E
SSE South.
The wind continued a strong gale, accompanied with showers of snow. Remained in the same opening of the ice. Whilst the ship drifted to leeward we prepared to repair the upper pinion of the rudder. For the security of the rudder in the mean time we fixed a long [strap?] twice round the rudder head, – crossing on the after part – to each side of the rudder, & by each end of the [strap?] we fixed a tackle & hauled them very tight when hooked upon a spring bolt in the stantion nearly abreast of the same. By this means the cross in the [strap?] formed a kind of hinge; so that the rudder was kept by means of these two & a third tackle to the mizen mast, steadily in its place, and allowed of a free and safe motion from one side to the other. In about two hours the armourer had united the broken pinion and we replaced it as firm as at first, leaving the alteration necessary in the two upper gudgeons for a more favourable opportunity.

In the evening the Mars joined us. As my father sent a boat for me I went on board – found all the people well but the ship a little damaged. The Mars had met with fully as coarse usuage[1] as the Esk, but it did not continue above half the length of time that we were in jeopardy. In the evening the wind recommenced with all its force & the weather became again disagreeable.

Saturday 4ᵗʰ of May Lat. 77°58′ Lon. 8°50′E
South SSW
Still blowing a hard gale of wind, which was rendered the more troublesome by the obscurity occasioned by a constant fall of granular snow. The grains of snow were about the size of those of common sea sand, and seemed to consist principally of the fragments of prismatic snow.

A slight [***] swell penetrated the ice, where we navigated but ['did' *deleted*] was prevented from annoying us, by a [*sic*] the shelter of some compact streams of heavy ice, under the lee of which we plyed too & froe and occasionally lay too.

The Mars and the Prince of Brazils were in Cᵒ but the former separated from us in the course of the evening.

---

[1] Considered an obsolete form of 'usage' in *OED*, with the latest citation in 1744.

In the afternoon a perceptible change of weather took place for the better. The crew at this time, having been prevented on the 1st of May from performing the ceremonies usually attendant on the suspension of the garland, now decorated themselves in the regular way and proceeded that routine of the ridiculous which is the ['regular' *deleted*] usual concomitant of this event. – During this day both fore & main top-sail sheets broke.

Sunday 5 May Lat. 78°10 Lon. 8°40′E
SW to NW. NNE
A rapid approximation of two streams of ice between which we plied took place about mid-night. We were obliged to make sail & with ['great' *deleted*] some difficulty worked through the windward stream, before their coarction[1] arrested the working of the ship, and gained an agreeable roomy situation.

At length towards morning, the storm which had now blown successively & with but a slight variation either in direction or force, began to subside. It is worthy of remark that this has ['the' *deleted*] been the longest & most considerable storm ['from' *deleted*] that I ever recollect having observed from the same quarter. Storms from the SE to E. are much more common at this season of the year, than those from the South which ['Observation on the Barometer' *in margin*] are particularly rare. It may also be mentioned, that the barometer did not vary until it had attained nearly its maximum when it began to fall – after settling about 1/10 of an inch it remained stationary until some time after the gale had abated – these observations confirm the general rule, that when the wind veers from the N^d to the S^d or SE^d a light wind of the former may become a severe storm in the latter quarter without any intimation from the barometer; and, on the contrary may subside without any ['Barometer & winds' *in margin*] change of the barometer provided the wind shift to the W^d or N^d. I may also mention that I have observed almost every southern or eastern storm of the spring of the year, has veered to the W^d or the N^d before it has subsided and, that after southerly storms a N.erly gale generally succeeds within two or three days, and frequently still more early. Saw several white whales.

The wind increased to a fresh gale in the course of the evening and the snow never ceased to fall all the day. Plyed a little to windward – made an attempt to reach to the eastward but were stopped by a compact aggregation of heavy ice. In the night lay too. 4 ships in sight.

Monday 6th May Lat. 78°5′ Lon. 8°40′E
NNE
Strong gales with snow showers and hard frost. Remained all the day under the lee of some heavy compact patches of ice, of great extent. Saw the Mars made fast by the stern in the center [*sic*] of a close patch apparently beset. Several ships seen working towards us.

---

[1] 'Obsolete' and 'rare' in *OED*. From the verb coarct: 'To press or draw together; to compress, constrict, contract, tighten.'

Tuesday 7th May Lat. 77°50′ Lon. 8°30′E
NNE to NNW Variable
The wind decreased about 4 am. at the same time veering to the NW. Snow showers continued with intense frost and frost rime. Thermometer 8° to 10°. In the cabin the temp. was 25° some time after the fire was kindled. Some cloaths which the steward had washed froze so hard and became so sonorous that I imagined as he brought them into the cabin, that it was the armourer bearing a quantity of metallic plates, such as sheets of copper, which the noise very much resembled. Saw a whale – pursued in vain.

A great number of ships gradually appeared in sight from the southward amount-ing to more than 20 or 25. ['NNW N. Var' *in margin*] Of these ships we recognized very few, and did not speak any or observe any that were fished.

Each of the ships as they passed us worked to windward and lay too near a compact body of very heavy ice lying 7 or 8 miles from us – as I was aware of its impenetrability we did not proceed that way but steered to the SE in search of some opening to lead us to the NE^d. We soon discovered that the sea was at a short distance and only separated from us by a sea stream of varying magnitude but consisting entirely of large masses of ice. We lay by the side of it expecting its ['*** opening' *deleted*] separation in a part which was not more than ¼ mile broad, whilst a number of the fleet returned from the windward ice and sought a passage to seaward at a great distance to leeward of us. Some succeeded after running 10 or 15 miles and others failed. In the afternoon the sea stream seemed slack – when with the help of all hands we drifted ['and ***' *deleted*] some pieces of intervening ice aside & then sailed through without striking any considerable mass. We immediately made all sail and reached by the wind to the NE–ENE near the edge of the ice. The Mars remained unmoved the last time we saw her.

Wednesday 8th May Lat. 78°30′ Lon. 8°E
NNW. N. Var.
We made several tacks in the course of the night when we met with streams of brash and bay ice.

In the forenoon we perceived the Mars to windward of us, having escaped about the time that we passed the sea stream. The weather was fine & we continued to ply to the N^d along the edge of the ice. At noon saw land but not sufficiently clear to be recognized. In the course of the day we saw 30 to 40 ships, many of which were running to the southward. In the Evening sent for Captain Munroe of the Neptune, late of the Clapham,[1] who came on board and supped with me, in the course of the

---

[1] See the journal entry for 15 May 1815. According to Lubbock, *Arctic Whalers*, p. 202, later in 1816 'Captain Munroe … sailed up the coast of Spitzbergen and reached as far north as Lat. 82°15′, where he found the sea clear of ice to the northward. He could have sailed even farther, but the absence of whales induced him to return.' It seems highly improbable that the *Neptune* reached so far north. Apart from the physical difficulties of pack ice that the ship would probably have encountered, such a feat would almost certainly have become known to Scoresby, and would have been mentioned in *Account of the Arctic Regions*, I, pp. 41–6. It seems more probable that the *Neptune* reached 80°15′, north of Spitzbergen and a respectable achievement in itself.

evening Capt. Johnstone of the Aimwell joined us. The former has one fish, the latter none. In the mean time the weather being still & fine we unhung the rudder and examined the state of the <u>bands</u>. I was concerned to find the 2^d 3^d & 4th gudgeon all ['partly' *deleted*] broken though none of them quite asunder, the upper one & the lower one therefore were the only ones sound, and as the lower one could only be seen through the water the examination was not very satisfactory. As however all the pinions were sound & the lower gudeons [*sic*] beyond our reach we could only repair the 2^d which was just above water. This being removed was soon [welded?]; the upper gudgeon was likewise better secured as well as the head of the stern post by the insertion of iron straps along the deck, connected with the gudgeon which encircled the head of the stern post; these straps were bolted to a beam & securely nailed. All the operations being performed within our power we re-hung the rudder. From Captains Johnstone & Munroe we heard various news. The Valiant of Whitby we were informed was seriously stove by the ice (at the west ice) in the easterly gale of the 15 & 16 ult*imo*. ['Greenland news' *in margin*] Several other ships likewise received damages. Several ships have captured fish of late in the situation in which we at this time lay – and many fish have been seen among bay ice further N. The rapid formation of the bay ice has driven the ships away from them.

Thursday 9 May Lat. 78°56′ Lon. 8°E
Calm. SW. S. SE. S. W.
Lay too all night. The sea entirely frozen over. A breeze which sprang up at noon and increased to a strong gale, nearly dissipated the bay ice. Of a sudden at 8 Pm. the wind fell in a shower of snow & veered to the westward. Reached towards the ice. Several ships in sight.

['Var. SWerly' *in margin*] As we approached the main ice we found a great quantity of bay ice yet undestroyed some of which was still extended in considerable sheets. This effectually prevented us from penetrating – as we were about to return we saw two or three whales, after which we sent 3 boats – but the bay ice was so tenacious, that they could not come near enough any of them. After this the wind abated to near calm & we had some difficulty in making our escape with a boat suspended by the jib boom for crushing the ice before the ship.

Friday 10 May Lat. 78°53′ Lon. 7°40′E
Var. NW. NE.
Our boats were in frequent pursuit during the night but without success. A fresh gale of wind commenced about noon, at NE, it soon blew hard, and was the occasion of a very sudden & turbulent swell. Perceiving we should not be able to keep to windward if the gale should continue for a length of time, we bore up and after running 5 or 6 miles to leeward found shelter under a point of ice, where the Mars was lying too. The ice opening rapidly to the westward, in the evening we pursued the crack a distance of 10 or 12 miles, when we were prevented proceeding by unbroken ice, consisting of a large sheets [*sic*] formed of heavy ice cemented together by bay ice. Here we were joined by the Enterprise of Lynn. Most of the other ships amounting to about 20 sail kept the sea.

The effect of solid ice on the density of the atmosphere was very evident during the gale. In the land water the sky was cloudy & very dark, and was apparently constantly discharging snow – whilst within the ice where we lay, few clouds were seen & little or no snow. The thermometer at 10 Pm. fell to 10°.

Saturday 11 May Lat. 78°45′ Lon. 7°E
NE. ENE N.erly. Var
The gale abated in the morning. Saw 4 or 5 whales, – one of which was observed to be wounded, a harpoon with a line attached being seen sticking in its back. Our boats were in frequent pursuit and approached very near the wounded whale, but its sudden disappearance disappointed our hopes.

As the wind subsided the ice began to close – we therefore worked out to sea ward, and reached the land water about 3 pm. In the evening the weather was fine and wind light. Different whales were seen and some <u>razor backs</u>. The Valiant got a fish. About 20 ships in sight. The Mars & Aimwell in company.

Sunday 12 May Lat. 78°40′ Lon. 7°50′E
N.erly Var.
In the morning, after a still night, the sea was again completely frozen over. The integrant flakes of ice were small & after being formed in a detatched state during the slight agitation of the waves, at length united in a continuous sheet & ['Appearance of bay ice resembles a pavement' *in margin*] bore a striking resemblance to a common pavement – each of the integrant flakes or pancakes, being about the size of a common pavement flint.[1]

We lay to from mid-n*igh*t to 2 Pm. The whales having then disappeared, and the ship having drifted into the lower part of a bight surrounded by ice from [SW?] south about to N. we made sail, but found at first the ship would scarcely move, so tenacious had the bay ice become in a few hours. We set every sail, and about 6 Pm. having reached to the edge of the eastern patch of ice, we found much thinner ice – the wind soon afterwards becoming more potent we made better progress: worked to windward until we weathered the NEern point and then reached eastward. Several ships in sight.

Monday 13 May Lat. 78°48′ Lon. 8°E
N.erly Very var.
All this day we had very light winds. We [doged?][2] in small holes of water which broke out among the bay ice, and almost as speedily froze over again. The weather was very fine – some showers of finely crystallized snow occurred. Made some observations on the anomaly of the magnetic needle when placed in different parts of the ship. As these observations however were not sufficiently conclusive for the establishment of a general principle I shall defer the particulars of them for to be completed by future investigations. A considerable number of Razor backs were seen, and

---

[1] 'Flint' not in *OED* in this context.
[2] Possible transcription error: 'dodged' intended?

among them occasionally a <u>whale</u>. One ship out of a fleet of 25 sail (in sight) made a capture. The land was seen.

Thursday 14 May 78°40′ Lon. 7°30′E
E. to NEbE NNE
A fresh breeze of wind prevailing, the bay ice began rapidly to separate itself from a point of heavyish ice lying to the NE^d of us, likewise to break into various openings and undergo a pretty considerable reduction. We reached to the edge of the main ice, under the lee of the point above mentioned and saw several fish. The situation however not being very favourable for their capture we in general drifted at a distance from the heavy ice, where an occasional whale was seen, but though vigorously pursued, without success. All the fleet but 5 or 6 sail worked away to the NE^d. One of those near us got a fish. Though the breeze blew strong, yet the weather continued very favourable for fishing throughout the day. At 10 pm we had a false alarm of "a fall" – the boat was nearly in the back of the fish & the harponeer struck, under water, and bent his harpoon. Whether he had made a bad stroke or his harpoon had fallen on an impenetrable spot of the fish is uncertain.

Wednesday 15 May Lat 78°38′+ Lon.7°E
NNE
Fresh gales of wind – fine clear weather but intensely cold. The fish continued in considerable numbers at the borders of the main ice, particularly in situations where the capture would have been rendered very precarious, by the extended masses of bay &

['John Harday' F.  No. 2 = 8. 8.' *In margin*]

intermixed heavy ice. In the open water several fish were also seen. About 2 am. our boats pursuing a fish towards the ice, were led among a great number of the species, ['and' *deleted*] one of which the harponeer struck. The ice being divided in the place & the fish fortunately keeping in the opening was soon killed. Towed it to the eastward clear of the ice and flinched it. The therm*ome*ter at this time stood at 8°. The cold to which the men were subjected in the boats, especially in the <u>fast</u> boat, was extremely painful. One of the boatsteerers when flinching, slipped against a knife & received such a severe cut in his foot, that it is expected he will for some time, be incapable of duty.

The ice here appears perfectly compact for several miles to the westward, but on the horizon may be seen a large expanse of water. In this place I could could [*sic*] discern 5 or 6 sail of ships some of which appeared to be making the attempt to reach the land water.

The Mars & Prince of Brazils each got a fish near us.

In the evening light winds – the freezing of the sea recommenced. Lay too, &c.

Thursday 16 May Lat. 78°40′ Lon. 7°35′E
Var. Calm SW. W
New ice having formed to a considerable thickness and all the fish having disappeared, we took the advantage of a westerly wind to steer to the eastward into a place more remote from the main ice & more likely to be speedily opened on a fresh breeze of

wind. By means of a boat ahead, suspended from the jib-boom end to break the ice, and to the operation of <u>sallying</u> which we had frequent occasion to resort to we accomplish [*sic*] a distance of 8 or 10 miles – seeing then a number of fish, though inaccessible to us on account of bay ice, we lay too. Shifted the top-sails. 20–30 sail in sight.

Friday 17 May Lat. 78°40' Lon. 8°30'[1]
Calm. Var. Nerly
The weather being calm & ship immovable we made off the fish captured on the 15th. The cause of the[2] Mars' leak being detected in a bolt hole being left open we lent the assistance of our carpenter to suspend the influx of water – which flowing through the side of the stomach piece[3] among the fortifications in the coal hole was with difficulty – but at length pretty effectually done.

   A number of fresh ships having made their appearance in the southern quarter about 40 sail were visible.

Saturday 18 May Lat 78°[4] Lon. 8°50'
SSW. Var.
Light winds to a strong gale. The greater part of the day the weather was clear and mild consequently pleasant. In the evening however we had, a continuous fall of prismatic & granular snow when the weather became disagreeable. In the morning we stretched to the eastward[5] a considerable distance and soon fell into an extensive opening which appeared never to have been encumbered (that is during the late frosts) with any bay ice. In this opening we saw a fish & pursued it with two boats. Stretching still nearer the land, among fine detached streams of bay & intermixed heavy ice, seeing no whales we returned a few miles westward & lay too when the gale commenced, under a compact patch of ice which completely sheltered us from any sea. The Mars in Co. 50 sail in sight! At 2 pm. the north end of the Foreland at E. dist*a*nt 8 or 10 lea*gu*es.

Sunday 19 May Lat 78°50' Lon. 7°50'E
SW. SSW
[Very?] fresh gales with squalls. We had a strong shower of <u>rain</u> in the morning. Fine clear weather prevailed during the ['greater part of the' *deleted*] forenoon & after-

---

   [1] Possibly '36'.
   [2] At this point, there is a marginal note:
'Made off. No. 2.
Casks filled with blubber.
7 casks of 252 gall*on*s
<u>5   </u>"   200 = 22 B
12'
   [3] Smyth, *Sailor's Word Book*: 'APRON, OR STOMACH-PIECE. A strengthening compass timber fayed abaft the lower part of the stem, and above the foremost end of the keel; that is, from the head down to the fore dead-wood knee, to which it is scarfed. It is sided to receive the fastenings of the fore-hoods or planking of the bow.'
   [4] The minutes of latitude are illegible.
   [5] Could be 'westward' but, two sentences further on, the journal indicates a landward direction.

noon, which in the evening terminated in a thick moist fog – whereby the rigging was completely encrusted with transparent ice.

About noon we made sail and stretched to the westward. finding much room, and the bay ice in a great measure destroyed we pushed forward under a <u>heavy press</u> of canvass on various courses in a westerly or northwesterly direction. At 4 Pm. we fell into a very large opening quite free from ice, indicative of fields or floes, and accordingly it proved for at 5½ pm. we saw a considerable heavy floe lying to the SW^d of us. As a number of ships [crowded?] along with us into the opening, and most of them steered for the edge of the floe, we went more to leeward, and though we saw several fish and missed some of them very narrowly yet we could not <u>get fast</u> to one – whilst as the fog was about to commence, we observed 8 sail of ships with their jacks already flying. After this we reached to the edge of the floe, near which we lay too occasionally for several hours.

Monday 20 May Lat. 78°58′ Lon. 5°50′E
SSW to WSW to SSW
The wind subsided – the fog cleared during a very short interval – and different fish were seen, both in the open water & by the floe edge. Several ships were already made fast to the ice and kept constantly fishing.

['John Greenwood [F.?]   No.3 = 4 . 2

John Dunbar **M.**   No. 4 = 6. 1' *in margin*]

At 5 Am. we had the "<u>good fortune</u>" to entangle a little whale & immediately afterwards we were surprised with the sound of "a fall" in an opposite direction. This to our satisfaction we found was likewise from our boat. The former fish was speedily killed, but the latter having run out 7 lines, died beneath the ice. We made the ship fast to the floe near the latter fish, flinched the first & had drawn the other to the surface of the water at mid-day. This we also flinched.

After this we saw no more fish during the day. The weather being foggy the opportunity seemed too favourable for ascertaining the temperature of the sea at great depths, to be ['be' *deleted*] missed. Accordingly, at my Father's request I took my <u>marine diver</u>[1] & other apparatus on board the Mars and let it down to various depths from which I determined the temperature of the surface of ['Experiments on the Temp. of the sea at considerable depths' *in margin*] the sea to be 29° of the water at 13 fathoms deep 31°, at 37 fathoms 33¾°, at 57 fathoms 34½°, at 100 fathoms 36, and at the depth of 400 fathoms or 2400 feet the temp. was likewise apparently 36°. At least the instrument had passed through water so war [*sic*] as 36° but no warmer & so cold as 29° (the temp. at the surface[)] but no colder. Whilst these experiments were performing the Mars was moved to a very heavy & extensive sheet of ice. The

[1] Illustrated in *Account of the Arctic Regions*, II, Plate 2, Fig. 2. A full scale replica is on display in Whitby Museum.

colour of the sea was <u>opaque green</u>.[1] As the apparatus sunk perpendicularly downwards there appeared to be no current. 12–14 sail near us. 30 in sight occasionally.

Tuesday 21 May Lat. 79.4 Lon. 5°35'E
SSW. South.
The wind being still moderate, weather foggy, and no fish in stir [*sic*], I borrowed from my father all his lead lines to which having attached our stock we made a total of 730 fath*om*s or somewhat more than 8/10 of an English mile.[2] Having on different occasions, seen wood which had been dragged to great depths by whales, become heavier than water; in consequence of the suggestion of Pro*fesso*r Leslie[3] also, I had prepared small blocks of wood of three dif*feren*t kinds, of nearly similar dimensions, with which I meant to ascertain the proportion of weight gained by immersion in the sea and subjection to ['Different kinds of wood sent down with the marine diver' *in margin*] immense pressure. Each block of wood was an inch square and two inches in length nearly, containing about two solid inches, in the form of an oblong with rectangular sides or double cube. Two corresponding masses were prepared from the same piece of wood, and made exactly of a weight when dry. The six pieces therefore formed a double set of Fir, Ash, and Hickory. One of these sets I attached to the *diving machine*, ['which when sent' *deleted*] the other I put into a pail of seawater upon the deck about two inches below the surface – and each set were immersed at the same moment, and each removed together; that is after being 1 hour & 14 minutes under water. The marine diver with the pieces of wood attatched was sent down the whole length of our lines or 730 fathoms – but either on account of the ice drifting to leeward, or a ['Course of the Current' *in margin*] windward current beneath[,] the apparatus & line trended to the SW (p compass) and was deflected from the perpendicular depth to about 600 fath*om*s but as it was probably in a great measure occasioned by the drift of the ice, the line would consequently form a curve, the lower and greater part of which would be nearly perpendicular; consequently the depth would be somewhat between the two – probably about 660–670 fathoms or 4000 feet. The results of this experiment were particularly interesting. I may premise that 26 minutes of time were expended in letting down the apparatus, that it

[1] The data from this experiment are repeated in the table on p. 187 of *Account of the Arctic Regions*, I, although the colour of the sea water is there given as 'Olive gr.' rather than opaque green.

[2] The experiment that is described in the following paragraphs was mentioned in *Account of the Arctic Regions*, I, pp. 193–4, though most of the data and the detail are absent, and the date and location of the experiment are not mentioned. It appears that Scoresby preferred to publish the results of a repeat experiment that took place on 7 June 1817. The *Account* (I, pp. 191–3) does however give the added information that the idea of the experiment came from an incident in 1794, when his father, on the *Henrietta*, had to retrieve a whaleboat that had been towed to a great depth by a harpooned whale. 'The sunken boat, which, before the accident, would have been buoyant when full of water, when it came to the surface required a boat at each end to prevent it from sinking.'

[3] Later Sir John Leslie (1766–1832), professor of mathematics in the University of Edinburgh from 1805 to 1819, when he became professor of natural philosophy. In a footnote in *Account of the Arctic Regions*, I, p. 194, Scoresby referred to him as 'My friend Professor Leslie'.

remained stationary at its greatest depth 15 minutes, and occupied 35 minutes more in drawing up. The greatest heat the instrument had passed through was marked by the Registering thermometer at 37° which ['was' *deleted*] is the greatest heat of the water, which have observed in these regions. The ['Temp of the sea at the depth of 4000 feet' *in margin*] temperature of the surface was at the same time 29° and of the air 38°. The great warmth of the sea ['at' *deleted*] below the surface in high latitudes, where the mean temperature is not higher than … degrees, proves the existence of a current from the southward running beneath, at the same time the current from the NE to the SW runs upon and near the surface, whereby the whole body of the polar ice is carried ['Effect of the pressure on the blocks of wood.' *in margin*] together to the southwestward.[1] The following are the relative weights of the blocks of wood in their different states.

	Fir		Ash		Hickory	
	oz	dr.	oz	dr.	oz	dr.
Weight when dry	0	10.75	1	1.45	1	0.05
Weight of the pieces immersed during 74 minutes at the depth of two to four inches beneath the surface	0	12.15	1	2.05	1	0.70
Weight of the pieces immersed 74 minutes below the surface of the sea, which decended [*sic*] 4000 feet in the water	1	7.15	1	13.60	1	11.70
Increase of weight produced by pressure.	drams	11.0		11.55		11.00

It is curious to observe the coincidence in the increase of weight occasioned by pressure in the three blocks of wood. It should be observed however that ['a change' *deleted*] an immediate change of weight took place in the wood on its arrival at the surface, or on its being removed into the air – at least such a change took place with regard to the fir, for when first detatched from the apparatus and thrown into a bucket of salt water, each of the blocks sunk to the bottom like a stone & remained there. When however the extraneous moisture was wiped from the fir, previous to weighing, it remained floating in both salt & fresh water. In the latter it was even with the surface. It was evident however that the expansion of the air in its pores, forced a considerable quantity of the water out again, which had added so much to its weight. Each of the pieces of wood were rubbed nearly dry with a towel previous to its being weighed. The hickory weighed, when immersed in fresh water temperature 58° = 2.11 drams,[2] and the ash 4.175 drams; hence the specific gravity of the hickory 1.082 ['Specific gravity of the wood after impregnation with water' *in margin*] and of the ash 1.164 whilst that of the fir when weighed was about 0.996 nearly[3] but when first

[1] See journal entry for 18 April 1815.
[2] In avoirdupois weight, there are 16 drams to the ounce.
[3] '996 nearly' appears to have been inserted after the rest of the text.

taken up (10 or 15 minutes previous) its specific gravity must have been about equal to that of the hickory or at least equal to that of sea water [viz?] 1.026.[1] The singular manner in which wood of the most light kinds as well as the most ponderous, become so impregnated with sea water as to render them heavier than ['sea' *deleted*] water, ceases to be surprising when we consider the immense pressure to which the wood then impregnated has been subjected. In the present instance the wood was sent perpendicularly downwards 4000 feet. The weight of a cubic foot of the water of the Greenland seas is 63 lb 15 oz 4 dr. avoirdupois nearly 64 lb. Now 64 lb divided by 144 (the inches in a square foot[)] leaves 0.444[2] to the weight of column of water a foot in height and one inch square, of course comprising 12 ['square' *deleted*] ['Prodigious pressure of the water at the depth of 4000 f[t.]' *in margin*] solid inches: and 4000 feet (the depth of the ['water' *deleted*] column of water pressing on the wood) multiplied by this sum of 0.444 lb gives the weight of the column of water one inch square & [two?] feet long, equal to 1777.8 lb; ['or 7 ' *deleted*] hence, as the blocks of wood were 2 inches in length and one square, they must each have contained ten square inches of surface, and therefore multiplying the weight of the above column of water by 10 (the pressure of water on the lower side being equal to that on every other part [***]) we have 17778 lb or 7 tons 18 cwt. for the pressure of the water upon each of those small pieces of wood!

In[3] consequence of a quantity of loose ice approximating the edge of the floe we were obliged to cast off – moored again on the leeward side further to the westward. The Mars and the Jane near us – all the rest of the fleet left us, and worked out of sight to the southeast. Here no fish were to be seen & as the fog was generally so dense as to preclude the possibility of searching for them among the floes to the westward, either with safety or the prospect of success – my Father conceived the plan of combining one half of his crew with the same ['An expedition for seeking whales' *in margin*] proportion of ours and searching round the boundary ice for whales. The force would of course be such as ['to be' *deleted*] would be sufficient to capture any whale however large and two or three small ones at the same time might be subdued. Having agreed that whatever benefit resulted from the expedition should be equally the right of each ship's company, and that altho' a single fish should not be subjected to an actual division yet whichever ship's crew should strike ['her' *deleted*] a fish & take her to their own ship – the other ship's C[o] should be considered as claiming one half. Having adopted a few requisite signals and made several regulations, the expedition superintended by father in person set out about 9 Pm. during a fresh gale of wind & in the midst of a continued fall ['**Wednesday 22[d] May** Lat 79°16′ Lon. 5°20′E[.] S. SSW Variable SSE' *in margin*] of rain. The Mars having more men than us, sent 4 boats – we equipped 3. The expedition had not been absent an hour before a fish was struck by my Father & soon killed. After [ranging?] about 6 hours without further success, the

---

[1] 'or at least … 1.026' is also a later insertion.
[2] There is a backslash through the final '4', presumably an indication of the recurring decimal. The backslash is used again when 0.444 occurs again later in this sentence.
[3] A 'South' wind indicated in margin.

[ 'Fish captured in a joint expedition with the Mars one half belonging to the Esk but the whole taken on board of the other ship' *in margin*][1]

boats returned and carried the fish on board the Mars, when lo! the Mars' harpooners &c. would not acknowledge that our crew had any claim upon the fish, notwithstanding the previous agreement! As however the wages of the crews may be regulated according to justice, the difference will (in the event of the safe return of the two ships to port) be adjusted. It is but justice to my Father to mention that he wished us to take the fish on board & sent word to that effect – but on our boats approaching the Mars, the men were so intimidated by the threats of her crew that they found it prudent to keep off.

About 3 Am. The wind still blowing a fresh gale and the weather disagreeable we began to make off, and soon put the[2] blubber of the last two captured fish into casks, as it only filled about 16 butts. The wind and rain continued until noon, when snow showers prevailed, with occasional lucid intervals. We therefore cast off and steered or drifted along the edge of the floe, searching every bight that was accessible, for fish. At length about 5 Pm. when we approached the termination of the opening on a NW.erly course, between masses of floes and bay ice we saw al [*sic*] considerable number of fish – 7 boats were immediately dispatched, and as we were entirely alone we had the prospect of doing much business. In a short time two fish were struck – but immediately afterwards three ships appeared in sight and soon joined us: by

['Thomas Fell **F.**   No. 5 = 6" 0']

[Thomas Scofield   Harpoon drew' *in margin*]

the combined boats of these ships the whales though at first very numerous were dispersed. One of the fish we killed, but the other concealed itself amongst bay ice, extricated itself just at the moment of time when we had discovered its retreat.[3] Made fast & flinched our capture. In the course of the evening several more ships approached us: we did not observe however more than one fish killed by the whole & this was a very small one. In the night we had variable, moderate winds, accompanied by much snow. Lay moored to a floe of ice.

---

[1] The tail is divided vertically: the left half is in-filled (grey/black), the right is outline only, to indicate the equal division with the Mars. Note that 'the whole' presumably refers to the blubber after flinching, not the entire carcass.

[2] There is a marginal note at this point:
'Made off.
filled with blubber.
5 Casks = 252 Gallo*ns*
4   "   200
9   Casks = 16 butts'

[3] In this case, 'retreat' probably means 'place of hiding' not movement.

Thursday 23 May Lat. 79°23′ Lon. 5°30′E
SSE SW SSE
We were just on the point of casting the ship loose from the ice, having seen no fish for some hours, when a fish unexpectedly

['John Dunbar **M.**   No. 6 = 4. 6' *in margin*]

appeared. ['and' *deleted*] was struck, and speedily killed. Having flinched this fish we cast off and worked to windward until 11 pm. When we reached the edge of a considerable floe to which 4 ships were moored. Near this place we saw a fish. The weather latterly was obscure with constant snow, attended with a strong gale of wind. Much heavy ice and many floes about us.

Friday 24 May Lat. 79°27′ Lon. 4°50′E
SSW to SSE Nerly NW. N.
About 2 Am. the Mars being near us stretched into a western opening, by[1] passing through a narrow strait between two floes. We followed and immediately the ice collapsed where we entered. Steered to the westward two hours among ponderous sheets of ice, and then before the wind towards the north during

['Thomas Scofield **M.**   No. 7 = 1.0' *in margin*]

two hours more. We then found ourselves (the weather being foggy) at the extremity of a bight where two fish were seen – a young one or sucker and its <u>dam</u>. The former we struck & captured & the latter was occasionally near our boats, but much nearer to those of the Mars. The ice being ragged, and slack or intermixed with bay ice in the interior, stifled our exertion in the pursuit, the prospect of capture being very indifferent.

At 9 Am. Made sail and worked to windward the way by which we entered, as the floes appeared to be <u>closing</u>.

One of the sailors having boiled a piece of the flesh or lean ['Flesh of the young whale, agreeable' *in margin*] of this whale, it really looked & smelt so much like beef that I was induced to taste it. I ate a tollerable <u>bite</u>, and though I tasted it critically I could perceive no unpleasant flavour whatever, but on the contrary it had so much the savour of lean beef that I might easily have been imposed on by it.

In the evening the wind ['fell' *deleted*] died away to a calm. The fog was uncommonly thick. About 9 Pm. A breeze from the NW[d] commenced and soon afterwards increased to a brisk gale: the fog had then dispersed. We were now enabled to ascertain our situation – we found ourselves completely enclosed, excepting a very narrow and crooked channel in the north east, a complete chain of heavy floes extended around from NE. southerly to NW. From NW to NE was a[2] compact aggregation of floes, drifts, and bay ice. Perceiving no fish and fearing to get beset, we passed through the narrow channel between the floes and lay too, among detatched floes and pieces of drift ice. 7 sail in sight.

[1] Originally 'between'.
[2] Originally 'an' but corrected after 'compact' inserted above the line.

The temperature of the air during the last 6 days has always been at or above 30°. At 10 it was 34° about 11 Pm. 26°.

Saturday 25 May
N. NW Var.
Moderate or light winds – charming fine clear weather.
The rough amusement of the sailors is a matter of astonishment to those who are unaccustomed to observe such <u>recreation</u>. A favourite sport is what is designated <u>sky-larking</u>:[1] it does not consist of any precise mode of ['On the recreation of sailors called sky-larking' *in margin*] proceeding, and can only be distinguished from playfulness by the coarseness of the method by which the sailors engaged ['therein' *deleted*] in it handle one another. In sky larking, a blow of the most painful description given either by the hand, a rope's end, a broom stick or other portable utensil, passes off as a <u>jest</u> – as likewise ['does' *deleted*] in the exertion of wrestling, does an unexpected slap of the face or unexpected trip of the heels. It is not uncommon therefore for serious accidents to arise from this mode of amusement. Not being confined to any number of persons sometimes several will attack one individual tumble him down & crush him most unmercifully by their combined weight, whilst his cries are unheeded because they do it out of <u>fun</u>, and the sufferer himself will be among the first to play the same trick to his companion. A circumstance of this description, though a sort of solitary skylarking, occurred this morning which was well might to have cost ['the' *deleted*] one of the men his life. The <u>watch</u> had for some time been amusing themselves in the various tricks of skylarking, trials of strength, feats of agility, &c. among which was the operation of swinging across the deck by means of a rope attatched to the main yard: some swung with both hands, others suspended by one hand supported themselves during two or three vibrations. One man (noted for his forwardness in all sports as well as for his activity in the way of duty) by the way of varying the amusement very thoughtlessly leaped on the ruff tree (the place of starting) and took a turn with the rope round his neck, whilst he held the end by his hand. Suspended, he cast himself off and when the greater part of his weight was ['suspended' *deleted*] supported by the rope round his neck one of his comrades, still more thoughtless, gave a violent pluck of his heels, observing very dryly at the same time that as the man was determined to hang himself, he was wishful to put him <u>out of his misery</u>! This act might however easily have effected in reality what they presented in the way of <u>fun</u>, and indeed it was wonderful that the fellow escaped as he did – for though he lossed his grasp, tumbled down upon the deck with crimsoned cheek and glaring eyeballs, and lay for all intents in a way that alarmed his companions, yet he presently recovered himself and suffered no ['Sky larking. Anecdotes of.' *in margin*] further inconvenience, than pain of the flesh produced by the friction of the rope.

---

[1] *OED* notes that this term was, in early use, chiefly nautical. The citations date from 1809 onwards, and include the following from Burney's 1815 edition of *Falconer's New Universal Dictionary of the Marine*: '*Sky-larking*, a term used by seamen, to denote wanton play about the rigging, and tops, or in any part of the ship, particularly by the youngsters.'

In the act of sky larking one of the seamen now with us when an apprentice received such a <u>wringe</u>[1] of his knee that the joint became disordered whereby he was reduced to the state of a cripple at the same time endured the most excruciating pains during some years before he was cured – yet it is remarkable that the same person has frequently since his recovery been among the first to engage in this rough sport. But a few days ago he struck a companion of his in a particular place (without design however) whereby he fell insensible on the deck! The consequences fortunately were not permanent.

['Ship enclosed by the ice – proceedings.' *in margin*] In the course of the day we discovered to our mortification and regret that we were completely enclosed by compact ice on every side with but an inconsiderable opening to range in and without any fish to amuse or console us. By the blink, as well as by a swell (which was apparent only by a slight rolling of the ship and by the disruption of the principal heavy floes around us) the sea appears to be at no great distance. The most promising direction of escape lay to the South or SSE where very small spaces was [*sic*] observable among the pieces of lightish drift ice of which the opposing pack principally consisted. Towards this we proceeded and though by the wind shifting to South the navigation was rendered as complex and arduous as[2] it was possible to be whilst navigable, yet we persevered during 4 or 6 hours and made most surprising progress considering the short tacks we had to make and the great difficulties we had to encounter. These difficulties indeed were so formidable, that of 7 ['accompanying' *deleted*] neighbouring ships, the Mars only proceeded in company with us. After about 6 hours hard labour, we found that the ice still offered great difficulties whilst there was scarcely a hope of making our escape – fearing also that should we get beset therin it would drift us far to the northward where our escape might be rendered doubly uncertain, whilst the junction between the <u>light</u> and <u>heavy</u> ice was more likely to form an opening with the first change of wind to the N. or W^d and whilst by taking refuge among the heavy ice should be enabled to preserve our situation without being much effected by the south wind – all these considerations duly weighed and their importance appreciated & confirmed by my father's superior experience, we bore up and returned the way we had worked in, ['and' *deleted*] having gained the opening which we left, as it was found to be closing, we maneuvered to the westward among very heavy ice & floes boring through a most massy stream, until we found an opening occasioned by some heavy floes on the south which had not being [*sic*] broken by the swell. Here we lay too in comfortable quarters. Three sail in company, 8 in sight. Thick weather all day – blowing hard. Moored to a floe.

Monday 27 May Lat. 79°36′ Lon. 5°20′E
S. SSW
Cast off at 2 am. on account of the approximation of a heavy NW.ern floe. Lay too – plyed about – moored again in the evening. The ice seems close around us, though a comfortable space yet remains among the floes.

---

[1] According to *OED*, an obsolete form of 'wrench'.
[2] 'S' (i.e. a south wind) in margin.

The wind was moderate – the weather frequently or generally very thick – fog and snow showers. A perceptible swell.

Tuesday 28 May Lat. 79°40′+ Lon. 5°40′E
SSW. S.
Though the swell which we had observed during the past day[1] was scarcely apparent, yet in the morning very early the floes about us began to break and in 15 minutes there was not a piece unbroken sufficient to moor the ship to. Plyed about therefore or lay too.

The atmosphere having cleared in the forenoon we discerned more clearly and certainly that we were completely beset, though yet we retained space sufficient to work the ship in. This [however?] appearing to contract, and a remnant of a floe yet remaining unbroken we moved to it along with the rest of the ships in company, consisting of the Dauntless, North Briton, Venerable & Mars. The first ship is yet <u>clean</u>, the 2^d has … fish, the 3^d 4 fish = 30 tons; and the latter 5 fish 30. Tons.

The existence of a SW. or Serly current[2] was fully proved since our detention here. Though the wind has blown almost continually from the southward for 8 or 9 days, and frequently with the force of a gale we found by observation in this day that our latitude was not ['in the least' *deleted*] much increased (of 3 days) whilst we well know that had the wind has blown with the same force from the N. during the same period our drift along with the ice would not have been less than 6 or 8 miles p day.

Wednesday 29 May Lat 79°45′ Lon. 5°30′E
SSW
Still blowing fresh with almost constant thick fog, though with occasional showers of snow, rain, or <u>haze</u>. The ice still more compactly around us, leaving a space of scarcely 150 yards square. We had occasion to move our birth in consequence of the ice accumulation in the place; from whence we hauled into an adjoining <u>bight</u> and moored the ship with her side to the floe. The ice is <u>tremendously</u> heavy; on the north is a very massy floe about 1½ miles square & the one on the south we are moored to though considerably reduced since we first saw it, contains[3] yet 6 or 8 square miles of surface. The 4 accompanying ships all lay within 200 yards of us. In the afternoon made off the blubber of the three fish last caught. In the evening the two floes approached each other with such force that some intervening pieces penetrated some

[1] Possibly 'days'.
[2] From the context it is evident that, then as now, Scoresby meant a current *towards* the south-west or south.
[3] There is a marginal note at this point:
'Made off.

Casks filled	Gallons
1 =	400
1 =	300
10 =	252
1 =	150
13	26 Butts'

distance into the body of the floes. Those pieces very happily prevented any pressure on any of the ships. The crang &c of our making off has induced a number of fulmars & other birds to remain with us & enticed 2 bears & some <u>sharks</u> to approach us.

Thursday 30 May Lat. 79°50′ Lon. 5°20′E
SSW. WSW. SW
The amazing long continuance of S.erly winds at this season together with the prevalence of mild weather and constant thick fogs, is a circumstance uncommonly rare. Some diminution of the wind took place in the forenoon when it veered to about WSW but the pressure of the surrounding ice, piece against piece remained undiminished.

The refuse of the blubber thrown overboard when we made off remaining floating about the ship, enticed several sharks and some bears to visit us. Of the former we caught 3 one of which was 12 feet in length & 6 in circumference. The liver affording a quantity of oil is the only part of the Greenland shark which is preserved. In the stomach of the largest of the three sharks which we caught was a fish about the size of a whiting; but on account of the work of digestion having commenced, the species could not be ascertained.

No alteration in our situation for the better.

Friday 31 May Lat. 79°55′ Lon. 5°10′E
SWbS
This day the wind blew a fresh gale. The weather was considerably clearer than heretofore. At 6½ am. my father in the Mars made a pre-agreed signal, signifying that some remove through the ice might possibly be accomplished. Accordingly I found that the floe to which we lay moored had divided & the two parts had separated so far as to admit a passage between them which led nearly to the windward side of the major piece, lying eastward of the other. Having called all hands – by means of warping, [sawing?], breaking ice with the boat, &c. we passed a neck of bay ice and gained the above mentioned opening. At this time I perceived the ice just where we left was slacking whilst to windward a contrary effect seemed to be produced – this circumstance, together with the evident movement of the floe in a circular direction, which had a tendency to twist us to the east side, induced me to push the ship behind a mass of bay ice, and moor there. The Mars meanwhile continued to persevere in the same direction when unexpectedly (to me at least) the passage opened at the top & closed near us and admitted her into an opening on the weather or SW side of the floe. The 3 remaining ships lay very near us – none of them attempted to follow the Mars though to each the act was practicable. Some of the people of the Venerable having built a <u>house</u>[1] of snow, excavated so as to contain two persons in an erect posture, with an entrance ['A peculiar method of shooting Birds &c.' *in margin*] and loop holes for shooting through, by means of some pieces of crang scattered on the ice a few yards distant they had the opportunity of shooting a number of birds, consisting

[1] 'hut' or 'but' inserted above the line.

principally of Burgomasters,[1] Kittywakes, & Snowbirds. The feathers of these birds are of a most beautifully delicate kind and are admirable for beds when clipped from off the fowls – if plucked the [pens?] are strong & an oily smell is communicated to the feathers.

Saturday 31 May[2] Lat. 80°0′ Lon. 5°15′E
SWbS to SbW
Wind moderate – atmosphere cloudy – snow showers but little or no fog. During the day the ice pressed against us & [***] us very forcibly. Hummocks of considerable magnitude were thrown up near us. Sheltered however by the berg and providentially never falling in the way of the heaviest <u>nip</u>, we remained tollerably secure. Unshipped the rudder to preserve it in the event of any great pressure that might endanger it. The Dauntless had a very narrow escape: whilst laying in a place unprotected by bay ice, – not above 100 yards from us, a tremendous point of ice approached her, and passed her with considerable velocity and even [toutch?] her obliquely. She could not remove – had it therefore <u>set up</u> two yards further to the eastward, the vessel must inevitably have been crushed.

In the evening, a crack which appeared in the floe to which we were moored and against which we intentionally lay in the event of its opening, enlarged with such celerity as to open a passage for the ship. We instantly called all hands & hove the ship into the opening & tracked her along it by means of the crew upon the ice, and passed through it in safety though the breadth in few places exceeded 10 yards & in places the ice (which was from 10 to 15 feet thick & perfectly even) touched the ship on both side. The shape of the opening resembled a Z and [was?] greatly very unfavourable especially in the angles. ['After this we [***]' *deleted*] We had not passed through it many minutes before the ice collapsed. In an hour afterwards however it again slacked & the three ships we left behind found a passage. – We now warped along the east side of the floe until we reached the SEern point, then deserted it & warped by another floe lying to the SE. of the one we so long had lain at. Here we had occasion to drag a great number of ['**Sunday 2**[d] **June** Lat. 80°1 Lon. 5°18′E[.] SEbS. EbS. SE *in margin*] heavy pieces of ice out of contracted openings before we could find a passage for the ship – after a continuance of arduous labour consisting of warping, tracking, sallying, milldolling, &c. &c. during about 11 hours we moored to a small floe about 1¼ miles to 2 miles from the place where we set out, being unable on account of the closing of the ice to get further. A few minutes before we arrived here the state of the ice was such that we

[1] In *Account of the Arctic Regions*, I, pp.535–6, Scoresby identified the burgomaster as *Larus glaucus*, but suggested that 'Larus imperiosus might perhaps be a more characteristic name for this lordly bird.' He continued 'The burgomaster is a large powerful bird. Its length is about 28 inches, breadth across the wings about 5 feet. Its colour, on the back and wing coverts, is bluish-grey, the rest of the body beautifully white. The bill is of a yellowish colour, with a little red on the lower mandible, and measures 2¼ inches in length; the irides are yellow; legs and feet yellowish flesh-red.' This description suggests what is now termed the Great Black-backed Gull, *Larus marinus*.

[2] This incorrect date was struck out in pencil, apparently at a later date, but the correct date was not inserted, although it does appear in correct form at the head of the continuing page.

could have proceeded at least a mile with ease could we have passed a single piece
of ice that lay jammed between a northern floe & the small one we moored to. The
Mars mean while had made some progress – she now lays to the west of us about
a mile – the other three ships to the NW ½ a mile. The land in sight. The Headland
at SEbE – 46 miles dist*ant*.

The ice among which we are entangled is of the most massy field ice. The regular
thickness of the thinnest pieces, consisting of a single sheet without hummocks below
or above, measured 8 or 9 feet below the water & excepting the snow scarcely 12
inches above, so that its density must have been very great. Indeed this ice is entirely
fresh where it is solid.[1] The side of one floe along which we warped frequently got
entangled with the fluke of the anchor which lay on the gunwale, and in many
['Prodigious weights of the pieces of ice about us estimated' *in margin*] places the
hummocks of the edge were 20 feet in height above the surface of the sea. This ice is
consequent [*sic*] immensely weighty. The regular size of the pieces may be about 60 to
100 yards square, the size of some of the floes, though much diminished by the large
[***] broken off by the late swells, may be about 2 to 3 miles square, and not any
part of these I believe less than 9 or 10 feet in thickness, besides 2 to 4 or 6 feet of
snow. Hence supposing the regular depth of water displaced to be 10 feet, which on
account of hummock, I believe will not exceed the truth then the quantity of water
displaced by the ice 100 yards square will be 900.000[2] and that by the ['Prodigious

[1] Scoresby's use of the term 'density' may be misleading here, because he did not use the term in its
modern physical sense of mass per unit volume, but in the more general sense of 'close-textured'. He
cited the ratio of submerged to exposed ice as an indication of its great density. The physical density
of ice is however less than that of liquid water, which is why it floats.

As seawater freezes, the salts are rejected by distillation so that, in principle, the ice is fresh. In
practice, however, 'The water from young sea ice may have a salinity of about 10 parts per thousand, dropping to 1–3 in old ice' (Wadhams, 'How does Arctic Sea Ice Form and Decay?'). This is
because the ice, as it forms, traps some of the rejected brine in small cells. 'They eventually drain out
of the ice, by way of a network of brine drainage channels which they create, and as the ice sheet
ages, the brine concentration drops' (ibid.). In *Account of the Arctic Regions*, I, Scoresby observed
that 'All young ice, such as bay-ice and light ice … is considered by Greenland sailors as salt-water
ice; while fields, floes, bergs and heavy ice consist of fresh water ice' (p. 233). Scoresby also accurately suggested that '… it is very probable that the retention of salt in ice, may arise from the seawater contained in its pores; and in confirmation of this opinion, it may be stated, that if the newest
and most porous ice be removed into the air, allowed to drain for some time in a temperature of
32°, or upwards, and then be washed in fresh water, it will be found to be nearly quite free from salt,
and the water produced from it may be drunk' (p. 230).

[2] *Sic*. Scoresby's calculations are not easy to understand, and some are clearly incorrect as transcribed. 100 yards square is 90,000 square feet; the displaced water from such an area of ice that is
10 feet in thickness is therefore 900,000 cubic feet. Dividing this by 35 gives the estimated weight of
the ice as 25,714.28 tons, as in the transcript. However, one mile square is 5,280 × 5,280 =
27,878,400 square feet, and one nautical mile square is 36,966,400 square feet. The displaced
water would be respectively 278,784,000 and 369,664,000 cubic feet, and the estimated weight of
ice either 7,965,257.1 tons or 10,561,828.6 tons, an order of magnitude less than in the transcript.
In a footnote in *Account of the Arctic Regions*, I, p. 247, Scoresby made a similar calculation for a
field of 30 nautical miles square, displacing water to a depth of 11 feet. He used the approximation
of 6,000 feet = 1 nautical mile, and accurately calculated the estimate of the field's weight as about
10,182,857,142 tons.

weight the piece of ice about us.' *in margin*] floes of three miles square (of[1] 6000 feet) will be 3,240,000,000 feet: now as by my estimations & experiments 35 cubical feet of the water of the Greenland seas will just weigh a ton, we have only to divide the above number by 35 and the weight of the smaller pieces will appear to be 25,714²/₇ tons each and of the floes 92,571,428⁴/₇ tons each! Moved about 100 yards SW.

Monday 3ᵈ June Lat 79°59′ Lon. 5°25′E
SE.erly. ENE, SE. Variable

At 8 Am. the weather being foggy & nearly calm, the ice slacked from the floe edge and we instantly exerted ourselves in warping, tracking, and towing until we had proceeded nearly a mile to the SEbE. A fresh breeze of wind then commencing from the ENE, the ice immediately collapsed and [arrested?] us between two small floes. In the afternoon the wind blew a gale accompanied by rain, sleet, or fog. The two floes between which we lay, squeezed so hard upon a piece of heavy ice lying intermediate, that a mass of from 60 to 100 tons was forced upon the top of one of the floes. The wind soon subsided, and veered to the SEᵈ directly in opposition to the wished for quarter.

Our situation is now become truly alarming, the force of the easterly wind of today has so compacted the ice in every ['Dangerous situation of the ship.' *in margin*] direction that scarcely an appearance of the [least?] water is to be seen from the mast head in a circumference of near 60 miles. We find the ice is daily more compact, and our distance from the sea gradually more considerable: the known dangers of the ice in this place are such, that the worst calamities are to be dreaded – ships having frequently been drifted several hundred miles to the westward from hence & have not made their escape (even those that escaped being wrecked) until the drift of the ice had carried them beyond Iceland to the South and west! As this drifting [occupies?] a length of time, such ships have frequently been detained beyond the termination of the year![2] Such ideas and well formed alarms are not at all calculated to afford happiness or content – however with help of Divine Providence to further our exertions with his direction and aid, we hope yet to escape the calamities which are forcibly exhibited in perspective.

Tuesday 4 June Lat. 79°58′ Lon. 5°20′E
SE.erly NE.erly. to SSE.

Light winds in the morning, attended with rain, sleet, or fog. The ice rather slacked at 8 am – we therefore by the united powers of capstern & windlass removed the piece of ice which lay between the two floes though it must have been at least 30,000 tons weight, into a small opening adjoining the ship's stern, and then warped to the westward through the narrow channel between the floes; directing our course then along the southern floe to the SSE we made a very little progress before we were impeded by

---

[1] This may be a transcription error: 'or' would suggest that Scoresby was approximating one nautical mile (6080 feet) to 6000 feet.

[2] In his paper 'On the Greenland or Polar Ice', Scoresby had described (pp. 310–11) the plight of the *Wilhelmina* and other Dutch whalers which, in 1777, had been carried by the drifting ice as far south as 62°N between June and October, all the vessels being destroyed in the process.

a point of ice. Finding it impossible to press the incumbent ice asunder we attempted to saw off the opposing corner which we accomplished in about an hour; the ice being only 4 feet in thickness & the length of the cut about 8 or 10 yards. Before we could heave the ship through, the ice began to squeeze so hard that we were just able with our whole powers of exertion to escape the dangers of the nip. After warping (assisted by the sails for the wind was now a fresh gale from the NEbE) about 60 yards we were completely arrested by the collapsin [sic] of the ice all round. In the course of the afternoon the ship was a good deal pressed by the ice, so that some pieces of 2 or 3 tons weight were squeezed upon the top of the adjoining floe piece. ['About 10 pm' deleted] Unshipped the rudder. Spent 4 or 5 hours in fruitless efforts to heave away from the ship's stern and turn athwart a very small space of water, an uncommon massy lump of ice: its depth appeared to 10 or 15 feet, and from one end of it a long tongue extended under water & toutched the ship's stern post at the depth nearly of the keel. About 10 Pm. the ice slacked – called all hands and warped in a very devious course a distance of about ¼ of a mile and afterwards proceeded with half watch, along a very ['**Wednesday 5 June** Lat. 79°58′ Lon. 5°20′E[.] SSE' in margin] extensive sheet of ice in a SEerly direction, by the side of which the ice was slack. Passed some hummocky pieces bearing the shape of arches, battlements, &c. of the elevation of upwards of 30 feet. At 3 am. the ice again collapsing we were stopped among some very heavy ice. The Mars SW from us one mile: the other 3 ships at W. 3 miles.

In in [sic] afternoon the wind blew a strong gale, and was accompanied by a continued fall of snow or sleet. The ice toutched the ship on both sides as well as astern and pressed with some force, but not dangerously. Our hopes of a speedy release were reduced very low by this apparently adverse wind.

Killed a bear: the stomach of this animal contained only a seal's paw of solids – it was singularly lean.

Thursday 6 June Lat. 80°2′ Lon. 5°10′E
SbE SbW
The gale continued accompanied with a quantity of snow until the evening – veering then to [SbW?] it became moderate. The North Briton (3 miles W. of us) appeared seriously pressed by the ice – her boats were on the ice and the ship careened to windward.[1] In the evening however she righted and was observed to remove a little astern. The three ships are now within 30 yds of each other. The Mars ['retreated to' deleted] as above. The ice pressed a little upon us, but being nearly perfectly close it had but a trifling motion.

Friday 7 June Lat. 80°0′ Lon. 5°0E
Variable. Calm. W.erly. Var.
A calm succeeded the gale. The day was fine and particularly warm.
Sent down the Marine diver to the depth of 120 fathoms where the temperature appeared to be 36°.3 at least the surface ['The sea still warm beneath the surface' *in*

---

[1] '… the terrible crushes of the ice that were apparent all round us, and which, in one instance, lifted the North Britain [sic] six feet above her usual water-mark' (*Account of the Arctic Regions*, II, p. 442).

margin] was 29°.7 and the register thermom*et*er had passed through the above temperature. A piece of fir wood att*at*ched to the instrument was still buoyant when it came up. As the thorough impregnation of wood does not probably take place above a certain depth, possibly its change of specific gravity when hauled up might be made use of to ascertain the depth of the water.

The apparatus set to the NNW (compass) at an angle of about ['Greenland Currents' *in margin*] 7 or 8°. Hence an upper current to the SSE or lower one to the NNW. The great warmth of the water below, where the mean temperature of the air is not more than [*blank space*]° is a circumstance that affords a strong presumption of a constant current flowing beneath the surface from a warm or at least temperate climate. And hence, the SW.erly upper current that constantly prevails here and carries the ice along with it, may be in a great measure occasioned by the return of the water to produce the level. The accumulation of some ice in the N. may possibly add to the effect just stated – for as 9/10 of the moisture which falls is brought by S.erly winds, and as Nerly ['Polar currents' *in margin*] winds from their chillness and inapt-ness to convey moisture do not rob the polar regions, it follows that there must be a continual increase of vapour in the high latitudes, which being deposited and formed into ice, returns again by the current to the regions from whence it was evaporated.

A small air of wind prevailed during the night from the W^d to NW^d but no effect was yet introduced on the ice – indeed ['Ther, 10 Pm.= 32° NB. It has not been any [lower?] but on one occasion since the 20th Ult.!' *in margin*] as it must first slack to sea ward, it may be some time before any alteration takes place calculated for our advantage

I retired to rest with the sanguine hope of being called up to remove the ship, but alas I was disappointed for not a sensible ['**Saturday 8th June** Lat. 79°54'+ Lon. 4°55'E[.] NWerly N.erly' *in margin*] alteration took place. Foggy weather during the night.

Though a little breeze of wind blew from the N. to NNE the whole of the day it had not the expected or wished for effect – the ice remained unslacked. Its [*sic*] true we [hove?] by immense power two pieces of ice asunder about 15 feet in the direction we wished to pursue, but the pieces being heavy (['being' *deleted*] the one about 50,000 tons and the other 30,000 in weight) and at the same time compressed on every side, they collapsed so suddenly & in such force that our 8 inch hawser (a good rope) was broken thereby. In the evening we had snow showers – the temperature of the air fell from 42° to 32° – water visible on the horizon from SSW to SSE in partial places. The 3 ships to the westward, though originally at NW have revolved to WbS without almost any movement thro' the ice – though during this day they warped about ¼ or ½ mile to the Southward. The Mars lays a mile from us – closely beset and like us immovable.

Sunday 9 June Lat. 79°49' Lon. 4°53'E
NNE

At 2 am. I was happily aroused with the information that the two pieces of ice, which we the preceding day had in vain attempted to separate were disjoined, and a passage of half the ship's breadth already formed, and that the ice in general had rather slacked. This prospect though indeed of itself but affording very slight hope was yet sufficient to put us on the alert who had become seriously alarmed for our permanent detention here and of course the total failure of the future fishery; accordingly I arose along with all the crew and with our united efforts made every progress possible. We passed through the strait formed by the two pieces of ice before alluded to, but not without the exercise of our utmost strength and ingenuity, because after the strait was sufficiently wide for the ship, she required to be turned very suddenly more to the south. This being at length accomplished we, were assisted by the sails in advancing (for the wind now blew a moderate breeze at NNE) and after 8 or 9 hours hard labour we were effectually barred in our further progress by a chain of very heavy ice extending from NE to SW, consequently directly across our course, and in which direction there was unfortunately a considerable pressure. Three hours having been spent in vain exertion, we relaxed, and in expectation of the ice slackening, we passed a short interval in performing the usual services of the Sabbath. No alteration having taken place we rested four hours and then renewed our labours – tho' we <u>sawed</u>, hove an immense stain[1] on our purchases, pressed the ice asunder by means of a long lever, consisting of a stout top-mast studding sail boom, yet we were able only to separate the pieces about 2 yards. Finding every hope of proceeding in this way, in the existing circumstances, extinguished, we found means to turn the ship, and attempted to pass on the opposite side of some of the pieces. Having the opportunity of heaving a few small pieces of ice out of the niche, we were enabled in ['four' *deleted*] six hours, to pass the first strait. ['**Monday 10 June** Lat. 79°47′+ Lon. 4°50′E. N.erly calm. W.erly. Variable.' *in margin*] The ice then began to slack, so that at 2 am. all hands were again at work, and our progress was considerable. The wind having subsided to a calm, we dragged the ship forward and twisted the opposing pieces of ice by means of lines on each side of the ship at the same time. About 8 am. we fell into a slack place and proceeded near half a mile with little interruption; here we shipped or <u>hung</u> the rudder. At noon we were again stopped in a chain of large masses of ice, which being closely joined and in the act of closing we were unable, notwithstanding every possible exertion to proceed. We therefore rested again for a short time.

This morning the weather was singularly warm, and the <u>light</u> so intensely power-ful, proceeding from a cloudless sky, and the reflection of the ice, that [pains?] in the ['Great intensity of Light' *in margin*] eyes and head, were common among our people in consequence. It was curious to see the men, winking, and looking upon dark objects, endeavouring to prevent the excess of light from penetrating the eye after the pupil was reduced its utmost state of contraction, by lowering the eyelashes, and partly closing the eye – every man seemed as if he had just arisen from his bed, or had just emerged from some extremely dark place. I made use of a pair of green spectacles which afforded me great relief, though I neglected to avail myself of them until my head was painfully disordered.

The weather in the afternoon became cloudy – and [breeze?] of wind from the east-ward commenced. This was against us. However as it was very light for sometime & the ice began again to slack, in about 5 hours (7 pm) we warped forward, under a cloud of fog, with tollerable effect insomuch, that at mid-night we found ourselves

---

[1] *Sic*. Presumably 'strain' intended.

['**Tuesday 11 June** Lat. 79°46′ Lon. 4°54′E[.] NE NEbE' *in margin*] on the exterior of all the floes and heavier masses of ice, among such pieces as with a favourable wind we could have managed pretty well in boring. Here then was a difficulty – the wind was directly against us, the ice compact, and the pieces too inconsiderable to warp by. The following method suggested itself to me. I selected, from the masthead, a pretty large and one of the heaviest pieces of ice to seaward – it was half a mile distant – a lot of men were sent from piece to piece towards, with a whale line, which with considerable difficulty (on account of the distortion of some of the pieces, and the abundance of ['heavy' *deleted*] deep tongues of ice intervening) they made fast by means of an ice anchor. By means of this line then, whilst we seperated the opposing ice, by means of other lines, ['and' *deleted*] grapnels, &c we hove the ship up to windward. It is true the resistance and reaction of the ship dragged the piece of ice to leeward, yet on account of the ice intervening, this was not very considerable. After hauling up to it, we did the same with regard to another large piece of ice about ¼ mile further to windward, to this we likewise hove the ship; when we were not above ½ a mile from the water. This envigorating prospect induced us to labour after even the probability of succeeding had in great measure vanished. The ice was heavyish about and we made no further progress to windward. There however appeared a possibility of boring out to sea, as the wind was fresh and the direction of the required course about SE which was with the wind abeam. We made the attempt but the ice being locked together by long deep seated tongues the ship fell to leeward and we were obliged to desist to prevent her penetrating further in. We therefore again furled the sails, seized on two or three of heaviest pieces of ice, and after heaving the ship nearly to them, we remained at rest. At 2 pm. we made another attempt to work forward, by means of lines attatched to distant pieces – the method now however partly failed on account of the increased force of the wind, and the consequent increased compactness of the ice. We nevertheless continued to get a little forward, though our distance from the water was undiminished, as loose ice kept settling on the seaward, ['side' *deleted*] edge of the pack.

At 4 pm. the wind began to blow a strong breeze – warps were substituted for lines, ['but little' *deleted*] and more effect produced.

The Mars at this time lay to the NbW of us, about two miles distance, and the three companions at NW. 3 miles; all of them firmly beset among heavy floe ice. Some ships seen at sea plying to windward.

Having, about 10 Pm. got within ¼ of a mile of the water we were in expectation of availing ourselves of a partial slack in the ice, but circumstances, such as the varying position of the ice, the unsuitableness of the direction of the wind together with its increasing strength, prevented us. We therefore lay moored, by the stern to the heaviest mass of ice near us.

Wednesday 12 June Lat 79°40′ Lon. 4°45′E
NEbE Variable to N ...
We experienced a fresh gale of wind during the night, attended with showers of snow. Saw 2 or 3 whales, and about the same time observed the Mars and one other of the ships we left beset, were fast to fish.

The different <u>unsuccessful</u> attempts which we made during the last day to extricate ourselves from among the ice, might construe a great deficiency of judgement & experience respecting the extent of the prospects[1] of a ship for performing the ['Reflections on the doubtful case between possibility & impossibility.' *in margin*] different operations connected with obstructions in the ice, – were it not observed that in every case of human circumstance where there is attatched possibility and impossibility of performance there must always be an intermediate case which is doubtful, and in the regard to which the most consummate wisdom of mortals is not always able to decide. Such was the case in our latter operations – the direction of the wind was such with regard to the position of the ice, as to be in the doubtful case: had the wind been two points more northerly, the possibility of succeeding would have been certain, and had it been the same angle more easterly the impossibility of effecting a release under the existing circumstances would have been equally certain.

About 6 am. we found our advantage in having quietly waited a change of circumstance when we had the advantage of a heavy piece of ice to moor to, which supported us well to windward, – for at this time the ice was found so generally slacked to seaward, whilst the wind was greatly lessened that there was no great difficulty attending our escape. We therefore set the sails, cast loose from the ice, and in less than half an hour <u>bored</u> out into navigable water, in which was a profusion of drift ice that had accumulated principally during the last 24 hours. We however found no difficulty in proceeding.

Thus after near three weeks of anxiety – after an amazing exercise of the most arduous labour, in the performance of which latterly we have been obliged to content ourself with ⅓ of our natural rest, after having almost destroyed the greater part of our ice ropes and several whale lines together with most of the handspikes and many of the boathooks, in the ship – after having endured a privation of every chance of furthering the object of the voyage for a similar period of nearly three weeks – at the same time that the safety of the ship when immersed among such prodigious masses of ice, was in continual jeopardy – after enduring these dangers, ['and' *deleted*] difficulties, and privations the effect of our providential release before our fellow sufferers; was of a nature so grateful, and pleasing in our minds as not to admit of very[2] ready or accurate description. Liberty is then proved, like every common mercy, to be appreciated only, when it is lost.

The effect of the want of our usual rest was strikingly apparent in ['the' *deleted*] a circumstance attending one of the boys. ['Boy fell asleep in a boat and tumbled overboard.' *in margin*] This lad being placed in a boat whilst we were engaged warping the ship forward in the ice, for the purpose of conducting it clear of the pieces, stood with a boathook in his hand in the stern of the boat & actually fell asleep in that posture and tumbled into the water! I fancy he did not long remain in his state of indulgence as he was instantly observed to struggle & with a tollerable imitation of swimming to make for the boat.

As the ice was very [crowded?] to the eastward, and especially as

[1] Possibly 'propriety'.
[2] Possibly 'any'.

['John Dunbar **M.** No. 8 = 3½ ft.' *in margin*]

different fish (which generally have a tendency to go to windward) had been seen near this place, we plyed by the edge of the pack to the northward. We had scarcely been at liberty half an hour when a fish appeared was pursued and struck. It retreated into the ice but was notwithstanding followed with such vigour that it was speedily subdued. Flinched it and then [proceeded?] again to the windward.

In the evening spoke the boats of the Grenville Bay,[1] from the harpooners of which we received the following information that in consequence of the blowing weather of late, together with the thick fogs which commonly filled up the interval, little progress had been made in the ['Greenland news.' *in margin*] fishery. The Grenville Bay had been as far to the southward as 75° without seeing any fish. That the bulk of the ships were seen 10 or 15 days ago, which were on the point of going to the southward that few of these had more than 2 fish each, and a great many were then <u>clean</u>. This intelligence had the effect of consoling us for our recent detention – not from the narrow [***] motive of wishing ill to our neighbours, but from the consideration that we had not suffered such a loss by our confinement as we imagined, for it appeared probable that had we been all the time at liberty we might have done but little good.

The Grenville Bay has 3 fish, the Norfolk[2] in company 6 (chiefly small[)], and the Sarah & Elizabeth clean – these three ships together with ourselves and companions are probably the only ships which are at present this far north. The John of Greenock (Brother Jackson) it appears was seen a week ago, with only one small fish.

Thursday 13 June Lat. 79°44′+ Lon. 4°55′E
Variable. SE.erly.
Light variable winds with fog or snow showers. Saw several fish during the morning watch which were pursued with vigour but without success. In the forenoon we ran to the northward a few miles, but meeting with no fish, plyed back again among loose ice by the edge of the pack. In the evening the Mars escaped from the ice – the other three ships were likewise near the edge but did not get out whilst we were within sight. A breeze from the SE springing up we reached all the night on a SSW ['**Friday 14 June** Lat. 79°0′ Lon. 5°0′E[.] Variable. NE.erly NEbN. NNE' *in margin*] course in open water – a few occasional pieces of ice seen & here and there a patch or stream. At 10 am. I saw a fish in the act of <u>thrashing</u>[3] (A kind of frolic it appears which the whale sometimes indulges in fine weather consisting of a violent motion of the tail which it dashes upon the water in a terrible manner and makes the water fly an

---

[1] The printed contemporary list for 1816 does not include this vessel, but it has been added in manuscript to the list in the Scoresby Papers, as a Newcastle whaler. See also Barrow, *Whaling Trade*, p. 69.

[2] This Berwick whaler (Captain Marshall) is shown in the 1816 contemporary list as 'intended for Davis's Streightes'.

[3] Termed 'tailslapping' by Würsig and Clark. See the section on 'Aerial Activity and Play', pp. 171–3 in their chapter on 'Behavior'.

amazing distance – sometimes it will leap entirely out of the water) this fish was pursued by three of our boats and two of the boats of the Gardener & Joseph[1] which had recently approached us from the southward; after the chace [sic] had been conducted about two hours our competitors being <u>over-pulled</u>,[2] left our boats to pursue their prey undisturbed: they in consequence pursued it in a circuit of 10 or 12 miles and when it reached an open patch of ice to the westward it rather stayed its speed and was struck by the mate. Five harpoons were struck at different times, two of which were <u>cutout</u> by the mate's harpoon that hung by a <u>wither</u>. It was with difficulty killed, some of the boats being in pursued [sic] of another fish at a great distance when it was struck. After 4 hours, however it was overpowered and killed. When brought to the ship it proved a fine prize, being by far the largest fish we have got this season. The wind blowing

['John Dunbar **M.**   No. 9 = 10..2' *in margin*]

strong from the NNE we took shelter under the lee of a point of ice and flinched laying too with the sails clewed down. In the course of the day we saw 3 or 4 other large fish. Spoke a boat of the Gardiner and Joseph from which the intelligence received from the Granville Bay with regard to the state of the fishing in general was further confirmed. This ship has 2 fish.

During a light breeze of wind from the eastward, in the forenoon, the land which was in sight assumed, in consequence of refraction, an appearance which whilst it was particularly curious, had beauty of expression peculiar to this country alone. The lower part of the hills had their usual appearance, but the upper ['Curious effect of a peculiar refraction' *in margin*] half appeared as if composed entirely of immense pillars or variegated basaltic columns. On some mountains stood erect and slender pillars like some monumental towers, whilst in one place an iceberg[3] was elevated immensely above its level & really appeared a prodigious elevation of <u>alabaster</u>. At this time to the north*war*d lay a fog bank – part of which extended in a slender sheet along the northern land, on which a similar effect was produced, but not so clear & striking as in the coast to the southward of the apparent density.[4]

Saturday 15 June Lat. 79°0′ Lon. 5°0′E
NNE. N.
Strong breezes, with fog showers. Strong southerly swell & considerable wind lipper from the north. In consideration of the propensity of whales to move to windward together with the observation that several of those laterally[5] seen were advancing to the N^d or NW^d induced us to ply all the day along the edge of the ice towards the

---

[1] Actually the *Gardiner and Joseph II* of Hull (Credland, *Hull Whaling Trade*, p. 123).
[2] Presumably meaning 'out-rowed' but not in *OED* with that meaning. See Smyth, *Sailor's Word Book*, s.v. PULLING.
[3] Here, presumably, Scoresby's usual term for a glacier.
[4] Scoresby included this occasion in *Account of the Arctic Regions*, I, pp. 386–7.
[5] *Sic*. A transcription error for 'lately'?

north, under a pressure of sail. Saw two[1] fish in the course of the day. Observed the Gardiner & Joseph and the Venerable (both to windward of us) in the act of flinching. When we approached the western ice, we found it excepting 2 or 3 miles[2] of slack ice on the exterior, a compact impenetrable body. Three ships seen to leeward, working towards us – but we soon left them out of sight.

Sunday 16 June Lat. 79°12′+ Lon. 4°50′E
N. NNW. W.erly
Charming fine weather, clear, and <u>warm</u>. Wind fresh breezes to nearly calm. Worked along the edge of the ice to the NE^d and in the evening searched the windward extremity of a considerable bight, where was compact ice and large floes within – but no fish to be seen. To the north we saw 4 ships separated from us by an extensive patch of loose ice. The Venerable and Gardiner & Joseph near us.

Monday 17 June Lat. 79°10′ Lon. 6°50′E.
W.erly. SWbS. S.erly.
Being considerably disappointed in not meeting with fish we took advantage of a fresh breeze of wind from the SW^d to make a long stretch to the eastward. At 1 pm. ['being' *deleted*] we were out of sight of all ice but 2 or 3 scattered patches, the Foreland (N end) bearing SEbS distant 12 leagues – tacked and returned by the wind to the W^d. In the evening as we approached a bight of the ice we saw two fish – one of them was struck by the boats of Venerable (but afterwards lost), and the other being pursued by 3 of our boats was overtaken, and one of them rowed completely upon its back – the harponeer struck his harpoon, but from some unaccountable mismanagement it instantly came out and the fish escaped! This was a mortifying circumstance – as the fish was a very large one, and the opportunity was as excellent as could be imagined.

Tuesday 18 June Lat. 79°0′ Lon. 4°40′E.
Variable. NW.erly. to SW.erly.
Very light winds in the night – fine weather. Worked into the midst of a patch of ice, but seeing no fish, reached again into the sea and then proceeded to the SW^d or S^d by the wind. In the evening saw two fish – pursued them in vain after having approached so near as to alarm both of them. The wind then veering to the SW ^{d} being very var. and attended with showers of snow we tacked, ['and' *deleted*] reached to the ice, and then worked along the edge of it to the S^d. 3 ships in sight.

Wednesday 19 June Lat. 78°40′ Lon 5°10′E
SW.erly. to W, WNW.
Continued plying or sailing along the edge of the loose ice to the SW^d accordingly as the wind suited, under all our sails. The weather was foggy and disagreeable all the morning and forenoon, in the evening in [*sic*] the wind was very light and the weather fine though frequent ['snow' *deleted*] showers of prismatic snow occurred.

---

[1] Possibly 'ten'.
[2] Could equally well be read as 'inches', but the context makes this unlikely.

Saw no fish throughout the day until evening though one ship caught a fish near us. About 5 pm. passed through a quantity of loose ice on a SSE course whilst the three ships in sight all tacked and plyed to the NW^d. Having again gained the sea I espied from the masthead at a great distance three large whales – all the boats were sent in pursuit and two and two [*sic*] chaced each fish for 4 or 5 hours without ['Inefficiency of the harpooners occasions great loss to the ship' *in margin*] success. One of them indeed by a blunder nearly as bad as that of Tuesday last allowed a fish to escape him under circumstances as favourable as could be wished – he erred in two points; first he pulled <u>from</u> the fish by the way of getting behind her to escape her eye and when [***]¹ at least 100 yards further than the occasion required – the consequence was, the fish was in the act of sinking as he reached it, and he finished the misconduct secondly by making a ['bad' *deleted*] insufficient and ill directed strike which instead of penetrating the fish, bent the harpoon. Thus two large fish have been sacrificed within 3 days by the most palpable misconduct or insufficiency of the harpooners. On this occasion, these officers on whom so much depends happen to be singularly deficient. – the loss to the ship is incalculable.

['Narwhale. male  Struck by the Mate' *in margin*]

The mate struck and killed a narwhale which came up close to his boat – it was a male – without a horn. The colour excepting the ridge of the back, the edges of fins and tail and the edge of the lips was perfectly white, and these other parts were ['Some particulars respecting the Narwhale.' *in margin*] bespotted with gray spots approaching to black on the back. The length was 15 feet 2 in. and its greatest circumference (at the distance of 4.6 from the extremity of the head) was 8^{ft.} 9ⁱⁿ. In its stomach were found a vast number of <u>sepia</u>, some of them perfect especially 2 in its mouth: they were about 4 inches long in the sheath. A vast number of their bills were found – several living worms 4 or 5 in. long – some ['crawfish' *deleted*] shrimps*² the backbones of a small fish and a substance resembling the eyes of fishes. The number of the sepia contained in the stomach was perhaps not less than 20 or 30.³ On the back of this narwhale was a remarkable ridge – it commenced at the distance of two feet from the front of the head and extended two feet in length along the back.

Killed three or four sharks which were found feeding on a ['Sharks killed: use of the liver and contents of the stomach' *in margin*] <u>crang</u> – preserved their liver, which when allowed to stand in the sun, yields a considerable quantity of oil, though it cannot be extracted by boiling, on account of the delicate and tender texture of the liver. In the stomach of one of these sharks were found three ['large' *deleted*] red animals of the shrimp kind – what we consider as the crawfish: I have seen within other individuals a

¹ Possibly 'rem*ov*ed'.
² Note in margin: '*There is a shrimp of this kind commonly caught among the common shrimps which is now by the name of …'.
³ In *Account of the Arctic Regions*, I, p. 544, Scoresby listed the *Sepia* as 'Cuttle-fish. – Found by myself in large quantities in the stomachs of different narwhals, and appearing to constitute their principal food. The species not known.'

small fish resembling a whiting in size and form, but on account of the process of digestion having commenced on it, I was unable to ascertain the species.

Whilst the boats were in pursuit of the fish alluded to I made some observations on the length of time occupied by the ['Remarks on the whale its stay down and up.' *in margin*] fish below and at the surface of the water. One fish blew 5 times per minute, remained at diff*eren*t times 2½, 1½, 1, and 1¼ minutes; and down in ['the' *deleted*] intervals of 4, 11, 6, & 6 minutes. I consider therefore the common stay of the fish below the water to be about 6 minutes; 10 minutes is rather long, though sometimes when feeding they will remain beneath 15 to 20' or ['longer' *deleted*] perhaps longer: I also consider that the usual stay of a fish at the surface is 1½ minutes – 3 minutes is reckoned a long time for a fish to remain up. It is therefore evident that great promptitude sagacity and activity is required in the harpooner to lay his[1] in a proper place and to improve any advantage which he may gain by a fish rising near him.

Thursday 20 June Lat. 78°20′ Lon.4°45′E
W.erly. SW.erly WSW
At 2 am. though we saw an occasional fish we set the watch. Worked the ship into a bight and among some loose ice where several fish were seen. All hands again pursued & happily better success followed. The mate (the only harpooner

['John Dunbar **F.**   No. 10 = 10.10' *in margin*]

we[2] has struck more than a single fish) again succeeded, struck a fish which was killed in about an hour and a half. Lay too and flinched, 2 to 4 boats meanwhile pursuing fish but without success. In the evening penetrated the ice to the NW about 8 miles ['about' *deleted*] when meeting crowded ice & no fish, reached 6 hours to the S, SbE, or SbW under a fresh gale of wind & being then to Eastward of a point of ice began to ply to windward.

Friday 21ˢᵗ June Lat. 78°7′ Lon.4°50′E
WSW
After plying to the southward all the night with a fresh gale of wind, we entered the ice about 10 am. and found it perfectly navigable & as we reached to the NWᵈ under a pressure of sail we constantly found more room for 8 or 10 hours sailing. About mid-night we were among very heavy ice, the fragments of floes, the pieces of which became so profuse that as the weather was thick with a dense haze we did not think proper to advance further; at the distance therefore of about 70 miles from the place we entered we ['**Saturday 22 June** Lat 78°16′ Lon. 1°E[.] SWbW' *in margin*] tacked, reached an hour to eastward into more ice, then calling all hands, reefed top sails and commenced making off.

---

[1] 'boat' presumably omitted in error.
[2] *Sic*; 'who' presumably intended.

Blowing a fresh breeze of wind all the day with constant fog or haze, except an interval of a few minutes about 1 Pm. and in the evening we had a strong gale. Lay too and drifted[1] to the eastward or northward (occasionally on either tack) whilst we made off and at 9 pm. finished. Spoke a Hamburgher – clean ship – has been to lat. 76° within this few days returned & just preceded us into this opening – saw no fish to the south – most of the ships he has seen are badly fished – 16 ships from Hamburgh this season & only 1 from Holland.

This bilge water was so strong that almost all of the linemanagers ['Effect of bilge water gass on the eyes' *in margin*] were obliged to leave the hold in consequence of blindness, and the second mate's eyes are so inflamed that is unable to keep his watch.

Sunday 23 June Lat. 78°16′ Lon. 2°E.
WSW WbS. W.erly
As we continued to lay too, until the deck, hold, &c. were cleaned and put in order – the weather being amazingly obscure in a dense fog – the wind blowing a strong gale at the same time we were unexpectedly embayed among very heavy ice, close patches of which were on every side but to windward. The ship fortunately wore readily, and the sails were set with great celerity and we were enabled to work the ship out to windward. The danger of our situation was considerably increased by the ship being out of trim in consequence of our making off; so much so that it was with the greatest attention and [science?] only that we were enabled to perform the evolution of tacking.

Lay too a few hours in the morning – and in the afternoon, the fog clearing away we stretched to the NNW[d] among crowded heavy ice, where we saw a fish. It escaped us. In the evening & night the wind was light and the density of the fog considerable. About mid-night the Resolution of Peterhead joined, us with 10 fish about 120 tons of oil. She has been fishing [to?] the southward these last 2 weeks where a number of fish were seen and many caught – gives account of the William & Ann 3 fish (about 19 instant); Lively 2; seen no other Whitby ships. They left the southward in consequence of the fish having disappeared and because the ice amongst which the fish were seen closed so much as to endanger their liberty.

Monday 24 June Lat. 78°11′ Lon. 0°30′E
W.erly. Var. Incl. Calm N.erly. NE.
Nearly calm the first half of this day – weather hazy or showery. The Resolution at the distance of little more than a mile from us killed two large fish whilst we saw not a single individual except those two which she got – neither could we approach the place where they were caught on account of light winds, and their [sic] constantly

---

[1] There is a marginal note at this point:
'Made off.

Casks		Gallons
13	of	300
35	"	252
6	"	200
54		110 butts'

veered gradually to the NW, N, to NE – whilst we unfortunately reached principally to the westward because the ice was more open that way – so that after 12 hours sailing, great part of which we had a fine commanding breeze of wind, the Resolution was still as far to windward as[1] us though she was all the while made fast. A fresh breeze of wind prevailed during the latter part of the day attended with cloudy or showery weather – perceiving a large floe or field to the NE^d we plyed towards it, worked through ['**Tuesday 25 June** Lat. 78°15' Lon. 0°0'. NE. NNE.' *in margin*] among the loose ice near the edge and reached it about 3 am. The Venerable with 7 fish = 50–60 Tons preceded us and three more ships

['John Greenwood F.  No. 11. Sucker' in margin]

joined us soon afterwards. Here though we had every prospect of an advantageous fishery, only two fish were seen during the 8 hours we remained near the field, one of these, a sucker, we happened to capture. The ice appearing open to the NW^d we made sail at 9 am. Stretched under the lee of the floe and proceeded until 6 pm. on a NW. course, amongst much heavy ice and some floes. During this navigation we saw three fish, one of which was within 6 yards of our boat but owing to the inexperience of a young harpooner it escaped. This is the third large fish which has been lost in 8 days by the unskillfulness of the harpooners!

Towards mid-night a thick fog commenced and the wind fell to near calm. A large floe surrounded with heavy ice being near, we [towed?] towards and made fast to a peice [*sic*] of ice lying against it. Here we saw 2 or 3 fish and the North Briton struck one. Different fish were seen after this which were pursued by the boats out of sight of the ship, so that for 4 hours we did not know where they were situated. Soon after ['**Wednesday 26 June** Lat. 78°20 Lon. 1°W[.] Calm. W.erly. SWbS.' *in margin*] mid night a breeze of wind sprang up at WSW and shortly veered to SWbS – this blowing towards the floe we cast off and stretched to the westward, through heavy crowded ice, into an open space which had been left by the floe when the wind was from the N^d. Here we saw several fish – three boats were sent off and the harpooner who yesterday failed succeeded in striking a fish under very similar circumstances. Before it made its appearance the mate shot a fish with the harpoon gun – he unfortunately being alone & far from the ship at the floe edge, he was obliged to hold a considerable strain, so that the harpoon [drew?].[2] This

['Thomas [Scofield?] F. No. 12 = 10.3' *in margin*]

['Shot by the Mate – harpoon drew' *in margin*]

fish was seen afterwards running to the westward. A number of fish were seen besides these two. About noon the first struck whale was killed – took it alongside & flinched

---

[1] Transcription error, 'of' intended?

[2] This appears to have been the first use of the harpoon gun by Scoresby's crews since the unsuccessful attempt on 9 July 1812.

while drifting to the NW^d along the western edge of the floe. This done we ran under the lee of the floe in expectation of meeting with fish, but being disappointed we plyed back with some difficulty along the edge of the floe & lay too among the windward ice. Saw one fish.

Thursday 27 June Lat. 78.16 Lon. 1°25′W
WSW
Light or fresh breezes – showers of prismatic snow. About 8 am. the John joined us with 9 fish, 60–70 tons of oil. Bro*the*r J. informed us that a vast number of fish had been caught in the ['neighb' *deleted*] vicinity of this place – that about 30 sail are fishing (though now with little effect) 50 miles SW from us where he yesterday left them – that most of the fish caught here are small, and that the fishing could scarcely be said to commence until 3 weeks ago, since which time several ships have procured 100 tons of oil or upwards – that the Resolution has 50 tons of oil – the Volunteer 2 fish about 20 tons.

After breakfast (Mr Jackson having breakfasted with me) we made all sail & plyed to windward amongst very crowded ice in which all my energies were engaged to get to windward of 4 accompanying ships which in consequence of several fish

['Thomas Fell. **M.** No. 13. = 10.6' *in margin*]

being seen we accomplished in the afternoon. About 4 pm. we were <u>solus</u> and met with several fish, one of which we were successful in striking and killing in the course of 1¼ hours – moored to piece of ice and flinched. Meanwhile we sent two boats to a windward floe where we had before seen several fish, but they returned without having met with a single whale. The fish being flinched we cast off and worked up to the windward floe where we stopped the night. 8^1 ships occasionally in sight.

Friday 28 June. Lat. 78.10 Lon. 1°30′W
W. to NW. N.erly
Blowing fresh the forepart with snow showers – latter part light winds to calm. Worked in the course of the day through an opening in crowded drift ice to the westward, where we entered among a number of detached heavy floes and at 8 Pm. reached a firm edge of fields to the [NNW^d?] of us. Saw 2 or 3 fish. 10 or 12 sail in sight. Lay too.

Saturday 29 June^2 Lat. 78°8′ Lon. 2°W
Variable Calm.
Light variable winds or calms. When I arose in the morning though we had been drifting all night to the SE^d I found we were still encompassed by floes, some of which were in rapid motion and approaching each other whilst they wheeled round. The

---

^{1} Possibly '5'.
^{2} Because of the events of this day, most of Chapter VII (pp. 444–88) in *Account of the Arctic Regions*, II, is devoted to this day and the remainder of the voyage.

fear of getting again beset urged me to endeavour to escape – we accordingly began to [tow?] with four boats through a considerable opening but just as we reached it the two sheets of ice joined. We then turned to the S^d and steered for an opening between two heavy floes which was not less than a mile wide. As we approached it we found this ['floes' *deleted*] opening was rapidly diminishing, we therefore called all hands and towed with 7 boats ['Ice in rapid motion.' *in margin*] about 2 knotts per hour, whilst the northern floe was [***] at the rate of above one mile per hour.[1] As the distance between the points of the floes was in general as considerable as our distance from them there was every encouragement to proceed. A ship[2] which preceeded us a few fathoms had just passed the strait when I perceived that were [*sic*] too late and that unless we instantly hauled astern the ship would be endangered – the boats were quickly removed to tow the ship back stern first when a boat was likewise dispatched to attatch a line to a hummock at a little distance to stop the headway of the ship. This line most unfortunately was found entangled and was hauled in to be cleared whereby not less than two minutes of time were lost – the ship meanwhile having passed a massy lump of ice that was likely to sustain a squeeze between the floes, which lump of ice was already forced to a junction within 20 yards, I feared we should be unable to effect the escape and in consequence determined if possible to advance about 40 yards forward, ['Ship in a dangerous situation.' *in margin*] in a still sufficient channel, and seek for shelter in a [considered?][3] sinuosity of the southern[4] floe where the ice was likewise favourable on account of its partial [***] & lesser thickness than the body of either of the floes. ['In' *deleted*] This attempt was extremely unfortunate; a small piece of ice being thrust partly in the ship's way, stopped her progress and ['the' *deleted*] two other pieces of intervening loose ice instantly pressed against her. Some minutes before this two points of the floes which were at some distance had joined, whereby I had expected that the motion of the ice would have been interrupted and that the floes would not have joined in the place where we were stopped[5] – one of the points of the southern floe however unhappily broke asunder & some thinner ice in the interior was crushed into prodigious heaps, and [yet?] the ice advanced. The ship was now forcibly pressed but the [rendering?] of the thin ice above mentioned prevented any dangerous pressure that was apparent. It however happened that [a?] danger threatened the destruction of the ship which was unseen and consequently unfeared, so that when the motion of the ice ceased we expected that we had escaped with impunity. But alas that was far from being the case – for after our attention had been engaged somewhat above an hour in endeavouring

---

[1] In *Account of the Arctic Regions*, II, p. 445, Scoresby stated that '... assisted by a light air of wind, the ship attained the velocity of about three miles *per* hour, while the northern floe had a velocity of about two.'

[2] In *Account of the Arctic Regions*, II, p. 444, this is identified as the *John*.

[3] Possibly a transcription error for 'considerable'.

[4] Possibly 'northern'.

[5] In a footnote in *Account of the Arctic Regions*, II, p. 446, Scoresby commented that 'While we were thus endangered, the John was in circumstances still more alarming. After she had passed the narrow channel through which we made the first attempt to escape, she was suddenly involved by distant ice, and made a very narrow escape from being crushed to pieces.'

to heave the ship forward into the bight where we at the first aimed for shelter, the ship moved and was directly observed to sink in the water above a foot – on sounding the pump we were astonished and terrified in finding 8½ feet of water in ['Ship dangerously stove.' *in margin*] the hold! I proceeded to the gunroom where I expected the damage was sustained from the circumstance of the rudder being lifted off the hinges, and soon discovered the water rushing upwards from an unseen depth with great violence. A signal of distress was no sooner displayed than boats from the neighbouring ships consisting of the John, North Briton, Elizabeth, Don, Superior[,] Perseverance, &c. came to our assistance. With the help of the men in them and a pump which was brought from the North Briton and which was kindly [hoisted?] out for our use, we worked three pumps and bailed at the same time in three places of the ship, especially in the fore hatch way from where a cask was removed that the buckets & specktubs[1] might be more readily filled. By these united means in the course of 4 hours the water in the hold was reduced to about 4 feet – the North Briton pump then sucked & the use of the specktubs at the fore hatch way were discontinued on account of the casks which prevented their being readily filled, the consequence was that the water again increased. At this time (6 pm) the floes having again seperated we hauled the ship through the strait and moored her on the weather side of the northern floe where a flat place of the ice was convenient for placing the cargo for the purpose of lightening the ship to endeavour to careen or heave her down to stop the leak. The water having been transparent the ['place of' *deleted*] [***] the misfortune was found to be no less than the removal of the after keel which with a part of the starboard sandstrake[2] attached was forced into an horizontal position. The cause of the accident was now apparent. a small piece of ice scarcely 3 feet above water which pressed against the ship's quarter & lifted (and as we afterwards found broke the main piece and otherwise twisted the [***] part) of the rudder, must have kept down a calf or tongue of so great a depth that the edge had forced the keel off when the ship by being pressed above was not perceptibly heeled or moved whereby the strength of the pressure must have acted with the worst possible effect, for had the ship been at all disengaged above she must have heeled to one side and relieved the violence of the crush.

Our first attention was to endeavour to fother[3] the ship, for which purpose a smaller thrumbed canvass given us by the North Briton was applied, together with a [fine] course to the place, but owing to the unfortunate position of the keel, which

[1] The word is not in *OED*, but is used again in the next sentence. The items were presumably normally used in the flensing process. In *Account of the Arctic Regions*, II, p. 447, Scoresby referred to them simply as 'tubs'.

[2] See Smyth, *Sailor's Word Book*, s.v. GARBOARD-STRAKE, OR SAND-STRAKE. Also the following footnote on p. 448 of *Account of the Arctic Regions*, II: '*Garboard-strake* or *sand-strake*, is the first range of strakes or planks laid upon a ship's bottom, next the keel, into which it is *rabitted* below, and into the stem and stern-post at the ends.'

[3] Another footnote on p. 448 is as follows: '*Fothering*, is a peculiar method of endeavouring to stop a leak in the bottom of a ship while she is afloat. It is performed by drawing a sail, by means of ropes at the four corners, beneath the damaged or leaky part, then thrusting into it a quantity of chopped rope-yarns, oakum, wool, cotton, &c.; or by thrumbing the sail, that is, sewing long bunches of rope-yarn all over it, before it is placed beneath the ship. These materials being sucked into the leaky part, the flow of the water into the ship is interrupted, or at least diminished.'

was not only driven out of its place at right angles but likewise forced above 12 inches to the starboard side, these means were unproductive of any good effect.

The carpenters of the neighbouring ships having assembled on board together with 4 of the captains I advised with them on the best means of proceeding to attempt to save the ship. The popular advice was to discharge the ship and heave her down to the ice.[1] We accordingly began to put on the ice our twin decks lumber and the blubber of the three fish last caught, whilst the pumps and buckets were kept in constant motion.

Sunday 30 June Lat. 78°6′ Lon.2°5′W
Variable Calm.

Meanwhile a lower studding sail had been thrumbed through a surface of 150 square feet, with bunches of rope yarns – about it were attatched numerous long shreds of thin old canvass, bunches of oakum, whalebone hair, straw, and a quantity of [ashes?]. Thus prepared a common leak under ordinary circumstances would have been instantly stopped, but on account of the peculiar awkwardness of the circumstances it could not be applied so as to produce any apparent advantage.

During the most of this day we were assisted by all the crew of the North Briton, most of those of the John, and a few from other ships, (the Symmetry and ['a few' *deleted*] some others afforded us little or no help) with which force the water was constantly kept reduced from 6 to 4 feet but never lower than the latter, the top gall*a*nt masts and all the yards except main & fore yards sent on the ice, & top-masts struck on account of the ship being extremely unstable, after a quantity of casks had been landed, together with other necessary labour. The men performed tollerably. Some of the Margaret's (Kay) crew and others of the Royal Bounty were added to our force, though many of our auxiliaries were become wearied and left us very early in the day. Towards ['our crew' *deleted*] mid night our crew began to fail – the exertion of strength and trial of their spirits discovered a serious want of energy in them general and several mean spiritless individuals. Our assistants at the same time relaxed their endeavours and became at length so careless that but a few persons out of 150 performed any work that was of service. It was distressing to my feelings to see men who had come apparently for our assistance retarding every operation by their carelessness and levity – the men at the pumps made no exertion, frequently stopped the discharge of the water by the way of amusement, and their conduct was all together so unseemly and unfeeling, that I could scarcely forbear turning them out of the ship.[2] At the same time the increase of

[1] See Smyth, *Sailor's Word Book*, s.v. HEAVING DOWN. Also *Account of the Arctic Regions*, II, p. 450: 'To *heave the ship down*, – that is, to discharge the whole of the cargo and stores upon the ice, turn the ship on one side, until the wound should come above water, and then repair it.'

[2] In *Account of the Arctic Regions*, II, p. 453, Scoresby expanded on this behaviour. 'It was peculiarly distressing to me to observe, that men who had come apparently with the intention of aiding us, not only were useless themselves, but relaxed the exertions of others by their open declarations, that the state of the ship was without hope. These inconsiderate men did not even scruple to converse, in the hearing of our people, on the subject of plundering the ship the moment they had the opportunity, and even were heard to name the particular articles of which they would endeavour to make prize.' In a footnote on p. 454, Scoresby noted that Captain Allen, of the Hull whaler *North Briton*, disciplined those of his crew who had behaved in this way.

water in the hold floated all the casks, ['and' *deleted*] stopped the operation of delivering the cargo, whilst the evident impossibility of [***] the ship caused us to relinquish the idea of heaving the ship down, as utterly impossible without the help of some ships to take the Esk alongside & heave her stern upwards whilst we careened by the ice.[1] As however no ship could easily approach us on account of the closeness of the ice, excepting ['**Monday 1 July** Lat. 78°6' Lon. 2°7'W[.] Variable E.erly' *in margin*] two, the masters of which were unwilling to risk getting beset, we had no recourse left but ['either' *deleted*] to allow the water to ['sink the ship' *deleted*] gain on the pumps and attempt the possibility of turning the ship bottom upwards, repairing the wound, returning her back, and then pumping out the water again.[2] This alternative though a distressing and alarming one was the only one left which I could imagine, unless we could remove the ['keel' *deleted*] loose keel, and thus be able to do something more effectual in the way of fothering, though this plan was strenuously opposed by most of the carpenters, as endangering the almost instant sinking of the ship. After placing a few empty casks in the hold to prevent the ship sinking too low, caulking the scuttles, dark lights, & companions, & securing the hatches, we discontinued the pumping in consequence of our being unable to less the depth of water in the hold below 7 feet, notwithstanding we had good assistance from 2 or 3 ships the men of which worked tollerably.

Before this was done all the dry provisions and seamens clothes, &c. were removed to the ice and two tents erected for the use of myself & the Crew. In this wretched apartment[3] I spread a sail on a few boards & with a mattress, a blanket & great coat indulged a short rest after having been on my feet about 50 hours. The crew at the same time received their first respite.

Although so much harassed my mind I could not help observing a phenomenon occasioned by the fog which at this time prevailed. ['Curious effect of fog in magnifying objects' *in margin*] Every object which appeared at the distance of from 100 to 200 yards, was strongly magnified, men looked like giants, the hummocks of the floe resembled mountains, and everything else in proportion; the effect was curious and in some respects magnificent.

Notwithstanding the chill disagreeable nature of the place where I slept I arose considerably refreshed,[4] and immediately proceeded with all hands to the ship which

---

[1] In *Account of the Arctic Regions*, II, p. 452, Scoresby emphasized that heaving the ship down was only feasible if the Esk could be emptied of water first, or if other ships could come alongside to take the strain.

[2] In *Account of the Arctic Regions*, II, pp. 449–51, Scoresby listed five possible ways of saving the ship. The last of these was: 'To *turn the ship keel upward*. – This plan, being a kind of desperate experiment, I was determined to adopt, in the event of all the others failing. To effect this, it would be necessary first to discharge the cargo, and to unrig the ship, then, letting her fill with water, after securing the cabin-windows and hatches, to turn her keel up, and repair the damage; and, lastly, to return her back to her proper position, and pump out the water. In performing these operations, the aid of some other ship to assist in heaving the Esk down, and returning her back, would probably be indispensable.'

[3] 'shelter' written above this word.

[4] 'I enjoyed a comfortable repose of four hours' (*Account of the Arctic Regions*, II, p. 457).

Figure 7. The unsuccessful attempt to invert the *Esk*, 1 July 1816

This engraving of the unsuccessful attempt to invert the *Esk* 'and bring her keel to the surface of the sea' on 1 July 1816 appeared as the frontispiece to the first volume of Scoresby's *An Account of the Arctic Regions* in 1820.

we found had yet only sunk to the 16 or 17 feet watermark on the outside, whilst within the water just washed the twin decks. As our case was now desperate the removal of the keel if it could be accomplished was an object of attention and whatever might be the effect it was of little consequence. We therefore put the <u>bight</u> of a towline over the end of the detached part of the keel, secured one end of the rope to a timber head on the starboard quarter & [***] the other to the capstern. Whereby in a few minutes the keel was hove off, seperated, but unfortunately slipped out of the rope & sank. This was a matter of regret only so far as the state of the keel would have enabled us to ascertain in some measure the extent of the damage. The piece of <u>sandstrake</u> yet remained attatched to the ship – a line was with some difficulty fixed to it but it was not sufficient to leave it asunder, a towline likewise failed until after several trials in different positions and situations it was torn off. This plank was about 10 feet in length & brought along with it about 6 inches thickness of the <u>dead</u> wood. As the ship now refused to sink further in the water on account of the empty casks, and buoyancy of her timber we applied our purchases the second time consisting of a 10 inches hawser clinched round the mainmast passed ['Attempt to turn the ship bottom up, failed.' *in margin*] under the keel and the other part taken to the ice;

the same as the fore mast and to each of the hawsers, a <u>canting</u> purchase was applied and to its pull a luff tackle, so that the power was increased to 36 times, [or abating?] friction, I suppose every man would be able to pull 20 cwt with ease – besides these we had suspended the two anchors from the main & foremasthead by towlines passed near the masthead, & under the bottom, and fastened on the opposite side in such a way that the bight of each lay over the keel, whereby should the ship be turned over the towlines could be cut and the anchors falling away would allow the ship to righten whilst another warp attatched to them & made fast to the ice would preserve them from being lost.

Thus prepared, assisted by the John's crew who after a short rest had again returned to us, was applied our force, but to our astonishment the ship could scarcely be heeled at all. This remarkable stability encouraged us to persevere and attempt to take the ship home at all events, for it appeared she would neither sink nor upset. On a former occasion (about 5 am) when all the North Briton's crew were on hand, besides a great part of the John's and some from other ships we applied our purchases when there was about 9 feet water in the hold. We then careened about 6 or 8 strakes, after which, with 200 men running from the higher to the lower part of the deck the ship did not fall half a strake. Thus we found without destroying her stability by the removal of every buoyant article, particularly all the empty casks it was impossible to upset her.[1]

We now prepared again the fothering sail, placed on it an additional quantity of whalebone hair, oakum, rope yarns, ashes, &c. and again hauled it under the ship's bottom, and with some hope of advantage, though the projection of all the keel bolts 12 or 18 inches in length at right angles to their proper position yet prevented any effectual application of this means. Three pumps were again put in motion at 5½ Pm. by our own crew and 30 men from the John. Our success was happy for after 11 hours hard labour the pumps ['**Tuesday 2ᵈ July** Lat. 78°4′ Lon. 2°10′W[.] SE.erly Variable Calm' *in margin*] sucked! In this space of time 13 feet of water was pumped out of the hold besides the leakage. On that occasion the John's crew performed to admiration – they exerted themselves with a noble spirit. This accomplished the John's crew, who were our sole assistant, all the other ships having deserted us to our fate, remained at the pumps 4 hours longer until all the after hold was cleared of casks and then they left us to procure that rest which they much needed.

---

[1] The activities described in this and the preceding paragraph were recounted by Scoresby in *Account of the Arctic Regions*, II, pp. 455–9, but with one important difference. In the *Account*, the effort to heave the ship with the hawser and blocks, and with the weight of men moving across the decks, is described as taking place *before* the removal of the keel and garboard-strake. Scoresby (p. 458) emphasized this sequence of events as follows: 'On account of the peculiar buoyancy and stability of the ship, it hence appeared, that the plan of upsetting her was not practicable, without the aid of some other ship to assist by additional purchases; and, as no other ship could with safety be brought to us, this method was at length relinquished.

The situation of the ship being now desperate, there could be no impropriety in attempting to remove the keel and garboard-strake, which prevented the application of the fothering: for, whatever might be the result, it could scarcely be for the worse.'

As the flow of water kept two pumps almost constantly at work the plan I proposed to secure against further leakage was the following. The ceiling[1] of the ship being so close as to be easily caulked, I conceived that provided we could stop the communication of the water between the place of the leak & the part of the ship before it by making a roomstead[2] or space between the timbers water tight, the ceiling would swim[3] the ship. Repeating our signal of distress or want of assistance and firing a gun brought two boats with 6 men each from the Prescot and the same number from our firmer[4] friend Mr Allen of the North Briton, who had in the time since he left us made a cruise in search of fish in consequence of the discontent of his crew at the handsome manner in which he assisted us. These men worked well. During their stay on board, assisted by several carpenters we cut away the ceiling directly across ['Attempt to swim the ship by caulking the ceiling and stopping the communication of the water between the place of the leak & the body of the ship' *in margin*] the hold at the distance of about 30 feet from the stern post. Unfortunately the timbers were so closely joined that we had a most laborious job to cut away so much as to [allow?] us to tighten the part between the timber & outside skin. This we attempted by caulking in the oakum, an improved woolen sheathing material, and occasionally the fat of pork to close the larger holes: the ceiling being nailed down & the extremities caulked between it & the timbers we wedged down the caulking with [connected?] slices and then caulked the space between them and every opening through ['**Wednesday** 3^d **July**. Lat. 78°0' Lon. 2°10'W[.] N.erly. NW. W.erly' *in margin*] which the water flowed in any considerable quantity. As however the separation of the ceiling had allowed a free course to the water for several hours it gained rapidly on the pumps flowed over the place where the carpenters were at work and obliged them to close up the openings with such expedition that the work was much less effectually performed than we had hoped. It however did not altogether fail, as it appeared by the water flowing through the seams of the ceiling at the height of 6 feet. Meanwhile that we had good assistance, I allowed our men who were completely overcome 4 hours sleep, half of them at a time, whilst the remainder were employed in stowing the main hold that was by the floating of the casks through[5] into a singular state of confusion, many of the casks damaged, and some of them stove and all the blubber lost. Swayed[6] top masts & some yards.

From the time that we happened our accident to noon of the present day the wind has been constantly light or calm and the weather generally foggy. The ice has been in

---

[1] In nautical use, this term has a very different meaning from that of land-based architecture. Smyth, *Sailor's Word Book*, made it synonymous with 'foot-waling' which he defined as 'the inside planking or lining of a ship over the floor-timbers; it is intended to prevent any part of her ballast or cargo from falling between her floor timbers.'

[2] 'Roomstead is the space between any two ribs or frames of timber in a ship' (*Account of the Arctic Regions*, II, p. 461, footnote). OED regards the term as rare or obsolete, but cites this definition by Scoresby.

[3] OED: 'To cause to float; to buoy up'. Scoresby used the term in this sense on pp. 450 and 478 of *Account of the Arctic Regions*, II, and OED cites the latter.

[4] Possibly 'former'.

[5] *Sic.* Evidently a transcription error; 'thrown' in *Account of the Arctic Regions*, II, p. 461.

[6] Smyth, *Sailor's Word Book*, s.v. SWAY: 'To hoist simultaneously; particularly applied to the lower yards and topmasts, and topgallant-masts and yards.'

constant motion but never completely closed on the ship though frequently we were completely [encaged?] among the floes, so that our auxiliaries were obliged to [launch?] their boats or walk over the ice. A little time before the carpenters had closed up the opening in the ceiling, the weather being ['clear' *deleted*] favourable for fishing, and a breeze of wind sprang up, whilst the clearing of the fog showed several ships at a distance were fishing induced first the North Briton's people & afterwards some hours the Prescot's to ['all our help' *deleted*] leave us ['except' *deleted*] & excepting the John all the ships worked out of sight. At the time that the ship was yet with difficulty kept with two pumps and the John was proposing to leave us I was informed that the men, being quite overcome with fatigue, dispirited, and even yet hopeless of being able to keep the ship at sea, were determined to leave the ship if the ['The men determined to leave the ship if the John sails away' *in margin*] John ['left us' *deleted*] sailed away. Expostulation was in vain for I had some time back discovered that one half of my crew were most despicable, spiritless, and altogether weak characters; their want of perseverance & their cowardice were alike evident and disgraceful, and prevented the hope of myself being able to detain them.[1] Through the whole course of the operations almost the whole of them and indeed every person who came near us saw no hope of saving the ship, nevertheless as I had still hopes: at least such an 'hope as keeps alive despair',[2] and even something more for I conceived that a sound, new, buoyant ship with sufficient assistance might possibly be saved, let her be damaged in almost any partial way. The men had indeed cause for apprehension if the John left us – the fishing season being so far advanced – our situation being surrounded by prodigious heavy floes – and enclosed by an extent of near an[3] 100 miles of ice in the nearest way of the sea – so that if the ship should eventually be through necessity deserted our lives would be at stake.[4] Now as my Brother Jackson had already sacrificed more time than was probably consistent with his duty as a commander, or at least as concerned the success of his fishing operation, I could not expect or require him to remain longer by us, and yet it appeared certain that if he quitted us the ship would be left and of course become a wreck. It was a proposal of the crew to hire the assistance of the John by a quantity of blubber – this method I at the first refused but in consideration of the absolute necessity of the case I conceived myself justified in entering into the following agreement which was voluntarily signed by every individual crew of each of the ships.[5]

---

[1] In *Account of the Arctic Regions*, II, p. 464, Scoresby's criticism is much more moderate. See Introduction, p. xxiv.

[2] Though not precisely in this form, there are many literary allusions to the coexistence of hope and despair. Perhaps the closest to Scoresby's formulation is from Seneca's 'Epistulæ ad Lucilium': 'Nec speraveris sine desperatione nec desperaveris sine spe'; 'Do not hope without despair, nor despair without hope.'

[3] Possibly 'on'.

[4] Note that Scoresby does not even mention the 23 degrees of latitude (1,600 statute miles) between the *Esk*'s position and Whitby.

[5] What follows in this journal differs considerably from what was subsequently printed in *Account of the Arctic Regions*, II, pp. 465–71. The latter source in fact contains the text of two contracts, one involving both crews, the other signed only by the two masters. What is in the journal identified as prepared on the 'Ship John' does not carry that location in the *Account*, but the

Ship John Greenland seas 3 July.

The Ship Esk of Whitby being in distress and her crew being unable of themselves to preserve her from sinking it is agreed between the undersigned masters, officers, and seamen of the ships Esk and John, that the crew of the John shall assist those of the Esk in the preservation of the ship to the utmost of their power, remain by her at all times ['As the only means of retaining the men by the ship or of saving her, hire the John's attendance and help by an award of 40 tons of oil & 1½ tons of whalebone, &c. &c.' *in margin*] except where the safety of the John may be concerned, take her in tow when necessary, and accompany her throughout the voyage from hence to some port in Shetland if required.

In consideration of which service, the sacrifice of future advantage in the fishery, and the consequent detention the crew of the Esk do agree I[1] to deliver up to the John 40 tons of oil or blubber accordingly after the rate of 8 butts to 2 tons, together with one half of the Esk's whalebone.

III. Should any dead fish be found or living whale be captured in the course of the passage out of the ice, it is agreed that whoever they may be seen or struck by they shall be ['Agreement' *in margin*] considered as the mutual property of the two ships.

II. But provided the John should by an [*sic*] casualty be obliged to separate from the Esk before the space of 7 days from the date hereof, and thereby not render that sufficient assistance required one half of the blubber and whalebone awarded to the John or the value thereof shall be returned to the owners of the Esk free of any charges for freight, demerage, or other circumstances, excepting only actual expenses thereon, on the arrival of the John at Greenock.

IIII. That provided the ship Esk shall by the united exertion of the two ships' companies preserved and arrive in safety at the port from where she sailed; and that the John accompanies and assists as agreed so far as Shetland, the master on the part of the owners of the ship Esk shall pay to the crew of the ship John (harpooners excepted) the additional sum of one hundred pounds, to be equally divided amongst every individual. And,

V. It is agreed that provided any of the John's crew should by an accidental separation of the two ships, be carried to Whitby, a reasonable allowance for conduct money shall be paid them by the owners or master of the Esk.

Account states that the contract between the masters was 'Done on board the Esk'. The text in the journal appears to confuse these two documents. For example, what appears in the journal as paragraph II of the agreement signed by the crew uses terms such as 'by any casualty' that only appear in Part III of the agreement signed by Scoresby and his brother-in-law. The numbering of paragraphs in the journal is also illogical. The agreements as they were published in *Account of the Arctic Regions* are inserted in the text for comparison.

  [1] This numeral inserted above the line.

[TEXT of two agreements between the *Esk* and the *John* as published in *Account of the Arctic Regions*, II, pp. 465–71:]

[I]

Greenland Sea, 3d July 1816.

The ship Esk of Whitby being in distress, and the crew of themselves unable to preserve her, it is agreed between the undersigned masters, officers, and seamen of the ship John of Greenock, and of the said ship Esk, that the former shall afford assistance to the latter, agreeable to the terms and conditions following:

I. That the ship John shall remain by the Esk, and shall accompany her to some port of Shetland, if required, and that the crew of the John shall, during the fitting of the Esk for the passage, and during the passage to Shetland, assist to the utmost of their power, in any measures necessary for her preservation.

II. In consideration of which services, the crew of the ship Esk do agree to give up to the ship John, forty-eight tons of oil, or blubber in proportion, after the rate of four tons of blubber to three tons of oil, together with one-half of the Esk's present cargo of whalebone, – and hereby they consider themselves as having relinquished all title and claim to the said oil and whalebone, as well as to any wages, oil-money, fish-money, or other perquisites, which might be dependent thereon.

III. It is agreed by the master of the Esk, on the part of his owners, that provided the ship Esk shall, by the united exertions of the two ships' companies, be preserved and arrive safe at the port from whence she sailed, and that the John accompanies, and the crew assists so far as Shetland, the sum of One hundred pounds shall be given by the owners of the Esk to the crew of the John, to be equally divided amongst each individual, excluding harpooners.

IV. It is likewise agreed by the master of the Esk, on the part of his owners, that provided any of the John's crew, by the unavoidable separation of the ships, shall be carried to Whitby, a reasonable allowance for their travelling expences homewards, shall be paid them.

And, V. It is mutually agreed by all parties, that should any dead fish be found or other whale be captured within the limits of this contract, whichever of the ships' crews it or they may be seen, struck, or killed by, the whale or whales so found or captured, shall be equally divided between the two ships.

[Signed by all Hands of each Ship.]

[II]

AGREEMENT, &c.

The ship Esk, of Whitby, lying at a vast distance from the sea, in a dangerous situation of the ice, being seriously damaged, extremely leaky, in a great measure unrigged, her cargo and stores discharged, the ship a mere hulk, and altogether in great distress, – her crew at the same time being worn out by hard and continued labour, and unable of themselves to preserve the ship from sinking and take her home, – are circumstances which render the assistance of some other ship indispensable. The master and crew of the ship John of Greenock, therefore, being willing to afford the requisite aid, it is hereby agreed between the undersigned masters of the two ships, the Esk and the John, that such requisite assistance shall be afforded on the one part, and that such certain award shall be presented on the other, as are expressed in the conditions and terms following:

PART I. – The undersigned Thomas. Jackson, master of the ship John of Greenock, on his own part, and on the part of his owners, with the unanimous consent of every individual of his crew, doth engage and agree to the four articles next following:

1. That he will, with his ship and crew, to the utmost of his power, assist and endeavour to preserve the ship Esk, to rig her, to stow her cargo and stores, and to fit her for the passage homewards.

2. That he will then take her in tow, when practicable, and use every exertion to remove her from the place where she now lies, and attend on and accompany her homewards, as far as some port of Shetland, if required.

3. That he will at all times furnish the Esk with as many of his crew as he can conveniently and safely spare, to assist in pumping and navigating the Esk on the homeward passage to Shetland. And,

4. That he accepts of *as*, and declares the award herein after mentioned *to be*, an ample and sufficient compensation for the services he hereby engages to perform; and that no claim in the way of salvage, demurrage, or other circumstance, shall or can hereafter be made by himself or owners of the John, on the master or owners of the Esk.

PART II. – In consideration of which services, the sacrifice of all future expectation from the fishery of the present season, the consequent detention, and so on, – the undersigned William Scoresby *junior*, master of the skip Esk, on his part, and on the part of his owners, with the free and unanimous consent of every individual of his crew, doth engage and agree as follows :

1. That he will abandon into the possession of the ship John 48 tons of whale-oil or blubber accordingly, after the rate of 8 butts to 3 tons, together with one-half of the whalebone, or thereabouts, which may at present form the cargo of the Esk.

2. That the above quantity of blubber and whalebone shall become the property of the owners of the ship John, on which himself or owners can have no claim whatsoever, on the conditions of Part I. being accomplished.

3. That provided the ship Esk shall, by the united exertions of the crews of the two contracting ships, be preserved, arrive at the port from whence she sailed, and that the John accompanies and the crew assists to the utmost of their power, so far as Shetland, as agreed; he, on the part of the owners of the Esk, agrees to pay, in addition to the whalebone and oil above specified, the sum of One hundred pounds, to be equally divided among the John's crew, harpooners excepted. And;

4. Should any of the John's crew, by the unavoidable separation of the two ships, be carried to Whitby, a reasonable allowance for their travelling expences homewards, shall be paid them by the owners of the Esk.

PART III. – It is furthermore mutually agreed by the undersigned William Scoresby *junior*, and Thomas Jackson, on their own parts, and on the part of their owners, and as far as concerns them, with the free and unanimous consent of their respective crews, as follows:

1. That provided the ship John shall, by any casualty, be obliged to separate from the Esk, and withdraw her assistance, within the space of seven days from the date hereof, the award mentioned in Article 1., Part II., shall be considered as the joint property of the owners of the two ships, and that accordingly, the one-half of the oil and whalebone, as therein awarded, or the value thereof, free of all charges for freight, demurrage, or other circumstances, excepting actual outlay, shall be returned to the owners of the Esk, as soon after the arrival of the John at her port, as conveniently may be.

2. That should any dead fish be found, or other whale be captured within the limits of this contract, whichever of the ship's crews it or they may be seen, struck, or killed by, the whale or whales so found or captured, shall be equally divided between the two ships. And it is declared,

3. That all the foregoing articles and stipulations of this contract are entered into, not from any regard of relationship, friendship, or other human tie, but from the sole principle of mutual obligation, consequently for the benefit of the owners of each concern. The award is thus given on the part of the Esk from the urgent nature of the circumstances, and accepted on the part of the John, from the small probability there is of procuring such an increase to her cargo elsewhere.

Done on board the Esk, at six o'clock P. M.
(civil day,) of the 3d day of July 1816.

Signed   THOMAS JACKSON,
           WILLIAM SCORESBY *jun.*

Signed *John Dunbar* ⎱
     Willm. Ward ⎰ Witnesses

Thursday 4 July Lat. 77°1 56 Lon. 2°02′W
NW, W. SW.

This agreement being signed and agreed to without any objection the John hauled alongside the ice which had fortunately opened in the place and took on board all our loose blubber estimated at 29 tons of oil, and 25½ tons in casks equal to 10 tons of oil, whilst in the mean time we hauled a little out of the way and employed ourselves in stowing the main hold – stowing the after hold and filling it with water, caulking and battening the seams of the ceiling, &c. &c. Placed two empty casks overend, in the forehold for pump well heads, one on each side: upper head [cut?], lower end full of holes.²

I may observe that I could with ['propriety' *deleted*] justice enough have made the above agreement with the John without the consent of my crew but as every individual was more or less ['concerned' *deleted*] interested in the blubber given up I conceived it proper to make the contract as the joint act of the two ships' companies. The stock of rum which was hitherto of essential service now failed us.

---

¹ Written over '78°'.
² This sentence was apparently inserted between lines written earlier. Scoresby provided a clearer explanation in *Account of the Arctic Regions* II, pp. 471–2. 'In the bilges of the ship, beneath the fore-hatchway, we placed two empty casks on their ends, with the upper heads taken out, and the lower heads bored full of holes, for the purpose of admitting the water which might accumulate in the ship when heeling, and freeing it from any substances calculated to choke the pump or pumps which might be introduced into the casks for extracting it.' Scoresby then added a footnote: 'This contrivance we found exceedingly useful; for on the passage homeward, the chips produced by the carpenters in making the stop-water in the hold, frequently choked our principal pumps, and annoyed us exceedingly. We were repeatedly obliged to hoist them out and clear the pump well; sometimes twice or thrice a-day.'

Every thing now going on favourably, whilst our men were in full and active employment, I was obliged to seek that rest which my wearied frame, could want no longer. I may observe that during nearly 120 hours I have only rested about 12 whereas in ordinary circumstances I should have rested between 40 & 50. The effect was most severely felt in my legs which swelled considerably and became so painful that I could scarcely walk. In justice to Mr Jackson I may likewise observe that in the course of our operations he has not slept more than myself. In what is thus far done towards the saving of the ship, however it may eventually prove, ['has been' *deleted*] could not possibly have accomplished by our own crew, but must be due principally to the assistance received from the John & the North Briton. The crew of the Prescot were likewise willing and useful, during their stay on Wednesday. I cannot say much in favour of the humanity of some of our neighbours. When we repeated our signal of distress and fired guns by the way or[1] urging the necessity of our case, though the ships ['Persever' *deleted*] Margaret, Don, Superior, Symmetry, and Brig Perseverance were at no great distance they never offered us the least assistance after the morning of Monday.

Blowing fresh all the day with snow showers. The floe we are moored to has revolved – of a circuit the way of the sun since Sunday morning last. We were then on the east side we are now on the NW side of it. A heavy body of floes seem to lay to the S^d of us and the same to the North*ward* and but a small passage between any [of?] them and many of them closely [united?] as appears by the blink. From this state of the ice the attendance of a ship is indispensible for the security our lives for should any accident happen further we should have but an indifferent chance of meeting with any ships within the distance of many leagues.

As the embracing or binding of the fothering sails to the ship's quarter was on account of its "concavity" a matter of some difficulty I made use of the following expedient which whilst it answered this purpose in a most admirable manner was likewise of service in preserving the sails in their places in the event of all the sideropes being cut away by the ice passing the lee quarter, a circumstance which considering the great quantity of ice between us and the sea, it is extremely probable cannot be avoided. First two ring bolts were put through the stern post at the water's edge, one on each side, and the same at the bows near the [stem?] – two warps were then clinched to the after bolts passed under the ship's bottom, through the bow rings, and the hawse hole to the windlass. Between these two warps were spliced a number of [spans ?] of whaleline 6 feet in length each and about 3 feet asunder, forming with the warps a kind or rope ladder the [spans ?] or steps of which embraced the sails and pressed them close to the wounded part of the bottom, at the same time that the spans [***] the warps down into the deepest "concavity."

Friday 5th July Lat. 77°50′ Lon. 1°25′W
W.erly. NNW
Moderate or fresh breezes of wind with frequent snow showers. The above warps had not long been applied before a sensible amendment was observed in the state of

---

[1] *Sic.* Presumably a transcription error for 'of' as in 'kind or' in the last sentence of this journal entry.

the ship – instead of the two pumps being kept constantly going, they now began to admit of a refreshing pause. The caulking of the ceiling abaft and the battening of the seams no doubt added to the effect of the warps, as the carpenters found constant employment for a length of time in stopping every opening from whence the water was seen to issue.

Assisted by all hands from the John, all our people after four hours rest set vigorously about getting the remainder of the stores on board, so that at 6 am. we had cleared the ice of all the materials, hoisted the boats up and made sail. When we cast off ['Ship unmanageable' *in margin*] we were surprised, grieved, and depressed to find that she would not steer – the helm had not the least effect upon her, even when assisted by the most favourable adaptations of the yards & sails, since with all the after sails furled & every other usual means, she could not be got to wear. The dangerous situation in which we had constantly lain since the accident happened, by being surrounded with many floes, the two between which the damage was sustained constantly threatening us and frequently paralising our exertions by approaching each other [within?] a [few?] yards and sometimes nearly touching both sides of the ship[.][1] This consideration together with the favourable navigation which offered for the first time an easy release induced us to use every exertion to reach a place of greater freedom and safety. Accordingly we sent a warp to the John, which immediately made sail with a view to tow us. Under almost any other circumstance it would have been a matter of the greatest amusement to observe the motion of the Esk. She first sheered out on one side to the utmost extent of the rope & obliged us to slack away to prevent its breaking, then ranging back on the other side without the rudder or sails producing an apparent effect. The rope on one occasion was broken, but after ['towing' *deleted*] shortening the tow rope the ship followed more steadily and fortunately [missed?] every piece of ice though she came very near some dangerous ['Bar. 29.83' *in margin*] pieces. Steering eastward in about three hours we came to an exterior floe, where we made fast with the John close by us. We now proceeded to attempt to rectify the want of steerage without which it was impossible to get the ship out of the ice. We first unshipped the rudder, and enlarged it on the lower part by the application of two twin decks hatches, one on each side extending about 4 feet abaft the rudder & of course increasing its breadth so much in the heighth of 6 or 8 feet. ['Means used to rectify the steerage of the ship.' *in margin*] This framing was secured by nails, bolts, and [clogs?] of wood at the back. I conceived this particularly requisite because on account of the distribution of the sails which it was impossible to [bind?] close to the ship's quarters, together with the increased thickness of the [rim?] of the ship by the quantity of the fothering and the projection of the keel bolts, on this account such an eddy of water was formed that no regular stream could reach the rudder, ['to effect the ship' *deleted*] and consequently no effect could be produced in the guidance of the ship thereby. As the clues of the sails[2] hung at a distance from the <u>quarters</u> or counters of the ship and thereby produced a great quantity of dead

[1] The ungrammatical nature of this sentence may indicate an accidental omission, especially as the following sentence begins a new page in the transcript.

[2] In *Account of the Arctic Regions*, II, p. 475, Scoresby made it clear that 'sails' here refers to those used for the fothering.

water about the upper part of the rudder, we securely lashed them to the [hollow ?] of the counter to staples driven into the plank; and as the ship being only 4 inches by the stern[1] and of an unusual light draught of water – a trim in which before the accident she would have scarcely been manageable we thirdly set about filling all the empty casks in the after hold amounting to 10 casks, whereby she was brought 11 inches by the stern. Whilst we lay here we likewise procured 3 butts of water from the surface of the floe.

Saturday 6th July. Lat. 77°48′ Lon. 0°50′W.
NNW. To SW
All this accomplished we should have cast off but the wind blowing strong from the NNW and the weather being thick with snow, we could not without imminent danger attempt to penetrate the compact body of ice which lays immediately to the eastward of us. I therefore took advantage of the opportunity to procure a long and refreshing rest, which I found of the most essential advantage after such an unusual exaustion [sic] and prostration. I arose after many hours quite refreshed, and in perfect health – thanks to a kind Providence.

We were obliged to remove on account of the floe revolving from S. to W., & N. &c. whereby several prodigious masses of loose ice came very near us, and about 10 am. the loose ice forced us to cast off, but at a time when we quite in readiness & when the attenuation of the fog and subsiding of ['Ship now succeeds tollerably' *in margin*] the wind, together with its veering to the SW. were a chain of circumstances that appeared favourable for making a trial to escape. When the ship was under sail we immediately tried the necessary experiments of wearing and tacking and found that though she reacted slowly and was particularly leewardly[2] yet she answered the helm and worked better than we could reasonably have expected.

On examining our boats we found some of our <u>kind</u> friends, who [at?] a particular time[3] merely ['Assistants have pilfered several articles.' *in margin*] encumbered us with their help, by resisting the operation of the discharge of the water by their untimely gambols, had taken a fancy to our boats' fids ['and axes' *deleted*], which by them with a musquet, a quantity of canvass and probably some other articles they had carried off, to compensate doubtless for their disappointment of an unrestrained plunder which they evidently expected from the wreck of the ship which they evidently endeavour all in their power to promote. In justice to Captains Jackson & Allen*[4] – I believe the charges they gave to their crew prevent any exploitation on their part, and as for the

---

[1] I.e. only four inches deeper in the water at the stern than forward. See journal entry for 29 March 1814, suggesting the normal difference was eight inches.
[2] Smyth, *Sailor's Word Book*, s.v. LEEWARDLY: 'Said of a ship which presents so little resistance to the water, when on a wind, as to bag away to leeward.'
[3] Originally 'timely', 'ly' deleted.
[4] Note in margin: '*Captain Allen enforced his command on his crew by the declaration that whichever of his crew should be known to be guilty of a single instance of plunder, unless the ship should be absolutely abandoned, should be deprived of his wages. And, some men it has appeared who boasted in having [***] our steward in by changing some part of their dress to procure a double allowance of spirits, were pointed out to Capt. Allen by the mate and he very justly ordered their future allowance of grog to be stopped during the voyage!'

aggressors their masters were doubtless ignorant of their proceedings. We knew that the idea of plundering prevailed from the circumstance of many of the strangers being overheard in conversation with each other, mentioning what particular articles should become the subject of their attention as soon as they could meet with an opportunity. One fellow had even the audacity to take up a musket in the Blacksmith's shop when the Armourer was present and perceiving it wanted the lock very seriously enquired where it was!!

We must certainly have uncommon cause of thankfulness to a Benignant Providence for having enabled us to bring the ship into her present state. At the time ['The improved state of the ship[.] Providential her situation being by all persons esteemed ['hope' *deleted*] hopeless.' *in margin*] we allowed the ship to fill, we had had the assistance of near 150 [fresh?] men who had worked the three pumps for many hours with the utmost ability and yet the water gained – every individual of our own ship's company as well as all our auxiliaries and even the Captains themselves considered our situation as quite hopeless. I even myself was sometimes inclined to despair, though thank God I always retained that hope which was sufficient to encourage me in the application and prosecution of other means. I know that in fothering the Almighty could easily direct my hand in the application of a bundle of oakum so as to produce an extraordinary effect, as well as the same merciful being could influence our carpenters to exert their energies with their best will & with the best effect – and this appeared to be the case for some of them, especially one Nicholson belonging to the North Briton, worked amongst water in the most disagreeable manner, in such a way as to receive my highest praise and admiration. ['Bar. 30.10' *in margin*] Should the ship eventually be preserved, which through mercy will be easy to be accomplished the services of this man must not be forgotten.[1]

We reached 2 or 3 hours to the SE[d] and fell in with a compact body of ice, which in the thick fog that had then commenced it was impossible to penetrate. We then attempted to ply to windward but with so little effect and at the same time with so much risk to the ship that we speedily relinquished this plan & lay too with a view to seek a passage more northerly. At mid-night made fast with the John to a heavy piece of ice. Very thick fog.

Sunday 7 July. Lat. 77°45'+ Lon. 0°10'W Bar. 29.95
W.erly[2] NW.erly Var. Calm. E.erly.
The attention of the carpenter to the stoppage of all visible leaks in the after hold, together with the advantage derived from the fothering has so reduced the leak that the two pumps require[3] to be worked little more than ¼ to ¾ of time at [rest?] Thus during divine service in the forenoon these pumps stood 76 minutes; in 20 minutes all the water 2½ feet was pumped out.

---

[1] He was not forgotten. Nicholson was again identified by name, and his efforts described as 'with a perseverance and assiduity that was really astonishing', in *Account of the Arctic Regions*, II, pp. 460–61.
[2] Originally 'SW.erly'.
[3] Originally 'required'; 'd' deleted.

Calm light variable winds the fore part of the day with constant fog or snow showers – the latter part we had a moderate breeze with occasional clear weather. During
an interval in the showers at 4 am. an opening of the ice was seen in an easterly direction – cast off & steered that way as well as the lightness & variableness of the wind
would admit. Having a steady breeze in the afternoon, the John took us in tow,
whereby we were enabled to work about 2 miles to windward until we entered an
opening leading as far as could be seen to the SSE – in this opening we were at first
annoyed with loose ice, among which however the ship was managed in better style
than could have been in any wise expected – we did not toutch [sic] a single piece.
['Three' deleted] In the course of the day our progress was about 10 miles ESE – floes,
a field, and heavy drift ice encompassing us on every side – but at mid-night a free
navigation lay in a SSE direction. 3 sail seen to the W^d supposed to be three of the
fleet which were in company when we met with our misfortune.[1]

Monday 8th July Lat. 77°20'+ Lon. 1°40'E
E. ENE to NNE
Fresh to light breezes of wind – snow showers. Continued our stretch to the SSE – SE
until 5 am. when a floe interrupted our course: after making a tack we weathered it,
being in tow of the John and reached amongst heavy crowded ice during 2 hours – the
weather then fortunately clearing we perceived a field to the E^d and a solid body of
floes to the S^d as far as SW which by the blink appeared to extend to a great distance.
Had to work up a narrowish channel to weather the field which in 4 hours we accomplished, continued then to ply to the NE where the most water lay until 10 pm. there
appeared a favourable [lead?] to the eastward which we therefore pursued steering
various courses from E to S: after passing a quantity of heavy ice, floes, and patches of
both, a very open navigation offered in an ESE direction. This we of course followed.
5 ships seen to the NE – 3 to the N^d [2]

Tuesday 9th July. Lat. 77. 24 Lon. 4°10'E
NNE N.
Having a light favourable wind with pleasant clear weather we pushed on in an E.erly
direction to the best advantage. We found the ice gradually diminish as we proceeded,
until the evening – when after some time that we had met an easterly swell we
conceived ourselves at sea, passing to the eastward of the last stream of ice within
sight about mid-night. Saw a whale in the morning – the John sent two boats and we
one. The land in sight at mid-night, but not very distinct being apparently 60 miles
distant. ['Bar. 30.00' in margin.]

---

[1] Here follows an insertion in pencil which, because of its mention of a 'tent' may well refer to the
period from 1 to 5 July, when Scoresby and his crew were on the ice, rather than to the entry for 7
July to which it is appended. This is more probable because the arrangement of the transcript left
enough space at the bottom of a page, after the entry for 7 July, for this insertion to be made:
'Surgeon drank 2 bottles wine [pint?] rum & brandy – lay on the ice which was wet without his
jacket where he must have perished, had not some of the men at my request carried him into my
tent, where a dog took compassion on him & ceased not to lick his face.'
[2] Originally 'NWd; 'W' deleted.

The carpenter was employed during the day in setting stantions between the after ceiling and the beams of the gun-room deck to prevent the ceiling from starting from the timbers by the pressure of the water. We find the leakage gradually less.

Wednesday 10 July Lat. 76°52′ Lon. 6°10′E
N.erly var. Calm. E.erly
Light winds or calm – charming clear weather – sun bright and warm. Dried all our wet sails. In the course of the day made progress of about 35′–40′ SEbS (p compass).

Saw several ships – the Valiant's boat was on board of us. They have 5 fish – 75 tons of oil. They furnished us with some nails, twine, & pump leather. In the evening the Phoenix approached us with 2 fish = 45 tons of oil. Mr Dawson came & supped on board along with Bro*the*r Jackson. Mr D. gives account of having seen the Mars on Thursday last with 13 fish = 80 t. of oil – in lat. 75½° moored to a piece of ice. The Phoenix having on board a spare pump it was a great matter of satisfaction receiving the loan of it. This with our own spare pump enables us to adapt two bilge pumps, which in the event of bad weather may prove of essential service.

Our ship sailing particularly heavy we are in constant tow by the John. The sails beneath the leak produce the effect of retarding her velocity in a remarkable manner, as well as injuring her steerage. Since however the application of the additional pieces to the back of the rudder, she has steered ['Refraction' *in margin*] pretty tollerably. The Valiant at a distance seemed divided asunder ['**Thursday 11 July** Lat. 76°20′ Lon. 8°30′E Therm. 38°Bar 30.04 E.erly NNE. E' *in margin*] between the main & fore-masts, by the action of a peculiar refraction the hull was perfectly distinct in every part but in mid-ships where there appeared a considerable vacancy.

Light or fresh breezes – occasional snow showers – a considerable S.erly swell. From the frequent and sudden subsidence of the wind during the day, and from the appearance of the southern sky, it is evident that a S.erly wind prevails at no great distance. At mid-night to 4 am. we were close hauled by the wind to clear a very large and extensive stream of ice or rather floe as it appeared, which after having doubled steered S. And at 10 am. SSW with a velocity of 1 to 4 knots. An appearance of land to the E^d probably Point Look Out. The William & Ann passed us within a mile, and though he must have observed our crippled state, he never attempted to speak us.

We have particular cause of gratitude to the protector of those of trust in him – that our leak continues to ['State of the leak improved.' *in margin*] diminish. The agitation of the sea which we feared would have a bad effect has probably been of service by agitating the fothering materials in the sails & bringing a quantity into the different places of indraught. On the 3^d of July – the day on which the contract with the John was made the flow of water kept two pumps almost in constant motion & the day preceding the water gained on three pumps though worked with the greatest vigour. On the 7th inst*ant* 2 feet of water flowed into the hold in an hour which could be exhausted in 16 minutes. At this time the water which flows in during an hour can be pumped out in about 7 minutes. Thanks be to God for directing our energies in the right way.

About noon we found a stream of ice to the westward ['Left the ice.' *in margin*] of us and did not afterwards see any more ice during the day. At mid-night fine weather, strong south swell, no ships in sight. Broke the towrope – took out a better warp. Received 12 men from the John which we classed along with our crew.

Friday 12 July Lat. 75°17′+ Lon. 8°55′E Ther. 38° Bar. 29.70.
East
We had a moderate breeze of wind attended with charming fine weather during the early part of the day but in the afternoon the wind increased, the sky became overcast, a prodigious SE swell rolled against the ship, so that we soon had the semblance of storm. The great agitation of the ship soon tore away the <u>after</u> fastenings of our fothering sails and they were seen spread partly behind the ship, though some of the foremost ropes retained their hold: all the staples under the counter were drawn and the loose fothering washed away. This circumstance occasioned at first considerable alarm for the effect it might have, as however the warps yet remained sound, though one of them was forced aside it is probable the lower part of the sails might yet perform their office.¹ Our alarm was not diminished to find the water accumulating in the lee bilges, whilst neither of the main pumps could withdraw it on account of the closeness of the ceiling. When however it had flowed about the depth of a foot into the cask we placed on the starboard side of the forehatchway as a pump well we put the pump we received from the Phoenix down and soon had the pleasure to find it decrease.

Steered SSW all the day under 3 courses, & topsails, & jibs, with a velocity of 3 to 7½ knots. The sea from the SE was very heavy, yet the fore bilge pump with an occasional spell at the lee main pump kept the water from increasing. Had a watch in the after hold.

The carpenter was employed most part of the day in increasing the number of stantions in the after hold to keep the ceiling down – for this purpose we cut up two studding sail booms. The sail maker was employed with help of 5 or 6 seamen in thrumbing a sail to be in readiness to replace those which are now in use, on the first occasion. The sail was formed out of a stay foresail as a perfect oblong 9 feet [***] and 8 yards long – this sail was thrumbed throughout. When applied it is expected that it will be more safely fixed, and answer a better purpose than the larger sails.

Saturday 13 July Lat. 73°20′+ Lon. 8°E. Bar. 29.50 Ther. 38–42.
E. SE. SSE S. to SE
Strong to fresh gales, rain, sleet, fog, clear, cloudy. The sea subsided in the forenoon & increased again from the S. in the afternoon. In the morning the fog was so dense that the John was frequently lost sight off [sic], though the two ships were connected by the same hawser! At 10 am. the sky cleared above first, and then the fog gradually dispersed and a fine clear interval succeeded. Sent the crow's nest down and rigged the main & fore topgallant masts. Porceeded [sic] on a SSW, SW, or SWbW course, laterally by the wind, under 3 boom courses, 3 jibs, 2 top gallant sails, and 2 stay sails.

¹ This optimism does not appear to have been justified. See the end of the journal entry for 15 July. In *Account of the Arctic Regions*, II, pp. 478 and 482, Scoresby indicated that from 12 July onwards survival of the ship depended on 'swimming the ship by the ceiling'.

Employed the crew in teazing oakum for fothering, [scouring?] the ships [rails?] and bulwark, cleaning decks, washing the remainder of the whale lines, &c. &c.

At mid night wind a fresh breeze – Very high SW. sea.

Sunday 14 July Lat. 72°19′+ Long. 5°40′E Bar. 29.70 Ther. 44–42
SE.erly Var. Calm.
The wind died away in the forenoon and a calm or very light breeze prevailed during the remainder of the day, accompanied in general by a thick fog: the swell remained though somewhat fallen – it however shifted from the SW, to W. The little progress we made the latter part of the day was in a SW.erly direction. A fresh supply of men came on board from the John in the evening to the relief of those who have been with us since the 11th inst*ant*.

The leak continues moderate, it does not much exceed 10 tons p hour. Hoisted both pumps out as they were become useless, cleared the pump well of dirt, [***] the lower part of the pumps, &c. they then [answered?][.]

Monday 15 July
Var. Calm. W.erly
It has for some days struck me that it would be a matter of much interest ['and' *deleted*] to ascertain the quantity of water which has been discharged from the Esk's hold, since the day of the accident to the present time – but most particularly if an estimate could be formed of the amount discharged during first five or six days when the quantity of leak was the greatest.

To come at the truth as near as possible I first made several experiments with the pumps to ascertain how many strokes of one pump was sufficient to fill a large tub which we had used for the purpose of bailing. With the greatest effect[1] ['Attempt to estimate the quantity of water discharged by the pumps.' *in margin*] of the men, it was filled with 6 strokes, but in the usual manner in which they generally labour it required 8 strokes. This latter number I therefore consider as one part of my data. During the very time of the greatest flow of water, namely in the day of the accident and the two following, I determined the rate of pumping to be from 55 to 75 strokes of each pump per minute – to be within [bound?] I shall take a stroke per second as the next part of my data. The tub above filled by 8 strokes 22 inches in diam*eter* at the top 20 at the bottom and 12 inches in depth – consequently its capacity in wine gallons 18. Therefore as this tub was filled by 8 strokes & 60 were always made in a minute it would be filled 7½ times in the course of a minutes [*sic*]. Hence 7½ x by 18 gall*ons* the contents of the tub gives 135 gall*ons* the quantity of water usually discharged by one pump in a minute, or 1 ton 18 gall*ons* by the two large pumps.*[2]

But besides the constant exercise of these two pumps a third pump was in use during the first 44 hours after the accident. This pump I estimate would at least deliver 60 gallons per minute.

---

[1] Possibly a transcription error for 'effort'.
[2] Note in margin: '*These pumps are of 9 inches bore in the chamber where the spearbox works.' In this context *OED* defines 'spear' as 'A pump-rod'.

To the water discharged by these pumps we have to add that discharge by bailing. In the fore hatch was 2 tubs (one of them ['as gauged' *deleted*] the same which I have just gauged; and the other considerably larger) each of these was filled whipped up and emptied 6 times every minute – but as a considerable quantity was always spilled in whipping up I reckon they would only discharge ¼ of their capacity. The smaller tub 9 inches deep gauges 13 gallons the larger at ¾ the depth about 17 gallons the two, which x by 6 gives 180 gallons the quantity of water discharged by them per minute.

To these we must add the effect of two pails of 4 gallons each, which, being well [plied?], would discharge about 60 gallons per minute.

Hence we have the following amount of water discharged ['Quantity of water discharged by the pumps, buckets, and tubs per minute.' *in margin*] from the ship during the first 44 hours after the accident

by the two large pumps	270 gallons per minute.	
.... small pump	60	ditto.
.... two large tubs	180	ditto.
.... two pails	60	ditto
	570 gallons or 2 tons 66 gallons per minute.	

But it must be allowed that the small pump occasionally sucked and the tubs were sometimes in disuse, by the way therefore of not exceeding the truth I shall allow the 66 gallons a minute to be struck off and reckon the discharge of the water at the general rate of two tons per hour.

From the preceding date [*sic*] we have the liberty of drawing the following conclusions.

Wine tons of
water discharged from the Esk's hold.

From the 29th June at 2 Pm. (The time when the damage was first discovered)) to the 1st of July at 10 Am. All the preceeding means were in general use for the discharge of the water and were plied by from 160 to 220 men – whereby an average of 2 tons per minute was discharged during the whole interval of 44 hours. Hence $44 \times 60 \times 2 =$ 5200

The next 9½ hours was an interval of rest = ...

['Estimation of the quantity of water discharged from the Esk's hold in the interval of 8 days' *in margin*] From the 1st July at 5½ Pm. to the 2d July, 5½ Am. the three pumps and all the bailing vessels were in the fullest possible play whereby 13 feet water was pumped out of the hold besides the leakage. I have not the least doubt therefore that in this 12 hours, 600 to 640 gallons per minute were regularly discharged. ['at the least' *deleted*] Supposing the quantity to have been 630 gallons or 2½ tons we x thereby 12 hours & by 60 the minutes in an hour gives us, the quantity of water pumped out =   1800

275

From 5½ Am. July 2^d to 3 Pm. of the 3^d July an interval of 33½ hours – two pumps were in almost constant exercise and sometimes three[.] I however estimate the quantity of water generally discharged at one ton per minute. Hence 33½ × 60 × 1 =   2010

From 3 Pm of the 3^d to 2 pm of the 7th of July – an interval of ['1' *deleted*] 95 hours I consider the average quantity of water pumped out at half a ton per minute. Hence ['1' *deleted*] 95 × 60 × .5 =   2850

Hence at a moderate computation it appears that between the 29th of June and the 7th of July an interval of only 8 days, were pumped out of the Esk's hold, ['the' *deleted*] of sea water, the enormous amount of =   Tons 11,940[1]

This amount enormous as it may appear I am persuaded does not exceed the truth. From this estimate it appears ['Progressive diminution of the leak – quantity per hour daily since the 29th of June' *in margin*] that during the first two days, the regular leakage was at the rate of 120 tons per hour! The third day about 100 tons – the fourth day about 60 tons – ['and' *deleted*] the fifth ['day & two' *deleted*] and the sixth days about 45 tons – the seventh about 30 tons – and the eighth about 20–25 tons per hour.[2] And, after this period the leak continued to diminish (from the labour which was bestowed in caulking the ceiling, and probably from some of the fothering materials having interrupted the course of the water) until this time when it does not exceed 10 tons per hour!

It has been mentioned that when the accident which ['Lat. 71°40' 5°34'E'.[3] *in margin*] occasioned the leak took place about 8 feet depth of water (allowing a few inches for what might have been in the ship) flowed into the hold in the space of about 90 minutes. By the way of proving the above estimate, I conceive that some satisfaction may be derived from the mensuration of the hold or rather the whole cavity of the ship. The external dimensions of the Esk for measurement are – Length

---

[1] In *Account of the Arctic Regions*, II. 480–81 these calculations are laid out in similar format, but with different values, leading to a final total of 15,690 tons. In both the journal and the *Account*, it appears that wine tons were the units, equivalent to 0.84 of an imperial gallon and 1 US gallon. But Scoresby in the *Account* revised his estimates of the number of gallons per minute achieved by the various methods of removing the water. The values for the large pumps and the large tubs remained unchanged at 270 and 180 gpm respectively, but the values for the smaller pump and the pails were each raised from 60 to 90 gpm, so that the total amount of water that could be discharged, using all available means, was raised from 570 to 630 gpm. He then used that value, equivalent to 2½ tons per minute, in the calculation for the period from 29 June to 1 July, yielding 6,600 tons instead of 5,200. The journal value for 1–2 July of 1,800 tons, based on 2½ tons per minute, was retained in the *Account*, but for 2–3 July the rate was raised from 1 to 1½ tons per minute and for 3–7 July from ½ to ¾ tons per minute, increasing the total for these periods from 2,010 and 2,850 tons to 3,015 and 4,275 tons respectively.
[2] These values were also revised upwards in the *Account*, the values for each day being as follows: 1 & 2: 150 tons per hour; 3: 130; 4: 100; 5: 70; 6: 52; 7: 34; 8: 20.
[3] The same value is inserted in its usual place at the end of this lengthy entry for 15 July.

from the fore part of the stem to the after part of the stern post 106 f^t 6 in. Extreme breadth 27.11. Depth of the hold from the deck ['Mensuration of the capacity of the Esk's hold' *in margin*] about 19 feet. Hence I suppose the internal dimensions will not be less than the following:

Mean length inside	90 feet
Depth of the hold ...	19 f^t
Breadth inside	25 f^t

Now if we consider the ship as a parallelopeidal body – her internal cavity would contain 90 × 19 × 25 = 42750 feet; but on account of the narrowing of the ends, the rise in the floors or their curvature, which especially occurs at the ends, I suppose we may deduct ⅓ which leaves 28500 – from this if we deduct say ⅒ for the beams, knees, twin-decks, bulksheads,[1] &c. there will remain 25650 cubic feet for the dimensions of the internal cavity of the ship for containing water. Now 33½ cubic feet are a ton of water wine measure, nearly:[2] if therefore we divide this remainder of 25650 by 33.5 we find the product 765 tons. If the ship had been empty of casks &c it would appear therefore, that when 8½ feet water was in the hold (which we may call about ⅓ of the internal cavity being the narrowest part) it would be equal to about ⅓ of 765 or 255 tons – but as in this space of 8 feet there were stowed about 100 tons of casks, &c. there remain 155 tons for the quantity of water which entered the hold during the first 90 minutes after the accident. ['The foregoing estimate proved by calculations.' *in margin*] But at the rate of 120 tons per hour this quantity, it might be supposed, should have amounted to 180 tons instead of 155. To this objection to the accuracy of the preceding statement we have a sufficient reply. It is true 120 tons of water entered per hour when there was only 2 or 3 feet in the hold but when that quantity was increased to 8 or 9 feet the ship not sinking in the same proportion in the water as the water flowed up within, the difference between the level of the water within the ship & without would be less as the quantity increased and consequently ['Alteration which would take place in the flow of water in consequence of the rise of the water within side of the ship' *in margin*] the flow of the water would be less considerable. From the known [law?] that the quantity of water which flows through any orifice is in proportion to the square ['of the' *deleted*] root of the depth,[3] it will not be difficult to ascertain the probable diminution which would take place in that flow as the water rose in the hold. For this calculation the following data are necessary.

---

[1] *Sic.* This may be a transcription error, but *OED* cites a 17th-century form 'bulkeshead'.

[2] In wine measure (or US gallons) 1 gallon of water weighs 8.33 lbs and 1 cubic foot of water equals 7.48 gallons. So 33.5 × 7.48 × 8.33 = 2,087 lbs.

[3] Torricelli's Law: The speed, v, of a fluid flowing under the force of gravity out of an opening in a tank is proportional jointly to the square root of the vertical distance, h, between the liquid surface and the centre of the opening, and to the square root of twice the acceleration caused by gravity, $2g$; or, in equation form,

$$v = \sqrt{2gh}.$$

Depth of the orifices by which the water entered the
ship when the accident occasioned the first flow – $11\frac{1}{2}$ ft $\sqrt{} = 3.4$

[*Ditto?*] when there was $8\frac{1}{2}$ ft depth of water in the hold ... $13\frac{1}{2}$
Deduct depth of water in the hold   – $8\frac{1}{2}$

Difference of level of the water inside & outside $\underline{5}$ $\sqrt{} = 2.236$

Hence the quantity of water entering at first & at the end of the 90 minutes would be
in the proportion of 3.4 to 2.24 nearly. Therefore as 3.4: 120 (the flow of water per
hour when the hold was nearly empty) : : 2.24 : 79 the flow of water when $8\frac{1}{2}$ feet
depth had entered. Hence it is evident that if the water rushed in at the first at the rate
of 120 tons per hour, $\dfrac{120 + 79}{2}$ when it had gained the depth of 8 feet in the hold, its
rate would be diminished to 79 tons per hour – but as this diminution would be
gradual we may take the mean of the extremes – namely; = 99.5 for the mean flow
of the water per ['Conclusions which further prove the foregoing statements.' *in
margin*] hour which × by $1\frac{1}{2}$ (the time that $8\frac{1}{2}$ feet of water entered in) the result
is 149.25 tons for the quantity of water which would flow in under the decreasing
rate as above mentioned. The estimation by the mensuration of the hold was 155
tons which approaches singularly near. And, as the water was supposed &
estimated at 120 tons per hour during the first two days when there was an
average depth of four feet water in the hold – its original force would appear to
have been something more than 120 tons per hour, and consequently that the
quantity of water which flowed in the hold during the first 90 minutes would
exceed 149.25 tons as above calculated.
   I think I may therefore consider it proven that the foregoing estimates of the
number of tons of water which were pumped out of the Esk's hold in the course of 8
days do not exceed the truth. Q. E. D.
   Very light variable winds prevailed during this day our progress was in consequence very inconsiderable. [The?] courses were SW to SE and velocity 1 to $3\frac{1}{2}$ knots.
Employed the watch in cleaning the ship – (scrubbing the sides, &c.) The carpenter
found employment in the after hold, in caulking several different places where the
water [forced?] out; which however I was happy to find were at a considerable elevation – some of them could not be above 4 or 5 feet below the surface of the water. It is
therefore evident the wedges are of essential service – and ['it' *deleted*] indeed that it is
through their means and the securing of the after ceiling that the water is kept out –
Especially since the two fothering sails appear to be almost totally washed away in
the place of the leak.

Tuesday 16 July Lat. 71°19′+ Lon. 5°59′E. Bar. 30.05 Therm. 44–52.
NW to SW. Variable calm.
Light variable winds – frequently calm. Fine weather. Called all hands early in
the morning and suspended 5 boats lines (which were previously washed) to dry.

Employed the people in the interval with making points,[1] roebands, &c. Having prepared an oblong thrumbed sail as before mentioned – we [marled?] it on two warps along the longest sides and connected the two warps by a chain of 3 feet in length which was intended to lay across the stern post ['The fothering sails renewed and the leak much reduced thereby' *in margin*] between it and the rudder at about the 3 feet mark, the lower part of the rudder having been cut away before we left the ice for the purpose. In our first attempt to get the sail under the ship, in consequence of the swell and a breeze of wind which forced the ship to lee-ward, we failed. In a perfect calm however, which shortly afterwards recurred we succeeded. The warps which were connected by the chain with the stern post were taken in at either bow and hove tight, several lines were taken from the sail to the quarters of the ship for stretching the sail across the damaged part. It was no sooner applied but a very sensible effect took place in the flow of the water. The leak was immediately reduced full one half. The long bunches of yarn with which it was thrumbed appeared to have drawn into some of the principal leaks.

In the evening coyled away the lines, which were in very good condition. A ship was seen in the morning, which approaching us in the course of the day proved to be the Phoenix of W*hit*by. The master when he supped with me on the 10th inst*ant* had some thoughts of accompanying us home, from the small prospect there appeared of further success. He was induced however to reach to the northw*ard* from us, I suppose from the clearness of the following day – and on the commencement of the coarse weather which followed he has probably made sail after us. At any rate – he joined us this night. Saw some sea weed – a symptom of approximation to land. Norway, doubtless[.]

Wednesday 17 July Lat.70°2′ Lon.5°7′E Bar.30.23 Ther. 46–50
N.erly E. ESE Variable
A charming fair wind all the day – blowing a fresh gale in the evening with heavy weather. In tow of the John under a brisk sail. Steered SW½W with a velocity increasing to 9 knotts. The Phoenix in company. Our new fothering sail though so well secured to appearance soon shared the fate of those which preceded it. It was split very soon after the ship attained the velocity of 8 knotts and the beam swell became considerable. The leak however continued throughout the day without any sensible increased [*sic*]. Passed an Archangelman, working to windward. The watch employed in the manufacture of points, roebands, gaskets, spunyarn, &c.

---

[1] Presumably what Smyth, *Sailor's Word Book*, termed reef-points (s.v.): 'Small flat pieces of plaited cordage or soft rope, tapering from the middle towards each end, whose length is nearly double the circumferences of the yard, and used for the purpose of tying up the sail in the act of reefing.' It is tempting to see the journal entries for this and the next day as evidence of Scoresby's psychological skill in keeping his crew occupied in activities similar to those of a normal return voyage, despite the continued peril for the *Esk*.

Thursday 18 July Lat. 67°16′ Lon. 1°59′E. Bar. 29.97 Ther. 50
ESE. to EbN
In the morning the SE.erly swell partly subsided – the wind continued fresh and fair –
weather hazy. Continued on a SW course. At noon during the 24 hours we had run a
distance of 184 miles by the log. In the afternoon a heavy swell from the ENE arose.
Our choice of fresh provision after near four months absence from home is so
remarkable that I cannot forbear mentioning the particulars. 1st Fresh beef for [boil-
ing?]; 2d chines for roasting, in excellent state; 3d Mutton for roasting or boiling yet
excellent; 4th fowls, killed three & half months ago, [failing]; 4th [sic] roast & boiling
pork. This pork was produced (pigged) in Scotland; bred on board of a ship; fed in
Greenland; killed in the North Sea; cured (at least may be) in the German ocean; and,
eaten (if we are spared) in England![1] In tow of the John. Phoenix in Cy. Leak on the
increase.

Friday 19th July Lat. 65°5′+ Lon. 0°56′E Bar. 29.70 Ther. 50 to 55.
EbN to SE, S. SW & var.
Fresh gales in the morning with considerable swell; thick fog showers. Steered SWbS.
At 3 am. the towlines by which we were towed, broke – the sea being ['very' *deleted*]
high we were three hours before we could get our hawser end on board the John.
Three different lines that were sent us floated by buoys all got entangled with the keel
bolts. In the afternoon the wind fell and veered into an unfavourable quarter – The
day was fine & clear which induced us to suspend our whalelines to dry, but in the
afternoon we were suddenly overtaken by a fog, which almost seemed to rise out of
the sea as it was not observed more than a few minutes before we were enveloped by
it, whereby the lines were considerably wetted before they could be got down. The
master of the Phoenix having come on board of us, the ship by the carelessness of the
officer of the watch lost sight of us and we had to fire a ['Saw more seaweed' *in
margin*] number of guns before the ship appeared to the relief of the master's anxiety.
Tacked at 7 pm. In the evening fine weather. Course SSE.

Saturday 20 July Lat. by observation = 64°39′23″ Longitude By lunar obser*vation* at
9h35′25 = 1°4′30″E[;] By Chronometer = 3.9.45E[;] By reckoning 1.6.0E Bar. 30.00
Therm. 60 to 57°
SW to S, SEbS.
This was a most agreeable day – the sky was clear, sea smooth, wind moderate, and
latterly fair. Suspended once again our whale lines which being shone on by a warm
sun soon dried and were taken down in the evening in an excel*lent* state. Employed
all hands a few hours in various necessary work. As our fothering sail the last applied
was quite removed from its place and had become useless we cut it away & took it
(['with' *deleted*] at least all that remained of it) together with some pieces of the other

---

[1] Use of the terms 'North Sea' and 'German Ocean' as if they were different locations seems to be
a literary flight of fancy by Scoresby. The names have always been interchangeable, with 'North
Sea' gradually replacing 'German Ocean' over the centuries. See Pokoly, 'On the History of Naming
the North Sea'.

sails that were towing astern, on board. Leak rather on the increase, but not yet very serious.

In the evening we met a heavy SW swell, at the same time we had a fresh breeze of wind (with hazy weather) at SSE. The water again accumulated in the bilge and obliged us to reduce sail, remove some lumber from the lee side to the opposite side of the deck, and to put in exercise the bilge pump. The carpenter again found employment in stopping some new leaks. About 10 pm. a light brig from Peterhead passed us bound to Archangel – she was spoken by the Phoenix. Stated Shetland to bear SWbW per compass and our longitude to be 2°50′E which corresponds very near with the observation of the Chronometer.

Sunday 21ˢᵗ July Lat. 63°44′ Long Chr. 1°36′E[;] [D.?] 0.29 W. Bar. 30.10 Therm. 58–60.
SSE to ESE
Blowing fresh in general but occasionally moderate. The fog which prevailed the greater part of this day was sometimes so very dense that the John could scarcely be seen at the distance of a short towline length. A strong swell from the SWᵈ. Reached by the wind to the SWᵈ until evening when it veered to the ESE – we then steered SbW½W under all sails, velocity 3 to 7 K. It is worthy of remark that the fog during its greatest density was composed of a stratum so thin that the sun shone through it with undiminished lustre. The Phoenix in company. Leak without alteration – kept [under?] by the lee bilge pump in a great measure. The large pump worked only at intervals of half an hour. Some stars seen!

Monday 22ᵈ July Latitude [indicated by?] Ob. 61°30′+ Long. By Chronometer 1°16 E[;] From lunar obs. 0.49W. By a/c 0.46W. Barom. 29.86 Ther. 56–62.
EbS to SbE
The easterly wind increased to a strong gale at 3 am. when the ship from pressure of sail (going 9 knotts) carried such a great <u>weather</u> helm that one of the stantions of the wheel gave way & the tiller ropes though newly rove were strained. As the great pressure of the water on our enlarged rudder seemed to endanger the stern post (which by the loss of the keel with its tenon & clamps together with the fractured state of the gudgeon braces of the rudder ['has lost its' *deleted*] is deprived of a great proportion of its support) and consequently the safety of the ship and with the increasing sea that had now become very turbulent the safety of our lives also, we found it necessary to reduce sail. We therefore took in the top gall*ant* sails, crossjack, stay sails, treble reefed the main top sail & double reefed the fore top sail. Sent down top gall*ant* yards and hoisted the lee waist boat upon deck. The John meanwhile having been furnished with our best hawser to tow us by, by carrying a great pressure of canvass continued our velocity at 8 knotts or upwards for several hours. A brig steering to the westward crossed our stern. The Phoenix being likely to be left astern was obliged to carry a very brisk sail. The bilge pump in constant play.

In the afternoon the wind began to subside and in the evening it became quite light, but a heavy swell continued. Our course was SSW most of the day, and SWerly when the wind veered about 6 pm towards the south. Struck soundings about 4 pm.

in 70 fathoms fine sand with brown specks & at 10 pm. 80 fathoms. Caught some mackerell. These soundings with the mackerell indicate our situation to be to the eastward of Shetland and the increase in the depth of water showed our near approach to Shetland.

Thursday 23ᵈ July Lat 60°10′ Lon. 0°20′W Bar.29.86 Ther. 59–64°
SbE to SE
Light variable winds with delightful, though hot weather. At 3 am. saw land bearing [NWbW?] and after steering SW for 7 hours discerned Hangcliff bearing WbN distant about 15 miles. The wind being considerably southerly we steered towards the land with the design of putting into Shetland until we should have a fair wind, but the wind shortly veering again to the SEᵈ we hauled up ['Curious swell' *in margin*] on a SSW course. During the day we had a constant heavy swell from the NE, SW, and E – sometimes two of these or even the whole three distinct swells could be observed at the same time. Mʳ Jackson & Mʳ Dawson of the Phoenix spent most of the day with me. About 10 pm having put the John's crew on board, received from them a supply of fresh water, &c. they left us to ourselves, their engagement being fulfilled which was to accompany us to some port of Shetland, if required and as we did not choose to put into port, when the ship passed the extremity of the Shetland islands ['Bent cables' *in margin*] on the south, so as to bring its bearing to NW½W – 20 miles distant, they accordingly steered away to the westward. The Phoenix in Cᵒ.

Wednesday 24 July Lat. 59°31′31″+ Lon. 0°40′W Bar. 29.87 Ther. 59°62
SE.erly NE.erly E.
Light airs of wind most of the day with a little rain – in the evening fresh breezes and showery. Steered SSW until 8 pm. and SbW½W afterwards, fearing the wind eastering and casting us on a lee shore. 2 fishing ships to the westward – Phoenix in company. Leak on the increase.

Thursday 25ᵗʰ July. Lat. 57°34′ Lon. 0°5′E. Bar. 29.06 Ther. 58–54
E.erly.NE.erly NNW ['S.erly SW' *deleted*]
Fresh gales in the morning – about noon light breezes – at night again fresh gales. Steered SbW until 8 am. then SSW and afterwards SW½S. when the wind veered to the NNW. The Phoenix took us in tow at noon. Passed a great number of Dutch fishermen. Velocity of the ship 3 to 8 knotts per hour. About 10 am supposed ourselves abreast of Peterhead, the land was not in sight. Under all sails. Set spare mizen as a lower studding sail. Blowing strong at night ['WNW' *deleted in margin*]

Friday 26 July Lat. [*blank space*] Lon. [*blank space*]
NW. SW.erly WNW
The wind decreased as the day advanced and the weather continued fine and pleasant. At 7 am. descried land and at noon Sᵗ Abb's Head bore NWbN distant 15 miles. Several ships and small vessels in sight. In the evening a S.erly breeze commenced which veered about 10 pm. to WNW under which we proceeded with a brisk sail on a SW course with a velocity of 5 to 7 miles per hour. The Phoenix left us

in the afternoon for the purpose of carrying the news – our ship being tollerably manageable. At 10 pm. saw the Staples lights bearing WNW. The wind continuing ['**Saturday 27 July** WNW W. Var. *in margin*] brisk in the morning we made such excellent progress that Whitby was in sight at 3 am. at 5 we were near Sandsend ness and though we had no signal or pilot we steered towards the harbour: when abreast of Upgang rock a cobble boarded us[.]

The tide having fallen but little we proceeded towards the harbour under all sails, studding sails and others and sailed above the Scotch head when the ship grounded. The Phoenix ran past the harbour and did not get in until the following tide. This happy termination of our adventurous voyage was enhanced by the circumstances of health in which I found my dear wife and child, together with my relatives. The congratulations of the inhabitants on our arrival after we had been deemed ship wrecked, were particularly gratifying after the hardships and hazards we had endured. Thanks be to that Divine being from whom our mercies are all derived.[1]

[1] In *Account of the Arctic Regions*, II, pp. 486–8, Scoresby described the aftermath of 'a voyage at once hazardous, disastrous, and interesting'. Although news of the state of the ship reached Whitby only a day before the *Esk* returned there, 'Some of the underwriters on the Esk, I was informed, had offered 60 *per cent.*, for the re-assurance of the sums for which they were liable; but such was the nature of the risk, as ascertained from the information of some ships' crews by whom we had been assisted, that no one would undertake the re-assurance even at this extraordinary premium.' I am grateful to Ms Sandra LaFevre, Reinsurance Association of America, for confirming that this meant that the underwriters would have been willing pay 160 per cent of the original premiums to anyone prepared to assume the insured liability. The underwriters subsequently rewarded Scoresby with 'a handsome piece of plate'. He mentioned in his autobiography that 'The underwriters of Stockton likewise proposed a subscription for a piece of plate; but the offer being made in an indelicate way I declined it.' The owners, Fishburn and Brodrick, similarly gave him a gratuity of £50, and the cost of repairs to the *Esk* 'did not, I believe, exceed 200 *l*'. Scoresby concluded as follows: 'I may add, in conclusion, that the whole of my crew, excepting one individual, returned from this adventurous and trying voyage in safety; and, in general, in a good state of health. Several of the men, indeed, were affected, more or less, by the excessive fatigue, and by the painful exposure to cold and damp while resting on the ice; but all of them were, in a great measure, restored, before our arrival at home, excepting one man; he, poor fellow, being of a weak constitution, suffered severely from the inclement exposure, and died soon after he arrived in port.'

APPENDIX

Scoresby's Navigation

George Huxtable

This section is intended to complement and expand on the information contained in Ian Jackson's Introduction to volume I of Scoresby's journals, particularly pages lv–lviii of that introduction, also titled 'Scoresby's Navigation', as well as his Introduction to the present volume. It is based on a reading of Scoresby's journals from 1811 to 1816.

Introduction

For a vessel involved in whaling in the Greenland Sea, navigation had many differences (though also some similarities) with that for an ordinary vessel making port-to-port ocean voyages. There was, for example, no specific destination to be aimed for, just a general area west of Spitsbergen, where the whales were known to gather. When within those deep-water whaling grounds, a navigator continued to record each day his best estimate of noon position, but with no fixed hazards such as shoals or reefs to avoid, it mattered little where exactly a vessel might be, so long as she could find 'fish' to follow and catch. It was of course necessary to avoid the rocky coast of Spitsbergen itself, particularly on the northward journey.

This situation was very different from the navigational needs of an ocean-voyaging mariner, who required his en route position with some precision, to enable him to approach his destination, or to round a headland on the way, with safety, and to choose an efficient route, in terms of known wind patterns and ocean currents. It was on the journey home, back from the ice at the end of the season, that such navigational needs became crucial for whaling ships. Even then, however, there were significant differences. Unlike a port-to-port ocean voyager, a Greenland Sea whaler was likely to set off southwards, for home, from an undetermined position, and there would be much guesswork in choosing a course to return to home waters.

Because arctic whaling was done at a time of continuous daylight, the principal navigational hazard – floating ice – was always visible, except in thick fog (e.g. 24 May 1816). Decades of experience had taught the Greenland Sea whaling fleet that there were no hidden keel-depth hazards to avoid, except right at the ice-edge. Because the sky was never dark during the whaling season, star and planet observations were unavailable to a Greenland whaler, and he had therefore only a low sun, and an occasional moon, available for astronomical observations. Within limits, he could often adapt his path through the ice floes to suit the wind direction of the moment, so he did not suffer from foul wind directions to the same extent as did the ocean voyager.

As the journals show, Scoresby recorded his position at sea in terms of latitude and longitude. Distances were given in miles, which were nautical miles, where 1 nautical mile is equivalent to 1 minute of latitude, or 1.15 land or statute miles. Because of the convergence of the meridians of longitude towards the poles, the length of a degree of longitude decreases from 34.9 nautical miles (40.1 statute miles) at the latitude of Whitby (54°30′N) to 10.4 nautical miles (12 statute miles) at 80°N, the normal limit of navigation by the whaling fleet.

The latitudes and longitudes listed in the logs of Scoresby and other early nineteenth-century whalers are however liable to convey a false sense of accuracy to the modern reader. In two important ways, what we can now determine with absolute accuracy was then accuracy only in relative terms. Not merely was a ship's stated position (in terms of longitude, particularly) no more than an approximation, due to the limitations of instruments, techniques and individual abilities, but the position of coastlines and places were known only in broad terms, especially in high latitudes. As Scoresby was later to complain in his *Account of the Arctic Regions*, 'In several particular situations I found an error of 10 miles of latitude and 2 or 3 degrees of longitude, in our most approved charts' (I, p. 113).

To the whaling captain, what mattered most in his navigation was the position of the ship in relation to land, especially on the homeward journey. It was necessary to keep away from the long lee shore of the Norwegian coast, and to bring the ship to the general vicinity of the Shetlands. The crucial question, when approaching the latitude of Shetland from the north, was whether the vessel would be passing that unlit archipelago, with its lethal outlying skerries, to the east or to the west. Scoresby's journals, at least before 1816, show that he could not rely on celestial longitudes to settle that matter, and that every possible clue had to be assessed (see especially the journal entries for 8 and 9 August 1812). Once Shetland had been sighted, the land and familiar landmarks acted as the navigational guide back to Whitby.

In the sections that follow, the navigational tools available to Scoresby, and their limitations, with their relevance to arctic navigation, will be considered. Then, the way that arctic navigation was conducted, by Scoresby in particular, using those tools. Lastly, I offer a personal, and necessarily subjective, appraisal of Scoresby's skills as a navigator and a mariner.

The Navigator's Tools.

In Scoresby's time, a navigator had available to him the following tools:

Compass. Compasses had several functions, and were in use all the time. If the sky was obscured, and if no landmarks were in sight, the steering compass enabled the helmsman to steer a constant course from minute to minute, the course that had been set by the navigator. The steering compass was placed behind a glass window in the binnacle, and lit at night. Usually, there would be two such compasses, placed so that one was always visible, straight in front of the helmsman, whichever side of the wheel he was standing. To determine the compass bearing of a landmark or a body in the sky, there was a bearing-compass or azimuth-compass. Sometimes a steering compass would be borrowed from the binnacle for that purpose, but more usually the azimuth compass was fixed in a spot which gave the best all-around view. Compasses were mounted in a gimballed box, to keep them independent of the heel of the vessel. They were marked in terms of the 32 'points of the compass', which are 11.25 degrees apart, rather than in degrees as they are today, and directions could be specified in terms of half-points or even quarter-points. A compass card gave the direction with respect to the local magnetic field, which differed from true north because of magnetic variation and deviation. Corrections had to be made to allow for those important errors. They will be discussed in a later section.

Sextant. The sextant is used to determine the altitude above the horizon of a celestial body; in Scoresby's case usually the sun. He also used it on occasion to measure a lunar distance; the angle, slantwise across the sky, between moon and sun. The sextant, when as usual it was made in brass, was then an expensive and precise instrument, and capable of measuring to better than a minute of arc. It was, at the time, gradually superseding the Hadley octant (or quadrant), a usually wooden instrument which was insufficiently accurate for taking 'lunars'. Even Charles Steward, the young supernumerary who sailed with Scoresby in 1814, had his own sextant, as his journal entry for 18 April shows. That was an expensive investment for his family at that early point in his career, but it was a navigator's badge of office.

Timepiece. Some sort of timepiece would always be carried on any vessel, to provide time of day and to relate to each other, in time, the various observations that were made. For those purposes, a constancy in timekeeping of a minute or so per day was perfectly acceptable. It might be a pocket watch, which might be referred to (though not by Scoresby) as the 'deck-watch' or 'hack-watch'.

Chronometer. This was an expensive instrument carried by a few well-equipped vessels, and was in a very different category. It lived below, cosseted in gimbals, and was expected to keep to a constant rate, over a voyage of several months, within an error of perhaps half a minute. Such a timekeeper could be used in determining the vessel's longitude.

Almanac and tables. In order to deduce latitude from sun altitude, a table of the changing declination of the sun was required. In order to determine Greenwich Time, a table of sun lunar-distances at 3-hour intervals was needed. These, with many other useful tables, were supplied in the Nautical Almanac, published each year from 1767 by the Board of Longitude. In addition, a set of mathematical tables, providing logarithms of trigonometrical functions, was necessary, with additional tables to ease lunar distance calculations.

Charts. Scoresby tells us little about what charts he carried aboard, other than stating that he found large errors in his chart of Spitsbergen. Charts of his British sailing areas had existed for many years, back to those of Greenville Collins, which included Shetland, published as early as 1693. Laurie and Whittle had published, in 1796, *A New Chart for the Whale Fishery and the Archangel Traders for the Navigation in*

the Northern Seas, from Great Britain and Ireland to Spitzbergen and the White Sea.
This would have been most useful to Scoresby, covering the whole extent of his
voyaging on a single large chart. It is likely to have been his working chart, though he
did not acknowledge it as such. The track of Phipps's expedition with HMS *Racehorse* and *Carcass* 'toward the North Pole' in 1773 was shown, and the chart was
presumably a product of that voyage. It agrees rather well with modern maps, though
the longitudes of Spitsbergen were somewhat in error, as Scoresby was aware. Point
Lookout, the southern tip of Spitsbergen, and much of the western coast, should have
been laid down nearly three degrees further to the east.

Because of the scale distortions, inherent in a Mercator chart reaching to high latitudes, Spitsbergen was shown on the 1796 chart at a useful scale, but Shetland
became highly compressed. Scoresby would therefore have needed a separate chart
covering the waters around Orkney and Shetland, and we know of two that existed.
The Hydrographic Office published chart 1419 'Orkney Islands, Shetland Islands' in
1807, the result of a survey made in 1795.[1] This appears to be a thorough piece of
work, and most useful to a mariner navigating those waters. It was in complete
contrast to the chart of 'The Shetland, Orkney, and Faro Isles', by Captain Ross
Donnelly, from his voyage in HMS *Pegasus* in 1796, published by Laurie & Whittle
in 1802. That chart is shoddy work indeed, showing grotesque distortions of Shetland, even though *Pegasus* had circumnavigated the islands. A mariner would have
been better off without that chart, than with it.

None of the charts mentioned above, except for the early one by Collins, carries
any warnings about the notorious tide-race of Sumburgh Röst.

Log and traverse board. The ship's log was usually a triangular wooden board, which
was cast over the stern at intervals, to measure her speed. It was attached to a long
line, paid out from a freely-running drum, by a triangular 'bridle', which kept it at
right angles to the direction of travel, so that it was not pulled through the water, but
stayed put. Knots were made in the line at a defined spacing, and the speed was
obtained from the number of knots counted, as the line slipped between the fingers of
a seaman in a defined time interval which was usually 28 or 30 seconds. That speed,
and the compass-course sailed over that 'leg', in points and half-points, were
recorded by pushing pegs into holes in a traverse board, which was similar to a dart-
board (see Fig. 8). There was therefore no need for a watchkeeper to be literate.

Lead. Our usual mental picture of casting a ship's lead is to avoid grounding on a
shoal, but Scoresby's journeys seldom took him into such waters, though no doubt
he carried a suitable lead for that job if required. Instead, his need was to sound
in much greater depths, in order to get clues about his position, from the depth
and from the way the depth changed. To that end, he would have carried a deep-
sea (often corrupted to 'dipsey') lead, with a heavy weight (28 or even 56 pounds)
attached to line reaching to 200 fathoms (1,200 feet). That much weight was
needed to ensure a quick fall to the bottom, and an obvious change in tension as

---

[1] This chart can be seen online at http://www.nls.uk/digitallibrary/map/early/scotland.cfm?id=1218.

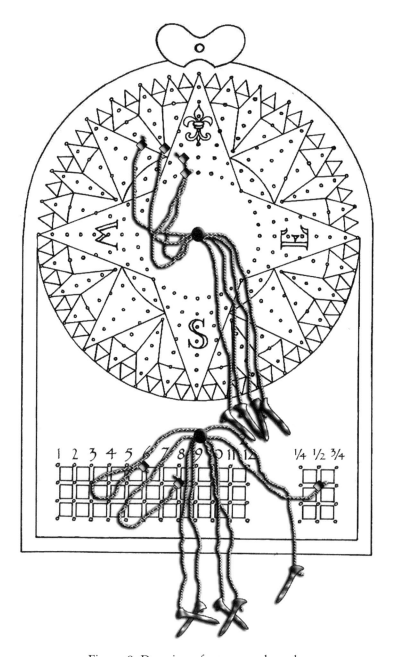

Figure 8. Drawing of a traverse board

The drawing shows a traverse board, which would be hung on a hook near to the helmsman and chartroom. It allowed the watch officer to record compass course and measured speed over a four-hour watch, even if he was illiterate. Details varied; this one allows eight courses, at half-hour intervals, and four speeds, at one-hour intervals, to be pegged. It is shown as it might be halfway through a watch, when courses at each 'bell' had been successively: N by W, N by W, NNW, and NW by N. The speeds measured were first 6 knots, then 8½ knots. The remaining pegs, here shown dangling, would be inserted as the watch progressed. When the watch ended, the navigator, usually the captain, would correct the courses for compass error, then resolve each segment in terms of Westings and Northings, which would be summed together. At the next noon, an overall sum allowed a new dead-reckoning position to be estimated. Traverse boards were often gaily painted, and some were real works of art.

(Drawing by Renée Mattie, based on an original by Duane Cline.)

the slack was taken up to lift it off. Dipsey-lead soundings were taken at rather long intervals, because retrieving the lead was a long and laborious business, and because the vessel was required to heave-to, taking the way off by backing certain sails. Often, a blob of tallow would be pressed into the foot of the lead, which would pick up a sample of the bottom material, and provide additional clues to an experienced navigator.

On 5 June 1815, Scoresby noted that when a whale had been taken by the *John* on the previous day, the sea bottom was at the great depth of 600 fathoms. From the context, it seems that this had been deduced, not by a sounding from the ship, but by the length of line taken out by the whale, which had sounded vertically after being struck, and had suffered injury on reaching the bottom.

Aspects of Navigation

Over the various phases of Scoresby's voyaging, the navigation took on different aspects. They will be discussed with the special problems of arctic navigation in mind, drawing from Scoresby's own methods of handling them.

Coastal navigation. When within sight of land, or having occasional sights of known headlands, the position of a vessel could be determined by compass bearings of such landmarks, together with measurement of the vessel's course and distance travelled through the water. Then the position was established with respect to that coast (which was what mattered), and could be plotted on the chart. It did not matter greatly whether that coast had been laid down precisely, in terms of latitude and longitude, on the chart. That was the situation that Scoresby faced off the coast of Spitsbergen, when he found his chart to contain serious errors in longitude.

Position by account. Out of sight of land, a vessel would be then navigated by calculating, usually between one noon and the next, her change in latitude and longitude. For each period spent steering a constant course, the ship's heading would be noted in terms of the magnetic compass. This would then be corrected by the previously-known (or recently-measured) variation of the Earth's magnetic field, to obtain the ship's heading with respect to true north. This presumed that there was no known deviation of the compass caused by iron in the ship or her contents; if there was, that too had to be allowed for.

A compass responds to the horizontal component of the earth's magnetic field, which points roughly in a northerly direction. However, as the magnetic pole is approached, that horizontal component becomes weaker, and the field points more and more in a vertical direction. This became a problem for navigators in arctic latitudes, who found that the compass needle became more sluggish and less precise as the directing force weakened.

The earth's magnetic field does not point directly north–south, unfortunately, but differs by an amount known to navigators as the magnetic variation, and to geographers as the magnetic declination. This variation changes with geographical position, and changes greatly, though slowly, over time. In Scoresby's day it differed from true north by an unusually high amount, about 25 degrees west, over his sailing grounds.[1] A navigator needs to know the variation, in order to correct his compass to obtain true courses and bearings, and Scoresby would have determined the local variation from time to time, using his compass with the Sun's azimuth as a reference.

A further correction needs to be made for magnetic deviation, which is caused by iron components of the ship, or iron items carried on board, affecting the local on-board direction of magnetic north. Commonly, those effects are enhanced in high latitudes, although they should not be great in a wooden vessel. On 22 July 1813 Scoresby described how he used a bearing compass to measure very different deviations from one part of the ship to another. This would have been due to the local presence of iron, although friction at the needle, which the weakened magnetic force may not be able to overcome, may also have been a factor. Deviation changes with the vessel's heading, and is corrected after 'swinging' the ship over the whole 360-degree range of headings, while measuring compass errors. Scoresby does not record any such exercise.

Scoresby lumped together the deviation with the variation, and referred to the resulting total compass error as 'variation'. As a result of the reduced directing force, the perturbing effect of nearby iron will increase in high magnetic latitudes. Scoresby was aware of this (journal entry for 22 July 1813), even if he got the mathematical details wrong.

A correction then had to be made for leeway angle, to allow for any crabwise drift of the vessel, which could be very significant for such round-bellied hulls, especially when sailed as close to the wind as possible. The result was an estimate of the true course of the vessel, which usually would not include any allowance for ocean current or tidal stream, these being imperfectly understood. It was this neglect of tidal streams that brought Esk near to disaster off Sumburgh on the night of 26 March 1814.

At intervals of perhaps three hours, the speed would be measured by the ship's log (though many navigators considered themselves able to estimate it equally well, just from experience) and, with the compass heading, entered on the traverse board.

At the end of a noon-to-noon interval, for each period over which the course could be considered constant, the ship's 'northing', or motion in a north–south direction, in minutes of latitude, and her 'westing' or motion in an east–west direction, in minutes of longitude, could be obtained quickly from a ready-reckoner called a traverse table. Then these northings and westings were summed up over the whole twenty-four-hour period. The result was the total change in latitude and longitude that had occurred since the previous noon, providing a new position at the current noon. Note that this did not relate to any actual *measurement* of the ship's new position. It was a position calculated 'by account', otherwise known as 'dead reckoning', and not a 'position by observation'. It was the only method of ocean navigation that was available if the sky was overcast.

There were unavoidable errors and uncertainties in deducing the change in position between one noon and the next by this method, particularly in regard to the

---

[1] There is a map of magnetic variation about 1800 at the website http://www.phys.uu.nl/~vgent/ magdec/mgdc1800.pdf.

effect of ocean currents and tidal streams. And then for the noon that followed that, there were further errors to add again, and so on.

Dead reckoning was therefore a method that provided reasonable accuracy over a short period, but if there was a long period in which a ship was unable to establish a true position by observation, then errors in her reckoning could accumulate to hundreds of miles. This could be particularly true in the case of a 'difficult' passage, in which a vessel had to spend long periods beating against a headwind, or in uncontrolled running before a gale.

The direction of north would be sensed from the reading of the magnetic compass. In Scoresby's journal, his courses and wind directions were always recorded in terms of magnetic compass reading, measured usually in named 'points' of the compass. However, to compute his northings and westings, for the purposes of navigation, it was necessary to convert those compass courses to true directions, based on true north, by applying the corrections described in the section on the compass. Those compass errors gave rise to considerable problems.

Scoresby noted some very significant differences between the readings of his three ship's compasses, mounted in different locations. This was an unsatisfactory state of affairs indeed, which he made the best of by averaging the three. For a discussion of the matter, see his journal entries for 22 July 1813, 20 April 1815 (which noted a remarkably low value for variation, of 15°37'W), and 30 June 1815. His compasses were evidently so badly affected by deviation that any recorded observations of variation in the journals must be somewhat suspect. To remove effects of local deviation, he could perhaps, when conditions were right, have taken a compass away from the ship on a wooden boat, or perhaps measured from the ice, but there is no evidence that he did so.

Scoresby wrote on 30 June 1815 'Where the anomaly was greatest; viz. on the main deck there was no iron longer than a nail or a bolt within 15 feet of the place, therefore it must be the attraction of the body of the ship which occasions the anomaly.' We now know this to be nonsense. It differs greatly from his earlier assessment of 22 July 1813 when he correctly attributed the compass deviation to the effect of iron. For a wooden vessel, the 'body of the ship' has no effect on the compass except in terms of its iron content. Had he properly considered the effect of out-of-sight objects below deck, such as the iron content of his armament? His journal for 27 April 1812 stated 'put the guns into a favourable situation for fishing. Thus 4 of the carriage Guns by the Main mast in the half deck, 2, 4-lbers in the Galley, and two 6s under the Bowsprit on the Forecastle the Cannonades [i.e. carronades] were lashed in different suitable places about the Decks.' Scoresby's journals (23 and 28 February 1814) also record the placing of twelve tons of pig-iron ballast in the bottom of Esk's hold. A frequent cause of compass problems was the position of the binnacle, if it butted up against a cabin skylight which usually included iron fittings, particularly a set of iron bars to protect the glass. We do not know what local iron was affecting Esk's compasses so badly, but iron it must have been.

Astronavigation. Astronavigation becomes important when the vessel is out of sight of land for a prolonged period, but is impossible when the sky becomes overcast. It allows positions, deduced by dead reckoning, to be updated from the result of an actual *measurement*. Dead reckoning allows interpolation over the interval between such measured astronomical positions. The two work together. Astronavigation has a number of facets, to be discussed below, in turn.

Latitude at noon. Provided that the sun can be seen around noon, together with a sharp horizon, this is an easy observation for a navigator to make, and a matter of routine. It involves using a sextant to measure the angular height of the sun's disc above the horizon, at a time when that angle reaches its maximum value, very close to the moment of noon. The aim is to measure that angle to a precision of a very few minutes of arc. No timekeeper is needed.

Several simple corrections need to be made to the observed Sun altitude. First, any zero-error (known as index error) in the sextant needs to be checked and allowed for. Then, the line from the observer's eye to the horizon will not be perfectly horizontal, requiring a correction for 'dip' of the horizon, due to his height, in the ship, above sea-level and also allowing for some bending of the light, due to refraction in the air, in its path from the horizon to his eye. Then there is a correction for refraction of the light from the sun, which bends its path from outer space to the observer's eye. Finally, what is measured by the sextant is not the sun's centre, but an edge or 'limb', usually the lower one, requiring a correction for the Sun's known 'semidiameter'. After all such corrections are made, the end result will be the noon altitude, in degrees and minutes, of the sun's centre above the true horizontal.

Next, the navigator needs to consult his Nautical Almanac for the current year to learn the sun's predicted 'declination' at his moment of noon on that day. Declination is no more than a fancy name for the Sun's latitude, as it slowly wanders between 23 degrees north (in northern hemisphere summer) and 23 degrees south (in northern winter). To that declination (taking north as positive, south negative) 90 degrees must be added, and the noon altitude subtracted. The result is the latitude at noon. It's just simple arithmetic, and requires no trigonometry. If the sun's altitude was observed to within a few arc-minutes (which is usually easy in clear conditions) then the latitude will also be known to a few arc-minutes, or a few nautical miles. The biggest source of error is abnormal refraction displacing the position of the horizon, an effect such as was apparent to Scoresby on 13 May 1814, but which can often occur without any evidence.

Any navigator would always measure a noon sun as a matter of routine, as long as both sun and horizon could be seen at that moment. The summer navigator in arctic waters, if he could observe a midnight Sun, could also deduce his latitude from its minimum altitude around 'midnight', by adding 90 degrees to that altitude, and subtracting the Sun's declination. Scoresby made use of that trick on several occasions; for example, to obtain his far-North latitude on 7 July 1814.

A difficulty faced by Scoresby and his fellow Greenland whalers was that there were weeks at a time when the weather was so bad that no noon (or midnight) sun observations were possible, for example between 7 May and 3 June 1814. In such a case all he had to rely on was his dead reckoning, noting the resulting positions in the log as 'by reckoning'. When the weather was kind enough to allow a noon 'sight', the resulting latitude was noted in the log with the words 'by observation', and Scoresby would mark such latitudes with a '+' sign.

Longitude. In the early nineteenth century, many vessels got by with the ability to measure latitude only, estimating longitude only by dead reckoning. In a voyage which crossed an ocean, eastward or westward, a navigator would adopt 'latitude sailing', aiming to reach the latitude of his destination while still well offshore, and would then sail along that latitude line, certain that it would take him to his destination. That policy was not available to a whaler in the Greenland fishery. He needed to know his longitude, toward the end of a northward voyage, to avoid Spitsbergen, or on the homeward voyage to avoid Shetland. He could not be certain whether he was east or west of those hazards unless his longitude could be measured, or perhaps guessed.

Longitude, the easterly or westerly displacement from the Greenwich meridian, was much more difficult to determine than was latitude. Longitude is derived from the time difference between local time, measured from the sun by means of a 'time-sight', and the time at Greenwich at that same instant. One degree of longitude corresponds to four minutes of time difference, which relates to the daily rate of rotation of the earth.

The time-sight. The moment of local noon is when the sun is at its maximum altitude, precisely on the local meridian, due south of an observer in the northern hemisphere. At sea, timing the moment of local noon *at* local noon is very difficult to do precisely, because the sun's altitude is then changing so slowly; indeed, not changing at all. Instead, a measurement is made of sun altitude at a moment, in the morning or afternoon, well away from noon, when the sun is rising or falling quickly; this observation being known as a 'time-sight'. The displacement of that moment in time from noon can then be calculated, as long as the latitude is well known, and that allows the error of an on-board clock on local time to be determined. A text-book example of such a procedure is Scoresby's sun altitude, taken at 3h 10m 2s after noon on 21 April 1812, when the sun altitude was measured to be 28°15'6".

Much more questionable is Scoresby's occasional practice of determining local time from the moment of sunset, such as he recorded on 26 March 1811. Because refraction at such low altitudes is so unpredictable, timings of sunset will never give a very precise result. But there is an additional uncertainty here. The usual mariner's definition of sunset is the moment when the last twinkle of the sun is level with the horizon. However, predictions of sunset time in most volumes of nautical tables are not of that moment, but instead of the instant when the sun's true altitude happens to be zero. It appears, from the numbers Scoresby quotes, that he was using the predictions of a table of that type. At the instant of zero true altitude, the whole sun appears (because of refraction) to float clear above the horizon by about two-thirds of its own diameter. Was Scoresby estimating, and timing, that moment, using a method suggested by Halley as early as 1692? If so, that table would give him a reasonable result. Or was he perhaps timing the moment when the last glint of the sun disappeared? If so, that table of sunset times would be very significantly in error.

Scoresby does not record how he defined his moment of sunset, for such timing purposes.

However, there is a clue to his practice in the journal for 7 April 1815 in which the sun's compass bearing, at the moment when the sun 'set clear', is noted. That phrase, 'set clear' is unfamiliar. What exactly did it mean? Working Scoresby's quoted result backwards, it seems most likely that he was indeed recognizing that moment of zero true altitude of the sun, perhaps just estimating the correct height by eye after long practice. In that case, 'set clear' is likely to refer to that definition of setting, i.e. clear of the horizon. If so, it could throw additional light on other journal entries, such as that of 29 April 1812 in which a similar observation may have been made, without use of the phrase 'set clear'.

Nevertheless, whatever the details of assessing the moment of zero altitude of the sun, because of the variability of refraction at low altitudes, timings of sunrise and sunset will never provide great accuracy for determining longitude. Textbooks recommend that such observations be taken only when the altitude of a body exceeds 5 degrees, and exceeds 10 if possible. However, in arctic latitudes the length of a degree of longitude, in miles, has become sufficiently small that the requirement for precise timing of time-sights can be greatly relaxed.

Obtaining Greenwich time. Taking a time-sight was only part of the necessary observations to determine longitude. To go with the time-sight, which deduced the local time in terms of error of the ship's clock, it was necessary to know Greenwich Time, which could be read from a chronometer if the ship was fortunate enough to carry one, or from a measurement of lunar distance, known as 'taking a lunar'. Scoresby was familiar with both methods, which will be considered next.

Timekeeper. Ideally, a ship's timekeeper would be a chronometer, of which any time-error on Greenwich time was known at the start of the voyage, and with a going-rate (of gaining or losing) that had been measured or 'regulated'. To the extent that the rate held constant, it would provide a measure of Greenwich Time at any moment in the voyage. Its corrected reading, at any instant at which a time-sight determined local time, would then allow the difference between local and Greenwich times, and so the longitude, to be determined. An additional correction, the 'equation of time', enters here, which allows for the irregular nature of the sun as a timekeeper.

However, a chronometer was an expensive tool for a vessel in the whaling trade, and Scoresby did not mention a chronometer until his voyage of 1816. In earlier years, he referred to his 'watch', about which he provided little information, but it was likely to be some sort of pocket-watch. Its going-rate would depend to some extent on its temperature and orientation, and the rate presumably was not sufficiently constant to keep good reliable Greenwich time over the duration of the voyage, even if it could be depended on for a few days at a time. It might be expected that Scoresby, on his way north, would take the opportunity of the stay at Lerwick to check that watch for time and regulating its rate, but his journals gives no evidence that he did so. Instead, his practice seems to have been to put to sea from Lerwick and then, later, to set his watch to Greenwich time, using a time-sight taken at sea.

There is a serious weakness in setting the watch in that way. To do so depends on a knowledge of the true longitude of the ship at the moment of the time-sight. If the task was done within view of Shetland, the ship's longitude would presumably have been accurate (to the extent that the longitude of Shetland was known). But once Shetland was out of sight, the longitude had to be deduced using dead-reckoning, perhaps (as on 21 April 1812) only over a day or two, which could be acceptable.

On another occasion (29 April 1812), ten days had elapsed since any previous sight of land, a gap which had to be covered by dead reckoning. In that latter case, I doubt whether the uncertainty involved in estimating the longitude allowed the watch to be set with any worthwhile accuracy at all. Contrary to footnote 2 on that page, it was not possible to deduce both longitude and time from that observation, which was no more than a time-sight. Instead, it required the longitude to be estimated by dead reckoning before an estimate of Greenwich time could be arrived at. About that same observation, in his Introduction to volume I (p. lvi), Ian Jackson states that, for a watch, 'the approximate error could be determined by solar observations ... and after allowing for this error the longitude could be determined ...'. However, without knowing longitude already, it was impossible to correct a watch from Sun observations alone.

It seems unlikely that any watch error derived from such an imprecise operation as that of 29 April 1812 could add anything worthwhile to that deduced earlier, using better techniques, on 21 April. Perhaps it had been necessitated by accidental stopping of the watch between those dates.

A mariner would normally set his watch to correspond to Greenwich time, and from then on would be reluctant to interfere with its setting. If an error was discovered by observation, that error would be noted, but the hands would not be altered. Not so with Scoresby, however, according to his journal entry for 3 August 1812. When he determined longitude that day by lunar distance (see below) he then reset his watch to show Greenwich time.

In the voyage of 1815 there are no references to longitude, no lunars, no mention of watch times. Times of events are given only to the nearest hour or half-hour. It seems possible that Scoresby was without a working timepiece for that voyage; perhaps his watch had let him down.

Things were very different in 1816, when for the first time a 'chronometer' was mentioned in the journal. This would have been a major investment. It was relied on to provide Greenwich Mean Time, and on 5 April the resulting longitude was deduced from a time-sight, a day after losing sight of Shetland. Presumably, the result matched what was expected from dead reckoning. No further observations for longitude were recorded until the return journey, approaching Shetland in a damaged condition on 20 July. Longitude then became important in order to ensure which side of Shetland the *Esk* would pass, and a lunar was taken, to compare with the chronometer, and also with the reckoning. Later that day a northbound brig was spoken to, which provided a longitude in good agreement with the chronometer. Shetland was sighted the next day. So the chronometer had indeed kept good time throughout the voyage, and the investment had paid off.

Lunar Distances. There was a technique available to Scoresby which allowed him to obtain Greenwich Time directly, at sea, and then use that to set or check his watch. This was by measuring a 'lunar distance', or 'lunar' for short. In the arctic summer, when stars were invisible, this could be done only when both sun and moon were visible in the sky at the same moment, though in Shetland latitudes, moon-star observations were sometimes possible.

A lunar called for very precise measurement of the angle subtended between the two bodies, slantwise across the sky, with a sextant. It relies on the predictable motion of the moon across the sky, in relation to the sun and star background, of about 360 degrees in a lunar month, or about 1 degree in two hours. If the angle could be measured to a precision of 1 arc-minute, which was about the ultimate anyone could aim for, then that would establish Greenwich Time within a couple of minutes of time. The earth turns through one degree in four minutes of time, so a lunar distance, determined to that accuracy, could establish longitude within half a degree. In the high latitudes that Scoresby frequented, the spacing between lines of longitude was shortened. At 80°N, half a degree corresponds to about five miles, which would be a very acceptable determination of longitude.

When Scoresby measured a lunar distance, he would note it in his log, using a phrase such as 'by observation of Moon and Sun', and mark the resulting longitude with a '+' sign to show that it was derived from observation rather than by reckoning. Lunars were mentioned in Scoresby's journal each year until 1814. In 1815 there was no mention of any timed observations. In 1816, Scoresby's chronometer took over.

As an example, on 24 April 1814, the *Esk* was approaching Spitsbergen from the south. Scoresby would have been aiming to pass to the west of its southern peninsula, but close enough to observe the land and be sure of his 'offing', so his longitude had become important. Luckily, the moon happened to be 'in distance' (see below), and the sky was clear. He wrote, tantalizingly, in his log for that day 'Long. by the mean of 5 sets of observations on the Sun & moon was [blank space] E'. However, Steward's journal for that date fills in the gap, when he tells us 'The longitude we made in the afternoon, by another observation, was 14°26′ East.'

On the next morning, 25 April 1814, at 9 am, with ship's latitude 75°54′, the mountains of Spitsbergen were first seen at a distance, and at 9h 23m 23s, 'the Longitude of the Ship as deduced from three sets of Observations on the Sun & Moon appeared to be 13°5′4″E …' This was a very reasonable result, although it was absurd to quote it to such high precision. A longitude stated to the nearest degree, as simply 13°, would have been quite sufficient and would have reflected better the uncertainties in the measurement.

Unfortunately, Scoresby's records of his longitude determinations by lunar distance are frequently incomplete or non-existent, and all we can learn is that such observations had been made. For example, on 29 April 1811, he wrote 'The Sun and Moon being both very clear took 9 Sets of Observations for finding the true distance from the mean of which the marginal Longitude was ascertained.' However, his journal provides no information about his position on that day. There are other occasions, when we can learn that a lunar distance has been measured only by inference from an indirect phrase in a journal.

It is unclear what reliance Scoresby placed on the lunar distance longitudes of these whaling voyages when in later years he came to write Appendix 1 of volume I of *Account of the Arctic Regions*. He listed the weather, day by day, with an estimate of his noon position; those taken by observation, rather than by account, being marked with a special symbol. No longitudes were so marked before the 1817 voyage. In his Introduction to volume I of these Scoresby journals (p. lvi) Ian Jackson correctly notes that from that source it might be inferred that no such longitude observations were taken. On the contrary, however, Scoresby's own journals show that such longitude observations were an important, though infrequent, aspect of his navigation; by lunar distance to 1814, and by chronometer from 1816.

Some problems with lunars. Measuring a lunar demanded great skill from an observer. Holding his sextant at an awkward angle, he had to get both sun and moon into view, simultaneously, in the restricted aperture of the instruments of that period, with an unstable deck underfoot. Then the edges of the sun and moon discs had to be made to 'kiss', brushing past to high precision, ideally to within an arc-minute. No horizon was involved in that measurement, but at nearly the same moment, altitudes of sun and moon above the horizon needed measuring. Then a complex series of calculations, involving five-figure logarithmic trigonometrical tables, was needed, to 'clear' the observed distance of certain vital corrections for parallax and refraction, though some short-cuts existed. Some of the difficulties of lunar observation were described (remarkably well for a sixteen-year-old) in Steward's journal for 24 April 1814. Finally, the apparent time at Greenwich was interpolated from a table of lunar distances, printed at three-hour intervals, in the Nautical Almanac for that day. Those operations were beyond the capabilities of many navigators.

Another difficulty was that lunars were only intermittently possible, especially in arctic summer, when lunar distances to stars were unavailable. The angle between sun and moon had to be in the range between 40 degrees and 120 degrees, which occurred only over two six-day periods in each month: one when the moon is waxing, the other when waning. Unless the moon's declination was somewhat northerly, it was too low in the sky to be properly visible, and that reduced the number of useful days for lunars still further. A low pale moon against a milky sky was very hard to make out. If the horizon was misty, the necessary altitudes could not be measured. If the sky was overcast, as happened so often in those waters, no astronavigation was possible anyway.

As a result, unless good luck intervened, a lunar was not usually available to meet a navigator's immediate need to know his longitude. If, instead, a lunar distance had been measured on the occasions when that became possible, it could be used to check the error of an on-board watch or clock (whether or not that could be classed as a chronometer). Then that timepiece could be used to provide an approximation to Greenwich Time until the next lunar observation could be made. Once Greenwich Time was known, any time-sight of the sun would provide the longitude, as for example on 7 August 1812. Unfortunately, Scoresby tells us little about the management of his watch, and its errors.

Scoresby's Skills as Navigator and Mariner – Some Examples

There is no doubt, from the consistency of his deduced positions, that Scoresby was remarkably precise in his sextant measurements. He was able to apply the mathematical procedures that were necessary to correct those observations; procedures that were particularly complex in the case of lunar distances, and beyond the grasp of many of his contemporaries. In overcast weather, a sequence of positions by account usually accorded well with a following position by observation, when that became possible. That showed Scoresby's professional skill in being able to estimate the going of his vessel, taking all the relevant factors into account; often a matter of informed guesswork. But more than that, Scoresby comes across as a deep thinker and acute observer, able to apply his intellectual powers to make the most of every scrap of navigational information that could be gathered.

In his Introduction to volume I (p. lviii), Ian Jackson picked out Scoresby's conclusion, on August 1812, that at a critical point in the approach to Shetland from the north, *Resolution* would be passing west, not east, of that archipelago. That was indeed an important matter, especially when setting a course at night to avoid running into outlying skerries in the dark. It may be of interest to examine, in greater detail, the evidence that Scoresby had assembled to come to that conclusion.

The watch had been set to Greenwich time, based on a lunar taken on 3 August, and on 7 August the ship's longitude had been updated using 'equal altitudes of the Sun' (a form of time-sight). Taken with that watch setting, assuming that it had kept good time over the intervening days, this indicated that the vessel would pass west of Shetland, but there was much uncertainty about such longitudes.

Scoresby took every factor he could think of in backing that conclusion. On the 7th, he had noted the presence of sea-birds, and on the surface 'Molluscous animals' (of the squid family?), indicating that he was then approaching land, without seeing it. The next day, a clear noon sky allowed a good observation for latitude, which indicated that *Resolution* had on the 7th been passing the latitude of Faroe, and not at a great distance, as was shown by the observed abatement of swell to leeward of those islands.

The presence of sea-birds on the 8th, but the absence of mollusca and seaweed, was taken as further evidence for the deduced longitude. However, this was shaken somewhat, next day, when soundings were obtained, at 73, 45, and later 60 fathoms; a surprise to Scoresby, who expected to find deeper water to the west of Shetland.

An additional factor, confirming the Westerly assumption, was 'the great variation', noted on 9 August. Magnetic variation increased slowly with more westerly longitude. Scoresby does not tell us of any local observations of variation, but to be conclusive on that point, such measurements would need to have a precision of better than one degree. Scoresby's magnetic observations at other dates, bedevilled as they were by local magnetic deviation, provide little confidence in the validity of any such deductions.

In the event, *Resolution* successfully steered a path taking her east of Faroe, west of Shetland, then east of Orkney without sighting any of these groups of islands, though the outliers of Foula and North Ronaldsay (which had been lit) were seen. This was not simply 'by the book' navigation, but an example of an intelligent man applying logical reasoning and sharp observation, putting everything together.

In the Introduction to this volume Ian Jackson refers to the 'near-catastrophe' at the outset of the 1814 voyage, when *Esk* was caught up in the tide-race south of Sumburgh Head on the night of 28 March. Scoresby appeared to be quite unaware of the dangers of that notorious race, which shows something of a blind-spot in his navigational knowledge. Someone aboard must have been remarkably alert to spot the nearby cliffs, quite unexpectedly appearing to leeward, on a black and murky night. The subsequent account, which tallies with that of Steward, is illuminating about the standard of seamanship aboard *Esk*.

Within half an hour, five more sails had been set with the aim of weathering Sumburgh Head, but it quickly became clear this would not be possible, as *Esk* was too far embayed. At that point, she had to be shifted from starboard to port tack, either by tacking or by wearing the ship round. With the sea 'running very high', a tack was a chancy business that might fail, leaving the ship in an even worse position. Scoresby decided to wear instead, an operation which could be done at short notice, requiring little preparation, and which he could be sure would succeed, as long as there was sea-room.

It must have been a heart-stopping few minutes. Wearing involved turning the ship downwind in the dark, directly toward those cliffs to leeward, trusting that the turn could be made within the confines of the bay, and that there were no outlying rocks to split her open. The gamble paid off, allowing *Esk* to gain a safe offing to the west. By then the tide was turning and by daybreak it had brought her back, northeast of Fair Isle, just where the intention had been to pass the previous night in safety and comfort.

It was a remarkable example of seamanship: a confident shiphandler ready to take decisive action in an emergency, even if that emergency had been largely of his own making. By such actions as that, and of *Esk*'s self-rescue from her grievous injury of 1816, we can judge the calibre of the man.

Works Cited

Admiralty Chart 1419 (Orkney & Shetland Islands), London, Hydrographic Office, 1807. Online at www.nls.uk/digitallibrary/map/early/scotland.cfm?id=1218

Allen, Grahame, *Inflation: the Value of the Pound 1750–2002*, Research Paper 03/82, London, House of Commons Library, 1999. Online at www.parliament.uk/commons/lib/research/rp2003/rp03-082.pdf.

Arnott, Neil, *Elements of Physics or Natural Philosophy, General and Medical, Explained Independently of Technical Mathematics, and Containing New Disquisitions and Practical Suggestions*, 2nd edn, 2 vols, London, Underwood, 1827.

Asher, G. M., ed., *Henry Hudson the Navigator: the original documents in which his career is recorded …*, London, Hakluyt Society, 1st ser. 27, 1860. (Facsimile reprint published by Elibron Classics, 2004.)

Barrington, Daines, *The Probability of Reaching the North Pole Discussed*, London, Heydinger, 1775. (Facsimile reprint published by Ye Galleon Press, Fairfield, WA, 1987.)

Barrow, Tony, *The Whaling Trade of North-East England 1750–1850*, Sunderland, University of Sunderland Press, 2001.

Bathurst, Bella, *The Lighthouse Stevensons: The Extraordinary Story of the Building of the Scottish Lighthouses by the Ancestors of Robert Louis Stevenson*, London, Harper Collins, 1999.

Brewer's Dictionary of Phrase and Fable (centenary edn, revised), London, Cassell, 1981.

Burney, W., ed., *Falconer Improved and Modernized, The Mariner's New and Complete Naval Dictionary …*, London, 1815.

Burns, John J.; Montague, J. Jerome; Cowles, Cleveland J., eds, *The Bowhead Whale*, Lawrence, Kansas, Society for Marine Mammalogy, 1993.

Butler, David, *Isle of Noss*, [Lerwick?], Garth Estate, 1982.

Coolidge, Susan, *What Katy Did Next*, London, Ward, Lock & Co, 1887.

Cranz (or Crantz), David, *The History of Greenland: containing a description of the country, and its inhabitants and particularly, a relation of the mission, carried on for above these thirty years by the Unitas Fratrum, at New Herrnhuth and Lichtenfels, in that country*, 2 vols, London, Brethren's Society for the Furtherance of the Gospel among the Heathen, 1767. (Note: Both the British Library and the Library of Congress prefer the author's name as 'Cranz', but the 1767 English translation was published as 'Crantz'.)

Credland, Arthur G., *The Hull Whaling Trade, An Arctic Enterprise*, Beverley, Hutton Press, 1995.

Dolan, Brian, 'Pedagogy through Print: James Sowerby, John Mawe and the Problem of Colour in early Nineteenth-century Natural History Illustration', *British Journal for the History of Science*, 31, 1998, pp. 275–304. Online through Cambridge Journals.

Falconer, William, *A New Universal Dictionary of the Marine* ..., London, 1815 edition modernized and enlarged by William Burney, online at www.mysticseaport.org/library/initiative/ImPage.cfm?BibID=10972&ChapterId=1

Gjevik, B.; Moe, H.; Ommundsen, A., 'Strong Topographic Enhancement of Tidal Currents: Tales of the Maelstrom', online at www.math.uio.no/maelstrom.

Greenland & Davis's Strait's Whale Fishery, 1814, 1815, 1816. (These annual lists of ships, masters and home ports preserved in the Scoresby Papers at Whitby Museum, are, for 1815 and 1816, similar to those for 1811–13 and probably printed in Whitby. The list for 1814 was prepared by the London 'Oil and Whale-bone Factors' Devereux & Lambert. All three lists are cited in the notes as 'contemporary printed lists'.)

Gyory, Joanna; Mariano, Arthur J.; Ryan, Edward H., 'The Spitsbergen Current', online at http://oceancurrents.rsmas.miami.edu/atlantic/spitsbergen.html.

Haldiman, Jerrold J. and Tarpley, Raymond J., 'Anatomy and Physiology', in John J. Burns *et al.*, *The Bowhead Whale* (q.v.), pp. 71–156.

Hamblyn, Richard, *The Invention of Clouds: How An Amateur Meteorologist Forged the Language of the Skies*, London, Picador, 2001.

Harington, C. R., ed., *The Year Without a Summer?: World Climate in 1816*, Ottawa, Canadian Museum of Nature, 1992.

Howard, Luke, 'On the Modifications of Clouds, and on the Principles of their Production, Suspension, and Destruction; being the Substance of an Essay read before the Askesian Society in the Session 1802–3', *Philosophical Magazine*, 16, 1803, pp. 97–107, 344–57; 1804, 17, pp. 5–11.

Kelly, Patrick, *A Practical Introduction to Spherics and Nautical Astronomy; being an attempt to simplify those ... Sciences. Containing ... the discovery of a projection for clearing the lunar distances in order to find the Longitude at Sea; with a new method of calculating this ... problem*, 4th edition, London, 1813.

Kidd, Thornhill, *Sermons. Designed chiefly for the Use of Villages and Families*, Pontefract, Boothroyd, 1812.

Krakow, Kenneth B., *Georgia Place-Names*, 3rd edn, online at www.kenkrakow.com/gpn/georgia_place-names.htm.

Layton, Cyril W., *Dictionary of Nautical Words and Terms*, 4th revised edn, Glasgow, Brown, Son & Ferguson, 1994.

Leier, Manfred, ed., *World Atlas of the Oceans, with the General Bathymetric Chart of the Oceans (GEBCO) published by the Canadian Hydrographic Service*, Buffalo, N.Y., Firefly, 2001.

Lubbock, Basil, *The Arctic Whalers*, Glasgow, Brown, Son & Ferguson, 1937.

Mason, B. J., *Clouds, Rain and Rainmaking*, London, Cambridge University Press, 1962.

McKinsey, Elizabeth, *Niagara Falls: Icon of the American Sublime*, New York, Cambridge University Press, 1985.

Naval Chronicle, The, London, Bunney & Gold, 40 vols, 1799–1818.

North Coast of Scotland Pilot: North and North-East Coasts of Scotland from Cape Wrath to Rattray Head Including the Caledonian Canal, Orkney Islands, Shetland Islands, and Froyar (Faeroe Islands), Taunton, UK Hydrographic Office, 2003.

Paclt, J., 'A Chronology of Color Charts and Color Terminology for Naturalists', *Taxon*, 32, 3, 1983, pp. 393–405. Online through JSTOR.

Paul, Harry W., *Bacchic Medicine: Wine and Alcohol Therapies from Napoleon to the French Paradox*, Amsterdam and New York, Rodopi, 2001.

Phipps, Constantine John, *A Voyage towards the North Pole undertaken by His Majesty's Command, 1773*, London, Nourse, 1774.

Pokoly, Béla, 'On the History of Naming the North Sea', paper presented at the Fifth International Seminar on the Naming of Seas, Seoul, 1999. Online at www.east-sea.org/article3/report3.htm.

Robinson, Francis K., *A Glossary of Yorkshire Words and Phrases, Collected in Whitby and the Neighbourhood: With Examples of their Colloquial Use, and Allusions to Local Customs and Traditions*, London, Smith, 1855.

Rye, Walter, *Norfolk Families*, Norwich, Goose, 1913.

Scoresby, William, *An Account of the Arctic Regions, with a History and Description of the Northern Whale-Fishery*, 2 vols, Edinburgh, Constable, 1820. (Facsimile reprint, with an introduction by Alister Hardy, published by David & Charles Reprints, Newton Abbot, 1969.)

Scoresby, William, *My Father, being Records of the Adventurous Life of the Late William Scoresby, Esq., of Whitby*, London, Longman, Brown, Green and Longmans, 1851. (Facsimile reprint published by Caedmon, Whitby, 1978.)

Scoresby, William, Jr, 'On the Greenland or Polar Ice', *Memoirs of the Wernerian Natural History Society*, vol. 2, part I, pp. 261–338.

Scoresby-Jackson, R. E., *The Life of William Scoresby, M.A., D.D., F.R.S.S.L. & E.*, London, Nelson, 1861.

Smyth, William H., *The Sailor's Word Book of 1867; an Alphabetical Digest of Nautical Terms*, London, Blackie, 1867. (Facsimile reprint published by Conway Classics, London, 1991.)

Syme, Patrick, *Werner's Nomenclature of Colours, with Additions, Arranged so as to render it highly useful to the Arts and Sciences …*, Edinburgh, J. Ballantyne & Co., 1814.

Tactical Pilotage Chart TPC B-1A, Scale 1:500,000, St. Louis, Missouri, Defense Mapping Agency Aerospace Center, 1986.

Wadhams, Peter, 'How Does Arctic Sea Ice Form and Decay?', online at www.arctic.noaa.gov/essay_wadhams.html.

Węsławski, Jan M.; Hacquebord, Louwrens; Stempniewicz, Lech; Malinga, Michal, 'Greenland Whales and Walruses in the Svalbard Food Web before and after Exploitation', *Oceanologia*, 42, 1, 2000, pp. 37–56.

White, Adam, ed., *A Collection of Documents on Spitzbergen and Greenland, comprising a translation from F. Martens Voyage to Spitzbergen: a translation from Isaac. de la Peyrères Histoire du Groenland: and Gods Power and Providence in the preservation of eight men in Greenland nine moneths [sic] and twelve dayes,*

London, 1855. (Facsimile reprint published by University Press of the Pacific, Honolulu, 2003.)

Würsig, Bernd and Christopher Clark, 'Behavior', in John J. Burns *et al.*, *The Bowhead Whale* (q.v.), pp. 157–99.

Yost, Robinson M., *Observations, Instruments and Theories: The Study of Terrestrial Magnetism in Great Britain, c. 1770s–1830s*, online at http://www.kirkwood.cc.ia.us/faculty/ryost/minneapolis.htm

Young, George, *A History of Whitby and Streoneshalh Abbey: with a Statistical Survey of the Vicinity to the Distance of Twenty-five Miles*, 2 vols, Whitby, Clark and Medd, 1817. (Reprinted in facsimile by Caedmon of Whitby in 1976.)

Index

Index of Whaling Vessels

Note: As in volume I, this index includes only those vessels mentioned in Scoresby's or Steward's journals. It includes a few vessels of the Davis Strait fleet. Home ports and masters shown in parentheses are based on the contemporary printed lists: *Greenland & Davis's Strait's Fishery, 1814, 1815, 1816*. These lists are not always consistent with the journals, especially in regard to spelling; in cases where vessels of the same name sailed from different ports, there is uncertainty in some cases as to which vessel the journals refer. The *Esk* is not included in this index.

[1] Scoresby also used the spelling 'Eggington'. See Credland, *Hull Whaling Trade*, where there is doubt (p. 122) whether *Egginton II* replaced *Egginton I* in 1815 or 1816. Credland (p. 138) lists Pickering as master in 1814, but also lists Pinkney as master from 1810 to 1815 which accords with the 1814 contemporary list. Kirby was master in 1816.

[1] Kings Lynn was normally abbreviated to 'Lynn' in whaling references.

[2] The contemporary lists have *Friendship* sailing from Dundee under Captain Ireland in 1816, but she reverted to Hull and Bowley in 1817.

[3] In all three years, the contemporary lists show the master as Hutchison or Hutchinson, the same name as the master of the *Superior*. In the 1816 list, however, 'Hutchison' has been deleted by hand and replaced by 'Mackie'.

[1] A London vessel according to Scoresby's journal, but there is no London vessel named *William* in the contemporary lists, whereas the *William* of Hull is well documented.